HOME
GROWING

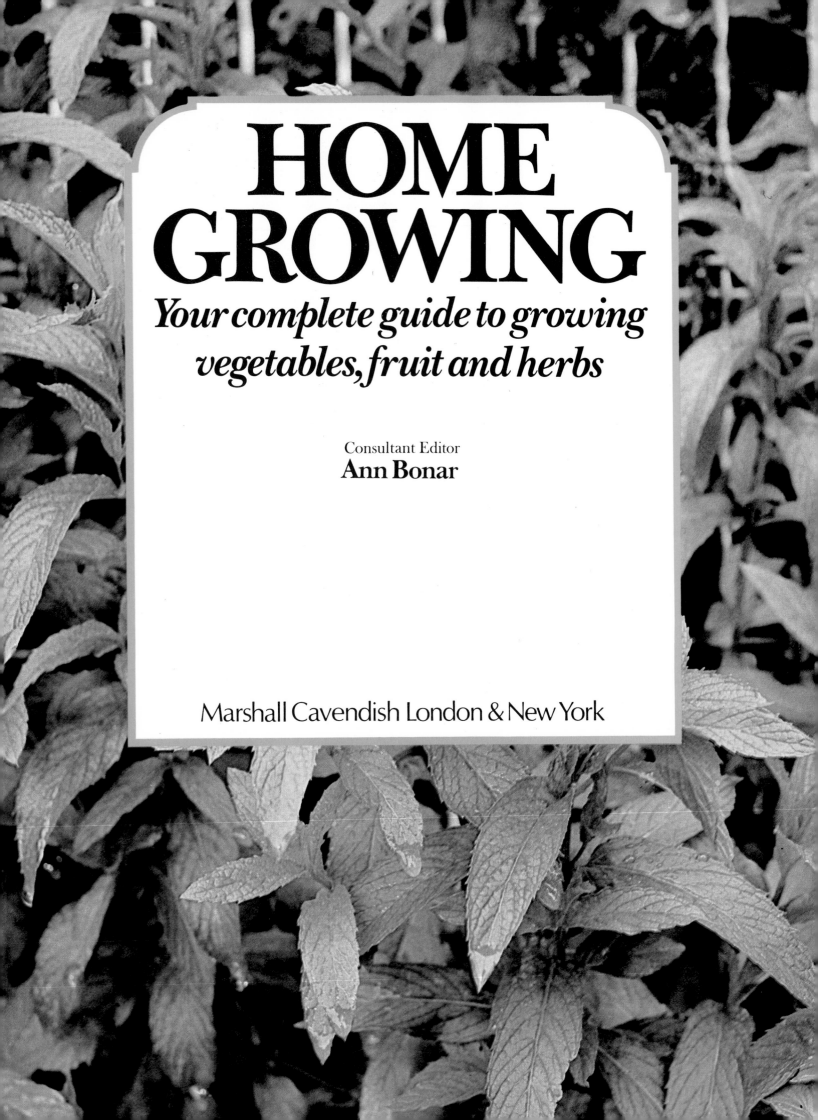

HOME GROWING

Your complete guide to growing vegetables, fruit and herbs

Consultant Editor
Ann Bonar

Marshall Cavendish London & New York

Contributors
Graham Andrews
Harry Baker
Ann Bonar
Guy Cooper
Peter Dodd
J.B. Duggan
Daphne ffiske
Brian Furner
Millar Gault
Nancy Mary Goodall
Cyril Harris
A.G. Healey
Joy Larkcom
P.J. Long
D. Macer-Wright
Cicely Mead

Ken Muir
Gay Nightingale
Horace Parsons
Peter Pashley
Ray Procter
Thomas Rivers
Keith Sangster
George Seddon
W.E. Shewell-Cooper
Donald Smee
D. Tostevin
James Trehane
John Warrington
Tony Webster
Richard A. Weeks
Ralph Whitlock
Jack Woodward

Editorial Staff:
Jean Wetherburn
Pepita Aris
Jonathan Elphick
Angela Errigo
Stella Hartwell
Elizabeth Holzer

Designed by:
Linda Palmer

Design Assistants:
Conal Buck
Keith Bloomfield

Picture research:
Ethne Rose

Published by Marshall Cavendish Books Limited
58 Old Compton Street
London W1V 5PA

© Marshall Cavendish Limited 1977

First Printing 1977

Printed in Great Britain

ISBN 0 85685 243 0

FOREWORD

Nothing beats the taste of freshly harvested crops. Crisp lettuce straight from the ground, plums still warm from the sun, the scent of fresh thyme – these are the delights and rewards of the home gardener.

Your own fruit, vegetables and herbs not only taste better and cost less than any you can buy – their food value is greater too. The vitamin content of many crops deteriorates rapidly once they are harvested, so that much of their goodness is lost on the journey from farm to kitchen.

In recent years more and more people have become aware of these benefits, and of the unique satisfactions of making their own garden – however small – as productive as possible. With an eye to the future in our increasingly crowded world, you too can enjoy the security of producing a significant part of your own family's food.

HOME GROWING is specially designed to help the new enthusiast. Beginners often complain that gardening books take the basics for granted, so we have taken care to explain the how, why and when of every step for successful growing.

Don't let anyone tell you that gardening is difficult or laborious – it isn't. With the right approach it can be a great source of relaxation and fun. But successful growing *does* require sound advice and information, and you will find all that you need in this book.

Here's wishing you many years of bumper harvests and happy home growing!

Ann Bonar

CONTENTS

A to Z GROWING GUIDE...

Angelica 10
Apple 11
Apricot 21
Artichoke, Globe 24
Artichoke, Jerusalem and Chinese 25
Asparagus 28
Asparagus Pea 31
Aubergine [*Eggplant*] 113
Balm 33
Basil 33
Bay 34
Beans, General 36
Bean Sprouts 36
Beetroot 38
Blackberry 41
Blackcurrant 44
Blueberry 48
Borage 51
Broad Beans 51
Broccoli 55
Brussels Sprouts 57

Cabbage 61
Calabrese [*Sprouting Broccoli*] 255
Cantaloupe [*Melon*] 166
Cape Gooseberry 66
Capsicum [*Peppers*] 210
Caraway 68
Cardoon 70
Carrot 72
Cauliflower 76·
Celeriac 79
Celery 81
Cherry 85
Chervil 90
Chicory 90
Chinese Cabbage 93
Chinese Gooseberry 94
Chives 96
Citrus Fruits 97
Collards [*Cabbage*] 61
Coriander 103
Corn [*Sweet Corn*] 269
Corn Salad 104
Courgette [*Zucchini*] 285
Crabapple 105
Cress 105
Cucumber 108
Damson 112
Dill 112
Eggplant 113
Endive 115
Fennel, Florence 117
Fennel 118
Fig 119

BASIC GARDENING GUIDE...

Planning your garden 288
Choosing your fruit 290
Garden hygiene 291
Tools 292
Improving the soil 293
Making a compost heap 294
Fertilizers 296
Seeds and seed beds 297
Cloches and frames 298
Watering 299
The Greenhouse 300
Pests and diseases 302

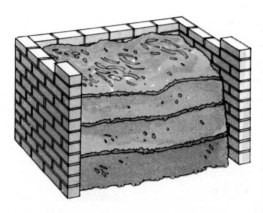

French Bean	122
Garlic	126
Gherkin	127
Good King Henry	127
Gooseberry	128
Grape	131
Greengage	139
Gumbo [*Okra*]	181
Hamburg Parsley	140
Horseradish	141
Kale	142
Kohlrabi	144
Lamb's Lettuce [*Corn Salad*]	104
Leek	146
Lemon Verbena	150
Lettuce	150
Lima Bean	155
Loganberry	157
Lovage	160
Mange-tout [*Pea*]	193
Marjoram	161

Marrow	162
Melon	166
Mint	172
Mulberry	175
Mushroom	176
Mustard Greens [*Chinese Cabbage*]	93
Nasturtium	179
Nectarine	179
New Zealand Spinach	180
Okra	181
Onion	183
Oregano [*Marjoram*]	161
Parsley	190
Parsnip	191
Pea	193
Peach	198
Pear	204
Peppers	210
Plum	214
Potato	219
Pumpkin	224
Quince	224
Radish	226
Raspberry	228
Red and White Currants	231
Rhubarb	234
Rosemary	236
Runner Bean	237
Rutabaga [*Swede*]	267
Sage	242
Salsify	242
Savory	245
Scallion [*Onion*]	183

Scorzonera [*Salsify*]	242
Seakale	247
Seakale Beet [*Swiss Chard*]	273
Shallot [*Onion*]	183
Snap Bean [*French Bean*]	122
Snow Pea [*Pea*]	193
Sorrel	249
Soya Bean	250
Spinach	251
Spinach Beet	254
Spring Onion [*Onion*]	183
Sprouting Broccoli	255
Squashes	258
Strawberry	261
String Bean [*French Bean*]	122
Swede	267
Sweet Corn	269
Swiss Chard	273
Tarragon	274
Thyme	275
Tomato	276
Turnip	283
Zucchini	285

Varieties	308
Glossary	312
Regional guide to seasons	314
Index	315

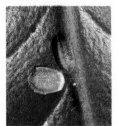

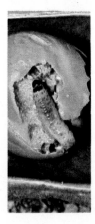

A to Z
GROWING
GUIDE

Angelica

**Angelica has a special flavour
rather like vanilla-scented celery.
It has many culinary uses, most popularly
in its brilliant green crystallized form.**

One of the largest and most handsome members of the *Umbelliferae* family, angelica *(Angelica archangelica)* was known as 'herb of the angels' in the sixteenth century. It is a biennial herb, generally dying out as soon as it has flowered and developed seeds in its second year of growth. The sweet-scented leaves spread out to form a magnificent plant, which may be as much as 2.1 m [7′] tall.

Cultivation

Angelica prefers semi-shady conditions and needs plenty of water. Ideally, a rich, moist soil produces the most flourishing plant. If soil is poor, rake in garden compost before sowing or transplanting.

Only fresh seeds will germinate, so be sure when ordering to ask specifically for seeds which have just ripened. Sow seeds in late summer or early autumn in finely raked open ground or boxes of seed compost. In either case germination temperature should be a fairly steady 15 to 21°C [60 to 70°F].

As soon as two or three true leaves appear, seedlings sown in boxes should be transplanted into open ground and watered in carefully. The young plants should be spaced about 45 cm [18″] apart so, if plants were started in the open, thin to this distance. When the plants are growing strongly thin again and allow a final planting distance of about 1.5 m [5′] between plants.

Water the growing plants regularly, taking great care not to submerge the crowns.

Keep the soil well dressed with organic compost. Except when young, the plant should not need much weeding.

Harvesting and aftercare

Leaf stalks are best cut for use in early and mid spring, before they become too fibrous.

A sturdy plant when established, angelica needs no

Angelica often grows very tall. Its sweet-scented leaves can spread out to form a truly magnificent plant.

training or supports. In winter, when the plant dies down, it will withstand moderate frosts. If flower-bearing stems grow up from the base in the second summer, cut them out or the leaves will turn yellow and die.

In its second summer, the plant should flower. It will then go to seed. If you wish to extend the life of the plant cut off the flower heads as they appear. You can enjoy a crop of angelica for perhaps another five years. Alternatively, if you wish to gather seeds for a successive crop, allow a few weeks for them to ripen then collect. Spread out and dry in the sun or a warm room for two or three days and sow as before. After harvesting the seed, dig up the plant and dispose of it, either by adding to the compost heap or by burning.

Using angelica

The best known way of using angelica is to crystallize the leaf stalk, preserving it for use in cakes, milk, steamed and baked puddings and sweetmeats. But it has several interesting uses as a fresh herb. The stalk, raw and grated, makes an excellent salad ingredient and adds flavour to seafood. Boiled and chopped, it can be added to poultry and vegetable stuffings. Boiled and puréed, the stalk enhances sauces, and braised angelica goes particularly well with game. The leaves can also be used in salads.

An elegant liqueur can be made from finely chopped angelica stalks and brandy. An infusion of angelica tea is good for the digestion and stimulates a poor appetite.

Apple

**This favourite tree bears numerous
crisp, juicy fruit.
According to variety, apples can be
eaten raw, cooked or pressed for juice
which is fermented to make cider.**

Today there are literally hundreds of apple varieties all descended from wild crabapple ancestors. They are all relatively hardy, flower in spring and bear fruit, according

Dwarf trees crop heavily and take up little garden space, so you can plant several varieties.

to variety, from midsummer to late autumn. From the culinary point of view, they divide into four groups of which the first two are the most important. Cooking apples

Apple
Malus pumila (fam. *Rosaceae*)
Hardy deciduous tree, with a useful life of about 50 years.
Size: from about 1.8 m [6'] tall for dwarf bushes to about 7.5 m [25'] for standard trees and up to 12 m [40'] for crab and cider apples.
Climate: cool to warm temperate.
Planting to harvesting time: dwarf trees on M9 rootstock start to produce fruit when 3 years old. More vigorous trees take a year or two longer.
Yield: dwarf bush trees may average about 14 kg [30 lb] a year, bush trees 28 kg [60 lb], mature cider trees may reach 500 kg [½ ton].

are sharply flavoured and are therefore never eaten raw. They quickly form pulp when cooked. The second group is dessert apples, sweeter in flavour and mainly eaten raw. These may be cooked, when they will hold their shape. Cider apples are grown solely for their juice. This may be combined with a smaller proportion of juice from dessert apples to make a drink which may or may not be fermented. Crabapples are very tart and are used for jelly and preserves. Both the last two trees can be planted as pollinators for the other two types.

CHOOSING YOUR TREES
A combination of cooking and dessert apples suit most families best. Tart cooking apples tend to have a longer season and to keep better than the dessert kinds, so a few carefully chosen varieties can keep a family supplied almost the whole year round, while bottled or frozen purée will bridge the few weeks between crops. Cookers are more tolerant of less-than-perfect conditions, but need more nitrogenous fertilizer than dessert apples.
Dessert apples are smaller than cooking apples, about 5-10 cm [2-4"] and sweeter to taste. They have a shorter eating

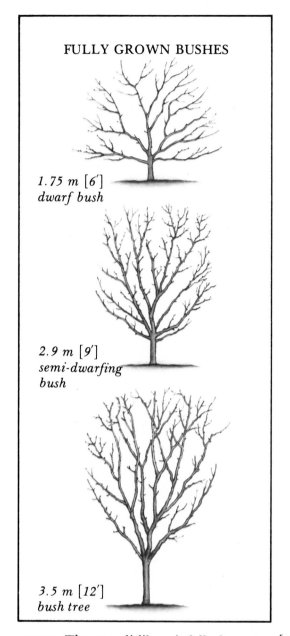

FULLY GROWN BUSHES

1.75 m [6']
dwarf bush

2.9 m [9']
semi-dwarfing
bush

3.5 m [12']
bush tree

Cider apple standards eventually grow very big for fruit trees. They are both ornamental and useful.

season. The trees dislike rainfall of over 1 m [40"] a year.

Choosing pollination partners

Most apple trees must have another variety in the vicinity, flowering at the same time, if they are to bear fruit, so you should plant a minimum of two. A very few varieties are self-fertile but all will give bigger crops if pollinated by another. The different apple groups will pollinate each other. The variety charts at the back of the book suggest suitable pollinators for your apple. Your specialist grower will advise you on varieties that flower at the same time and will pollinate each other.

Tree shapes

The simplest form of tree for the small garden — and the one most appropriate for cooking apples — is the bush, or if you are short of space, the dwarf bush, which needs only a 1.5 m [5'] space.

Old-fashioned standards or half-standards grow far too big for the modern orchard or vegetable garden and are best planted in the ornamental part of the garden. It may be ten years before such trees come into cropping. Most space saving are apples grown on walls or boundary fences, and instructions for cordons are given later.

Rootstocks

Modern apple trees are formed by joining the apple variety to a separate root system or 'stock'. The fruiting habits of the resulting tree are that of the top, or scion, but the size is determined by the rootstock. The development of what are called dwarfing rootstocks now means that small but abundantly fruiting trees are available. By choosing between rootstocks you can select the variety you want at the size you want. The research was carried out at East Malling Research Station and at Merton in England and their rootstocks, referred to as M (Malling) and MM (Malling Merton), are used throughout the world.

Where space is very limited, you can plant a 'family tree'. These are trees with several varieties (usually three) grafted on to the same roots. Thus they will pollinate each other and you will have a choice of types of apple.

Age of tree to buy

If you are going to train your apple on a wall or fence yourself, then you should buy a maiden (one-year-old tree). If you are growing bush fruit, then a three-year-old tree will bear fruit sooner. Do not let them bear more than a couple of sample fruit each during their first summer. You must give the roots time to re-establish.

CULTIVATION

A sunny site which is sheltered and frost-free at blossom time is necessary to ensure that insects can pollinate. Apples will grow successfully in most temperate areas. They will not grow in gardens waterlogged for long periods in wet weather, though a method of overcoming this is suggested below. In coastal areas salt-laden winds can cause damage. Rainfall over 1 m [40″] a year will make the control of disease difficult.

Cooking apples are more tolerant of heavy clay soil, high rainfall and indifferent drainage, and will put up with less sunshine than dessert varieties.

The ideal soil is a brick earth or medium loam, slightly acid and well-drained. If you can organize it, prepare the soil for your apple trees in summer. Deep digging will improve surface drainage, while perennial weeds must be eliminated.

If you cannot prepare the soil so far in advance, firm the ground well by treading or rolling it after digging, and leave it to settle for at least two weeks before planting.

Test your soil with a simple soil-testing kit. If it is very acid, make it less so by applying lime. A neutral or only just alkaline soil is more of a problem. Improve it by working in manure and use acid fertilizers such as sulphate of ammonia when necessary. Modern artificial fertilizers and foliar sprays can correct the lack of nutrients caused by highly alkaline soil.

You can improve both light, sandy or gravelly soil, as well as heavy clay ones, by working in liberal quantities of manure, garden compost, peat or leafmould. Peat has no feeding value, but improves the consistency of the soil. If you are contemplating planting apples in an existing kitchen garden, be cautious. Where there has been a high level of feeding, for dessert apples in particular, tree growth will be stimulated to the detriment of fruit blossom. In this case plan a year's delay with no fertilizing, when you can go on growing vegetables.

When to plant the tree

You can plant at any time during the dormant season — when there are no leaves on the tree — provided the soil is neither frozen hard nor too wet to work freely. It is best to plant soon after leaf-fall so the tree can start to develop as soon as possible in spring.

Spacing

It is important to leave enough space between individual trees and also between trees and walls, fences etc. For bush trees on M7 or MM106 rootstock in soil of average quality, allow a radius of 2 m [7′] around each bush. If soil is rich, allow a radius of 2.8 m [9′].

For bushes on semi-dwarfing M26 rootstock allow a radius

of 1.75 m [6′]. For the smallest trees on M9 rootstock, allow a radius of 1.5 m [5′]. For vigorous growers on dwarf M9 rootstock allow a radius of 1.75 m [6′]. Family trees need a spacing of at least 4.25 m [14′], as they are more vigorous than the dwarfs.

Starting to plant

Plant the trees as soon as they are delivered, provided the soil in your garden is working well so that it is crumbly and not pasty. If the roots have dried out in transit soak them in water in a dustbin or similar container for about an hour. Trim any damaged roots back to a good one, making slanting cuts on the underside of the thicker roots.

If for any reason planting has to be delayed, heel the tree in temporarily in the open. Make a trench deep enough to bury the roots in, with one side of the trench sloping at an angle of about 45°. Lay the trees in this trench, against the sloping side, and return the soil over the roots. Cover them just up to the soil mark on the stem, which shows the depth the tree was previously growing in the nursery, and tread in lightly.

It is easier to plant trees if you have someone to help you. Dig the planting hole deep and wide enough for all the roots to be spread out fully in their natural growing positions.

Lay a stick across the planting hole to show you the ground level and ask your helper to hold the stem of the tree against this. Your aim must be that when you have finished planting the tree and treading down the soil, the tree will be at exactly the same soil depth as it was when growing in the nursery. The join of the stock and the variety (top part) must not be below ground level, or the variety may put out roots, nullifying the dwarfing effect of the rootstock.

Staking

All bush trees need stakes, and these should be treated wood. Drive two upright stakes into the planting hole so that they will be about 23 cm [9″] away from the tree. In light soil they should eventually be buried 60 cm [2′] below soil level, in heavy soil 45 cm [1′ 6″]. After planting fix a crosspiece to the two stakes so that it comes to a little below the lowest branch, and fasten the tree to it.

Finishing planting

Put a spadeful of soil into the bottom of the hole, spread out the roots, sprinkle over a few handfuls of moist peat and start returning the soil.

If your soil is on the poor side, mix a couple of handfuls of sterilized bonemeal with the soil waiting to go back into the planting hole, but not in immediate contact with the roots. Your helper should wriggle the tree a little so the soil filters well between the roots. Tread the soil down to firm it as you go.

Water with one 12 L [2½ gal] bucket, and if there is no rain within a week, give it another bucket.

Level off and surround the tree as far as the branches extend with a surface mulch (layer) of well-rotted compost, manure, leafmould or damp peat, but do not let this touch the tree stem, or it may rot the bark.

PLANTING AN APPLE BUSH

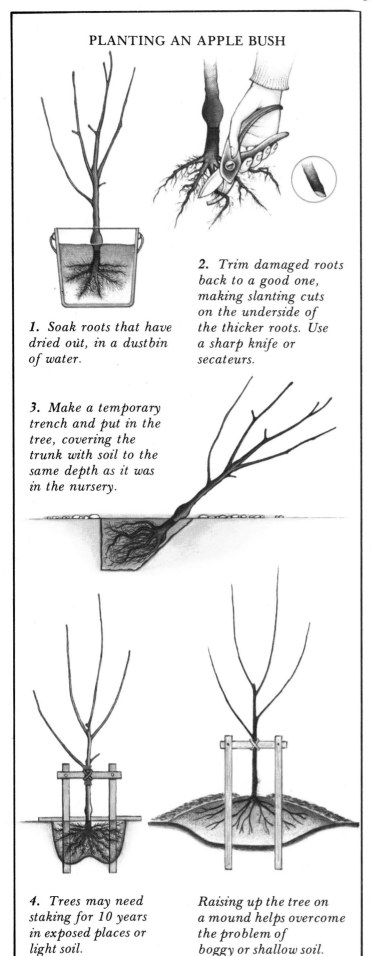

1. *Soak roots that have dried out, in a dustbin of water.*

2. *Trim damaged roots back to a good one, making slanting cuts on the underside of the thicker roots. Use a sharp knife or secateurs.*

3. *Make a temporary trench and put in the tree, covering the trunk with soil to the same depth as it was in the nursery.*

4. *Trees may need staking for 10 years in exposed places or light soil.*

Raising up the tree on a mound helps overcome the problem of boggy or shallow soil.

Support

Immediately after planting fasten the tree to its stakes. Use an easily adjustable plastic tree tie, or failing that, wrap a piece of cloth around the tree to protect the bark and tie over it with cord. Finish by twisting the cord between the tree and stake to prevent chafing.

Inspect the tree's fastening frequently in early months because the soil will settle and it may be necessary to reposition the tie. The tree may be able to dispense with support in two to three years.

Planting in badly drained ground

Dessert apples, and in particular Cox's Orange Pippin, are less tolerant of heavy clay soils and indifferent drainage than cooking apples. Deep digging and, wherever practicable, the laying of land drains are the first step. If you are still doubtful about the drainage, but want to grow dessert apples, you can plant on a slight mound.

Instead of digging a normal-sized planting hole, make only a depression. Stand the tree in this, insert the usual stakes, and then remove topsoil from some other part of the garden and mound it up to the previous soil mark on the stem. The mound should be wider than the existing extent of the roots, to encourage them to grow out. Mulching should extend further than the branches and therefore each year you will have to topdress further out.

As the tree is on an individual mound, the roots will have to grow further before they encounter the inhospitable wetter layers. This method is also effective where shallow topsoil overlies chalk at a depth of about 45 cm [1′6″]. The disadvantage of mounding is that the tree is more vulnerable to drought, and generous watering is vital in dry periods, particularly in its early life. A mulch of garden compost will arrest surface evaporation.

Watering

The surface mulch will help to prevent evaporation and keep the soil moist during the first spring. This is a critical period for newly-planted trees and you must water freely and in adequate quantities in the first few summers if there is a drought.

Feeding

Apart from the sterilized bonemeal at planting, give no other manure the first season. In succeeding winters, dress the ground around each tree, a little further out than the branches extend, with 38 g per sq m [1¼ oz per sq yd] of sulphate of ammonia and 22 g per sq m [¾ oz per sq yd] of sulphate of potash. Do this in late winter, just raking the fertilizers into the surface.

Then every other year also rake in, at the same time, 54 g per sq m [1¾ oz per sq yd] of superphosphate. If the harvest has been heavy an extra fertilizer dressing is beneficial.

Thinning

If you let an apple tree bear an exceedingly heavy crop in any one year, it may take a rest the next season. The big crop, too, is likely to be of undersized fruit.

Dessert apples are thinned out to improve the appearance

and size of the individual fruit. Cookers tend to be naturally larger and are not thinned. Fruit thinning is less likely to be required on dwarf trees growing on M9 rootstock and trees trained as cordons and espaliers.

Some shedding of fruit occurs naturally about midsummer or just after, but the earlier you do any thinning the better for the tree. As soon as the fruitlets have 'set' (when a tiny but obvious fruitlet has replaced the blossom and you know a heavy crop is possible) take a thin pointed pair of scissors and cut out the king apple, the central fruitlet, from each cluster. The king apple often proves to be misshapen and of poor keeping quality. Remove any blemished fruitlets and, having done that, continue thinning until only one or two fruit remain out of each original cluster. These fruit should never be closer than 10 cm [4″] to the next cluster.

PRUNING THE TREE

The purpose of winter pruning is to build up a framework of robust main branches. Standards and half standards are pruned the same as bushes.

Immediately after planting give the tree its first pruning. Hard winter pruning stimulates the wood growth and at this stage of the tree's career that is what you want. Make sure your secateurs are really sharp. If it is an unpruned maiden (one-year-old) tree cut it back to half its height, leaving three or four good buds.

Second year: If you have bought a two-year-old tree, it will have only three or four branches. If these are strong and long, cut each back half way, making your cut close beyond a growth bud pointing outwards. If, however, these first branches are not very long and look thin and wispy, you must be more drastic and cut off two-thirds of the length of each. Cutting back these first branches causes growth buds near the cut ends to develop.

Third year: By the tree's third winter each of the three or four primary branches will have made three or more secondary branches. Cut back the previous summer's growth by a third of its length if strong, by a half if thin and wispy.

Meanwhile, by this time some sideshoots (also known as laterals) may have grown from the secondary branches. If these laterals are badly placed to make new branches, cut each back to its fourth bud. Slice off, flush with the stem, any sideshoots springing from the trunk of the tree just below the main branches.

Fourth year: The four-year-old tree may be regarded as adult. From now on restrict winter pruning to the minimum necessary to build up a continuing supply of fruiting wood rather than extending the size of the tree. Crossing branches and cankerous and broken branches should always be removed.

Encouraging fruiting wood

If you do not prune a sideshoot, it will make fruit buds in its second year. These are bigger, fatter and rounder than growth buds and the year after will burst into blossom in spring. Each winter leave some sideshoots untouched to bear fruit.

If more sideshoots are needed, cut back some to the second

bud from the base, but generally you should cut back the three-year-old sideshoots which have fruited to a 5 cm [2″] stump. Don't touch the tips of the branches once fruit-bearing has begun — unless a branch is growing in an undesirable direction and you want to replace the season's new extension growth with another one.

Under this system the tree will produce a good balance of fruiting laterals and vegetating ones, to provide fruit later. Some varieties also form fruit buds at the tips of one-year-old shoots. Leave such shoots intact.

TRAINING APPLES ON WIRES

A wall facing the midday sun may well be too warm for an apple and you would do better to plant one of the varieties of *Prunus*. Most economical of garden space is the cordon, where three different varieties can be grown in a 3 m [10′] row. Espaliers require a 4 m [14′] space and you must plant a pollinator. For training an espalier tree *see* PEAR.

Planting cordons

A cordon consists of a single stem bearing fruiting spurs. The tree is planted at an angle to restrict growth and to encourage early fruiting and an even production of buds on the stem.

If you have no suitable wall or fence, you can erect one as a garden divider, perhaps to separate the patio or lawn from the vegetable garden.

Put in sturdy posts about 2.1 m [7′6″] tall and about 3 m [10′] apart. Between these strain three 0.25 cm [1/10″] gauge galvanized wires at heights of 60 cm [2′], 1.25 m [4′] and 1.8 m [6′]. Use an adjustable fence strainer at the end of each wire to keep it taut. If possible, arrange the row to run from south to north.

Buy two- to three-year-old cordons and space them 75 cm [2′6″] apart in the row and, if you have more than one row, allow 1.8 m [6′] between rows. Plant them at an angle of 45° with the tip of the tree pointing away from the midday sun.

About 10 cm [4″] above the ground level mark, you will find a swelling, called the union. This is where the scion, the upper part of the tree or variety, is joined to the rootstock. You should hold the whole tree at an angle for planting, with the scion uppermost on the rootstock. Planted the other way round, the tree could break off its root.

Immediately after planting, tie the cordon to a 2.4 m [8′] long bamboo cane which has previously been secured to the three horizontal wires at an angle of 45°. Three ties are necessary, using soft string, with the lowest tie near the bottom end of the cane and 5 cm [2″] above the union.

Pruning cordons

No pruning is usually necessary during the winter except in the case of tip-bearing varieties. With these, cut back the main stem only, by a quarter of the previous season's growth, and repeat this in subsequent winters.

The main pruning of cordons is carried out in midsummer in warmer districts and as much as a month later in cooler ones. Start when you see that side-shoots growing directly from the main cordon stem are maturing — that is, they are more than 23 cm [9″] long, the leaves have lost their

Apple blossom needs shelter from wind to aid pollination.

THINNING FRUITLETS

Cut out the central fruitlet in each cluster and then any diseased or smaller fruitlets.

WINTER PRUNING PROGRAMME

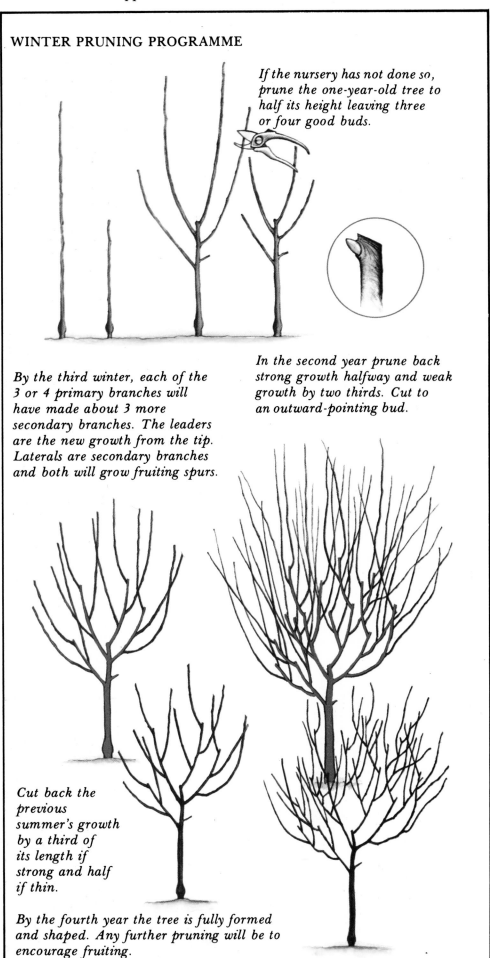

If the nursery has not done so, prune the one-year-old tree to half its height leaving three or four good buds.

In the second year prune back strong growth halfway and weak growth by two thirds. Cut to an outward-pointing bud.

By the third winter, each of the 3 or 4 primary branches will have made about 3 more secondary branches. The leaders are the new growth from the tip. Laterals are secondary branches and both will grow fruiting spurs.

Cut back the previous summer's growth by a third of its length if strong and half if thin.

By the fourth year the tree is fully formed and shaped. Any further pruning will be to encourage fruiting.

PLANTING CORDONS AND SUMMER PRUNING OF LATERALS

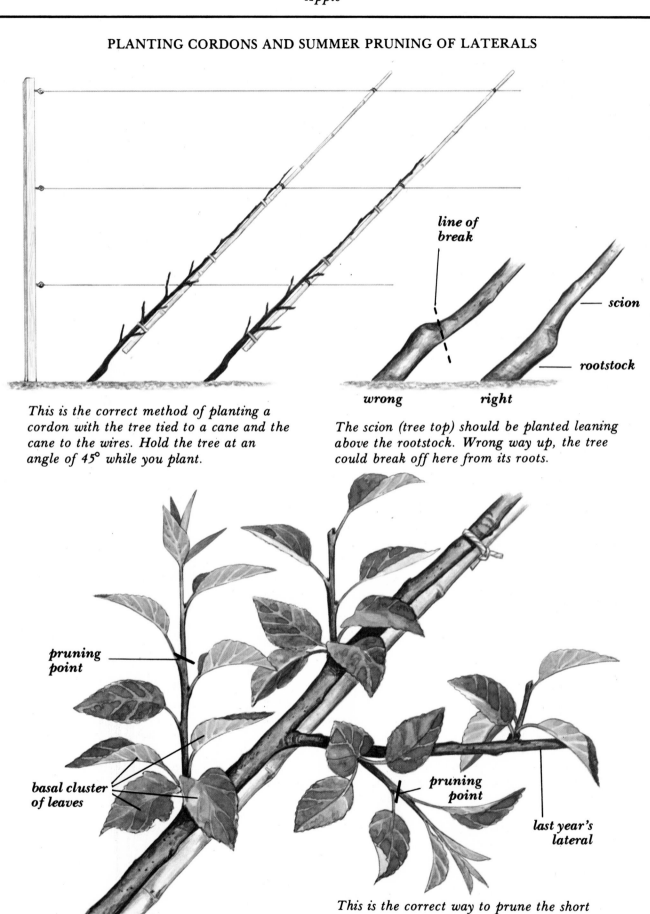

line of break

scion

rootstock

wrong   **right**

This is the correct method of planting a cordon with the tree tied to a cane and the cane to the wires. Hold the tree at an angle of 45° while you plant.

The scion (tree top) should be planted leaning above the rootstock. Wrong way up, the tree could break off here from its roots.

pruning point

basal cluster of leaves

pruning point

last year's lateral

This is the correct way to prune the short spurs of the cordon in summer to encourage it to produce fruit buds.

early brightness and become a deep green and the skin of the shoot has stiffened and begun to look definitely bark-like for the lower part of its length.

At the base of such a shoot you will usually find a cluster of leaves. Disregard these, count three leaves from the base of the shoot and then cut close after the third leaf. Then there may also be growths springing from laterals made and pruned a previous year. Cut each of these back to the first leaf beyond the basal cluster.

If some of the new shoots are not mature, wait till they are and then prune them. If secondary growth occurs in late summer from near the point where you made your first cuts, prune such shoots back to one leaf or bud in mid-autumn.

When the cordon reaches the length of its cane, probably after about three years, unfasten the cane from the wires and bend the whole tree down about 5° and refasten the cane. This can be repeated again a few years later.

Usually there comes a time when the mature tree stops producing further extension growth each summer but if it reaches the limit of space available before that happens, cut it back as necessary soon after new growth begins in the spring.

Except in the case of tip-bearing varieties, the leader should not normally be pruned until it must be checked for reasons of space. However, if the desired fruit-bearing sideshoots are scarce, stimulate the production of more by pruning the season's new extension growth of the leader by a third during winter. Individual buds in a bare length of stem can be encouraged by cutting a half-moon notch from the bark just above them.

At the other extreme, if after some years there are too many fruiting spurs and they are becoming crowded, cut some of these back and take out some entirely, doing this in winter.

HARVESTING AND STORING

A dwarf bush on M9 rootstock should start to bear fruit in its second garden summer. It will give crops of up to 28 kg [60 lb] in good seasons, but will probably average less than half this over the years. Very strong growers and those on rootstocks more vigorous than the dwarfing M9 will take longer before bearing.

Lift the apple in the palm of your hand and give it the slightest possible twist. If it is ready to pick it will come away easily. Handle dessert and cooking apples carefully; they bruise easily and this can spread rot among the stored crop. Cider and crabapples grown in grass may be allowed to drop off, or you can spread sheets underneath and shake the tree.

Cooking apples may be used before they are ripe, but their full flavour will develop with keeping. Cider apples must be allowed to mature off the tree before being used. When fully ripe, their flesh is easily bruised by thumb pressure. Pick and store dessert apples before they are ripe, otherwise they quickly deteriorate.

Apples require a well-ventilated, cool, slightly moist dark storage place, just below 5°C [40°F], possibly in a garden shed, garage or loft above the ceiling insulation. All these places would normally be too dry for storing apples, but

you can overcome this by storing the fruit in plastic bags. Only store sound dry fruit and put different varieties in different bags. Use a lot of small bags, rather than a few large ones, so that any rot cannot spread far. Seal the bags, then snip off a fingernail sized triangle from each bottom corner to admit a little air. Examine the apples periodically and use immediately any that begin to show soft bruising or brown; if left too long, these apples will be inedible.

PESTS AND DISEASES

Apples can be the victim of a number of pests and diseases: scab, mildew, caterpillars eating leaves (winter moths etc.) or fruitlets (sawfly), aphids of various kinds, capsids, apple suckers, red spider mite and scale insects. These can all be controlled by a routine spray programme.

There are also a number of troubles that could occur and which will not be controlled by the spray programme: canker, brown rot, American blight (woolly aphids), codling moth, bitter pit and birds.

Scab is a fungus disease producing black spots on leaves and fruit, which later cracks and may become infected with brown rot. It is worst in a wet spring and is treated with captan. Mildew produces white powdery patches on leaves and young shoots in spring, and infected flowers turn cream in colour and do not set. Remove infected shoots and spray with dinocap.

The white maggots of apple sawfly eat into the fruitlets and leave ribbon-like scars on resulting apples. Derris should be sprayed when most of the flower petals have fallen. Apple suckers feed on the undersurface of the leaves in the same way that aphids do and are controlled by the same insecticide. Capsid damage is mainly in the fruitlets. These develop pale scabs and become distorted in shape. Control as for aphids. Codling moth grubs have a brown head. From midsummer they go into the fruit through the eye and eat the centre. Spray with fenitrothian in early and midsummer.

American blight or woolly aphids are covered with white fluff and commonly feed on the junctions of the branches. The bark cracks, which allows the entry of canker and other fungal diseases. Malathion sprayed in early summer, repeated two weeks later, or brushing with methylated spirits, will control the aphids.

Canker is a fungus disease of the wood of the branches, trunk and shoot, which causes trouble in humid climates. The bark flakes and dies where fungus enters through tree wounds. If it encircles the stem, the branch above it will die. Wherever flaking bark is seen, the wood should be cut back below the infection to healthy growth, making a clean cut just above a joint. Paint large wounds with a fungicidal wax.

Bitter pit causes small brown pits in the flesh, giving it a bitter taste. Spray the leaves with calcium nitrate at two-to-three week intervals from early to late summer; less hard pruning, less nitrogenous fertilizer and regular watering will keep it in check. Brown rot infects the fruit, which then either drops, or remains mummified on the tree to infect next year's fruit. Fruit with brown skin or flesh should be destroyed as soon as seen, not stored.

VARIETIES OF DESSERT APPLE

Crispin is a heavy cropper but pollination is difficult.

Rome Beauty flowers late and bears well in warmer climates.

James Grieve is best eaten direct from the tree.

Charles Ross is not juicy but will tolerate chalk.

Sturmer Pippin is compact and likes warm dry areas.

Cox's Orange Pippin is famous but is tricky to grow.

Egremont Russet has a good flavour and yellow flesh.

Lord Lambourne is easy to grow and a heavy cropper.

Kidd's Orange Red is crisp, juicy and full of flavour.

Worcester Pearmain is juicy but is best grown as a bush, as it is a tip bearer.

Golden Delicious has a pleasant flavour but only succeeds where there is a lot of sun.

Granny Smith is a famous Australian apple, useful both for dessert and as a cooker.

Treatment

You can do one of three things with these troubles; if you adopt a simple regular spraying programme, you can keep most of them in check. Secondly you can spray only if troubles appear. Thirdly you can rely on natural predators, and hope regular feeding will aid the tree to resist fungal disease. You will get some marked fruit and occasionally lose a crop, but cultural care and cutting out should restrain most troubles.

A spray programme could be as follows:

Every three years: spray with tar oil during the tree's dormant or leafless period, to control the eggs of aphids, winter moth and suckers, and adult scale insects, and to clean the bark of lichen, moss etc., which harbour troubles.

Every year: the first spray, when the leaves are unfolding, is with captan to control scab, and malathion and derris against aphids, capsids, apple suckers and winter moth caterpillars.

The second spray, about two weeks later when the blossom buds are showing pink, contains captan, dinocap (for mildew) and the same insecticides.

The third spray is at petal fall when nearly all blossom is off. Never spray fully opened flowers, because of the danger to bees and helpful pollination insects. This spray is against pests and diseases already mentioned and also apple sawfly caterpillars and red spider mites. Pesticides can usually be applied together, but not all are compatible, so follow the maker's instructions.

Apricot

Luxurious, orange-fleshed fruit,
apricots grow on small trees and
are therefore very suitable for
the home garden.
They flourish in warm climates.

The Romans, who introduced the apricot tree into Europe, named it *Praecocia,* meaning early, and this evolved into the word 'apricot'. It is one of the earliest fruit trees to flower. It is more tender than the plum, to which it is related, but less tender than the peach. In cooler temperate areas, unprotected blossoms are all too often damaged by cold and the tree needs the shelter of a wall facing the midday sun.

Suitable site and soil

In the coolest parts of the temperate zone you would be unwise to plant apricots except under glass; a cool well-ventilated greenhouse will afford adequate protection. A slightly heated greenhouse is suitable too but the fruit will not be much earlier than the normal season — it is difficult to force apricots into fruiting early.

In relatively frost-free parts of the cool temperate area the tree will still need the shelter of a wall, which should be a minimum of 2.5 m [8'] high. Because it blooms in very early spring, when some of the bleakest cold winds are experienced, the flowers have difficulty in setting, that is, becoming fertilized so that fruit will form. The tree produces best results when fan-trained on a wall. In a Mediterranean climate apricots grow successfully as bushes.

The apricot dislikes clays or soils which are wet and cold; good drainage therefore is essential. It likes a chalky loam.

Buying the tree

Buy a two or three-year-old tree and specify either a fan or a bush according to where it is to be planted. With a fan it is advisable to let the nurseryman carry out the initial shaping. A dwarf fan, which has no central leader but is formed from a Y-shape, is recommended.

A bush tree in the open needs 3.5 m [12'] square. On a wall, if space is limited, ask for a fan on semi-dwarfing stock, which has a height of 2.5 m [8'] and a spread of between 4.6 m [15'] and 6.1 m [20'] according to soil conditions. A tree on vigorous stock will eventually grow to 3.5 m [12'] in height and 7.5 m [25'] in spread.

Apricots can be grown from seed by sowing the stones 7.5 cm [3"] deep and 60 cm [2'] apart. However, this could be an unrewarding labour, as apricots do not grow true from seed, and you will wait for several years for the result.

Planting the tree

To prepare the site, fork the soil, adding a 10-12 L bucket of compost or peat per sq m [2-2½ gal per sq yd] plus bonemeal at 125 g per sq m [4 oz per sq yd]. Test the soil and if the pH shows acidity, add powdered lime at 212 g per sq m [7 oz per sq yd] as a top dressing. This dressing

---

Apricot
Prunus armeniaca (fam. Rosaceae)
Hardy deciduous tree, with heart-shaped leaves, and a useful life of about 50 years.
Size: 2.5-4.5 m [8-15'] tall.
Climate: cool to warm temperate.
Planting to harvesting time: two years for three-year-old trees.
Yield: for mature, semi-dwarf tree 15-20 kg [35-40 lb].

will gradually be washed into the soil by the rain.

Plant allowing 4.5 m [15'] to 7.6 m [25'], according to the vigour of the stock, between fan-shaped trees to be trained along a wall. Plant 15-22 cm [6-9"] from the wall. In the case of bush trees planted in the open, allow 3.5 m [12'] between trees each way.

Plant no deeper than 20 cm [8"]. Dig out a hole 15 cm [6"] deep and 1m [3'] across. Prune back any damaged roots. Spread out the roots evenly in the hole.

Place a spadeful of soil over each root and stamp this down firmly. Then fill the hole, firming after each few spadefuls. When you have finished, there should be a slight mound toward the main stem of the tree. This allows for settling later on. If this is not done, the soil tends to become concave and trouble may be caused by water collecting there.

Watering

Water liberally during dry weather. Trees growing against a wall are particularly susceptible to drought, as are greenhouse trees, and lack of water may cause immature fruit to drop.

Feeding

Mulch the ground 2.5 cm [1"] deep all round the tree for 1 m [3'] or so using compost or peat. Wood ash may be applied each early spring at the rate of 155 g per sq m [5 oz per sq yd] and bonemeal at 90 g per sq m [3 oz per sq yd]. These are very lightly raked in. Hydrated lime may be applied every 4 or 5 years at 185 g per sq m [6 oz per sq yd] if the soil test indicates that acidity is present.

Pollination

In cold areas during blossoming give the tree shelter on cold nights by hanging hessian or plastic sheets over it. Nail a batten above the tree and hang your cover from this; it should not touch the flowers.

The fine pink flowers are self-fertile but in cool temperate areas they need help to set. At mid-day when the flowers are fully open, stroke the centres of the blossoms with a fine paint brush — this will artificially transfer the male pollen from the anthers to the stigmas.

Thinning

When the fruit are formed and are as big as peas, remove

In the coldest parts of cool temperate areas, apricots should not be attempted, and even in milder parts they need the shelter of a wall facing the midday sun.

Apricots make small trees and can be grown in pots. Ensure good drainage and fill with potting compost. Keep this moist in summer, drier in winter. Restrict pruning to the minimum that is necessary.

half of the smallest. Repeat the operation when they are the size of small walnuts, leaving the apricots spaced out evenly all over the tree 10 cm [4″] apart.

Pruning and training

A fan-trained apricot should be pruned and tied in the same way as a peach (*see* PEACH) in its formative years.

Fruit is produced on the shoots of the preceding year's growth and on short spurs carried on the older wood. Do not prune in winter, because of the danger of die-back disease in temperate areas.

For a fan, in midsummer cut back any vigorous current season's shoots to just above the fifth leaf from the base of the shoot. Leave untouched both weaker shoots and those required to extend the framework for a fan. After cropping, cut back the same pruned shoots to three leaves from a spur which will then bear fruit next year.

Pinch out unnecessary crowding shoots in the course of the summer when they are only 2.5 cm [1″] long. As soon as the fruit has been picked, any shoots badly placed for a fan can be removed and the branches re-tied to leave them evenly spaced over the wall.

Harvesting and storing the crop

Fruit should be gathered when just ripe, usually in late summer. The top of the fruit, near the stalk, should be slightly soft. Pick very carefully to avoid bruising. Pick in the morning as soon as the fruit is perfectly dry. If you have a cool room like a larder, you can extend the eating season by two or three weeks by picking the fruit when fully coloured but still hard, letting it ripen slowly. It is, however, difficult to force fruit to ripen early by additional heat in the greenhouse.

Pests and diseases

Die-back is the most damaging disease of apricots in temperate areas, and is not easy to cure. If a branch does die, saw it off so that the wound is smooth. Paint the cut with a wound-sealing compound to prevent the growth of fungus, and destroy the branch. See the diagrams in CHERRY for the correct way to remove a branch.

Other troubles are the fungus disease silver leaf (*see* PLUM) and red spider mites and scale insects. Every third year spray with a 5% solution of tar-oil wash against wintering eggs. Spraying with water keeps down red spider mite.

Stroke flowers with a paintbrush to transfer pollen.

In Mediterranean climates apricots are successful on bushes.

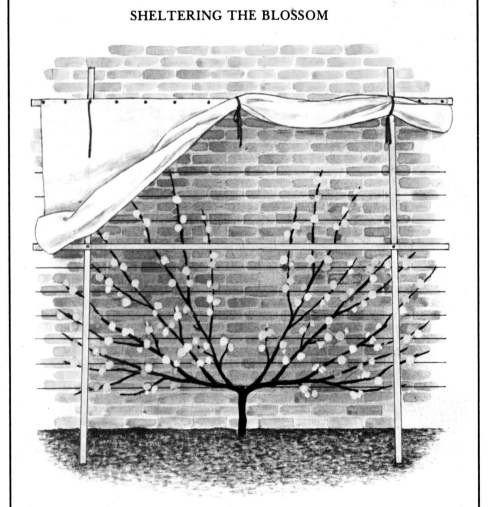

SHELTERING THE BLOSSOM

Blossom needs shelter on cold nights. Support a batten on the wall by two poles, and suspend netting or plastic from it. This should not be allowed to touch the flowers.

Artichoke

This strikingly handsome, thistle-like plant has arching, grey-green leaves and looks attractive enough to plant among shrubs or in a herbaceous border.

The globe-shaped flower buds consist of numerous edible 'leaves' or scales on a fleshy base. Always choose varieties with green globes, which are delicious and tender: purple globes have beautiful flowers but are not worth eating.

Suitable site and soil

The ideal position is sunny, well protected from wind and away from trees and hedges. If you are planning your kitchen garden on a rotation system, remember that artichokes must stay in the same place for four years and will develop into large, bushy plants.

Globe artichokes like a rich soil which is moist but well drained (not water-logged in winter). Light sandy soil is best. If you have a heavy soil, break up the subsoil, then lighten the topsoil with ashes, coarse sand, peat or grit. These plants will give three good years of production only if they have a deep bed, rich in nutrients. To prepare poor soil for planting, apply some garden compost or well-rotted farm manure. Dig either of these in well during late winter or early spring, at a rate of about half a barrow-load per 5 sq m [6 sq yd]. A general fertilizer should be incorporated before planting; dig over the soil and distribute the fertilizer over the area to a depth of 10 cm [4″], at a proportion of 100 g per sq m [3 oz per sq yd].

Artichoke, globe
Cynara scolymus (fam. *Compositae*).
Hardy perennial with a useful life of four years.
Size: the bushy, herbaceous plants reach about 1-1.75 m [3′-5′] high, 1 m [3′] in diameter.
Climate: cool temperate to sub-tropical.
Planting to harvesting time: the plants crop in the second year from offsets, in the third year from seed.
Yield: about 5 king heads and 10 side heads per plant per season.

A crop of globe artichokes heads ready for harvesting.

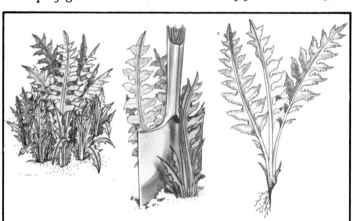

Propagate new plants by cutting offsets (side shoots) about 25 cm [10″] high from the base of the plant in spring. Plant with a piece of root attached.

Both the main kingheads and the smaller laterals are delicious to eat.

Lay leaf-mould over the crowns of cut-down plants in autumn to protect them from frosts.

Sowing and planting

Artichokes can be grown from seed but the results are often erratic and it is better and easier to start with suckers, known as offsets, from a well-proven plant. Buy your offsets in mid-spring. Plant firmly 10 cm [4"] deep, in rows at least 1 m [3'] apart, with 75 cm [2'6"] between plants. Water well and mulch with garden compost or rotted manure.

If you wish to try seeds, sow after the last spring frost 1.5 cm [½"] deep and 30 cm [1'] apart. Care for seedlings as for offsets, thinning to 1 m [3'] apart when they grow too closely together.

Watering and feeding

Water the artichokes well and often through spring and summer, especially in dry periods. They must never be allowed to become dry at the roots.

In spring, a sprinkling of sodium nitrate, 15 g [½ oz] per plant, on damp soil provides a good start to growth.

Substitute ammonium sulphate on clay soils which are made even heavier by sodium salts. Fork garden compost between rows every spring.

In summer, apply a good liquid fertilizer at 10-day intervals. In this mid-season of vigorous growth, two weak doses of chelated iron (marketed under several names) are of great help. Lawn mowings spread around from time to time help retain moisture in the soil. Tall plants may need staking. Choose stakes strong enough to bear the full weight of the plant and insert them firmly. Tie the main stem to the stake, allowing room for the plant to sway naturally, otherwise the flower heads may snap off.

Harvesting the crop

First year: there will probably be no big heads the first year, as the first main crop matures in the second year of growth. Some small buds will appear and should be pinched out at the first sign of formation to build up the basic plant and make it more productive for next year's harvest.

Second year: large terminal buds, known as king heads, should be picked for eating when firm. These will be about 10 cm [4"] in diameter. The leaves should be green, tightly packed and not yet opened for flowering. Each plant should produce at least five king heads. If the heads are left to mature to full growth they become inedible and the chokes open out into immense purple-blue thistles. Once the king head is picked, lateral (side) shoots then develop and smaller heads will grow, which can also be picked and eaten.

Care after harvesting

After all the good heads are gathered, cut down the artichoke stems and most of the large leaves, except for a few leaves to protect the crown. If your area is liable to suffer frost or biting winter winds, protect the plants in mid autumn with straw manure and a covering of bracken, wood shavings, a raked-up 10 cm [4"] covering of earth, or a mulch of compost or leafmould. Remove these coverings after danger of hard frosts is over in the following spring. No row should be left to grow after it is more than four years old. Plant a new row of offsets each year so that the old rows can be dug up and replaced.

Propagation

To propagate new plants for the following season, take offsets from the base of an established parent plant when about 25 cm [10"] high in early or mid spring. Use a sharp knife to remove the offsets and see that a piece of root is attached, to help growth. Plant offsets immediately after cutting them.

Pests and diseases

Artichoke hearts may be infected with a fungus disease called blight fungus which rots the petals. Remove infected heads as soon as seen.

Other problems which may occur include slugs, aphids and earwigs.

JERUSALEM AND CHINESE
Artichokes

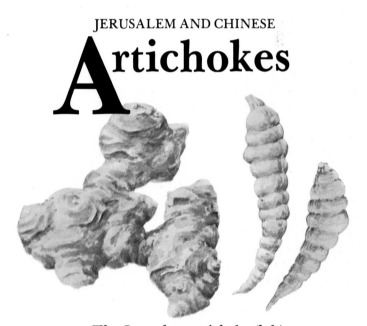

The Jerusalem artichoke (left)
and Chinese artichoke (right)
are both unusual and tasty
tubers which will grow in almost any
soil and give high yields for
very little gardening effort.

The Jerusalem artichoke is a hardy vegetable native to North America. It is related to neither the globe nor the

---

Artichoke, Jerusalem
Helianthus tuberosus (fam. *Compositae*)
Perennial, treated as an **annual.**
Size: about 1.5-2.5 m [5-8'] tall.
Climate: temperate.
Planting to harvesting time: about 9-11 months.
Yield: about 1 kg [2 lb] per plant, with 5 plants per 3 m [10'] row.

1. Dress the soil with wood ash before planting, to remedy any potash deficiency.

2. Another way of planting out. Make drills 10 cm [4"] deep, 75 cm [2½'] apart. Set tubers 38 cm [15"] apart.

3. Tying-up to avoid wind damage. Use string to tie the plants to strands of wire between stakes.

4. At the approach of winter, cut off the dead stems and foliage fairly close to the ground.

5. Forking up. Take care not to spear the tubers, and be sure to clear the ground. Any remaining portions will grow next year, spreading like a weed.

6. In a severe winter, store tubers in dry peat or sand in a cool place. Rub off any soil and arrange them sandwich fashion in containers.

Chinese artichoke, being a member of the sunflower (*Helianthus*) group of the family *Compositae*. It is straightforward to grow and provides an excellent winter crop. The tall stem and broad leaves resemble those of the annual sunflower.

The swollen edible roots, or tubers, are knobbly with either 'white' (buff-coloured) or purple skins. The 'white' type is better flavoured and far more widely available. The tubers are about the size of a small potato tuber, extremely irregular in shape but usually with a rounded base and tapering to a long thin end.

Jerusalem artichokes are underrated vegetables perhaps because, in their raw state, they are rather unattractive to look at. But properly prepared they have a subtle flavour and can be used in an interesting variety of dishes, from soups to desserts.

Suitable site and soil

Although these plants will grow in almost any position in the garden and in almost any soil type, a sunny site is preferable and fertile, well-drained soil is the ideal. The tubers can be planted in early spring for harvesting the following autumn and winter. In a rotation system, however, it may be a better use of space to plant them in late autumn in ground which has been used for summer crops of peas, beans, potatoes or cabbages.

Planting out

The tubers themselves are planted because, like potatoes, they bear tiny buds which will sprout into new plants. You should be able to obtain tubers from seedsmen or grocers.

Use a garden line to mark out straight rows spaced 1 m [3'] apart. A trowel or a dibber may be used to make planting holes 15 cm [6"] deep at 60 cm [2'] intervals. Plant the tubers, cover them and fill in the planting holes. The tubers should sprout in about 2-4 weeks.

Care and development

In temperate regions, Jerusalem artichokes usually require little watering because rainfall provides sufficient moisture, but give plenty of water in dry areas.

Prevent weed growth either by hoeing the weed seedlings in spring or by applying a mulch of straw or lawn mowings around the plants in early summer.

In sheltered areas this vegetable may be grown as a windbreak or as a screen to hide an unsightly view from the garden. In windy areas, however, gales can damage the plants severely. To prevent such damage, pinch off the top of the plants when they reach a height of 1.5 m [5']. Hammer stakes into the ground at either end of each row with additional stakes at 1.5 m [5'] intervals in the rows. Link the stakes together with two or three strands of wire and tie the plants to the wires with garden string.

Harvesting the crop

When the stems and foliage die and turn brown in autumn, the tubers are ready to use. Stored tubers have less flavour than freshly dug ones, so the tubers should not be dug up until they are required in the kitchen.

They can be lifted at any time from late autumn to late winter. The tubers are not loose, like potatoes, but are found growing tightly packed together.

Storing the crop

Where winters are severe and the ground may freeze solid, remove the tubers from the roots, rub off any soil and store them in dry sand or peat in a cool place.

Take care that all the tubers have been cleared from the site after harvesting. If you are not replanting immediately, keep enough large tubers in store to use for planting the next crop.

CHINESE ARTICHOKE

This is a rare vegetable, and tubers for planting are not easy to obtain. It was introduced from China less than 100 years ago and was first grown in Europe at Crôsnes in France — hence its alternative name, crôsnes. Like the Jerusalem artichoke, it is grown for the sake of its tubers, which are long and tapered, with billowing rings. They need to be thoroughly washed before use. It is a low, bushy, undistinguished plant.

Cultivation

This crop needs a rich but not heavy soil. If necessary, lighten a heavy soil by an application of peat. Dig in a generous quantity of garden compost or farmyard manure the autumn before planting.

Propagation is by means of tubers, like potatoes. Plant in early spring, about 10 cm [4"] deep, and 25 cm [10"] apart, in rows 45 cm [18"] apart. Protect against late frosts by covering with sacks, straw or cloches. There is no transplanting.

Water lavishly, particularly in dry weather. Feed plants frequently — every week or ten days — with liquid manure. Chinese artichoke tubers are quite small — much smaller than those of the Jerusalem artichoke — and need coaxing to grow to a worthwhile size. Hoe frequently between the plants. Slugs are the main pest.

Harvesting and storing

In autumn you can lift the tubers and either use them immediately, or store them in damp soil. Alternatively you can leave them in the ground until required, making sure that you provide protection against frost. However you store your tubers, remember to retain enough for next season's planting. Once the crop has become established, it is difficult to eradicate without very thorough digging.

After cropping, dead stalks and leaves go on the compost heap. You can grow Chinese artichokes for several years on the same plot without deterioration in quantity or quality.

Chinese artichoke
Stachys affinis (fam. *Labiatae*)
Perennial, but treated as an **annual.**
Size: to about 45 cm [18"] high and 50 cm [20"] wide.
Climate: temperate.
Sowing to harvesting time: about 8 months.
Yield: 11 or 12 plants per 3 m [10'] row.

Asparagus

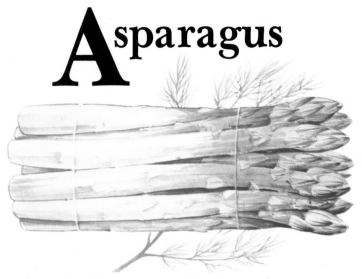

**Freshly cut spears of asparagus have
such an outstanding flavour that
the effort involved in growing
this luxury vegetable is very worth while.**

One of the oldest of cultivated vegetables, asparagus was grown by the Romans as early as 200 BC. Asparagus is a superb delicacy but it is becoming increasingly expensive to buy as a vegetable, which makes it all the more worthwhile to grow.

At least 12 flourishing asparagus plants are needed to provide a weekly portion for a family of four during harvesting. Young asparagus shoots are cut in spring and early summer when 0.5-1.5 cm [¼-½″] in diameter and 7.5-10 cm [3-4″] high. Any shoots that are not harvested grow to bear elegant, fern-like foliage.

Provided instructions are followed with care, growing good crops of asparagus is a rewarding project which should not present great problems. The main deterrent is the three-year gap between sowing and your first harvest. However, that gap can be bridged by buying one or two-year-old crowns from a nursery. In this way you can have an established bed in a comparatively short time.

The seed bed

Young plants are going to stay where the seed is sown for a full year before being transplanted, so take care to select a sunny, sheltered site where the plants can grow undisturbed, and prepare the bed well. Make sure it is completely free of weeds, particularly perennials. The soil should be rich, with a good humus content — preferably

> **Asparagus**
> *Asparagus officinalis* (fam. *Liliaceae*)
> **Perennial** with a useful life of at least 20 years.
> **Size:** grows in bush form to a height of about 1.5 m [5′].
> **Climate:** temperate to sub-tropical.
> **Planting to harvesting time:** from seed 3 years; from transplant 2 years.
> **Yield** per plant (once established) is about 25 spears per year.

well-rotted garden compost or farmyard manure. Autumn is the best time for preparation: the manure can then be well buried and the bed left rough during the winter.

Sow the seed in mid spring, thinly in rows about 2.5 cm [1″] deep, with 45 cm [1′6″] between the rows. Tubs, boxes or flower pots can also be used as seed beds in a small garden. The seed should germinate within 7-21 days.

Keep the bed well watered and free from weeds throughout the summer. When the seedlings are about 15 cm [6″] high, thin out to about 30 cm [1′] apart.

In autumn, when the feathery foliage begins to turn yellow, cut the plants down to almost ground level. Some of them will probably be bearing berries. These are the female plants, which are not such good croppers as the males. If enough male plants are available the females can be rooted out and destroyed. If doubtful, mark the females so that the males can be transplanted first in the following spring. Pick up all berries and either burn the berry-bearing foliage or bury it deep in the compost heap.

The main bed

Preparing the main bed is without doubt the most important factor in growing asparagus successfully. It takes time and trouble but is essential. Remember that once the bed is established it will continue producing an annual crop for at least 20 years; 50 years is not unknown.

The ideal soil is a sandy loam. If your soil is too light, dig in plenty of garden compost or farmyard manure. If too heavy, treat with coarse sand to break up its close texture. If very heavy and waterlogged, it is better to grow the asparagus in raised beds. Work on the soil should begin in autumn.

Traditionally asparagus beds are 1.2-1.8 m [4-6′] wide. A bed 1.2 m [4′] wide takes two parallel rows of plants; a bed 1.8 m [6′] wide takes three staggered rows. Alternatively, if it suits your layout better, you can grow the plants 30 cm [1′] apart, in rows 90 cm [3′] apart.

It is a good idea to run a path on either side of the bed so that cultivation and harvesting can be carried out without treading on the soil, and without damaging the plants. In autumn dig in garden compost or well-rotted manure, and remove all weeds, especially perennials, from the site.

If the soil is extremely stony, waterlogged or otherwise unsuitable, the bed should be raised completely above ground level. For this you will have to construct a retaining wall all round, about 60 cm [2′] high, built with brick, concrete, stone or old railway sleepers. Fill the beds with soil to the top of the wall, dig in a layer of garden compost or well-rotted manure, then build a mound of soil on top about 30 cm [1′] high in the centre.

Setting out the transplants

Transplanting is done in spring. If you have grown from seed, you should be transplanting the one-year-old plants. If you are buying plants from a nursery make sure they are one or two-year-old plants: do not be tempted to buy three-year-old crowns because they are far too old to

Asparagus is a delicious vegetable delicacy, and the taste of spears fresh from the garden is unsurpassed.

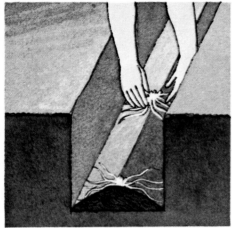

1. *Placing asparagus crowns in a trench. Spread the roots out well.*

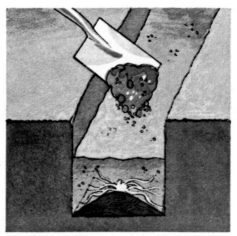

2. *Cover the roots with fine soil and gradually cover the crowns.*

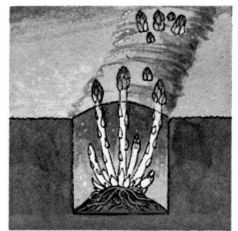

3. *Fill the trench gradually during the first year, as the plant grows.*

4. *Harvesting the shoots, using a sharp knife, cutting at an angle.*

5. *In autumn, all foliage should be cut down, almost to ground level.*

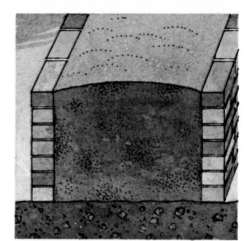

Asparagus can be grown in raised beds if soil is stony or waterlogged.

A traditional asparagus bed will probably look like this: they are usually 1.2-1.8 m [4-6'] wide.

Weed-free asparagus in the seedling stage. The beds should always be kept well watered, particularly during hot, dry weather, and they should also be weeded regularly and carefully during the growing season.

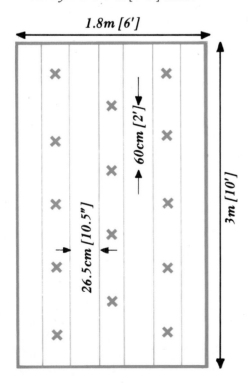

survive unscathed the shock of being transplanted.

In early spring dig trenches about 25 cm [10″] deep and wide, then put a little more garden compost or well-rotted manure and loamy soil along the bottom of the trench in the centre to make a small ridge. If you have bought crowns — which should arrive from the nursery in mid spring — get everything ready beforehand so that they can be planted immediately to avoid danger of drying out.

Allow 45-60 cm [1½-2′] between the plants in the rows. In fertile soils in warm climates allow 90 cm [3′] between plants. Asparagus roots are long and must be spread out well over the ridge. Cover the roots with fine soil, burying the crowns completely so that they are about 10 cm [4″] below the surface, and water well. Do not fill the trenches immediately; fill them gradually during the first year as the plant grows so that by the end of the year the land is flat, that is either level with the ground or the top of the curve of the raised bed. Build up the retaining walls if necessary.

Care and development

If one-year-old plants have been transplanted, a two-year waiting period now lies ahead. Even if two-year-old plants are used, they cannot be cropped in the first year and they will benefit in the long run from a two-year rest. But, meanwhile, there is useful work to be done on the asparagus bed.

The beds always need to be kept well-watered, particularly during hot, dry summers. Weeding must be carried out regularly throughout the growing season. With the advance of summer, any female plants retained will bear red berries. These berries should be removed — without damaging the foliage — as they only weaken the plants. In autumn, cut down all foliage almost to ground level and put it on the compost heap.

Harvesting the crop

The time invested in growing is repaid by the fact that only people who grow their own asparagus can ever hope to taste this delectable vegetable at its best. Ideally, asparagus should be cut only an hour before using. The succulent spring shoots are cut when they are 7.5-10 cm [3-4″] above the surface of the bed. Scrape the soil away and cut the shoot about 7.5-10 cm [3-4″] below the surface, taking great care not to damage adjacent shoots.

In the second year after transplanting, the first harvesting year, cut about three shoots only from each plant. These should be some of the earliest shoots; leave all the later ones, otherwise you will kill the plant.

In subsequent years, cut every shoot that appears for about two months but never after midsummer. Some of these shoots will be thin and straggly, and are known as sprue. They are good only for soup, but if allowed to grow they will use up resources that should go to the more vigorous shoots.

Care after harvesting

Stop cutting after about two months. After then, any shoots that appear should be allowed to grow to maturity so that crowns are built up for the next year. The plants should be kept well watered, with occasional applications of liquid manure until winter. The foliage is cut back to within 2.5 cm [1″] of the ground in autumn (as in its first unproductive years), and a topdressing of farmyard manure, garden compost or seaweed applied. This not only feeds the plants but also helps to protect them from any winter storms and severe frosts.

Before spreading the layer of manure, clear off any remaining weeds from the site and lightly fork over the surrounding soil.

Pests and diseases

Asparagus has one fairly common specific pest: the asparagus beetle *(Crioceris asparagi)*. This beetle has reddish wingcases bearing a double black cross. Its grubs are grey, with black heads and legs. Both beetles and grubs (of which there may be several generations in the course of a summer) feed on the shoots and foliage of the plants, and can seriously weaken them. Apply an insecticide, such as derris or pyrethrum, preferably in powdered form wherever the insects are observed. Several applications may have to be made at intervals throughout the summer. In autumn the debris cleaned from the bed should be burned, as the pests can overwinter in the dry hollow stems.

Other troubles which affect asparagus are slugs and snails and the fungus disease violet root rot.

Asparagus Pea

The square-shaped pea pod is eaten whole and has a delicate flavour similar to that of asparagus.

This unusual vegetable is native to Sicily. Quite different in growth and appearance from the common garden pea, the asparagus pea makes a low, spreading plant which bears reddish brown flowers. Asparagus peas are easy to grow, and are becoming very popular with gardeners who appreciate delicately flavoured vegetables. The pods must be eaten while they are young and tender, otherwise they become very stringy.

Cultivation
Plant in an open site which receives plenty of sunshine, in light sandy soil. If possible, give the ground a dressing of rotted farmyard or stable manure or garden compost, which should be dug in during the winter months. If these are not available, rake into the surface a well balanced, complete fertilizer at the rate of 90 g per sq m [3 oz per sq yd] about ten days before sowing.

Make a V-shaped drill about 5 cm [2″] deep, space the seeds about 10 cm [4″] apart in the row, allowing 40 cm [15″] between rows. In warmer areas seed can be sown any time in mid spring, whereas the early part of late spring is preferable in colder areas. To ensure a continuous supply of peas, make a second sowing about 3-4 weeks after the first one.

As soon as the young seedlings break the surface of the soil, hoe through the soil as close as possible to the plants to kill off any weed seedlings and to promote healthy growth of the plants. Repeat when necessary during the life of the plant. If the soil has been well prepared, no further feeding during growth should be necessary. Unlike the garden pea, this plant does not produce tendrils, and support is not required.

Harvesting the crop
Pods should be ready to pick about 12-13 weeks after sowing, in mid to late summer, according to climatic conditions prevailing during growth. It is essential to gather the pods when very young and tender, the ideal being about 2.5-3 cm [1-1¼″] long and certainly before the 'peas' in the pod have reached any size. After harvesting pull up plants and add to the compost heap.

Pests and diseases
None.

Asparagus pea
Lotus tetragonolobus, synonym *Tetragonolobus purpureus* (fam. *Leguminosae)*, also known as winged pea or Goa bean.
Hardy annual.
Size: grows to about 30 cm [1′] high.
Climate: temperate; will not withstand extreme heat or frost.
Sowing to harvesting time: 12-13 weeks.
Yield: 14 kg [30 lb] on average per 3 m [10′] row.

Aubergine
See EGGPLANT

Asparagus pea in flower. The plant grows in a low, spreading formation. The young, tender pods are an unusual and delicately flavoured vegetable.

Balm

**Balm is very easy to grow and is one
of the first herbs to appear in the spring.
Its strong, fresh lemon scent attracts
bees to the garden.**

Balm *(Melissa officinalis* — which translated means 'bee
plant') grows in clumps with erect branches, nettle-like
leaves and small, tubular, white flowers. The green-leaved
variety is used in cooking to give a sweet, lemon flavour
and for making a refreshing tea.

Cultivation
Balm is native to the Mediterranean but will grow in
almost any situation, resisting both moderate frosts and
high temperatures. It prefers fairly rich, moist soil and in
dry, light soils benefits from a little shade. In towns, balm
can be grown in pots, tubs or window boxes, but must be
kept well-watered. A pot of balm will also grow well indoors on a sunny windowsill and is a useful fresh herb for
flavouring food in winter.

It is best to start balm from a young nursery plant in mid
spring or mid autumn. Balm has invasive roots that may
need restraining in a herb garden. A common and reliable
method is to plant the herb in a bottomless container, such
as a bucket without a bottom or part of a drainpipe, which
has been sunk into the ground and filled with good soil.
This will prevent the roots spreading into neighbouring
plants.

If you cannot get young plants, sow the seed in a shallow
drill about 1.5 cm [½"] deep and thin the seedlings, which
appear after three to four weeks, to 30 cm [1'] apart.

An established balm plant will set a lot of seed and this can
be a nuisance in a herb garden. Keep a watch for unwanted seedlings and weed them out as they appear.

Harvesting and aftercare
Pick leaves for immediate use as required throughout the
spring, when they are most tender. After the plant flowers

*An attractive bush of lemon-scented balm. This
easily grown herb can also be raised in pots.*

in early summer the leaves begin to grow tough. Mid to
late summer is the best time for harvesting the leaves for
drying. Dried balm should be kept in a dark screw-cap jar
and stored in a dry, dark place.

Cut the stems down to the ground in autumn, and in exceptionally frosty areas protect the balm plants with straw.
To propagate new plants, you can divide and replant the
roots in autumn or spring. Space the root sections 30 cm
[1'] apart in soil that has been dug over and treated with
compost.

Basil

**Basil originated in tropical India and
is still regarded by Hindus as a herb
sacred to the gods Vishnu and Krishna.
Excellent in cooking, basil's spicy-flavoured
leaves can be used fresh or dried.**

Although basil *(Ocimum basilicum)* comes from tropical
Asia, it will grow outdoors in temperate climates. Bush
basil *(Ocimum minimum)* is a smaller, more compact,
slightly hardier type which is more suitable for cool
climates.

Cultivation
Ideally, basil should be grown in a warm, sheltered
position facing the midday sun. In very warm climates it
benefits from semi-shady positions. Basil prefers light,
rich, well-drained soil. Before sowing dig the soil and add
some well-rotted garden compost, peat or leafmould.

Sow the seed 20 cm [8"] apart in mid spring. In a cool
region you may wish to start the seed under glass. Sow two
or three seeds spaced apart in a 5 cm [2"] pot filled with
potting compost. Maintain a fairly constant 15°C [60°F],
when germination should take about 14 days, then
gradually get the seedlings used to cooler temperatures
until they are planted outside in late spring. Plant the
whole root ball of the seedling without breaking it up.

33

In late summer pinch off the flowers and stem tips to encourage a leafier plant, water in dry weather and hoe lightly to deter weeds.

Harvesting and aftercare
Cut the leaves freshly as needed throughout summer. Take leaves for drying, just before the plant flowers in late summer. Hang them upside down in a dark, warm place and when they are dry crumble the leaves and store in a tightly-sealed jar for use through the winter.

After harvesting, pull up the plant and add it to the compost heap. Before doing so you may take cuttings to propagate a supply of new plants. These should be potted and usually produce roots after a few days. Bush basil grows very well in pots and is a useful winter herb. Dig up the selected plants in late summer and pot them up individually using 10 cm [4"] containers.

Using basil
Basil is considered invaluable among herbs in Italy, where it is used extravagantly, and in India, where it is a common ingredient in curry dishes, but it is less familiar elsewhere. It is especially suited to any tomato dish, but also gives a special flavour to cheese, egg and fish dishes. Unlike most herbs basil actually becomes stronger in flavour in cooking, so it should be used more carefully in cooked dishes than in salads and sandwiches.

Bay

Bay is the only tree whose leaves are used as a culinary herb. The ancient Greeks knew it as laurel, a symbol of glory and honour for poets and heroes.

Bay *(Laurus nobilis)* is a handsome, dense evergreen tree with smooth, pungent, dark green leaves and in late spring it produces small yellow flowers, followed by glossy black berries. The leaves may be used in cooking either fresh or dried and are one of the ingredients in the classic French *bouquet garni*.

Cultivation
Choose a sunny, sheltered site, allowing about 1.8 m [6'] clearance all around. A few weeks before planting in mid spring, dig some well-rotted garden compost or manure into the soil.

When ordering your bay, try to obtain a three-year-old, well-rooted tree with healthy, dark, shiny foliage and about 1 m [3'] high. Water the plant in its container before planting.

Dig the planting hole deep enough to cover the roots to the original soil line on the stem, and wide enough for the roots to be well spread out. Return a little soil to the hole, carefully remove the tree from its pot and place it in the hole. Fill in with soil, shaking the plant gently so that the soil can settle naturally between the roots and continue to fill the hole gradually. Firm the soil all the way around at intervals until the hole is full, then tread it in firmly, fill in again if necessary and rake the surface lightly.

Water occasionally during the first few years, especially in hot weather, and during dry spells spray the leaves with water in the cool of the day. Protect from frost in the first few years by surrounding with plastic bags or sacking. Do any weeding by hand to avoid damaging surface roots. If pruning is required cut outer shoots in mid spring.

Take off the leaves sparingly during the first few years so that the new growth is not weakened. Thereafter, pick the leaves as required. Always leave the young foliage. When collecting for drying, clip the leaves singly.

Propagating
Bay cuttings can be taken in late autumn. Choose firm side shoots 7.5-15 cm [3-6"] long and pull them off gently with a strip of the main shoot. Trim this heel neatly and place the cutting in damp, sandy compost under glass in a shady position. When it has rooted, after about 12 to 18 months, pot it in potting compost in a 7.5 cm [3½"] pot and return to frame or greenhouse. Keep moist and shaded and plant out the following spring.

Growing in containers
Bay is a good choice for container growing. The restricted root area of the container limits the size of the tree and makes it a decorative plant for doorsteps and patios. There are three traditional shapes for container-grown bay — pyramid, 'mop-head' and bush — the first two of which are pruned to shape by the nursery. The trees sold are usually six-year-olds, about 1.5 m [5'] high and in 25-30 cm [10-12"] containers.

Bay likes to be pot-bound and will grow in its original container for about six years after its purchase. After that time, or when the roots show through the drainage hole, get a container about 5 cm [2"] larger than the original.

Before re-potting, water the plant well. Fill the base of the new container with pieces of broken clay pots for drainage

Bay makes a most attractive and useful pot plant.

and repot the plant in a good standard potting compost. Firm the soil down very thoroughly to retain moisture. Water in and take extra care to make sure the compost does not dry out at all during the next few weeks.

Bay grows best outdoors, but can be grown in a conservatory or cool greenhouse. Water the plant well and often in dry weather, but never during frosts. A well-established tree can be left outside during a mild winter, but take it indoors to an unheated place or cover with protective sheeting during frosty weather.

In late spring or early summer, prune the tree lightly to shape by clipping individual shoots. Feed in summer with liquid fertilizer and replace the top layer of compost to a level of about 2.5 cm [1″] each year, in early spring.

Pests and diseases

Watch for scale insects that look like little brown blobs and live on the underside of leaves and on the stem and trunk. These commonly infest bay trees grown in containers, particularly if the plant becomes short of water. Cover the surface of the compost with sheeting or newspaper and scrape the insects off very gently with the blunt edge of a knife on to the covering. Then spray the whole tree thoroughly with an insecticide and repeat 10 to 14 days later.

BEANS

COMMON TYPES OF BEANS

There are many different kinds of beans, and the variety of names given to them can be very confusing. For convenience they can be divided into four categories: French beans, runner beans, dry beans and shell beans.

French beans are picked when green and the pods are cooked whole with the beans inside. There are both bush and climbing varieties available.

Runner beans belong to a different species from French beans. These climbing varieties are very popular in Britain and, like French beans, they are picked when green and cooked whole.

Dry beans are those which are allowed to ripen on the plant before harvesting; they are taken from the pod and dried or processed. A common example are the haricot beans — certain varieties of French beans which are allowed to mature fully before harvesting. Soya beans, too, are treated in this way, so are red kidney beans and navy beans — the dried version of a white-seeded kidney bean used mainly for canned baked beans.

Shell beans are picked when green and the beans are taken from the pods to be cooked. Broad (butter) beans are an example. For cultivation *see* BROAD BEAN, LIMA BEAN, FRENCH BEAN, RUNNER BEAN and SOYA BEAN.

Bean Sprouts

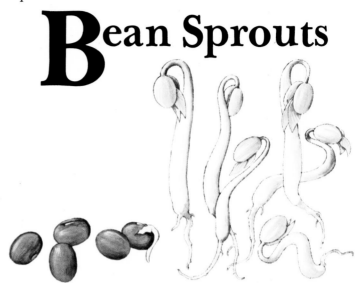

Ready to eat in as little as six days, the new sprouts of these beans require little effort to grow and are an extremely nutritious vegetable.

Bean sprouts and seed sprouts are exceptional vegetables, with a number of unique features. The seeds can be planted or sown at any time of the year; they can be ready to eat in three to six days from the sowing date; they will grow in any climate, needing neither soil nor sun, and you do not even need a garden. They are highly nutritious, being particularly rich in vitamin C.

Because they are so quick and easy to grow, bean sprouts and seed sprouts are an inexpensive source of fresh vegetables all the year round. Excellent in salads or as a substitute for lettuce during winter, bean sprouts and seed sprouts are much used in Chinese cooking. They make an attractive and tasty base for many cooked dishes, especially rice dishes like curry and risotto, and can be used in breads or cooked with other vegetables. Cook quickly to prevent loss of their valuable nutrients.

Types of bean sprouts

The most popular types are mung beans and adzuki beans. Mung beans, or Chinese bean sprouts, are the best known and are a familiar ingredient in many popular Chinese dishes. Mid-green in colour with white sprouts, mung beans may be used raw or cooked when they are 5 cm [2″] high. Adzuki beans are also from the Far East. They have

Bean sprouts
Phaseolus aureus, mung bean, also known as Chinese bean sprout, green or golden gram; *Phaseolus angularis*, adzuki bean; both fam. *Leguminosae*.
Size: mung sprout, about 5 cm [2″] long; adzuki sprout, about 2.5 cm [1″] long.
Climate: grow indoors anywhere.
Sowing to harvesting time: 3-6 days.
Yield: mung sprouts, about 225-275 g per 25 g [8-10 oz per 1 oz] of seed; adzuki beans, about 125-175 g per 25 g [4-6 oz per 1 oz] of seed.

1. The easiest way to wash the seeds is in their growing container. Pour about 5 ml [2 teaspoons] of seeds into the jam jar.

2. Pour cold or tepid water into the jar to cover the seeds.

3. Place your hand over the top of the jar and shake vigorously.

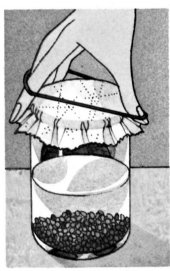

As the seeds sprout, their goodness grows. Mung beans will be ready to eat after three to five days or when they are 5 cm [2"]; they deteriorate if left longer.

4. Secure muslin lid over neck of the jar with an elastic band.

5. Drain off the water and then repeat the process 2 or 3 times.

6. The jar can be placed anywhere out of direct light. Seeds germinate to give sprouts at a temperature of 13° to 18°C [55° to 65°F].

been grown for centuries for their crunchy texture, nutty flavour and their filling bulk. They have an attractive, rich mahogany-red colour with white sprouts, and are also suitable for use raw or cooked. They are eaten when 2.5 cm [1″] high. Other types are triticale, alfalfa and fenugreek, each with their own distinctive flavour.

Jam jar growing

The simplest, cheapest and most effective method of growing bean sprouts is the glass jar method. All that is needed is a jam jar or a similar glass container, a rubber band and a piece of muslin. The muslin should be large enough to fit comfortably over the jam jar opening and be secured with the band.

Take about 5 ml [2 teaspoons] of the seed and rinse it thoroughly. This is most easily done by placing it in the container, filling the container with cold or tepid water and shaking vigorously. Drain, then repeat the rinsing and draining several times. This initial saturation aids germination.

Do not exceed the suggested amount of seed when you first start to grow bean sprouts. By the time they are ready to eat they will have increased their volume as much as tenfold. Too many will fill up the jar and push out the top. Secure the muslin lid and leave the container on its side to allow the remaining water to drain off.

Repeat the rinsing and draining process twice a day, in the morning and evening. The beans need to be kept constantly moist, but not really wet otherwise they may go mouldy. Place the jar anywhere out of direct light — in a corner, on a shelf or in a cupboard. They need a temperature of between 13° to 18°C [55° to 65°F].

As the seed sprouts, the fats and starches in it are changed into vitamins, sugar (which provides quick energy) and proteins, which make the sprout more digestible, less fattening and even more nutritious than it was as a seed.

Less than a week to harvest

Mung beans will be ready to eat within three to five days, or whenever they have reached about 5 cm [2″] in height, when they will have increased eight or ten times over their weight as a seed, and many times over in volume. Left any longer in the jar they will continue to grow, lose their crispness and begin to discolour.

Adzuki beans are ready within four to six days, or whenever they have reached about 2.5 cm [1″] in length, when they will have increased their weight by four to six times as much as the bean.

Continuous cropping

Bean sprouts are filling; the crop from one jar gives four serving portions if the bean sprouts are prepared as a separate vegetable, and many more if they are served as part of a dish.

If you do not eat the shoots all at once they will keep a few days in the salad compartment of a refrigerator. But fresh foods always lose some of their vitamin content the longer they are kept. It makes sense to grow only what you can eat immediately and keep a fresh supply of beans growing, rather than storing them.

Beetroot

As well as the well-known red beet, there are also varieties with yellow and white roots. Beet is usually eaten cold in salads but can be served as a hot vegetable.

The most common type of beet is round (also called globe or ball) and deep carmine-red. There are two other shapes — oval (known as intermediate or tankard) and long, and two other colours. Long beet is rarely grown today and then only as a stored crop for winter eating. It is the least sweet and succulent variety.

The advantages of the yellow and white types, which are round in form, is that they do not 'bleed' in salads. The green foliage of both types can be cooked as spinach.

Suitable site and soil

Beet is part of the root-crop in a rotational system, and should be grown on land in the vegetable plot which was well fed with compost the previous season. It needs plenty of light and a well-drained soil.

Dig heavy soil in late autumn and leave rough. Dig light soil in spring. Remove all weeds and their roots. If you plan to make successional sowings later, dig the soil to a depth of about 17.5 cm [7″]. Before sowing, rake the soil level and remove any large stones or debris. A very light soil should then be firmed slightly and raked again.

Sowing

Sow in mid to late spring when the soil is warming up.

Beetroot
Beta vulgaris (fam. *Chenopodiaceae)*, also known as beet.
Half-hardy biennial, grown as an **annual.**
Size: plants about 30 cm [1′] tall, swollen roots between 2.5 cm [1″] and 9 cm [3½″] in diameter, according to form and variety and picking time.
Climate: cool to warm temperate.
Sowing to harvesting time: round and intermediate types 8-10 weeks; long types about 19 weeks.
Yield: round and oval types, about 40 roots per 3 m [10′] row; long beet about 20 roots per 3 m [10′] row.

There are several types of beet;
most common is the round (globe or
ball) type. Another is oval
(intermediate or tankard). Long
beet, with a tapering end, is
seldom grown now. The other
two round types, distinguished
by their colours, yellow and
white, are ideal for use in salads
as they do not bleed into the
other ingredients.

Plant seeds 2.5 cm [1"] apart in
rows 30 cm [1'] apart. Germination
takes place within 1-2 weeks.

Thin out round and intermediate
seedlings when 2-7 cm [1-3"] tall
with spacing of 10 cm [4"].

Thin out long beet seedlings when
15 cm [6"] tall with a spacing of
15 cm [6"]. Protect from birds.

Water plants regularly, especially during dry weather, and hoe between plants, removing weed seedlings by hand.

Seeds are usually sold as clusters, each containing four or five seeds (a few exceptions come as one single seed). Plant each cluster about 2.5 cm [1″] apart, in rows 30 cm [1′] apart. The seeds should germinate within 1-2 weeks of sowing. Thin out the seedlings when they are between 2-7 cm [1-3″] tall for round and intermediate varieties, and 15 cm [6″] for long beet, giving a spacing of 10 cm [4″] and 15 cm [6″] respectively. Protect from birds.

Care and development
Keep the plants supplied with adequate water at the roots, especially during periods of drought, to maintain steady growth, and prevent cracking and toughness.
Start hoeing between the rows as soon as the seedlings show. Remove weed seedlings growing close to the beet plants by hand since the hoe may damage the roots.

Harvesting and storing the crop
Round and intermediate beets are ready to start pulling up when they are 2.5 cm [1″] in diameter. Pull them here and there in the rows to leave space for the rest to grow larger. Continue pulling more beet as and when needed. Dig up long beet in mid autumn and store.
All beet may be stored; choose a dry day to harvest for storing. Shake each root to remove adhering soil. Twist off the foliage at about 5 cm [2″] from the crown, i.e. the top of the beet. Sandwich the beet in single layers between 2.5 cm [1″] layers of peat or sand in boxes. Store the boxes in a cool place such as a garden shed, outhouse, garage or cellar. If kept at a temperature of about 10°C [50°F] the beet should remain in good condition for six months.

Container-growing
Choose round varieties for container-growing. Large tubs are most suitable but if using pots the smallest useful size is 30 cm [1′]. Sprinkle seeds thinly over a standard compost mixture and cover with 2.5 cm [1″] of the mixture. Water well, using a fine rose on the watering can. Thin the seedlings to allow each plant enough room to develop, leaving only eight plants in a 30 cm [1′] pot. Water frequently in warm weather.

Growing under a cloche or frame
Choose round varieties of beet for growing under cloches or in frames. Tent and tunnel cloches are suitable for one single row; wider sorts of cloches may take two or three rows spaced about 17.5 cm [7″] apart. Sow thinly in early spring in seed drills 2.5 cm [1″] deep, about 17.5 cm [7″] apart. Thin the seedlings to 5 cm [2″] apart. Ensure that they are never short of water.
After germination, provided that the days are not excessively cold, open the frames or cloches slightly to admit air. Close when night temperatures fall below about 10°C [50°F]. Remove the glass panels or cloches entirely on days when temperatures average about 16°C [60°F], but replace in the evening if frost threatens. Remove the cloches or frame lights (glass panels) when the weather is warmer (usually 4-6 weeks after sowing).

When ready to harvest twist foliage off 5 cm [2″] from crown.

Round varieties of beet are the best sort for container growing. Water well and thin seedlings to allow plants room for development.

Pests and diseases

The deficiency disease known as speckled yellows may occur if the soil lacks manganese, causing the leaves to go yellowish between the veins at first and then brown. This can be controlled by watering with a solution of manganese sulphate at 30 g per 12 L [1 oz per 2½ gal]. Some aphids, particularly blackfly and greenfly, may also infest the plants.

Blackberry

This fruit is composed of numerous drupelets, each containing a seed. They are suitable for cooking or for eating raw. They grow on canes, which may be smooth or thorny.

Wild blackberries, also known as brambles, are found in hedges and copses throughout Western Europe and North America. Varieties which are cultivated in the Northern Hemisphere are often a pest in the Southern. Because blackberries come true to seed (as well as reproducing by rooting canes) scores of species are known.

Blackberry
Species of *Rubus* (fam. *Rosaceae*), in Europe derived from *R. fruticosus*, which has itself been subdivided into many species, in America from crosses of *R. alleghaniensis*, *R. argutus* and *R. frondosus*.
Hardy perennial cane usually prickly, with a cropping life of about 15 years.
Size: 1.8 cm [6′] in height and up to 4.5 m [15′] wide when trained.
Climate: cool to warm temperate.
Planting to harvesting time: two years.
Yield: about 2.25-4.5 kg [5-10 lb].

The dewberry, with black fruit similar in appearance but composed of fewer and larger drupelets, and ripening earlier than the blackberry, is closely related to it. In Europe the name is given to *R. caesius*, in America to trailing native species, chief among them *R. canadensis*. Some varieties are cultivated.

Because *Rubus* berries interbreed so easily, many crosses have been made between the different sorts of blackberries and with raspberries, and the cultivation of these hybrid berries is covered under LOGANBERRY.

Although wild blackberries are delicious, they tend to be small and hard to pick because the brambles have sharp thorns and quickly form impenetrable bushes. In the garden therefore blackberries are trained to make picking easier. Some modern varieties are thornless, which are easier to handle but less vigorous.

Garden varieties produce larger fruit and more abundant crops than wild ones, and the fruiting period is longer. The berries are borne on canes of the previous year's growth, in dark purple or black clusters.

The pinky white flowers are self-fertile and are produced in succession throughout the summer. This means that blackberries will fruit in cold regions where other earlier-flowering fruit fails to set (form fruit from the flowers).

Suitable site and soil

Blackberries will crop adequately without much care. They are often the solution for the problem corners because they will crop in shade or facing north, or in frost pockets. Flowers continue to appear through the summer and these will set, even if earlier ones are killed. A bigger more regular crop will be obtained in a sunny site sheltered from wind and frost.

Canes are trained against a wall or shed, or on wires supported by posts. A row on a slope should run up and down, not across, or it will trap cold air.

Well drained medium loams are ideal; light soils need additional organic matter. A chalky soil is least suitable. Acid soils should be treated with lime. On poor soil choose a more vigorous variety.

Eradicate all perennial weeds before planting, because blackberries have a 15-year life. Dig in organic matter to about 45 cm [1½′], adding roughly 2.5-6.5 kg per sq m [5-15 lb per sq yd].

Training wires and fences

If wire fences are to be erected, do this before planting. Use metal or treated wooden posts 2.3 m [7′6″] tall, with 1.8 m [6′] above ground, carrying four 25 mm [⅛″] plastic coated wires 30 cm [1′] apart, starting 90 cm [3′] above the ground. Length will depend on the number of canes. The wires will bear the full weight on the canes, so the post should be propped with a strut; or run a guy-rope from the top of the post outward to a well-secured peg.

On a wall, fence or shed the same intervals should be used and the wires well secured. Vigorous canes are trained by the weaving method.

Planting out

The best time to plant is late autumn. Vigorous varieties

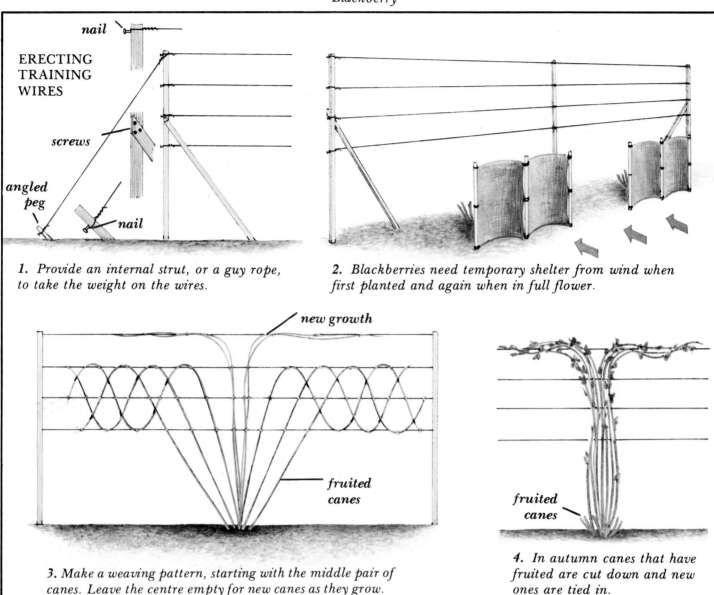

ERECTING TRAINING WIRES

nail

screws

angled peg

nail

1. *Provide an internal strut, or a guy rope, to take the weight on the wires.*

2. *Blackberries need temporary shelter from wind when first planted and again when in full flower.*

new growth

fruited canes

3. *Make a weaving pattern, starting with the middle pair of canes. Leave the centre empty for new canes as they grow.*

fruited canes

4. *In autumn canes that have fruited are cut down and new ones are tied in.*

should be planted 3.5-4.5 m [12-15'] apart, the thornless varieties 2.5-3.5 m [8-12'] apart. Leave 1.8 m [6'] between any rows.

Dig the planting hole 10-12.5 cm [4-5"] deep. Cut off broken roots and set the plant in with the roots spread out naturally to their full length. The crown should be level with the soil surface. Crumble the soil over the roots, firming it gently and fill the hole. After planting, cut down the canes to 23 cm [9"].

Providing shelter

Provide temporary protection from strong winds until plants are established, and again when in full flower. Sacking, polythene sheets or wattle hurdles should be erected on poles in front of the plants.

Training

Blackberries do not need much attention during the growing season. The first summer only a few canes will grow, and these will not fruit. Wearing stout gloves against prickles, gradually tie them in. The fruiting canes are woven between the bottom and the third wire *(see diagram)*, leaving the centre empty for the new canes.

Choose the two canes nearest to the centre. Take them up to the next-to-top wire and attach them one on either side, leaving the centre empty with a 75 cm [2'6"] space between them. Now weave them down to the bottom wire and up again, working outward from the middle, tying the cane along its length, and taking care that all the curves are gentle. Now take the second pair of canes up to the next-to-top wire, about 23 cm [9"] outside the first pair, then repeat, and so on, until all the canes are tied in.

Sometimes the main canes and sideshoots outgrow their space. If so cut them back in late winter, the main canes by about 60-90 cm [2-3'], the sideshoots to within a handspan of the main stem.

In the second summer, when these canes are fruiting, new canes will be produced. Tie these vertically up the middle and, when they reach the top wire, spread them out on either side and tie them along the top wire to stop them whipping about. These canes will bear next year's crop.

Watering

The best method is a perforated hose laid along each side of the row in turn. In a normal year, watering increases yield; during drought it is vital to ensure canes produce

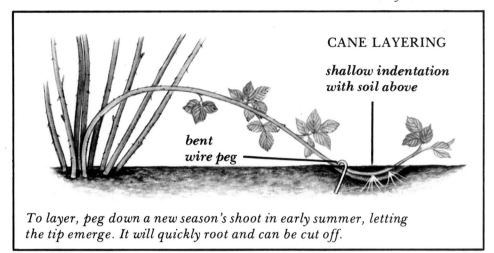

CANE LAYERING

*shallow indentation
with soil above*

*bent
wire peg*

To layer, peg down a new season's shoot in early summer, letting the tip emerge. It will quickly root and can be cut off.

Blackberries are suitable for shady corners, and can be trained for easy picking on walls, fences and garden sheds.

both fruit and new growth. Without adequate moisture, fruit will mature at the expense of new shoots and hence next year's crop.

Feeding
Top dress in early summer every year with garden compost 2.5 cm [1"] thick. If this is not available use a compound fertilizer and mulch with straw.

Harvesting the crop
Fruit is produced on the previous year's wood, so there is no crop the first year. Picking starts in late summer with early varieties, when the berries are fully black, and can continue till mid autumn. Pluck off berries with the plug, the white centre of the fruit. Pick every few days to encourage more fruit to ripen.

Pruning and after care
After cropping has finished, cut out the canes which produced fruit, either completely or to the strongest new sideshoot low on a cane.
Untie the new canes, wearing stout gloves, and disentangle them if need be. Lay them out singly on the ground and

Dewberries (top) are sweet and black. They are similar to blackberries but their canes have a trailing habit. Blackberries (above) grow best in rich loam but once planted they need little attention. Thornless varieties have been developed to make picking and handling easier. Pick every few days to encourage more fruit to ripen.

sort them into two groups. It is usual to retain only 8-10 canes on each plant. These are then tied in the pattern previously described. Any winter die-back can be removed in early spring by cutting the dead tip back to a bud or sideshoot. Destroy all prunings.

Propagation
Blackberries are easily increased by cane layering, which simply means pegging down a new-season shoot near the tip in early or midsummer until it makes independent roots. Make a hole a hand-span deep and lay the end of the cane in so the tip shows but the stem just behind it is buried. Peg the stem with a piece of bent wire. The new plants should be well-rooted by the late autumn, when they can be cut off and planted out in their permanent positions. Cut back the parent canes to ground level.

Pests and diseases

Blackberry dwarf disease is spread by aphids. Instead of producing a few strong canes, infected plants grow a lot of very short new shoots which never grow. Diseased plants must be destroyed. Other pests can be capsids, greenfly or leaf-eating caterpillars.

Blackcurrant

These delicious dark-juiced berries
are the richest in vitamin C of
all the garden fruit.
The flavour is sharp and the fruit
is cooked before being eaten. The
leaves are also useful for flavouring.

Blackcurrants are an easy soft fruit to cultivate and require a moist climate. Wild species of blackcurrant occur all across America, Europe, Russia and temperate Asia as far as the Himalayas and north almost to the Arctic circle. *Ribes americanum* is closely related to the cultivated species. Though the plant itself will withstand frost, the blossom is borne in early spring and is consequently prone to frost damage.

Unlike other soft fruit bushes which are grown on a single stem like a miniature tree, blackcurrants are encouraged to be shrubby, with several main shoots rising from below soil level. It is the tallest of the soft fruit bushes. Both leaves and stem have a strong smell when crushed. The

---

Blackcurrant
Ribes nigrum (Saxifragaceae)
Hardy deciduous shrub, with a useful life of 15 years.
Size: about 1.5 m [5′] high and across.
Climate: cold to warm temperate.
Planting to harvesting time: two years.
Yield: 4.5 kg [10 lb].

---

fruit begins to ripen after midsummer and cropping from different varieties continues for about two months.

Suitable site and soil

Choose the warmest, most sheltered spot available because the flowers are prone to frost damage. A place in full sun is best, though they will tolerate partial shade. Shelter from wind is vital to allow insects to pollinate the flowers (*see* the diagram in BLACKBERRY).

Blackcurrants are more tolerant of indifferent drainage than most other fruit, but the very best results will be obtained on a deep loamy well-drained soil.

A slightly acid soil is best, and a soil test should give a pH value of between 6 and 7. If it is less than 5.5, scatter hydrated lime (never mix it with manure or fertilizer) at the rate of 90 g per sq m [3 oz per sq yd].

Dig the ground over a couple of months before planting — preferably in late autumn. Pay special attention to weed eradication, as perennial weeds can be a great nuisance later on. If possible, dig in manure or compost at this time.

If neither is available, add leaf mould or peat at the rate of a wheelbarrow-load per 1.5 sq m [2 sq yd]. Blackcurrants like plenty of nitrogenous fertilizer. Extra plant food will be provided by forking into the surface a dressing of 46 g per sq m [1½ oz per sq yd] each of sterilized bonemeal and hoof-and-horn meal, and 30 g per sq m [1 oz per sq yd] of sulphate of potash. A dressing of general garden fertilizer at 122 g per sq m [4 oz per sq yd] may be used instead.

Planting

Most families will probably find that about four bushes are sufficient. A range of varieties, although not necessary for cross pollination, will spread the picking season and provide some insurance against a single frost causing crop failure.

Planting can be done any time during winter when the soil is not frost bound or wet, though early winter is best. Buy two-year-old plants and, if possible, make sure they are from government certified healthy stock.

Plant the bushes 1.8 m [6′] apart. Dig a planting hole large enough for you to spread out all the roots fully in their natural direction. An established blackcurrant has a number of main stems. To encourage this growth habit, the bush should be planted between 2.5-5 cm [1-2″] deeper than it was in the nursery. Firm the soil back round the roots.

Immediately after planting, cut down every shoot to within 2.5 cm [1″] of the ground, to just above the first or second visible growth bud. Though this means you will get no fruit the first year, it will ensure that the bush develops a good root system. It also encourages the bushes to form a good crown below ground.

Watering

Start early in the growing season if the weather is at all dry. Watering is essential, as blackcurrants need more moisture than comparable fruit. Mulching with manure in early spring will help reduce water loss through evaporation.

PLANTING AND PRUNING

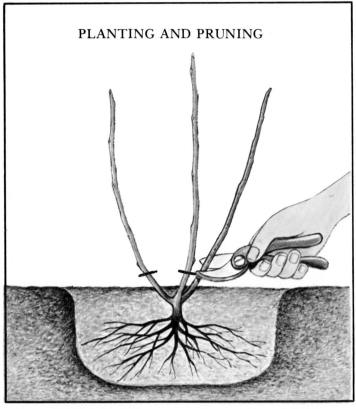

Blackcurrants are planted lower in the ground than the original soil mark. This, and pruning after planting, encourages new shoots from below soil level.

Blackcurrants grow taller than all the other soft fruit bushes. They need heavy quantities of both nitrogenous feed, water and moisture-retaining soil, to do well.

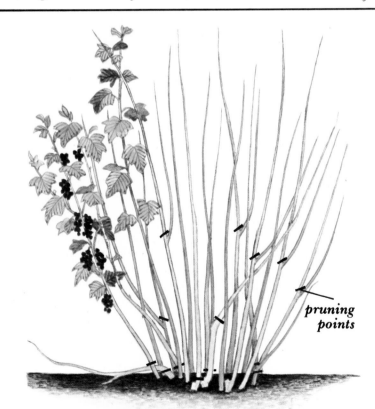

pruning points

PRUNING FROM THE SECOND YEAR

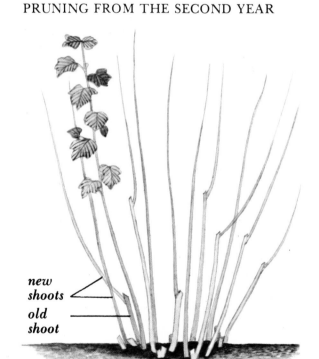

new shoots
old shoot

Pruning from the second year is to encourage new wood, as this bears the most fruit the following year, and to build up a good bush shape. Prune to the ground, or to a low-growing shoot, and ignore new growth at the tip of old wood.

Low growing branches, crossing branches and those which are diseased are cut out first, followed by branches in the centre of the bush, to let in light and air. Finally a proportion of old wood is cut to a low shoot, or removed entirely.

Feeding

Blackcurrants thrive on heavy manuring. First, in early spring every year, scatter and rake in 30 g per sq m [1 oz per sq yd] of sulphate of ammonia and 15 g per sq m [½ oz per sq yd] of sulphate of potash over the bed. Where the soil is acid, use nitro-chalk instead of sulphate of ammonia. Then mulch the bed with manure or compost at the rate of a wheelbarrow-load to every 2.5 sq m [3 sq yd]. If no manure is available, double the quantities of fertilizers and mulch with moist peat.

Frost protection

The greenish white flowers are borne in drooping bunches like grapes, and appear in early and mid spring. Cover the bushes at night with hessian or any sort of cloth if frost is expected.

Pruning

Little pruning will be necessary in the winter after planting, though you can cut any weak growths back to the first bud above ground level.

In the second season, you should prune immediately after your first harvest. Blackcurrants bear most of their fruit on the new shoots produced the previous summer, so the aim in pruning is to encourage the growth of strong new wood from the base of the plant. Most of the new shoots will be retained, and a proportion of the older wood which also bears a quota of fruit and produces more young wood. First, cut away low-growing shoots which hang down to the ground, any which are dead or are obviously diseased, and any which are crossing or awkwardly placed. If the centre of the bush is crowded, next remove some of the shoots there to let in light and air.

Finally, remove about a fifth of the older wood that remains. Make your cuts above a good new low-growing shoot or close to the ground to encourage new growth lower down and ignore promising growth at the tips of these shoots.

In subsequent years old wood with sideshoots on it will be cut right to the ground.

When the bushes are well established, after about four seasons, you should remove about a third of a bush each winter, following these rules. If growth is very vigorous remove less and if it is weak and needs stimulating remove more.

Harvesting and storing the crop

Blackcurrants reach maximum cropping capacity after four or five years. They are ready to eat when deep black. For speed strip them straight off their stalks using a kitchen fork, but berries plucked in a truss are less likely to get mouldy and will keep five days.

Propagation

Blackcurrants are easily increased by hardwood cuttings taken in mid autumn from healthy bushes. Never take cuttings from diseased bushes to replace those about to be destroyed.

Cut off shoots of ripening wood about 20-25 cm [8-10"] long just below a bud. Put them about 15 cm [6"] deep in the ground with two buds or so showing and, unlike red currants and gooseberries, retain the buds under the soil. Space them about 20 cm [8"] apart. The following autumn transplant the cuttings to their permanent positions.

Pests and diseases

Reversion is the most serious disease, so-called because bushes revert within about three years to the form of the wild species. Fruit bearing deteriorates and eventually ceases. There is no cure, although you can help guard against it by buying certified disease-free stock. As soon as you have identified reversion, burn affected bushes, roots and all, and plant new healthy stock in a different site.

The virus is carried by the big bud gall mite. Thousands of mites grow within a single bud which swells up prematurely to an abnormal size. In spring the buds open and the mites migrate to the developing shoots. Pick off and burn swollen buds as soon as you see them. Some varieties are more susceptible than others to attack. As soon as you see big buds suspect an attack of reversion.

Unfortunately there is no way of destroying the pests inside the buds. Spray with a 3% solution of lime-sulphur just before the flowers open and repeat after three weeks. A strong lime-sulphur spray causes leaf scorching and reduction of crops in some varieties. Your nursery will advise you when you buy your plant if it is susceptible, in which case use a ½% solution. This spray will also protect against American gooseberry mildew.

Bushes infected with reversion grow vigorously which makes identification tricky. First check for signs of disease just before the blossom opens, when the buds are like little bunches of grapes. Healthy flowers are covered with tiny downy grey hairs. Infected buds have fewer hairs, so that they appear a much brighter pink. Some varieties, however, are more hairy than others.

In midsummer look for signs of leaf reversion. In a healthy blackcurrent leaf there is a definite cleft between the bottom edge of the leaf's basal lobe and the stem of the leaf. In an infected leaf this angle becomes much less pronounced and the leaf is flattened straight across. Also, in a healthy leaf you will find that the top lobe in the centre of the leaf has five or more main veins on either side of the central rib and at least 14 serrations along each edge. A reverted leaf will have fewer than five main veins and less than 12 serrations. Compare leaves of the same varieties if you can.

The brown spotting blackcurrant leaf spot, a fungus disease, can severely weaken growth. Spray with zineb or thiram immediately after flowering and three more times at four-weekly intervals.

Birds will eat your ripening fruit if you don't prevent them. If you cannot grow it in a fruit cage, cover the bushes with netting or rayon web while the fruit is ripening, and in some areas you will need to protect the buds also.

American gooseberry mildew may inflict blackcurrants (*see* GOOSEBERRY for treatment). Birds, capsids and greenfly are also pests and should be discouraged by a winter spray of tar oil at 5%. Spray again in summer if they appear, with malathion.

Blackcurrants are very easy to
increase. Take hardwood cuttings
in mid autumn and insert them
in the ground, retaining the
buds below ground level.

Left: Blackcurrants reach maximum
fruiting after 4-5 years, and
continue bearing for 15 years.
For speed strip the fruit
straight into a collander.

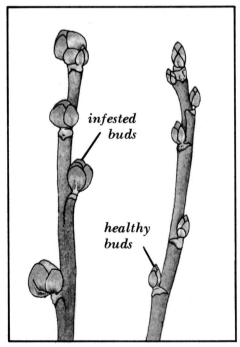

infested
buds

healthy
buds

Gall mites, carriers of incurable
reversion virus, invade the buds
in spring, causing them to swell
up to an unnatural size. There
is no way of stopping them growing
inside the bud. Pick off and burn.

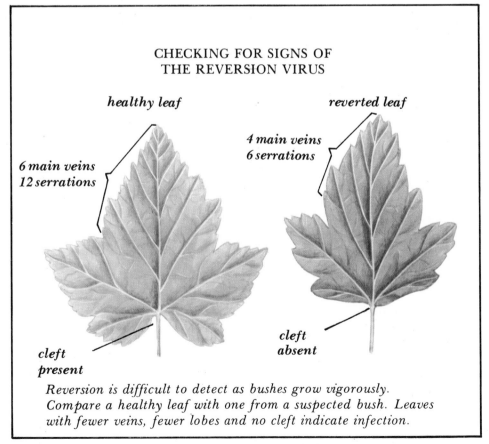

CHECKING FOR SIGNS OF
THE REVERSION VIRUS

healthy leaf

reverted leaf

6 main veins
12 serrations

4 main veins
6 serrations

cleft
present

cleft
absent

Reversion is difficult to detect as bushes grow vigorously.
Compare a healthy leaf with one from a suspected bush. Leaves
with fewer veins, fewer lobes and no cleft indicate infection.

Blueberry

**Sweet-tasting and full of
juice, blueberries grow
in bunches on woody bushes.
Though they contain many seeds,
these are unnoticeable when eaten.
They are good for canning, pies and tarts.**

Blueberries grow well on rather poor ground, where other fruit would not flourish. Light, acid, sandy soil suits them well and if your garden is on the edge of heathland you might well make good use of reclaimed land by growing this delicious fruit.

The high-bush blueberry is ornamental as well as useful, with a brilliant autumn leaf colour. The shrub produces long new growths from the woody crown each year, as well as fruiting sideshoots from last year's wood. The flowers, which smell like cowslips, appear in mid spring. They are white and urn-shaped and hang downward in clusters. They open in succession for some weeks which helps to diminish frost damage.

Other types of blueberries

There are a number of sweet edible species of the *Vaccinium* genus, and also sour ones including the cowberry, *V. vitis-idaea*, and cranberry, *V. macrocarpum*, most of them native to America.

The European wild bilberry (also called blaeberry or whortleberry), *V. myrtillus*, produces edible fruit on a shrub up to 45 cm [1′6″] high. The fruit are small and are produced singly, unlike the American blueberries which are borne in clusters and are therefore easier to pick.

Another small shrub, up to 20 cm [8″] high, is the American *V. angustifolium*, the low-bush blueberry, with small sweet fruit. It grows in colder areas than the high-bush blueberry, where it is protected in winter by the snow covering it.

The rabbit-eye blueberry, *V. ashei*, is a tall semi-deciduous shrub up to 5.5 m [18′], which will grow freely on poor, dry, less acid soils. It likes a sub-tropical climate, which the high-bush blueberry will not tolerate.

Suitable site and soil

The blueberry needs a period of winter cold to crop successfully and is therefore limited to places where frost occurs. Sites which suit them are often moorland or heath; poor land not usually suitable for cultivation. Wherever rhododendrons grow successfully, you can try this fruit-bearing shrub.

The ideal site is flat or gently sloping land in full sun with an open aspect and free air circulation to dry the heavy fruit clusters. Like blackcurrants, blueberries should be sheltered from the wind, though their bell shape helps protect them from frost.

Do not grow blueberries with other fruit, even to use the same fruit cage. Other fruit require lime and manure but the blueberry will not tolerate them.

The best soil is light sand, high in peat content, as moisture retention is important. The soil should be acid and if it is not, blueberries should not be attempted. A soil test should give a pH of 4 to 5.2. If it is 6, sulphur may be added at 60 g per sq m [2 oz per sq yd]. The shrub needs good drainage. Soils on which water stands after heavy rain should be ridged.

If a tract of heathland is being incorporated into the garden for the first time, the hire of a cultivator will save much weary work. This will turn in and bury heavy growths of heather and gorse, which will then create an ideal rooting medium. This preparation is ideally carried out in the summer months when the weather is at its driest and warmest.

Planting out

A single blueberry can be planted and the flowers will set (form fruit), but crops will be increased if you plant two or more varieties together. Buy two-year-old bushes, which will be about 30 cm [1′] high. Plant in autumn or winter, spaced 1.8 m [6′] apart. The bush makes a slow start, but it has a long life.

If the soil lacks organic matter, spread sphagnum peat 7.5 cm [3″] deep evenly over the area you intend to plant, and mix it in while digging.

Dig a hole big enough to contain the natural spread of the roots and place the plant in it to the same depth as its nursery planting. Crumble the soil back over the roots until the hole is filled. Mulch round the bush with sawdust, then sprinkle over 60 g [2 oz] of general fertilizer. After planting tip the shoots to remove any flower buds; the bush should not be allowed to fruit in the first year.

Blueberries may be the answer to poor sandy soils, particularly the edge of heathland. They will grow wherever rhododendrons are successful, and their red leaves in autumn are very ornamental.

Blueberry
Derivative of *Vaccinium corymbosum, V. australe* and *V. lamacrkii (Ericaceae),* all high-bush types.
Hardy deciduous shrub with a useful life of 30 years.
Size: 2 m [7′] high, rather less wide.
Climate: cool to warm temperate.
Planting to harvesting time: two years.
Yield: 4.5 kg [9 lb] per bush.

The British bilberry. This species is less productive than its American relative, the blueberry.

Watering

A well-mulched soil should need no extra watering in areas that receive well-dispersed rainfall over 75 cm [30"] a year. Watering will be necessary where summers are continuously hot and dry. The leaves will go red prematurely when short of water. Tap water (which may be too alkaline) can safely be used for infrequent watering.

Feeding and soil improvement

In winter mulch the ground 10 cm [4"] deep with sawdust. This helps retain moisture, and also stimulates growth. Extra nitrogen will be added to help rot down the sawdust, otherwise it would take nitrogen from the soil as it decomposes. You can wait until spring to spread 45 g [1½ oz] sulphate of ammonia or 60 g [2 oz] of dried blood and 30 g [1 oz] of sulphate of potash per sq m [yd] on top of the sawdust.

In early summer spread a further 45 g [1½ oz] of sulphate of ammonia or 60 g [2 oz] of dried blood, and if necessary water in. Do not make the two applications together. If sawdust is not available, use pulverized fir bark or peat (though this has no nutrients) and for the latter omit the sulphate of ammonia and dried blood applications. Do not use spent mushroom compost or any dried animal manures.

Weeding

If weeds get into the mulch, they are likely to be perennial, and herbicides should be used. Watch out especially for blackberry seedlings among the bushes, introduced by birds. If they are not quickly removed they are likely to become ineradicable.

Pruning

Growth is in two stages. First, sideshoots grow from below the flower clusters formed the previous year. These pause in early summer and then grow again to form flower buds. Then in mid summer new shoots thrust from ground level from the woody crown and by late autumn these may be 1.8 m [6'] high with the top 25 cm [10"] covered with flower buds.

Pruning proper begins in the third winter after planting, when the original branches of the young bush have become dry and twiggy.

Fruit is carried on the previous year's shoots. These may either be new long growths from the crown, or sideshoots on the growths of the year before that.

Each winter cut most of the stems which have borne two crops, that is, all the stems that have branches which have also fruited. Cut them to the base, or to a strong low side shoot if there is one. This encourages strong new growth and heavy cropping. After a dull cold summer, prune back any green soft growth from the tip to tough brown wood.

Harvesting and storing the crop

The first small crop will ripen the second summer after planting. Blueberries should reach their maximum

cropping after about four to eight years.

The clusters should be picked over four or five times, starting in midsummer and finishing in early autumn. Berries are rolled off with the thumb and finger, dropping their stalks in the process.

Pests and diseases
Blueberries may be attacked by birds, rodents and the fungus *Botrytis.*

During a dry spring water the plants well until they are established. Hoe lightly between plants to keep the soil friable and weed free.

Using borage
Fresh leaves may be added to salads or to give an exhilarating lift to summer drinks and punches. Pick the young leaves from the lower stems before the flower heads show in midsummer. The flowers are also good in salads, both for decoration and for their cucumber flavour.

Clip the seed-head before the seeds have a chance to self-sow to save them for sowing the following year.

Borage

**Borage is a sturdy plant with a
fresh, cucumber scent and the most
beautiful, intensely blue flowers.
Both the leaves and flowers are edible.**

Borage *(Borago officinalis)* is a hardy annual which grows to about 30-75 cm [1-2½'] high. Its heavily veined, deep green leaves and hollow, rounded stems are very rough and prickly. The abundant blue, star-shaped flowers attract bees and produce plenty of seeds for subsequent sowing. In sheltered gardens it can flower through the winter, and will only succumb to a bad frost.

Cultivation
Borage grows well in a sunny or shady position, whether in bank or border, rockery or herb garden, and in any type of soil. It is also suitable for growing in containers about 12.5 cm [5"] in diameter, filled with potting compost.

Before sowing fork the soil deeply so that the tap root — the long primary root — can grow down unimpeded. Sow in early spring, covering the seeds with about 2.5 cm [1"] of soil. When the first pair of true leaves are well-developed thin the seedlings to 30 cm [1'] apart and firm the soil well around the remaining plants.

Borage is an attractive herb and easy to grow. Its leaves give a delicious flavour to drinks and salads.

Broad Bean

**This bean comes in three types —
long-podded, short-podded and dwarf.
Though usually shelled for cooking,
the pods can be eaten whole when young.**

The broad bean is one of the oldest of cultivated vegetables. It belongs to the vetch group of the family *Leguminosae,* which includes several species grown as fodder for cattle and horses. The varieties grown for human consumption, however, have been developed for a more delicate flavour and are a very nutritious vegetable.

The broad bean is hardy and easy to grow. Each seed sown sends up several succulent, square-sectioned stalks, usually

> **Broad Bean**
> *Vicia faba* (fam. *Leguminosae*) also known as English or fava bean.
> **Hardy annual**
> **Size:** plants grow to about 60-90 cm [2-3'] tall.
> **Climate:** temperate.
> **Sowing to harvesting time:** 14 weeks for spring sowing; 24 weeks for autumn sowing.
> **Yield:** 5 kg [11 lb] per 3 m [10'] double row.

to a height of 60-90 cm [2-3′], though there are a few dwarf varieties. Its grey-green leaves are large and rather fleshy; the white and black flowers are borne in clusters from the stem and have a strong, pleasant scent. One group of broad beans has short, broad, flat pods with about 6 seeds inside — these are the Windsors. They are sown in spring. Several varieties have green beans, which keep their colour when deep-frozen and are therefore popular for that purpose. Another type has very long pods — as much as 38-50 cm [15-20″] with 9 or 10 seeds in each. The pods hang down from the stem. These beans, known as Longpods, are sown in autumn, and show an inch or two of shoot above ground before the first winter frosts. The chief variety in this section has white beans in its pods. The broad bean is a cool climate crop. It is sown in late autumn or early spring so that it produces its crop before the arrival of very hot weather. Beans sown later in spring, in the hope of getting a succession of crops throughout the summer, seldom do well.

Suitable site and soil

Broad beans, when fully grown, will be like a fairly dense hedge up to 1 m [3′] high across the garden, so when planning their site keep in mind the needs of the crops that will be next to the beans. Some crops will appreciate the shade and protection, but others will not. Arrange the rows so that they run north-south to ensure that plants growing on either side of the beans get sunlight for some hours during each day.

Broad beans like a rich, deep and fairly heavy soil but will tolerate almost any type. They do best in ground manured for a previous crop, rather than on freshly-applied manure or garden compost. They do not like an acid soil, which can be corrected by an application of lime.

There is no need to fuss with broad beans. If the soil is naturally rich or has been manured for a previous crop, just dig it deeply and thoroughly. If the soil tends to be acid, work in hydrated lime, at the rate indicated by the result of a soil test.

Sowing

Broad beans are large seeds, so they are sown individually. One method is to draw a shallow, flat-bottomed drill, about 6.5 cm [2½″] deep and about 10 cm [4″] wide, across the garden plot. Place two rows of beans in the drill with the rows about 7.5 cm [3″] apart and the beans spaced about 5 cm [2″] apart in each row. Ideally the seeds should be arranged so that each one is opposite a gap in the opposite rank but this is not absolutely essential. Cover with soil, using a draw hoe, firm the soil by treading on it and rake it over.

Most gardeners leave a space of 45-60 cm [1½-2′] between each double row drill, but broad beans have a low germination rate — no more than 75% of the seeds usually grow — so it is a better use of space to plant a second double row only 10-15 cm [4-6″] from the first. It is very unlikely that severe overcrowding will result. The effect is to make a hedge of broad beans 30-45 cm [1-1½′] wide across the garden. With this arrangement it is impossible to walk between the ranks for picking, but all the beans

are within easy reach if you walk along first one side and then the other.

The bean seed will germinate at almost any temperature above freezing point. The normal period from sowing to germination is from 1 to 2 weeks. Broad beans can tolerate moderate or even severe frosts, down to −7 to −9°C [20-15°F], provided they are not too prolonged. However, those sown in autumn should not be put into the soil too early (late autumn is ideal) or they will make a vigorous initial growth and then bend over at the first frost, with possible damage to the stems.

The seedlings are quite distinctive — they are among the largest seedlings in the vegetable garden. They have sharp-pointed, bright green leaves when they first emerge. No thinning is required.

Transplanting

Once planted, broad beans are seldom transplanted. The seed has a low germination rate, however, and because occasionally unfavourable weather produces a failure, many gardeners provide an insurance by raising a small stock of bean seedlings in pots, under cloches or in the greenhouse. They are used to fill the gaps in the ranks in early spring.

Care and development

As the broad bean usually completes its life cycle before the onset of severe summer droughts, it will probably not need much watering. However, in the event of a drought, water generously.

The crop will be making its maximum growth when weeds too are growing strongly, so they need frequent hoeing. Tall weeds, such as thistles and milk-thistles, often take advantage of the cover provided to grow within an inch or two of the bean plants, and these persistent weeds should be pulled out by hand.

The broad bean is not a climbing plant; it will not twine itself around a pole, as a runner bean will, and has no tendrils to hook on to a support like a pea. It is, however, shallow-rooted and tends to flop over as it approaches its maximum height or in windy weather. There are two ways of combating this tendency. One is to earth up the bases of the plants, gathering the soil around them with a hoe. The other is to stick a row of twigs alongside each rank.

Pollination is carried out by bees. When the flowers have just begun to bloom, many gardeners pinch out the top shoot of the plants. This encourages larger and earlier bean pods and, as the top shoot is a favourite place for aphids to congregate, also reduces blackfly attacks.

Harvesting

Harvesting is a matter of individual taste. Some people like well-matured broad beans, leaving them on the plants until the pods are turning bronze and are well-filled with hard beans. Most, however, prefer them fresh and young,

A row of broad beans supported by stakes. As the plant is shallow-rooted, it tends to flop over when reaching its maximum height. Stakes or strong twigs alongside each row help to combat this, and are particularly useful in windy weather.

Broad bean

Sow in double rows, with staggered spacing, to avoid crowding.

Pick out the top shoots to encourage earlier and bigger pods.

Spray against blackfly — remember the underside of leaves too.

Bean pods reaching maturity. The lowest clusters of beans will mature first. At this point it is possible to cut off the top shoots of the plants and cook the leaves in the same way as spinach.

picking the pods as soon as they can feel sizeable beans inside. It is also possible to pick the pods before the beans inside have properly developed and cook them whole in the same way as runner beans.

For spring-sown crops, the normal time from sowing to harvest is about 14 to 16 weeks. Autumn-sown crops take longer — about 24 to 28 weeks. The pods should be picked by splitting off the pod from the main stem with a quick downward movement of the hand. When the lowest clusters of beans, which mature first, are beginning to form, the top shoots of the plant may be snipped off and — if clean and not already attacked by aphids — cooked as spinach.

After-care
Generally, broad bean plants are disposed of as soon as they have finished bearing crops, about midsummer. The space they occupy in the garden is then ready for other crops. The best thing to do is to plant brassicas in the soil — a good crop rotation, because brassicas benefit especially from the nitrogen that broad beans release in the soil.

Because of the nitrogen-producing bacterial nodules on its roots, the broad bean plant, like other leguminous plants, enriches the soil for the next crop. When clearing the ground after a crop, therefore, dig in the plants, stems, roots and leaves — chopping them up into short lengths if necessary.

Growing under glass
The broad bean is so hardy that glass is only used to bring on a reserve to fill in the gaps in outdoor rows. Broad beans can also be planted or sown in pots under cold glass in mid winter, ready for transplanting in early spring. When this procedure is followed, it is as well to sow one bean per pot and to transplant very carefully, with a minimum disturbance of the roots.

Harvesting the beans — split the pods from the stem with a sharp downwards twist.

Pests and diseases
The most important and troublesome pest that attacks the broad bean is the black dolphin aphid *(Aphis rumicis),* often known simply as blackfly. This juice-sucking insect saps the life of the plant and fouls the leaf surface with sticky honey-dew. The earliest broad bean crops usually bear their pods before the aphid attacks, but the later ones are often heavily infested.

Pinching out the top shoot of the plant is an effective deterrent, as that is the favourite place for the aphids to congregate. Derris and malathion are effective against the pests, but the later crops may have to be dusted or sprayed several times. Spray in the evening after pollinating insects have finished working. Bear in mind that many aphids are tucked away in crevices on the underside of leaves. Experiments in companion plantings have revived the old farmer's belief that summer savoury sown among the broad bean ranks can keep black aphids away.

Chocolate spot *(Botrytis fabae),* may appear on the leaves of late broad bean crops. It is not usually very serious and, as it chiefly attacks weak plants, as good a treatment as any to encourage strong growth. Lime helps to prevent an attack on acid soils and, if the plants are thought to need an extra feeding, a fertilizer rich in potash can be given.

Broccoli

**The head or 'curd' of the large-headed
broccoli is a closely packed
mass of flower stems and buds,
tightly enclosed by leaves**

Broccoli is a cold climate crop, despite the tenderness of the seedlings. Like most cabbages, the plant will survive hard frosts but in harsh conditions the flower head may be damaged and so is generally given some protection. In common with most other garden brassicas, broccoli has been evolved from the wild cabbage.

Broccoli comes in two shapes, the loosely packed sprouting broccoli *(see* SPROUTING BROCCOLI) and the compact, large-headed broccoli covered here. The large-headed broccoli has been evolved from the sprouting, but in appearance it is more like a cauliflower. It has a compact white head and is often listed in seed catalogues with

---

Large-headed Broccoli
Brassica oleracea botrytis (fam. *Cruciferae*), also known as winter cauliflower.
Hardy biennial plant, grown as an **annual.**
Size: 60-90 cm [2-3′] high and 20-45 cm [8-18″] in diameter.
Climate: cool temperate.
Sowing to harvesting time: 9 months to a year.
Yield: 217 kg [6 lb] per 3 m [10′] row.

---

cauliflower. There is also a purple-headed variety, called Cape broccoli.

All the tiny, independent flower heads of sprouting broccoli have been merged into one. The head is knobbly and consists of several rounded sections, unlike the cauliflower which has one compact crown forming a single smooth dome. The cauliflower head is set in a loose frame of upright leaves, but the inner frame of broccoli leaves fits tightly around the flower head and folds over it in winter.

Planning a succession of crops

Between them cauliflowers and broccoli are always in season. Early broccoli mature in late autumn or early winter, mid season varieties come to harvest right through the winter, though frost holds up their development. The later varieties crop the following spring and the last crop is almost in midsummer and can coincide with the earliest cauliflowers.

Suitable site and soil

Broccoli likes a sunny site. Ideally, there should also be some shelter from wind, but very protected spots in low-lying country encourages frost to collect. In these cases a position where wind prevents intense frost is better. Do not choose a site that was used the previous year for any other brassica crop, as your broccoli may get club root and the cabbage root fly. Choose a different site for all brassicas each year.

Improving your soil

Like all brassicas, broccoli prefers a rich, heavy soil — it also needs good drainage. If possible, broccoli should be grown after a crop for which the ground was previously manured, otherwise dig in manure or garden compost at the rate of 3 kg per sq m [6lb per sq yd] early in the autumn before planting. This will give the soil time to consolidate, which is very important to ensure compact heads.

If the soil is at all acid, apply sufficient hydrated lime, at least six weeks after adding the manure, so that a soil test gives a pH of just over 7. A very acid soil is unsuitable for growing broccoli.

Sowing

Where a succession of varieties is planned, sowing is done from early to late spring for cropping the following autumn to spring. Broccoli needs a long growing period so that it can establish itself before the cold weather comes. For the earliest crops, sow seed thinly in drills about 1.5 cm [½″] deep and 15 cm [6″] apart under a frame in early spring. Seed can also be sown the same way outdoors in mid or late spring. A temperature of about 16°F [60°F] is needed for germination, which takes 7-12 days. Thin when the seedlings are large enough to handle.

Planting out

The ground should be trodden down well before planting to ensure that it is thoroughly firmed. When the young plants have grown four or five leaves they can be transplanted. If they are left longer than this the head will be

1. Sowing in a frame for early crops. Seed should be sown thinly in drills, in early spring.

2. The seed should germinate in 7-12 days. Thin out the seedlings when large enough to handle.

3. Before planting out, tread the ground well.

4. Winter protection: pushing plants into a shallow trench, made by scraping the soil away on one side.

5. Cover the roots and stems with soil again.

Right: the inner frame of leaves of the compact, large-headed broccoli fits tightly around the head in winter.

6. Another method of winter protection to prevent the curd freezing and thawing — cover the heads with dry straw in times of hard frost.

poor. They should be hardened off before planting in their permanent positions, from late spring to midsummer.

Plant the seedlings fairly deep in the holes made with a dibber, so that the base of the leaves is only a finger's breadth or so above the surface of the soil. The plant will finish up with a heavy superstructure and needs firm anchorage. Push the dibber into the soil alongside the plants at an angle towards them. This will firm the soil up against the roots and also produce a hole for watering in dry weather. Firm planting also ensures that the heads are compact and do not become 'blown'.

Plant in rows 60-75 cm [2-2½'] apart, with about 60 cm [2'] between plants. In dry weather, take extra care with transplanting. Dig a hole for each plant, fill with water and press the soil firmly around the roots as soon as the plant is inserted. Or the roots may be dipped in a bucket of mud just before planting.

Care of plants

While broccoli will not stand having permanently wet roots, it should never be allowed to get dry during the summer and especially after planting. A light mulching will help to keep the soil moist without waterlogging. Providing the ground was well fed as advised, there will be no need to feed during the growing season. Hoe round the plants frequently to keep down weeds.

Protection in winter

Some winter protection may be necessary in cold areas. Remove the soil from the roots on the side away from the midday sun, then push the plants gently on to their side so that they face away from the sun. Cover the roots and stem with soil again. This prevents alternate freezing and thawing of the curd. Alternatively the heads may be covered with dry straw in times of hard frost.

If the curds are showing, they may be covered by breaking the mid-rib of some of the leaves and bending them over.

Harvesting and storing the crop

If you have planned a succession of broccoli varieties, your first harvest will be in late summer and will continue through the autumn and winter to the beginning of the following summer.

Varieties which come to maturity in winter, or which have to survive the winter to expand in the following spring and summer, are less reliable. In a cold climate they may be badly checked by severe weather and a proportion of the crop destroyed.

Large-headed broccoli should be picked when the enclosed leaves unfold, revealing the curd. For the early and late crops, wait until the unfurling process is complete. In winter it is often advisable to forestall frost damage by cutting broccoli early.

Large-headed broccoli may be pulled out of the ground and the leaves trimmed off afterwards with a sharp knife. Or it may be cut on the site, slicing through the stalk to leave the outer leaves on the stem and the inner leaves, which are edible, around the curd.

If too many heads are maturing together, the surplus may be pulled up with the roots and soil still attached, and hung upside-down in a cool, dark shed. Cover the curd with tissue paper and store for up to three weeks.

Care after harvesting

Once the heads have been cut the crop is finished. The ground may now be finally cleared. Surplus leaves and the fleshy part of the stalk may be dug in or composted if you are sure they are free from disease or pests, but the roots and stem are very woody and should be burnt, to prevent spread of pests and disease.

Pests and diseases

Broccoli is susceptible to all the pests and diseases common to other brassicas (*see* CABBAGE), but it also suffers from a deficiency disease called whiptail, caused by a shortage of molybdenum in the plant. The leaves become badly malformed, being reduced to only the midribs with an edging of leaf. Any curd which develops is small and leafy; seedlings will be yellow, with the leaves turning inwards. It appears on acid soils, so liming is advisable, which will make the soil neutral to alkaline.

If these same symptoms occur when the plant is young, it may be due to a check in growth, caused by cold, dryness or too much fertilizer too soon, and not necessarily the result of whiptail.

Brussels Sprouts

This popular vegetable
belongs to the cabbage family.
The tiny compacted 'sprouts'
grow all the way up the stem.

Like most of the other brassicas, Brussels sprouts have been developed from the wild cabbage *Brassica oleracea*. The stem of the plant is crowned by a head of inward-curling leaves. From the crown almost down to the base of the stem are leaf axils, or joints, and careful plant breeding has ensured that tight little cabbage-like heads are produced in these right up the stem. Each of these miniature cabbages is called a sprout. The buds in the leaf axils of most brassicas do not form until the second season of growth but Brussels sprouts develop theirs during the first year.

The natural tendency of the plant is for sprouts to form first near the base of the stem. After these have been picked those further up the stem grow bigger, and so a succession of picking can be made from the same plant. For many years plants were developed to produce greater quantities of larger sprouts. Commercial growers, however, began to select varieties which produced a mass of medium to small sprouts of uniform size which all came to maturity at the same time.

It is helpful to bear this in mind when choosing varieties. For general kitchen use the gardener will probably prefer the larger plants which produce a succession of sprouts throughout the winter. If, however, the sprouts are chiefly grown for freezing, a variety used by commercial growers might be more suitable.

The picking season can be further extended by using a range of varieties bred to produce sprouts which mature early or late in the winter. The harvesting season for sprouts is from early autumn through to early spring.

Brussels sprouts are a cool-climate crop. They are hardy and will withstand considerable frost, but they do not like extreme heat. A hot dry summer seems to inhibit their capacity to produce tight sprouts in the following autumn. Throughout the germination and growing periods, the plants need a temperature at least a little above freezing point. In the following winter, when they are mature and cropping, they will stand quite severe and prolonged frost. The plants will not grow during such extreme conditions but they will remain alive and will resume growth when the frost is past.

Suitable site and soil

Brussels sprouts are nearly always transplanted into their final positions as young plants. For the seed bed any available plot of fairly fine soil will do. The seedlings will be there for only a few weeks. They may also be cultivated in boxes or pots or under cold glass.

When deciding where to plant, remember that Brussels sprouts plants grow tall and that they are in position for a long time. If possible, arrange the rows so that other plants on either side get a share of sunlight. Remember to choose a plot that has not been occupied by brassicas in the previous year to avoid the build up of pests and diseases. Sprouts are rather top-heavy plants, so try to choose a site which gives some wind protection.

Brussels sprouts
Brassica oleracea gemmifera (fam. *Cruciferae*)
Hardy biennial, usually grown as an **annual.**
Size: about 90 cm [3′] tall.
Climate: temperate
Sowing to harvesting time: about 28-36 weeks.
Yield: 6 plants per 3 m [10′] row, each producing about 1kg [2 lb] of sprouts.

Brussels sprouts will grow in almost any type of soil, though they do not like over-acid conditions. Preferably, choose a site that was manured for a previous crop or, in the autumn before planting, dig the site deeply and work in a heavy dressing of well-rotted farmyard manure or garden compost. This will allow time for the soil to become firm, very important if 'blown' sprouts (open, leafy ones) are to be avoided. If you have not manured the land the previous autumn, apply a topdressing of a compound fertilizer in spring at the rate of 90-125 g per sq m [3-4 oz per sq yd], to improve the soil.

Sowing

As with all brassicas, the seeds of Brussels sprouts are small and round. In the open ground they are sown in drills about 1.5 cm [½″] deep and as close together as is convenient, about 15 cm [6″]. For a main crop, this sowing should be made in mid spring, and the seeds should be sown thinly. Germination should take place within 7-12 days of sowing.

Planting out

When all danger of frost is past in late spring or early summer, the plants should be moved to their final bed. It is essential to allow plenty of space for Brussels sprout plants. Allow 75-90 cm [2½-3′] between rows, and 45 cm [1½′] between each plant in the row.

The Brussels sprout plant is rather shallow-rooted, and its roots have to support a tall, heavy-headed superstructure. So it is important to plant deeply. At transplanting time the plants will be from 10-15 cm [4-6″] high, and they should generally be planted so that their lower leaves are resting on the soil. Try to choose a day just after rain has fallen and water the holes before planting. Make sure the plants are firmed in well to anchor the roots and encourage the development of tight 'buttons', or sprouts.

The plants should be allowed to remain in the seed bed, without pricking out, until the time for the main transplanting. Some gardeners transplant part of the crop but leave plants about 45 cm [1½′] apart in the rows in which they were sown. This can be satisfactory but the plants left in their original site are seldom as good as those which have been transplanted. The transplanting seems to benefit the plants; they grow stronger and produce an earlier crop.

Buying transplants

Rather than taking the trouble to sow seed and grow seedlings, many gardeners prefer to buy their plants at the transplanting stage. There are always plenty of Brussels sprout plants available at markets and garden shops, and a delay of a day or two between pulling the plants and replanting them usually does no great harm.

Early crops

As sprouts require a long growth period and, as the last frost sometimes comes late in spring, many gardeners try to bring on an early crop under glass. The soil temperature for germination needs to be 10° to 13°C [50° to 55°F]. The seed is usually sown in boxes, in an unheated

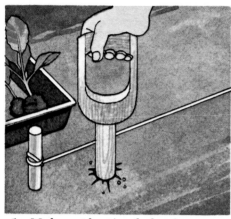

1. Make a planting hole about 10 cm [4″] deep, using a dibber.

2. Unless the soil is moist, fill the dibber hole with water.

3. Push the dibber into the soil near the plant to firm the roots.

4. Fill the hole beside the plant with water when the weather is dry.

5. Test for firmness of planting by pulling at one of the leaves.

6. Draw up soil around the stems to anchor them 1 month after planting.

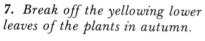

7. Break off the yellowing lower leaves of the plants in autumn.

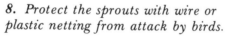

8. Protect the sprouts with wire or plastic netting from attack by birds.

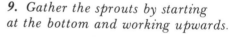

9. Gather the sprouts by starting at the bottom and working upwards.

greenhouse or conservatory, or under cloches.

In districts which have a mild winter the seed is sometimes sown in sheltered borders in autumn and protected by temporary arrangements of glass or plastic against any winter frosts, ready for transplanting early in spring.

Early sowings of Brussels sprouts are transplanted twice. As soon as the seedlings show the first pair of leaves they are pricked out, or transferred from seed boxes to pots or trays which, like the seed boxes, also need the protection of glass or plastic. The seed boxes, pots or trays should contain a fine soil or potting compost. Transplant the seedlings about 5 cm [2″] apart in every direction. An advantage of using boxes is that they can be placed outside the greenhouse or frame on mild days to allow the plants to harden off. If the transplanted seedlings are growing in open ground under cloches, the cloches may be removed on mild days.

Care and development

Remember that sprouts need plenty of water when they are young, so keep them well watered. Also water well in dry weather, so that they can grow without check.

A mulch of garden compost or farmyard manure will help to keep the soil moist and supply a little more plant food. Too much nitrogen while growing results in blown sprouts later, so any addition of compound fertilizers should be done with caution, and preferably in the light of experience. Summer care consists mainly of keeping the surrounding soil free from weeds. The hoeing involved is also beneficial to the plants as it keeps the soil aerated, but hoe lightly across the surface to avoid damaging the shallow roots.

Harvesting the crop

As the crop reaches maturity — 28-36 weeks after sowing, depending on variety — the lower leaves of the plant will start to yellow. Cut or pull them off. They come off easily if pulled downward. The sprouts mature from the bottom of the stem, though sometimes the bottom few are too poor for use. Split each sprout off from the stem by a sharp downward tug. After the lower ones are removed, those higher up will grow more quickly.

At this stage the tops of the plants can be cut off and cooked as a cabbage. Once this is done, remaining sprouts will mature quite quickly. Some gardeners who want all their sprouts early and small for freezing cut off the top several weeks before the crop is ready for picking. Most of the sprouts will then mature at the same time.

If more sprouts are grown than can be used in the course of a winter, the sprouts themselves will unfold and form flower-stems and heads in spring. Some gardeners leave a few plants for this very purpose. The young shoots, picked as they are expanding, make delicious spring greens at a time when vegetables are scarce.

Care after harvesting

Almost every part of the Brussels sprout plant is used. The sprouts and crown are both eaten and all that is left is the stout, woody stem. This will rot in time but should be chopped up with a sharp spade to aid decay. It can be dug

Sprouts of this semi-dwarf variety, ideal for the small garden, can be harvested as early as mid autumn.

Chop up the stems of the sprouts plants and, if free from pests and diseases, put them on the compost heap.

into the soil but is probably best incorporated in the compost heap, if free from pests and disease.

A Brussels sprouts crop is quite a heavy drain on soil, which will benefit from a generous manuring before being used again.

Growing in containers

Brussels sprouts can be grown in boxes, tubs, barrels or other containers in a small garden. Each plant requires a large container about 30 cm [1'] deep and quite wide. Even just one is worth growing for its high yield — about 75-100 sprouts.

Pests and diseases

The pests and diseases of all brassicas are the same; *see* CABBAGE for those attacking Brussels sprouts.

Cabbage

**Cabbage is a vegetable of major value,
for varieties suitable for sowing
in different seasons make it
possible to grow a fresh supply
throughout the year.**

A biennial grown as an annual, the cabbage was evolved from the wild cabbage which grows in many coastal regions of northwestern Europe. It is anchored in the soil by a shallow root and consists of a rather short woody stem and an edible head, or heart, of tightly packed leaves surrounded and enclosed by looser, coarse leaves. Different varieties provide crops all year round.

The first Savoy was developed in the area of France known as Savoy in the Middle Ages. This cabbage-like plant, which is actually more closely related to the Brussels sprout, is hardier than true cabbages.

TYPES OF CABBAGE

There are two main ways of classifying cabbages — one is according to shape and the other is by their season of use. The shape simply means whether the head is pointed or round. The season of use refers to the harvesting time: one group (spring cabbages) is sown in late summer or early autumn for harvesting the following spring; another (summer and autumn cabbages, including red cabbages) is sown in very early spring and harvested in summer while the third group (winter cabbages and Savoys) is sown in late spring and early summer for harvesting in autumn or winter.

Most of the autumn and winter varieties are round headed, while virtually all the spring cabbages are pointed. Young spring cabbages, harvested in early spring before they have developed hearts, are called 'spring greens'.

Red cabbages are always round-headed and are usually sown in spring for autumn harvesting.

Savoys are treated much as winter cabbages. The different varieties are highly specialized in that they mature at different times — the range is wide enough to provide crops ready for harvesting in every month from late autumn to early spring. If you live in a city, however, it would not be a good idea to grow Savoys, for the deeply crimped leaves soon become ingrained with dust, soot and other pollutants.

Each group of cabbages needs rather different treatment, though there are some general rules for growing all types of cabbage, as there are for growing all types of brassica. The cardinal rule for brassicas is never sow or plant them in a plot that contained a brassica crop the previous year.

Spring cabbages

Sown in summer, spring cabbages are moved in autumn to a permanent bed — e.g. a plot which has just produced a crop of potatoes or peas. Protect the crop with cloches during the winter.

Summer and autumn cabbages

To prepare a permanent bed for summer or autumn cabbages, which are sown in spring, dig the ground deeply the

---

Cabbage
Brassica oleracea capitata (fam. *Cruciferae*)
Biennial, grown as an **annual**.
Size: 22.5-45 cm [9-18"] high and 15-60 cm [6-24"] wide.
Climate: cool temperate to sub-tropical.
Sowing to harvesting time: 20-35 weeks for red and autumn cabbages, 28 weeks for winter cabbages, 35 weeks for mature spring cabbages.
Yield: about 10-12 cabbages, each 0.5-1.4 kg [1-3 lb] per 3 m [10'] row.
Savoy
Brassica oleracea bullata major (fam. *Cruciferae*)
Size: to about 20 cm [8"] high and 50 cm [20"] wide.
Climate: cool temperate.
Sowing to harvesting time: about 32 weeks.
Yield: about 6-7 Savoys per 3 m [10'] row.

Savoys are much more hardy than other types of cabbage.

Red cabbages need longer maturing than green varieties.

Most varieties of spring cabbage have pointed heads.

previous autumn and work in a heavy application of farm-yard manure or garden compost. At the same time, apply lime if the soil is acid. Alternatively, if you cannot afford to let the land lie fallow, grow a crop — such as leeks — that needs generous manuring.

Winter cabbages

In more temperate regions, winter cabbages can be planted after any crop, such as early peas or broad beans, which is harvested in late spring and for which the ground was well manured in the previous autumn. In cooler areas where the growing season is shorter, however, it is not possible to grow another crop beforehand on the same land.

Most of the details of cultivation are the same for winter cabbages as for the summer varieties, but the land must be well enough drained so that it does not become sodden in winter. You should allow at least 45 cm [1½'] of space between each plant, the larger varieties requiring 60 cm [2'] in each direction. It is a good idea to earth up the cabbages to enable them to withstand strong winter winds — pile up soil around the stems.

Winter cabbages need less nitrogen and more potash than summer cabbages, and a tomato fertilizer may be used for this crop instead of the usual general fertilizer.

You can also give the soil an extra dressing of sulphate of potash, at the rate of 60 g per sq m [2 oz per sq yd], which will help them stand up to hard weather and soot, at the rate of 1.3 kg per sq m [2½ lb per sq yd], which gives the plants a healthy dark green colour.

Red cabbages

These need a longer period of maturing than the green varieties. To have red cabbages ready for harvesting in late summer, sow seed in the open in early spring, transplant the young plants as soon as possible and water well if the weather is dry. For winter harvesting, sow the seed a little later and put the young plants under cloches or in a cold frame in winter months.

Remember that if the plants are exposed to any frost they will be damaged. General methods of cultivation for red cabbages are the same as for the green types.

Savoy cabbages

These are hardier than the other types of cabbage, and can be grown well on poor soil. Savoys have a rather different texture and flavour from other cabbages, and make a welcome change. You should grow relatively few plants in rich soil, as they can grow to a huge size.

Collards

Collards, or coleworts, are dwarf cabbages, about the size of a lettuce, which can either be cut as spring greens in early spring or allowed to mature to mid-late spring, when they produce excellent miniature cabbages. They have the advantage of being very hardy and of reaching the edible stage very quickly.

(Facing page) Plant cabbages so they will just touch each other when mature, without being overcrowded.

Cabbage

1. *Prepare the seedbed by raking the soil to a fine consistency.*

2. *Make a tiny trench, or drill, in the bed, using the side of the hoe.*

3. *Sow seed in the drill, 1.5 cm [½″] deep, about 8 seeds per 30 cm [1′].*

4. *Cover the seeds with a thin layer of fine soil or peat, using a trowel.*

5. *Smooth and firm the surface of the seedbed with the back of the rake.*

6. *Thin the row of young cabbage plants to about 30 cm [1′] apart.*

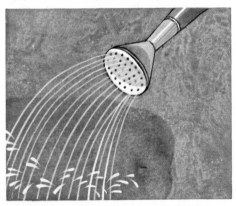

7. *Water the ground well before transplanting the young plants.*

8. *Dig a hole with a trowel, fill it with water and firm in the plant.*

9. *Water the young cabbages liberally as they grow.*

10. *To harvest hearted cabbage, cut the heart out with a sharp knife, leaving the large outer leaves on the stump. In time shoots will appear which produce greens.*

CULTIVATION

There are three main sowing periods for cabbages. The first is in late winter or very early spring, to provide crops for early summer harvesting. The second is the maincrop, sown outdoors in mid spring, for autumn and winter harvesting. The third is from mid to late summer, to provide a crop for overwintering which can then be harvested the following spring.

Sow the earliest crops under glass, either in seedboxes in a greenhouse or frame or in seedbeds protected by frames or cloches. Sow the other crops in a fine seedbed outdoors.

Suitable site and soil

Cabbages grow best on a medium light soil, though they can be grown well on most types of well-drained soil that retain a reasonable amount of moisture. Prepare the soil well in advance of sowing.

Sowing techniques

For starting outdoors. sow in drills (tiny trenches) about 1.5 cm [½"] deep at the rate of about 8 seeds per 30 cm [1']. Thin out alternate seedlings when one cabbage-like leaf shows. Under glass, sow the seed thinly or prick out seedlings at the two-leaf stage, to give the plants room to develop. The same spacing applies as for outdoor plants.

Planting out

Generally speaking, cabbages are transplanted to their permanent beds when five or six leaves have appeared and the stems are the thickness of a pencil. If left too long in their seed-bed growth will be stunted, so be sure to transplant at the proper time.

Assuming you prepared the permanent bed in advance, the soil should be moist at the time of transplanting. Dig a small hole and fill it with water. Place the plant roots in it before the water soaks away, then firmly press the soil around the root using a trowel, a dibber or your hands.

The final spacing should be 30-45 cm [1-1½'] for spring cabbage, depending on whether it is to be hearted or spring greens; 30 cm [1'] between plants and 45 cm [1½'] between rows for summer cabbage, and 45 cm [1½'] between plants and 60 cm [2'] between rows for the main winter crop.

Watering, feeding and weeding

Never allow cabbages to become dry. Water liberally during dry weather, and during the growing period feed occasionally with a liquid feed. Give spring cabbages a dressing of nitrogenous manure and hoe it in well to give the plants a good start at the end of winter.

Hoe around the plants frequently, not only to control weeds but also to aerate the soil and to deter insect pests from laying eggs near the crop. Break off any outer leaves that start to turn yellow.

Harvesting and storing

The cabbage is ready for harvesting when the heart is hard. Cut the stem with a sharp knife, a little above the base of the lower leaves, and remove the outer leaves which are much too coarse for eating.

Spring cabbages are often harvested, as spring greens, in very early spring or even late winter before the hearts are properly formed. The fully formed cabbage is picked, as its name suggests in mid spring.

Red cabbage is usually harvested in autumn or winter. Mature, hard, round-ended cabbages, stripped of their outer leaves, can be kept in a cool shed for several weeks. This applies especially to red cabbages. Spring cabbages do not keep long once they have been harvested.

After harvesting

Once the cabbages have been cut, the crop is finished and the ground may be cleared. Dig the surplus leaves into the soil. Burn the stems or chop them up well and add them to the compost heap if free from pests and disease. The stems of cabbages harvested in autumn and winter are sometimes left in the ground to shoot again in spring, thus providing another welcome source of spring greens.

Pests and diseases

Cabbages can be attacked by the following troubles: clubroot, cabbage root fly, flea beetles, wirestem and ring spot. These will also invade other brassicas and are specific to these crops.

Clubroot is a fungus disease which infects the roots and is soil-borne. The roots become swollen and distorted, and rot; the leaves become blue-green and wilt. The disease can be spread on tools, shoes, machinery and infected roots left in the soil; it is worst on acid soils and wet, badly-drained sites. Control consists of liming the soil to make it slightly alkaline, improving the structure so that water drains away, and dusting seedbeds and planting holes with calomel dust if the disease has been troublesome in the past. Infected roots should be removed complete and burnt; soil should be rested for at least five years. To ensure that the disease does not appear, rotation of crops should be practised as a matter of course.

Cabbage root fly causes wilting of the young plants, because the small white maggots eat into the main root. Trouble can occur first in late spring, and continue all summer as successive broods hatch. Since the eggs are laid on the soil surface close to the plants, squares of tarred felt with a central hole or flat plastic collars placed round the plants on the soil will prevent this, otherwise dust the soil with diazinon.

Flea beetles can decimate seedlings and young plants by biting small round holes in the leaves, and completely destroy a crop before it has even started to grow. They are black and hop when disturbed; dust the leaves when dry with derris, and hoe frequently to disturb their egg-laying.

Wirestem is a fungus disease of the seedlings, in which the base of the stem withers and browns; the seedling either dies or survives to produce a stunted, poor plant with a constricted stem. Avoid by using sterilized seed compost or soil and sow the seed thinly, in non-acid soil.

Ringspot is a fungus disease which produces round brown spots about 1.5 cm [½"] diameter on older leaves; the latter then turn yellow. The younger and inner leaves will also gradually be infected. Remove affected leaves, and give a light dressing of potash fertilizer to harden the growth.

Other troubles which can affect cabbages are: whitefly, mealy aphid, caterpillars of the cabbage white butterfly and cabbage moth, slugs, birds, rodents, and cutworms and leatherjackets, soil-inhabiting grubs which eat roots.

Calabrese

SEE SPROUTING BROCCOLI

Cantaloupe

SEE MELON

Cape Gooseberry

The fruit is a juicy little golden ball enclosed in a 'chinese lantern' which protects it from birds and insects. It needs a fairly warm climate.

Cape gooseberries or physalis have a sweet to sharp taste and are eaten raw as dessert or cooked in chutneys and curries. A confection is made by folding back the calyx and using this to dip the berries in fondant.

Though they are associated with South Africa, the berries originated in Peru, and were named for the Cape of Good Hope. In sub-tropical climates it will give quite large crops on relatively poor soil. Although it is a perennial, replanting every year gives better yields. The plant is a member of the tomato family and requires similar conditions, being very sensitive to frost. It forms a bushy but rather sprawling plant which requires support.

Suitable site and soil
In a cool temperate area choose a site in the full sun, which is sheltered from the wind. A well-drained sandy soil is ideal. Treat poor soil with well rotted manure at the rate of a 10 L (2 gal) bucket per sq m (yd). Do this at seed planting time, which will give it time to break down. A general fertilizer, at the rate of 45 g per sq m (1½ oz per sq yd) about two weeks before planting out, can be used instead.

Sowing and planting out
Sow the seed in early spring in a greenhouse in a peat-based proprietory seed compost. Sow them 0.5 cm [¼"] deep in 5 cm [2"] pots. Place a sheet of glass over the seeds to increase humidity. A temperature of 18°C [65°F] is needed for germination.
Seeds sprout after 10-14 days. Early pricking out is essential when the seedlings are about 1.5-2 cm [½-¾"] high, putting them into 7.5 cm [3"] pots, which should then be kept in the greenhouse. If seedlings are planted out at this time, the plant will produce too much growth and will not fruit early. Transplant to permanent positions in the open when there is no more risk of frost. Allow 1 m [3'] between them. From mid spring you can plant out under cloches.

Care and development
Stake the plant with a 1.25 m [4'] bamboo cane at the time of planting out, and tie it with soft string. Overwatering reduces fruiting. The leaves may be allowed to turn dull grey-green, but do not let the plant wilt. Feeding encourages luxuriant growth at the expense of fruiting. Feed only after the plant shows its first flowers, at the rate of 60 g per sq m [2 oz per sq yd] with a general fertilizer. Proprietary tomato feeds are suitable as they are low in nitrogen. The root system is shallow, therefore hoe carefully to remove weeds. If the plants reach 30 cm [1'] high without producing any sideshoots, the growing tip of the plant should be pinched out. Later on tips of sideshoots can be removed to keep the plant within bounds, and sub-sideshoots completely removed.

Cape gooseberry
Physalis peruviana edulis (fam. *Solanaceae*)
Herbaceous perennial, usually grown as an **annual.**
Size: 1.5 m [4-5'] out-of-doors, 2.5 m [8'] under glass.
Climate: warm temperate to sub-tropical.
Planting to harvesting time: minimum 4 months, 7 months as a half-hardy annual.
Yield: 1-2 kg [2-4 lb].

A member of the tomato family, the cape gooseberry requires support and should be staked with a 1.25 m [4'] bamboo cane when planted out. A row can be staked out like raspberries with posts and wires strained between them.

The 'Chinese lantern' of the cape gooseberry protects the fruit from birds and insects. Though cape gooseberries are ready to pick when golden-brown, they reach their flavour peak a few weeks later.

The cape gooseberry should be grown on a site which is in full sun and sheltered from the wind. It will crop well on poor, sandy soil, the main requirement for its success being good drainage and adequate watering.

Growing in the greenhouse

If you have sufficient heat in your greenhouse to keep out frost, the plant may be grown as a perennial. Crops in the second year are substantially larger, as they get an early start. Pot on your transplants into 20-25 cm [8-10″] containers containing compost with a high proportion of sand. Don't use old tomato soil, which might carry over pests and diseases.

Cut the plant down to about 25 cm [10″] at the end of the season. Winter watering should only just keep the soil moist, to reduce the risk of root rot. Do not water from above after pruning as grey mould (*botrytis*) can develop. The following spring pollination must be aided by shaking the plant when the flowers are open.

Train plants on a trellis or with a system of wires: erect two 1.8 m [6′] wooden poles — making sure the poles are far enough apart to accommodate the plants when full grown. Tie two wires horizontally, between the two poles, one 60 cm [2′] and the other 1.2 m [4′] above ground level. Tie each plant on to the wires where they cross.

If the plant is to be staked, it may be necessary to pinch out the growing tips when 4-6 fruits have set, otherwise it will grow too tall.

Growing in a warm climate

The cape gooseberry is not very fussy about its site. The main requirement is adequate drainage and provision for watering in the dry months. It will crop well on poor sandy soil; on rich silty soil the plant grows prolifically at the expense of fruiting.

Fertilize the site as before, and plant out seedlings when about 10 weeks old and a height of 30 cm [1′]. Allow 45 cm - 1 m [1½-3′] between plants, depending on soil fertility. A row of cape gooseberries may be staked like raspberries (*see* RASPBERRY) with posts and wires at 75 cm [2½′] and 1.25 m [4′]. Water thoroughly after transplanting and, if there is no rain, water at 2-3 weeks intervals until well established. Though a perennial, plants are usually treated as annual because mortality rates from root-rots and virus diseases increase during the second season. Cape gooseberries should not be planted in rotation with tomatoes or potatoes, due to eel worms and other problems.

Harvesting

Fruit is ready to harvest when the calyx changes colour to golden-brown and acquires a papery texture. The fruit will hang for several weeks when ripe, though this may not be practicable in some areas where birds attack the crop. Pick the fruit complete with calyx. If the fruit has been grown out-of-doors in a temperate climate, gather all berries showing a hint of yellow when a severe frost threatens. These will continue to ripen in a sunny position. In warmer climates first pickings are in autumn, or when the calyx changes colour, and continue at 1-2 week intervals. The fruit develops its flavour peak 2-3 weeks after assuming its deep golden colour.

Storing the crop

Storage time depends on humidity. In cool climates drying the husk is essential, by spreading the fruit in a single layer on a warm windowsill or greenhouse. They can then be kept a few weeks in a dry atmosphere at 10-15°C [50-60°F]. Do not dehusk them until they are required. In a warm climate they will keep up to five months.

Pests and diseases

In a temperate climate there are no problems because the fruit has natural protection from its husk. If cape gooseberries are grown in the greenhouse, greenfly and whitefly can be a nuisance; if they occur, spray with a proprietary insecticide. In a sub-tropical climate cutworms, red spider mites, caterpillars, the potato tuber moth, root-rots and virus diseases cause problems.

Capsicum

SEE PEPPERS

Caraway

Caraway is an aromatic plant most often grown for its seeds, which are used in cooking, baking, confectionery and flavouring liqueurs.

Caraway (*Carum carvi*) is a biennial in the *Umbelliferae* family and in its first season will produce feathery shoots about 20 cm [8″] high, like carrot tops. In its second season it will grow to 60 cm [2′] and produce white umbels, ribbed umbrella-like flower heads.

Producing an aromatic seed which has a wide range of uses in the kitchen, and is best known in rye bread, caraway is an undemanding plant to cultivate.

The name caraway is thought to derive either from the Gaelic word 'caroh' meaning ship, or 'karawya', the Arabic word for seed. Caraway seeds are recorded in Egyptian and Roman days, and in Elizabethan times, the seed were served, either in a dish by themselves, or with roast apples, after a meal to help digestion and reduce flatulence. They were also added to herb bags, along with flower petals and other fragrant herbs and spices.

The fragrant seeds are the most useful part of the caraway plant. Dried, they are best known as a seasoning in rye bread, but are also particularly suitable for flavouring cream cheese, cooked brassicas, such as steamed Brussels sprouts or sauerkraut, and are common in German, Austrian and Jewish dishes. The young leaves may be used in soups or salads and the tap roots may be eaten like parsnips. Oil of caraway is used in making the unique liqueur called Kümmel.

Found wild in Europe, North America and India, caraway is undemanding, unaffected by either dry weather or frost, and can be grown either in or out of doors in a herb garden, window box, tub or other container.

Cultivation

Caraway will grow satisfactorily in semi-shady conditions but it does not need much water and should never be planted in soil that tends to stay damp. The best soil for it is fine, sandy and well-drained. Heavy soil should be treated with a mixture of sand and peat.

Sowing can be done outdoors in mid spring or late summer, putting the seed thinly in drills 45 cm [1½'] apart. Seeding to germination is approximately three weeks, and the seedlings should be thinned to a final spacing of 30 cm [1'] between plants.

Since caraway produces a long tap root, it is not advisable to transplant it. When growing in containers, therefore, two or three seeds should be sown in the container in which it is to grow, and the weakest seedlings discarded as soon as possible. Seedlings sown in the spring will not flower until late spring the next year. Seedlings sown in the autumn will reach maturity the following midsummer.

During the very dry spells, the plants should be kept damp by light watering every two or three days. The plants need no special feeding or support, but tend the ground around the plants regularly to make sure that it is kept completely free from weeds.

Harvesting and aftercare

The leaves should be cut sparingly 8-10 weeks after planting out. The seeds are ready for collection when the stems start to discolour and the fruit is dark green. The roots can be used once the seed heads have been collected. The seed heads should be removed from the plant with care, put into paper bags and kept in a dry place until the seeds fall. The seeds should be put in an opaque airtight container; dampness impairs their flavour. Stored in this way they will keep their pungency for at least one year.

Caraway seeds are ready for harvesting when the stems begin to discolour and the fruit goes dark green. If they are left the seeds will fall and be lost in the garden. The heads should be kept in paper bags until the seeds loosen.

Cardoon

**An aristocratic vegetable for the
adventurous gardener, the cardoon is a
large, handsome thistle-like plant
which yields delicious stems after blanching.**

The cardoon is a hardy, herbaceous plant, a native of
southern Europe that was introduced to Britain in the late
16th century. Its botanical name *Cynara cardunculus*
comes from the Greek *kynon*, a dog; its abundant spines
are rather like dogs' teeth. The cardoon is similar in appearance to its close relative the globe artichoke (*C.
scolymus*), but it is hardier. It is often grown solely for its
appearance at the back of a flower border, where it towers
majestically over the other plants.

The flower buds of cardoons can be eaten exactly like
those of globe artichokes, but they are much smaller; if
picked when very young, they can be cooked and eaten
whole. Usually, however, it is the stems that are eaten,
after blanching in the same way as celery.

Suitable site and soil
Cardoons need plenty of sunlight and warmth for ordinary
growth, but to produce lush leaves you must also water
them generously in dry weather. They need a rich soil; on
dry soils they are best grown in a trench, but in heavy, wet
soils they can be grown normally.

Sowing under glass
If the ground is cold, you should sow the seeds in pots under glass in mid spring. Sow three seeds to each 7.5 cm [3″]
pot and later thin to one seedling per pot. Plant the young
cardoons outside in their permanent positions in late
spring. Alternatively, raise young plants from seed sown in

Cardoon
Cynara cardunculus (fam. *Compositae*)
Perennial, usually grown as an **annual.**
Size: to 1.8 m [6′] or more high.
Climate: cool temperate to sub-tropical.
Sowing to harvesting time: 24-34 weeks.
Yield: 6-7 plants per 3 m [10′] row.

---

early spring in a heated greenhouse or propagator.

Sowing outdoors and thinning out
If sowing outdoors in a permanent position, the ground
should be warm. Prepare trenches 30 cm [1′] deep and 45
cm [1½′] wide, as for celery, with 7.5 cm [3″] of well-rotted
manure or good garden compost mixed with soil at the
base of the trench. Allow this material to settle, when
there should be a hollow for retaining water.

Sow the seed in the trench in mid to late spring in groups
of 3-4 seeds at 45 cm [1½′] intervals, and 2.5 cm [1″] deep.
Place an inverted flower pot over each little group of seeds
to prevent mice or other animals from eating them. If you
are sowing more than one row of cardoons, the trenches
should be 1 m [3′] apart so that you will have enough room
for cultivation later.

As soon as the seeds have sprouted, remove the flower pots
covering them. When the seedlings are big enough to handle (at about 5 cm [2″] high), thin them out from 3 or 4
seedlings per group to a single one, leaving the strongest.

Care and development
From late spring to early autumn, water your cardoons
well; when the weather is very dry, flood the trenches.
Prevent the soil from becoming a solid mass and remove
all weeds by hoeing regularly. At the end of midsummer,
give the plants a mulch of moist horticultural peat or garden compost. Throughout late summer, feed them weekly
with diluted liquid fertilizer.

When the plants have reached 30 cm [1′] high, push a
stake into the ground alongside each plant and tie the
leaves lightly to it.

Blanching
To blanch cardoons, remove all dead or yellowing leaves
in late summer to early autumn, bunch all the leaves
together and tie them together at their tops with twine.
Then wrap long strips of thick brown paper 15 cm [6″]
wide around the plant, starting at the bottom; alternatively, you can bind the plants with strong black plastic
film. Leave several centimetres (inches) of the leaves free
so that the plant can still make its own food. Next, pack
soil around the tied-up plants to exclude all light.
An alternative method of blanching requires no earthing-
up. You should thatch the plants with layers of straw 10
cm [4″] thick to cover them completely. The straw can be
tied at the top and turned over on one side so that it resembles an old-fashioned night-cap. This method, although
more painstaking, gives quicker results than the previous
one: the cardoons should be ready to eat in four weeks or
less, instead of six to eight.

Instead of blanching your cardoons at the end of late summer, you may prefer to wait until winter and eat them
when there are few other fresh vegetables available. If
frosts set in before you have started blanching, you should
cover the plants with a mulch of straw or other light
material, removing this in the morning. If blanching has
not been completed when winter arrives in earnest, dig up
the plants with as much soil as possible on their roots and
move them to a storage room such as a shed, cellar or

1. *To blanch, tie each plant lightly to a 60 cm [2'] cane when it is about 30 cm [1'] high.*

2. *To avoid cutting your hands on the leaves, gather them with two sticks and some string.*

3. *Bunch all the leaves together and tie them at the top with raffia, soft strings or twine.*

4. *Wind strips of brown paper round stem upwards from soil level, leaving the leafy tops exposed.*

5. *Pack earth or soil round the tied-up plant to stop all light from getting through.*

An alternative to earthing-up is to thatch with layers of straw 7.5-10 cm [3-4"] thick.

Black plastic sheet can be used in place of brown paper for blanching. The thatching method however, produces cardoons to eat in four weeks or less instead of the 6-8 taken with the earthing-up technique.

garage; heap soil, sand or peat over the roots and keep them moist. Provided you follow these instruction, they should remain in good condition for several weeks.

If the storage place is completely dark, you can remove the wrappings — otherwise leave them on until you are going to use the cardoons.

Pests and diseases

There are few troubles, apart from rare damage by slugs.

Carrot

Carrots are one of the easiest vegetable crops to grow, provided the soil has been well prepared. They are rich in vitamin A and, harvested young, sweeter and more tender than market crops.

Carrots are herbaceous biennials, grown as annuals. The swollen 'tap roots' of the most cultivated varieties of carrot are orange, but some types do produce white, yellow or even purple roots.

There are three main types of carrot: the finger-sized, shorthorn or 'stump-rooted' type ideal for an early or forced crop; the medium-length thin-ended type with a cylindrical, tapering root, suitable for both storage and im-

---

Carrot
Daucus carota (fam. *Umbelliferae*)
Herbaceous biennial, grown as an **annual.**
Size: 23 x 4 cm [9 x 1½"] for long-rooted varieties,
12.5 x 6.5 cm [5 x 2½"] for stump rooted types.
Climate: cool temperate.
Sowing to harvesting time: early or forced crops are ready for pulling after about 9-11 weeks, maincrop after 14-18 weeks.
Yield: about 90 g [3 oz] of roots per plant.

---

mediate use, and the long tapering type which makes a good late-maturing crop and is particularly suitable for exhibition growing.

Suitable site and soil

Carrots prefer a deep, light loam and a sunny or partially shaded aspect. Early crops grow best in full sun. Maincrop varieties can be grown on well-prepared, heavier soil. Soil conditions are all-important because the carrot is a root vegetable and must penetrate and build up its structure within the soil. Carrots require a deeply dug bed of friable (crumbly) soil about 45 cm [1½'] deep, rich in finely-divided particles of humus. The bed should have been manured in the previous growing season. If manure, garden compost or similar materials are introduced into the structure of the carrot bed in the season of sowing or during the immediate preparation of the bed, some of the crop will tend to be malformed, the roots being forked into two or more branches. Large stones can also result in crooked roots.

On a plot where crops are being grown in a rotation system, carrots should, ideally, be grown in the previous year's pea bed.

Preparing the soil

Carrots grow best in sandy loams, but even heavy soils can be adapted for growing them by thorough digging and the incorporation of humus-forming manure or garden compost, provided this is done well in advance of the growing season. Leafmould can be introduced while you are digging the bed. You should sift the soil thoroughly with a garden sieve to remove all stones and large lumps of soil and work plenty of moist peat into it. The reason for adding peat is that carrots like a well-drained soil but not a dry one. The peat helps to bind loose, fast-draining sandy soils and also encourages better drainage and crumb structure on heavy soils that need lightening.

Leave the surface of the carrot bed rough until a week or ten days before sowing. Rake it level and create a good tilth (a fine crumbly layer) to ensure maximum germination. After raking immediately work in a handful per sq m (sq yd) of a good general fertilizer to give the seedlings a good start. Rake the fertilizer well into the surface of the bed.

When you have raked the bed level, position a line of string between two stakes across the bed to mark out the row of carrots. Run the corner of a hoe or rake along the line to cut out a V-shaped furrow at least 2.5 cm [1"] deep. Rows should be 23 cm [9"] apart for early crops, and 30 cm [1'] for maincrops.

Sowing

Maincrops are sown from mid spring to midsummer, the later the better, to avoid attacks from carrot fly. Early crops are sown in early spring.

Carrots prefer warm soil and grow best in the early days of the season. If you sow too early however, before the cold

Rich in vitamin A, carrots should be harvested when young and tender and eaten soon for the best flavour.

weather has cleared, there is a danger of seed failure. If the weather is bleak at the time you planned to sow, use cloches of horticultural glass or plastic, or plastic mini-tunnels to protect the seedlings. The cloches can go on to the seed-beds three weeks before sowing to warm the soil; after sowing they can be replaced to give the seeds a good start in their early growth.

Sow carrot seed either in pinches between finger and thumb or by carefully shaking the seed into the drill direct from the packet with the hand held just a few centimetres above the drill.

After sowing, replace the soil by gently covering the drill, using the back of the rake. A better but more painstaking method of doing this job is to place your feet on either side of the V-shaped drill in which the seed is lying at a depth of about 2 cm [¾"]. Then shuffle forward along the row with the toes pointing outwards and the heels pushing soil into the row. This action safely covers the carrot seed and at the same time gives the row a gentle firming. After covering the seed, rake the soil level by lightly pulling the rake down the row — never across it. Raking across the row would disturb or actually displace some of the seeds. Germination normally occurs from 14-18 days after sowing.

When sowing carrot seed the rule is to sow as thinly as possible, thus avoiding waste and the back-breaking task of thinning out. The most painstaking method for a successful crop is to sow the seeds singly, but a less time-consuming method is to mix a little dry horticultural sand with the seed in the packet. Alternatively, mix radish seed with the carrot seed. The radishes are soon ready for harvesting and this is an easy way of thinning the carrot row early on.

Thinning and general care

The essential task of thinning, by pulling out the smallest seedlings in each cluster, should begin when the greenery is about 2.5 cm [1"] high.

The best time to thin your carrots is after a rain shower; the water loosens the bed and makes the seedlings easy to lift. The first one or two thinnings will be tiny, but the last one or two in the early crop can be used in the kitchen. The early crop should have a final distance of 5 cm [2"] between each root, the maincrops are thinned progressively to a final spacing of about 10 cm [4"].

You should remove discarded seedlings from the area immediately. From time to time during these thinning operations, scatter a very light dressing of general fertilizer around the rows and allow the rain to wash this food into the soil; if it is dry, water it in. Keep the weeds under control, and do not allow the crop to run short of water, otherwise the roots split.

Harvesting and storing the crop

Once they have reached the desired size, short-rooted early varieties can be harvested from midsummer and harvesting can continue for several weeks. Maincrop varieties should be harvested from early autumn onwards.

Choose a dry day at the end of the season to lift the crop. Use a garden fork pushed into the soil well away from the

vegetables to avoid damaging their skins. After lifting, cut off the foliage near the crown and put it on the compost heap. They are now ready for use or for storing.

Choose sound roots for storing and use during winter. Carrots can be stored outdoors in a hole filled with dry sand and covered with straw or in a clamp, like potatoes. To store indoors, place the carrots in boxes of sand, soil or peat in a frostproof shed.

Frame cultivation

Forcing varieties of carrots can be grown to mature at times when bought carrots are expensive.

Sow the seed in an outdoor cold frame in a layer of soil above a hotbed — a mixture of manure and other humus-containing materials that creates its own heat by fermentation (brought about by the bacteria living in it).

The hotbed for out-of-season carrots should be a mild one, consisting of a basic layer of straw and rotted manure mixed with rotted leaves. Stack up this mixture until it is about 15 cm [6"] deep. Turn it over and moisten it every day for about a week to encourage fermentation, then flatten it and cover it with about 15 cm [6"] of good garden loam. Scatter seeds of a stump-rooted carrot variety thinly onto the soil, work them in below the surface with a hand-fork, and firm the bed with a wooden board. Water frequently, give ventilation when the weather allows it, and cover the frame with sacking or other protection on frosty nights; do not allow the night-time temperature to fall below 7°C [45°F].

Consign the first carrot thinnings to the compost heap; subsequent thinnings, to about 5 cm [2"] apart, can be used in the kitchen.

Pests and diseases

The greatest pest is the carrot-fly (*Psila rosea*), which is attracted by the pungent smell of the carrot foliage, and finds small areas of disturbed soil near the rows ideal places to lay its eggs. The small, pale yellow maggots that emerge from the eggs then burrow into the roots and may devastate the crop. Wilting, reddened foliage is usually the first symptom above soil level.

The chief carrot-fly attack occurs in late spring, so by delaying sowing until the end of early summer it is possible to miss it altogether. The second generation of adult flies does not start laying eggs until late summer, and the maggots hatching from these hardly ever cause damage.

Since thinning the young plants unavoidably releases the smell of the foliage, sowing the seed as thinly as possible in the first place is a great help in reducing the possibility of attack. Do this in the evening when the fly is less likely to be about, and destroy the thinnings. Never use a hoe to thin out young crops; this damages the foliage even more.

Some veteran gardeners sow parsley between the carrot rows because the scent of parsley is said to counteract that of the carrot leaves and so distract or deter the fly. In the same way a rag soaked in paraffin oil can be pulled along the rows occasionally to introduce a camouflage scent. You can also use bromophos dust as the makers direct. Other troubles that may occur are wireworm, violet root rot, eelworm, greenfly and soft rot.

Ball-shaped carrots are ideal for shallow soil.

Long tapering varieties for a late-maturing crop.

The medium-sized cylindrical types of carrot are good for both storage and immediate use.

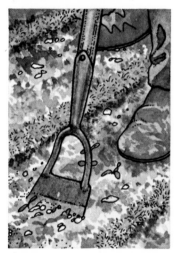

1. *Hoe regularly between the rows of seedlings to remove any weeds.*

2. *Thin the seedlings to 2.5 cm [1"] apart after watering thoroughly.*

3. *Firm in and water the remaining seedlings to deter carrot fly.*

4. *Sprinkle general fertilizer between the rows of carrots and water.*

5. *Water the night before, then young carrots can easily be pulled by hand.*

6. *Use a fork to lift mature carrots which can be stored in early autumn.*

Store carrots between layers of dry sand in a box in a frostproof shed. Cut off tops and pack evenly. They can also be stored outside covered with straw or in a clamp.

Cauliflower

Although more difficult to grow than other brassicas, this popular vegetable is well worth the effort.

The cauliflower is a highly specialized member of the brassica tribe. Generations of selective growing have developed the stalks of the opened flower-buds to form a compact head or 'curd'.

The plant produces a short, woody stem, 7.5 - 15 cm [3-6"] high, crowned by a cup of leaves which encloses the curd. When the leaves unfurl to disclose the entire top surface of the curd, the cauliflower is ready for cutting. There are many varieties, ranging from those which mature in early summer to those which are ready in late autumn. In the latter part of the year the range overlaps with heading broccoli. These are also called winter cauliflowers.

Suitable site and soil

Like other brassicas, cauliflowers are usually transplanted, so they need two sites. The seedbed can be any bed of fine soil, or a box of seed compost. Work on the permanent bed should be done in autumn. The site should be sunny and sheltered from wind, but must not contain hollows that trap frost. The soil should be either double-trenched or dug to a sufficient depth to take a good layer of rotted farmyard manure or garden compost in the bottom. The lighter the soil, the more organic matter it needs. It may also be reinforced by a dressing of about 125 g per sq m [4 oz per sq yd] of a compound fertilizer worked into the soil about a week before planting. Correct any soil acidity by an application of lime well before planting, at a rate determined by the result of a soil test. The lime should be added at least six weeks after the addition of the manure.

As with all brassicas, avoid using a plot on which a brassica crop was grown in the previous year. Cauliflowers are even more susceptible than most other brassicas to the pests and diseases encouraged by continuous cropping.

Cauliflower
Brassica oleracea botrytis (fam. *Cruciferae*)
Biennial, usually grown as **half-hardy annual.**
Size: Head 7.5-38 cm [3-15"] across; stalks 7.5-15 cm [3-6"] long; leaves 45-60 cm [18-24"] high.
Climate: cool to warm temperate.
Sowing to harvesting time: 18-24 weeks.
Yield: 0.5-1 kg [1-2 lb] per plant; 5-7 plants per 3 m [10'] row.

The spreading leaves of the summer cauliflower, the 'true' cauliflower. The winter type is a kind of broccoli.

A freshly-cut cauliflower. Harvest cauliflower while the head is still firm and compact.

Sowing

Cauliflower varieties are divided into four groups, according to the time of harvesting:

Group 1 contains the earliest cauliflowers, which are intended to be harvested in late spring and early summer. They are all dwarf cauliflowers, only 30 cm [1′] or so high. They should be sown under glass from late autumn to mid winter, and will require a constant temperature of 10·15°C [50-60°F]. They produce a minimum of small, pale leaves that give little protection to the curd, which is pure white and of a delicate flavour.

Group 2 contains the second earlies, consisting of rather hardier varieties, for harvesting in midsummer. They are also dwarf, but not as small as those in Group 1, and the leaves are rather larger and darker. They should be sown in boxes, pans or pots under glass at the same time as Group 1 cauliflowers. A second sowing may be made outdoors in early spring, although this should be protected by cloches against night frosts and chilly daytime weather. The plants will come to maturity a month or two later than those brought on under glass.

Group 3 contains the maincrops, consisting of a number of larger, hardier varieties of cauliflower, for harvesting from late summer to mid autumn. Sow in an outdoor seedbed in mid spring, giving some protection against night frosts. Sow in drills about 1.5 cm [½″] deep, in rows 23-30 cm [9-12″] apart.

Group 4 consists of a number of dwarf, very hardy varieties, originating in Australia and introduced to Britain and the United States within recent years. Sown at the same time and in the same manner as those in Group 3, they come to maturity rather later and will tolerate a moderate amount of autumn frost. They have compact, high quality, uniform curds protected by tightly incurling leaves.

The small, round cauliflower seeds tend to be expensive, so it is as well to sow them economically, — ideally about 2.5 cm [1″] apart. Sowing time to germination is from 1-2 weeks. With those sown under glass, prick out the little plants into boxes, pans or even small pots when they reach the two-leaf stage. Allow 5 cm [2″] between plants in each direction. Alternatively, you can use smaller pots, but put only one plant in each.

Planting out

Transplant to the prepared outdoor bed when the plants have about five leaves and cloche the varieties in Groups 1 and 2, if frost is still likely. For crops in Groups 1 and 2, plant 45 cm [1½′] apart in rows 60-90 cm [2-3′] wide. For crops in Groups 3 and 4, allow 60 cm [2′] between the plants.

Take great care to avoid a check to the plants when transplanting them, as this is one of the main reasons for small or non-existent heads. In times of drought, water both the plants and the prepared bed before transplanting. Keep a ball of soil intact around the roots of each plant during the transplanting. It is as well to work with a trowel rather than a dibber. In warm, sunny weather, dig a small hole in the soil, fill it with water, insert the plant roots, and press soil firmly around them.

Buying cauliflower plants from a nursery, for transplanting, is less satisfactory than for other hardier types of brassica — cauliflowers suffer much more from the slightest check. Also, few nurseries carry more than a limited range of varieties.

Care and development

The secret of success with cauliflower is rapid and continuous growth. From transplanting time onward they need copious watering. Even though the soil may be very rich as a result of its preparation it can do with even more feeding where summer cauliflower is being grown. There

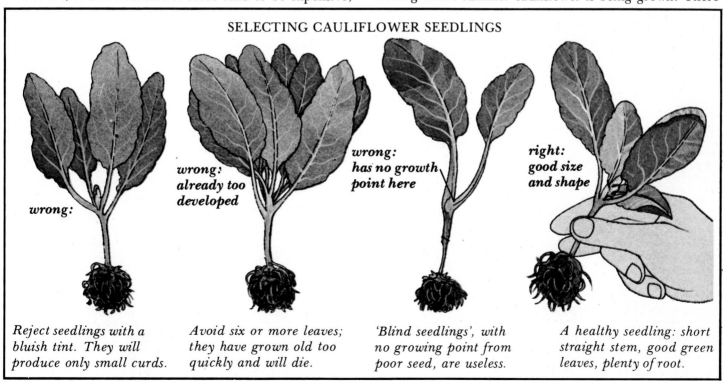

SELECTING CAULIFLOWER SEEDLINGS

wrong:

wrong: already too developed

wrong: has no growth point here

right: good size and shape

Reject seedlings with a bluish tint. They will produce only small curds.

Avoid six or more leaves; they have grown old too quickly and will die.

'Blind seedlings', with no growing point from poor seed, are useless.

A healthy seedling: short straight stem, good green leaves, plenty of root.

1. *Before planting out seedlings at the four-leaf stage, dip roots into pesticide paste to avoid club root.*

2. *Keep a ball of soil around the root when transplanting, and in warm weather fill the holes with water before inserting the seedling. Take care to avoid any check during the operation.*

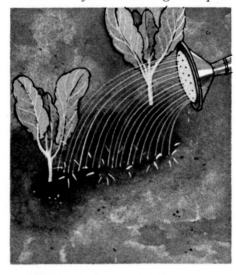

3. *Dust with insecticide to guard against pests, particularly the flea beetle which eats the leaves.*

4. *Water gently around the seedlings, using a rose on the can. Water the soil, not the plants.*

5. *Fold back the inner leaves over the curd to protect it from direct sunlight.*

6. *Tie the leaves in position over the top of the curd with raffia or with a rubber band.*

7. *Harvest before curd opens. Cut horizontally with a sharp knife, leaving a few leaves round curd.*

8. *One storing method is to hang upside down in a cool, dark place, syringing with water every night.*

are several methods. One is to mulch the soil around the plants with rotted farmyard manure or garden compost three weeks after planting, drenching it with water afterwards. Another method is to work a topdressing of a nitrogenous fertilizer, such as ammonium nitrate or nitro-chalk, into the soil around the plants with a hoe, again followed by a generous watering. This should be done five weeks after planting. Alternatively, the nitrogenous fertilizer may be dissolved in water and the solution used for watering the plants two or three times at regular intervals during the growing period.

As cauliflowers, especially the early varieties, are not strongly competitive plants, they should be thoroughly weeded throughout the growing period. A heavy mulch does have the effect of suppressing weeds for a time.

Harvesting the crop

One advantage of choosing your seed from seed catalogues instead of buying plants from nurseries is that you can make a selection of varieties which will extend your harvesting period from late spring to the beginning of the following winter.

A cauliflower is ready for cutting when the upper surface of the curd is fully exposed, and the inner leaves no longer cover it. If left in the ground longer, the head expands and loses its compactness. Cauliflowers can be held back if too many are maturing at once. Gather up the leaves and tie them together over the curd so that they cover it, using a piece of garden twine, a rubber band or raffia. This should take care of the plant for a week or more. Breaking the ribs of some of the leaves and bending the leaves over the curd will delay maturing for a few days. Another method is to pull up the plant complete with its roots, and hang the cauliflower upside down in a cool shed, away from strong light, spraying it with water every night. This will keep the plant fresh for up to three weeks.

When harvesting cauliflower, cut through the stem with a sharp knife, leaving sufficient leaves attached to the curd to form a 'frame' around it. Cut in the early morning, when the plant is freshest — ideally with dew on it. Cauliflowers can also be frozen successfully.

Aftercare

Unlike some brassicas, the cauliflower will not produce worthwhile shoots after its head has been cut. Clear the remains of the crop as quickly as possible, either burning the surplus leaves, stems and roots or putting them on the compost heap if they are free from pests and disease. Chop up the stems and roots first.

Pest and diseases

All the pests and diseases common to brassicas attack cauliflowers, but two additional troubles affect cauliflowers and broccoli in particular.

Whiptail is a disorder in which the leaves become distorted to thin, whiplike thongs and the curd may be deformed, or not form at all. It is caused by a lack of the element molyb-denum in the soil, usually as a result of continuous or too intensive cropping. Molybdenum is a 'trace' element, that is, one that is essential for the healthy growth of plants but

which is needed only in minute amounts. The remedy for this deficiency is to give the plot a rest from brassicas, to allow the soil to replenish its molybdenum resources. The natural process may be aided by applying a solution of sodium molybdate at the rate of 30 g [1 oz] dissolved in 1 L [2 gal] of water to every 8. 4 sq m [10 sq yd].

Another deficiency disease is caused by lack of the trace element boron. This causes browning and sometimes stunting of the curd, a hollow stem and distorted leaves. It is best dealt with by applying a fertilizer containing boron, according to the manufacturer's instructions.

Celeriac

Celeriac is a swollen root which tastes very much like celery. It is delicious eaten as a cooked vegetable or in salads, either raw or blanched.

Both celeriac and celery are cultivated crops that have evolved from wild celery, which grows in marshy meadows and ditches near the sea in north western Europe. But while celery has been developed for the sake of its stem, celeriac is grown for its root and is sometimes called turnip-rooted celery. Celeriac is not nearly as well known a crop, having been developed mainly in Germany and introduced elsewhere only in recent years. It has an aroma and flavour similar to that of celery and it is used for flavouring soups, fish stocks and other dishes, as well as

---

Celeriac
Apium graveolens rapaceum (fam. *Umbelliferae*)
Hardy biennial, grown as an **annual.**
Size: about 30 cm [1'] tall; edible roots are about 7.5-10 cm [3-4"] round.
Climate: temperate.
Planting to harvesting time: 24 weeks.
Yield: 8 to 10 plants per 3 m [10'] row.

1. *For indoor sowing, first prepare a seed tray and firm down compost.*

2. *Sow the celeriac seeds thinly and evenly in the seed tray.*

3. *Cover the newly-planted seeds with finely-sifted compost.*

4. *Water the surface of the compost lightly using a rose on the can.*

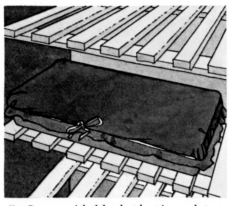

5. *Cover with black plastic and put in airing cupboard to germinate.*

6. *After germination, replace with inflated clear plastic bag.*

7. *Plant (but not bury) 30 cm [12"] in shallow drills 40 cm [16"] apart.*

8. *After plant has grown remove side shoots from swollen root.*

Though the shoots of celeriac can be eaten like celery, the plant is usually grown for its tasty root.

9. *Scrape the soil away with a hoe so that at least half the root is exposed.*

10. *Earth up the root in mid autumn to protect against the frost, until it is lifted.*

for serving as a cooked vegetable or grated raw as a salad.

Suitable site and soil
Choose a fairly sunny, sheltered plot. Celeriac likes a reasonably rich soil, though not excessively so. The soil should be well-drained and, ideally, celeriac should be planted on a site which had a generous application of farmyard manure or garden compost in the previous autumn, well dug in. However, do not be discouraged if the soil does not match up to the ideal; celeriac will grow in most soils, provided they are not dry or very wet.

Sowing and planting out
Celeriac seed requires a soil temperature of 15°C [60°F] for germination. In most temperate climates this is reached in mid spring, but celeriac requires a long growing season and it is advisable to sow the seed in boxes under frames or cloches or in a heated greenhouse in early spring.

Sow about 0.5 cm [¼"] deep and cover lightly with soil. When the seedlings are big enough to handle, which will be shortly after they have reached the four-leaf stage, prick out either into boxes or the open ground under cloches with about 5 cm [2"] between seedlings. Whether in boxes or in the open ground under cloches, the seedlings should be gradually hardened off during spring by removing the glass or plastic covering — for a few hours around mid day in sunny weather at first, and then for longer periods until it is dispensed with entirely.

Transplant seedlings into the permanent bed in late spring, putting them in rows that are 30-38 cm [12-15"] apart, with the plants about 30 cm [1'] apart in the rows. At this stage, the plants will already have slightly swollen root-bulbs. Plant with these at about surface level — above rather than below — and handle carefully to avoid any unnecessary disturbance to the roots.

Care and development
Water the young plants frequently after transplanting, and also during drought, but do not saturate. When nearly mature, the need for water lessens, and they can withstand a moderate drought with an occasional watering, but the final size will be decreased.

For most of the summer the crop requires little attention, except to be kept free from weeds — use the hoe frequently. Towards the end of summer side shoots will start to sprout from the root. These should be removed. Scrape away soil around the root so that at least half of it is exposed, but in mid autumn earth up the root to protect it from frost until lifting.

The leaves can be used as celery, but if so they should be blanched, as for celery. It is more usual, however, to take just one crop — the roots.

Harvesting and storing
Lift the roots as required from mid autumn onwards. They will tolerate moderate frost if left in the ground during winter. Do not lift for storing until hard frosts make it absolutely necessary, because the roots retain their flavour better if left in the ground. However, in very cold districts they should all be lifted at the end of autumn and stored in boxes of sand or soil in a dry shed for use at any time during winter and early spring. Remove all the leaves except the small ones in the centre before storing. There is little clearing up to be done after harvesting. The rather sparse foliage may be consigned to the compost heap or dug into the soil.

Pests and diseases
The same pests and diseases attack celery and celeriac, including the fungus disease celery leaf-spot, the larva of the celery fly and the carrot fly larva.

Celery

Winter celery needs time in preparing trenches and blanching, but the summer varieties are self-blanching. Both types are delicious eaten raw or cooked.

Celery has been developed from the wild celery, a plant fairly common in meadows and roadside ditches in maritime areas in many parts of the world. It has been bred mostly in Italy (first by the Romans) for its tall, thick stalks or 'sticks' which, when blanched, are used both as a salad and a vegetable, also for flavouring soups and

---

Celery
Apium graveolens (fam. *Umbelliferae*)
Biennial, grown as an **annual.**
Size: 30-50 cm [12-20"] high, 7.5-10 cm [3-4"] in diameter.
Climate: temperate.
Sowing to harvesting time: 6-8 months; mature plants may be left in ground for several more months and lifted as required.
Yield: 12-15 plants, each 0.7-1 kg [1½-2 lb], per 3 m [10'] row.

'American green' is one of the unblanched varieties of summer celery. These are transplanted earlier than winter celery, set out in blocks on a flat bed.

savouries. It was not commonly grown in the rest of Europe until the 1800s.

Celery has been considered a specialist's crop, largely because of the labour and skill thought to be involved in trenching and blanching. In fact, these operations are not particularly difficult or time-consuming. For those who wish to avoid them, however, there are now self-blanching varieties of celery.

The trench or winter varieties may be white, pink or red while the summer varieties which may be white or green, require little or no blanching.

The winter varieties are quite hardy, but, as celery requires a long growing season, it is normal practice to start off the seeds under glass or cloches. The mature plants of winter varieties will tolerate moderate frost and, indeed, this seems to improve the flavour. In severe weather, however, any plants left in the ground should be protected by covering with straw, bracken or sacking. The summer varieties are less hardy than the winter ones, and they mature earlier.

Suitable site and soil

Celery does not grow well in shade, so choose a sunny, open situation. The soil should be very rich, having been treated with farmyard or other organic manure in the previous autumn rather than immediately before planting. Deep, easily worked soil, moderately free from stones, is ideal. Avoid soils prone to waterlogging and also those such as light, sandy ones which dry out too quickly.

Sowing

You can avoid sowing by buying plants ready for transplanting from your nursery in early summer. A dozen plants will suit most households.

Celery seed requires a temperature of 13-16°C [55-61°F] for germination. It is possible to wait until the outdoor temperatures rise to this level in spring, but you may prefer to gain a few weeks by sowing indoors in a greenhouse, or under frames or cloches.

Sow in seed compost in a propagator, or in a seed-tray in a heated greenhouse in early spring. The seed is very small and it is easier to sow if you mix it first with a little moist sand or vermiculite. Sow it 2 cm [¾″] deep and cover lightly with sifted compost. Water carefully and allow to germinate in darkness. Seed is treated with chemicals so do not use left-over seed as a herb in the kitchen.

Celery may take a long time to germinate — from 10 days to well over three weeks, depending on the temperature. The seedlings have the distinct celery scent and leaves with serrated edges. When they are large enough to handle, prick them out into trays or boxes of potting compost, setting them out at 5 cm [2″] apart.

The succulent leaf-stalks of winter celery have a strong flavour, whether eaten raw in salads, or as a cooked vegetable. Green leaf tops make successful soups.

1. *Dig trench 30 cm [12"] deep by 38 cm [15"] wide and lay down manure. Return soil short of ground level.*

2. *Plant in a single row 30 cm [1'] apart then water. Remove side shoots and wrap newspaper around stems.*

3. *Earth up when about 30 cm [12"] high. Earthing up should continue until the trench becomes a ridge.*

Catch-cropping summer celery: plant in blocks with lettuce (raised indoors from seed sown before celery).

4. *To harvest, first scrape back the soil.*

5. *Thrust fork well down to avoid damaging stems.*

For white summer celery, erect framework of stakes and sacking or plastic. Move this in as plants are taken.

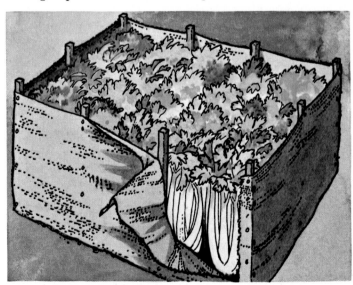

Instead of sowing indoors, you may sow outdoors in fine soil under cloches or in a frame and thin the seedlings to 5 cm [2″] apart. In both cases, harden them off gradually by placing the seed-trays outdoors on sunny days, or by removing the cloches or opening the frames for a few hours each day.

Planting out winter celery
Plant out in late spring or early summer. Winter celery should be planted in previously prepared trenches. These should be about 38 cm [15″] wide by 30 cm [1′] deep and 90 cm [3′] apart. They can be dug at any time during the previous winter or early spring. Before planting, clean them out, removing the soil that has been disintegrated by frost and has fallen into the bottom of the trench. Fork over the bottom of the trench and put in a 10-15 cm [4-6″] deep layer of rotted farmyard manure or garden compost. Cover this with 7.5-10 cm [3-4″] of soil. Transplant the celery plants into the soil at the bottom of the trench in a single row, at a spacing of 30 cm [1′]. Plant them firmly and water well.

Care and development
Water the plants frequently — never allow the soil to become dry. Applications of liquid manure will be beneficial, but avoid splashing the leaves. You may also give light applications of a dry balanced fertilizer, but work these well into the soil with a rake or hoe, and water in. If the plants throw out any side shoots, remove them.

Blanching
When the plants are about 30-38 cm [12-15″] high, begin earthing them up. Choose a fine day, when the ground is fairly dry. First, tie the stems together just below the leaves, loosely with raffia, string or a rubber band. Then rake the loose soil from the edges of the trenches down into the trench around the bases of the plants, until it is about halfway up the stems.

Carry out further earthing-up operations at intervals of 2-3 weeks. Press in the soil quite firmly around the plants, but not too hard. Continue with the earthing-up process until only the leaves are showing above the soil. Your celery trench will then have become a ridge.

When earthing up celery, you should be very careful to prevent soil from penetrating into the spaces between the stems. Once this has happened, it is almost impossible to get the sticks completely clean in the kitchen. Tying the stems together and forking in the soil with care should prove satisfactory. A better method is to tie newspaper or cardboard around the plants before earthing them up, or shortly after transplanting, encourage the plants to grow through earthenware drainpipes. The blanching process will continue right through late summer and well into autumn.

Summer celery
With self-blanching varieties, a trench is unnecessary. These varieties are usually sown a week or two later than the others, as they are more inclined to bolt (run to flower); they will therefore be ready a little later for trans-planting. Prepare the soil as for winter celery, digging in plenty of garden compost or well-rotted farmyard manure, but do not dig trenches; summer celery is grown on a flat bed. Set out the young plants in a 'block' arrangement not in rows, spaced 23 cm [9″] apart each way. The white varieties of summer celery, although often called 'self-blanching', do in fact need to be shaded from the light for complete blanching. By growing them in blocks, the outer plants cast shade on the inner ones and so blanch them. Erect a framework around the plants, and cover it with sacking, hardboard or black plastic sheeting to keep the outer plants blanched. The green varieties of summer celery do not need blanching at all.

Harvesting, storing and aftercare
Lift winter celery as required, during autumn and winter. Light frost improves the flavour. Start at the end of a row and walk along it, lifting each stem carefully to avoid damaging the next in line. The bigger the plant, the crisper it is likely to be. The summer varieties are normally ready earlier than the other, from the beginning of late summer onwards. As you harvest the white types, move the framework up to the next plants in the block to keep them blanched. You can leave winter celery in the ground until you need it. Cover the plants with straw or bracken in very cold or rainy weather. Summer celery is not frost resistant and should be used as soon as it is ready.

After harvesting, put the leaves, outer stems and roots on the compost heap, and level the ridges. The soil is already well enriched for succeeding crops, but avoid replanting with carrots which are a member of the same family, to prevent a build up of pests and diseases.

Pests and diseases
The chief pest of celery is the celery fly (*Philophylla heraclei*). The eggs hatch into tiny, leaf-mining maggots which tunnel into the leaf tissues of the plant during late spring, producing transparent blotches which turn pale brown and eventually shrivel the leaf. A second attack may occur in summer. Handpick badly affected leaves, and spray the remainder in spring and summer with malathion. Carrot fly larvae occasionally attack the roots of the plants (*see* CARROT) and, if celery is not thoroughly earthed up slugs can find their way into the heart and cause considerable damage.

The most troublesome fungus disease is celery leaf spot (*Septoria apii-graveolens*), prevalent in wet summers. Small brown spots appear on the leaves and may spread rapidly. Seed advertised as "thiram-treated" should produce plants resistant to leaf-spot. If an attack develops, remove infected leaves promptly and spray the remainder with Bordeaux mixture or other fungicidal compound containing copper. Give the plants an extra application of a potash-high fertilizer.

Soft rot makes the centres of the plants soft, brown and slimy. Once the plants are affected they cannot be cured. The disease enters through wounds caused by pests, careless cultivation or severe frost. Virus diseases may also cause trouble; if these occur, the only course is to destroy the affected plants.

Cherry

These yellow, red or nearly black stone fruit can have a sweet or tart flavour and are eaten raw or cooked according to variety.

Cherries belong to the same genus, *Prunus*, as the peach, plum and apricot. They bloom early and need a sheltered site. They also require a period of winter cold to crop well. They do not thrive where summer temperatures are high, though sour cherries tolerate heat better than sweet cherries.

Fruiting cherries are divided into two species, the sour *Prunus cerasus* which need cooking, and the sweet *Prunus avium*, which can be eaten raw. The Duke cherries are a cross between the two, useful for both dessert and cooking, but their fruit is inferior to the best of the other two groups.

Sweet cherries

Sweet cherries are not suitable for a small garden as they form big trees, up to 14 m [46'] high and even wider. There is no really dwarfing rootstock. Tree sizes and shapes vary greatly within the group, but they are usually grown as standards or half-standards. Birds are a great problem as the tree size makes them difficult to net. They

---

Sweet Cherry
Prunus avium (fam. *Rosaceae*)
Hardy deciduous tree, with a useful life of 50 years.
Size: 10-14 m [33-46'] high, 15 m [49'] across.
Climate: cool to warm temperate.
Planting to harvesting time: up to 6 years.
Yield: 100 kg [220 lb] per tree.

Sour cherry
Prunus cerasus (fam. *Rosaceae*)
Hardy deciduous tree with a useful life of 50 years.
Size: 4 m [13'] high, 6 m [20'] in diameter.
Climate: cool to warm temperate.
Planting to harvesting time: 2 to 3 years.
Yield: 15-20 kg [33-44 lb] per tree.

---

flower before apples, from mid to late spring, and are therefore susceptible to frost. To do well they need a sheltered site open to the sun. They are also particular about soil.

Sweet cherries need a pollinator, so you must plant two different varieties flowering at the same time, and in compatible pollination groups, to ensure that the fruit sets satisfactorily.

The fruit is generally heart-shaped and varies in colour from nearly yellow to black. They are the earliest top fruit to mature, cropping from midsummer. In nursery catalogues sweet cherries are often divided into two groups by the colour of their juice. 'Black' varieties have dark red juice and 'white' varieties have colourless juice. They can be further subdivided into Heart cherries with soft tender flesh, and Bigarreau with firm breaking flesh.

Sour or 'pie' cherries

Sour cherries are easier to cultivate than sweet cherries. Both are demanding as to soil, but sour cherries will tolerate a heavier soil. They will also tolerate a greater degree of cold — they flower after sweet cherries — and so are more likely to miss the frost.

Unlike sweet cherries the sour ones are self-fertile, so a single tree will set fruit. They are usually grown in bush form and make smaller trees than sweet cherries. A morello, one of the best varieties, may form dense bushy growth, often wider than it is high.

Most of the varieties are red, but the Morello turns almost black when left to ripen on the tree. Sour cherries come into bearing more quickly than sweet, and the crop of the mature tree is of a more manageable size.

Morellos can be successfully fan-trained and for that require a wall of 2.5 m [8'] high and up to 6 m [20'] wide. They will also tolerate a sunless wall, but not deep shade. A wall has the advantage that it is easier to net against attack from any birds.

CULTIVATION

The crucial consideration for cherries is drainage. Plums and apples will tolerate a degree of poor drainage but the cherry will yield poorly. Heavy soils are therefore best avoided as are dry sandy soils which will, in a drought, give small fruit and the minimum of flesh. Look to see if there are ornamental cherries in your area and how well they are doing as these need similar conditions to sweet and sour cherries.

A warm site is ideal, sheltered from prevailing winds which could rock the tree on its roots, as it will not be staked. Frost at flowering time can be a problem. In cool temperate areas, therefore, avoid valley bottoms and frost pockets. A slight slope with room for cold air to drain away at the bottom is ideal.

The soil should be well drained but capable of retaining water; a medium loam is therefore best. A soil test should show either a slight acidity or neutrality, a pH reading of 6.0-7.0.

Buying the tree

A stone sown in the garden will not produce as good a tree

Montmorency is the best known of the American cherries. It is very popular for use in pies and tarts.

Sour cherries are successful wall-trained, and are one of the few fruit that will tolerate a sunless wall.

The Merton Bigarreau sweet cherry, one of the mid season varieties developed this century, is a heavy cropper with a fine flavour. Sweet cherries are very fastidious as to soil. They make large trees, so you need plenty of room to grow them successfully.

as recommended varieties, and may take as long as 15 years to fruit.

Sour cherries are self-fertile and can be planted singly. Morellos will pollinate sweet cherries if they are flowering concurrently. However, it is essential for sweet cherries to have a pollinator. They are divided into 13 pollination groups. One group contains what is known as universal donors, which will pollinate any other variety, but varieties in the remaining 12 groups will only pollinate those of another group. The two you choose must also flower together, so check carefully. The charts at the end of the book will help you.

Buy certified virus-free trees if they are available. These offer some protection against disease, and they grow and crop better.

Cherry trees are budded or grafted on to rootstocks. The best is the East Malling Mazzard F 12/1, while a tree on *Prunus avium* rootstock is always preferable. A semi-dwarfing rootstock Colt is being introduced. Nurseries offer sour cherries as bushes, half-standards, standards, fan-trained trees or maidens (one-year-old trees and therefore untrained). Sweet cherries are usually grown as standards.

Cherry trees are particularly susceptible to bacterial canker at the base of the branches. A staddle is a form of rootstock designed to overcome this. A few inches of the branches of the rootstock, which is more resistant are retained about 1.8 m [6′] from the ground, and the variety is grafted onto each branch.

Planting out

Autumn planting is best, but this can be done any time in winter when the soil is workable. The tree may be heeled in (*see* APPLE) to wait for suitable conditions. If the roots are dry when the tree arrives, soak them in water. Before planting, trim any damaged roots and remove entirely any dominant downward-pointing root.

If you are planting more than one sour cherry, allow 6 m [20′] between them. Plant standard sweet cherries 7-10 m [23-33′] apart, depending on the vigour of the variety and plant trees on semi-dwarfing rootstock 5-7 m [16-23′] apart. Cherries are very susceptible to some weedkillers so remove all persistent weeds by careful digging. If they are to be planted in grassland, 3 sq m [10 sq ft] should be cleared around the tree position.

Dig a hole big enough to take the root system when fully spread out. Fork over the bottom and add a 10 L [2-gal] bucket of rotted manure, or the same quantity of moist peat with the addition of 60 g per sq m [2 oz per sq yd] of sterilized bonemeal. Plant the tree at the same depth as in the nursery, with the union with the rootstock (a slight swelling) 7.5 cm [3″] above the soil level. Hold the tree upright while you replace the soil, shaking it gently to settle soil round the roots. Firm each layer well before putting in the next.

Following planting and a good watering, dress the soil round the tree with two buckets of rotted manure or a mulch of straw. If the land is very dry or there is a prolonged rainless period after planting, regular watering of the young tree may be necessary, but otherwise the mulch should help to retain sufficient moisture.

A mid season white variety of sweet cherry, Napoleon is a good regular bearer which does well as a trained tree.

Morello is the best of the sour cherry types, and is self fertile, so you need plant only one.

Care of the tree

It is not wise to stake cherry trees, as any rubbing that occurs between the tie and the tree can lead to bacterial canker infection through the wound. If branches have to be tied (for a fan tree) this should be done with a length of plastic tubing, which does not wound the branches. Cherry roots are vigorous and penetrate deep down into the soil. After the first watering when the tree is planted, watering is only necessary under drought conditions in the first few years. Remember that trees trained against walls are always more susceptible to drought.

Mulch around each tree in spring, before the soil dries out, with manure at the rate of a 10 L [2-gal] bucket per sq m [yd]. In addition trees on most sites will benefit from a spring application of 30 g per sq m [1 oz per sq yd] of nitro-chalk and 15 g per sq m [½ oz per sq yd] of sulphate of potash. Every third year supplement this with 20 g per sq m [⅔ oz per sq yd] of superphosphate.

Keep a minimum of 3 sq m [10 sq ft] clear around the tree by hoeing. If the cherry rootstock produces suckers, these should be cut off where they are attached to the roots with a sharp knife. Once the tree reaches maturity, at ten years or more, grass may be grown up to the base of the tree, though this should be mown regularly.

TRAINING AND PRUNING

All cherries can be grown as standards. Sour cherries are usually grown as bushes and can also be successfully fan-trained, but sweet cherries are really too vigorous for this form. A new form for both types is the central leader pyramid, and the cherry may be trained in the same way as a pear (*see* PEAR).

When young, standard sweet cherries are pruned like apples to shape the head, but subsequently they need almost no pruning, as fruiting spurs are freely formed on older wood. After the shaping of sour cherries, pruning continues in order to encourage the production of new wood, which bears fruit the following year.

It is essential to remember never to winter prune cherries. Because of the risk of infection the very minimum of pruning is recommended. They should only be pruned in late spring, when the leaf buds are bursting open, or summer. All the cuts should be made very smooth, without snags, and the larger ones painted with bitumen wound paint.

Training a sour cherry as a fan

You will need a wall 2.5 m [8'] high and 6 m [20'] across. Wire the wall horizontally with 3 mm [⅛"] gauge wire at a spacing of 30 cm [1'] each. The best form is that used for peaches, with the central leader pruned out entirely and the fan built up from two opposite diagonal branches (*see* PEACH).

Training bushes

For a sour cherry bush, buy a maiden (one-year-old) and

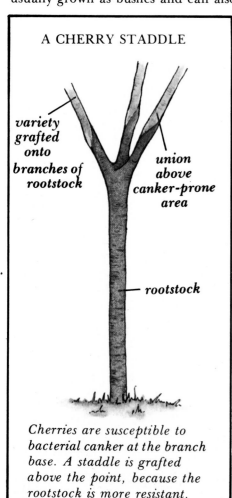

A CHERRY STADDLE

variety grafted onto branches of rootstock

union above canker-prone area

rootstock

Cherries are susceptible to bacterial canker at the branch base. A staddle is grafted above the point, because the rootstock is more resistant.

Birds are one of the most common pests to attack cherries. A great advantage of growing the smaller sour cherry is that a net can be thrown over the whole tree and be secured underneath for protection.

prune it off in the spring about 1 m [3'] from ground level, just above a good bud. This will induce lateral branches to grow out in subsequent years. No further pruning will be required for four to five years, with the exception of cutting out branches which rub each other, or any canker.

Pruning sour cherries to encourage fruit

In addition to any shaping, sour cherries need a light prune after harvesting. They fruit on the previous year's growth, so the aim is to encourage new side-growth and gradually remove old shoots, when these are not needed for the shape of the tree. Prune back to a new sideshoot.

HARVESTING AND PROTECTION

Birds are a major pest of cherries; they attack the buds in winter and consume and spoil fruit in summer. Net the tree with a 2.5 cm [1″] mesh plastic net. Stand on a pair of steps and throw it over while a helper adjusts and ties it in below. Sweet cherries do get too big to net effectively. Individual sprays can be protected with plastic bags.

Sour cherry maidens will carry a small crop in their fourth year, while standards may carry small crops in their sixth year (probably its second year in your garden), but will not reach full cropping until at least ten years old. Fruit is ripened on the tree to develop flavour, so protect against birds.

For sweet cherries several picks at two or three day intervals are required. Cut through the stalks with blunt-nosed scissors and handle the cherries by the stalk. Take care not to damage the tree spur. A pair of steps will help you pick the higher branches. Sweet cherries can split if there is rain just before harvesting, so if rain threatens it may be better to harvest partially unripe.

Pests and diseases

Bacterial canker (*Pseudomonas mors-prunorum*) is the most serious disease of cherries in Northern Europe, and the most frequent cause of death among the stone fruits. The bacteria gain entry through wounds and the scars left by leaves falling in autumn, and the disease develops during the winter to kill the bark and young growth, producing raised, cracked and flaking bark from which gum is often produced. If these cankers surround a stem or branch the portion above the canker will die the following summer; it may produce leaves but only of a pale green or yellow colour. The disease first appears on the foliage; sometimes buds are killed in spring, or 'shot-holes' appear on the leaves. Therefore trees should never be pruned in winter, and in late summer should be sprayed with Bordeaux mixture, repeated twice at three-weekly intervals.

The cherry fruit fly is a major pest in most cherry-growing countries outside Northern Europe. When it is sighted in spring, spray with derris or malathion 2-4 times at 10-day intervals. For 'silver leaf' fungus *see* PLUM.

Bacterial canker, the main disease attacking the cherry.

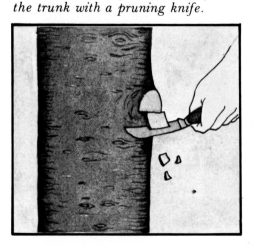

1. *Saw below cankerous growths.*

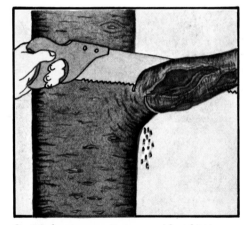

2. *Make two cuts to avoid splitting.*

3. *Trim the stump to the line of the trunk with a pruning knife.*

4. *Cover scar with bitumen tree-wound paint.*

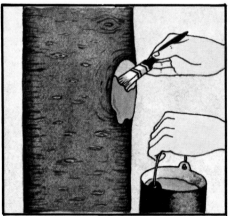

Chervil

**A pretty plant which is one of the
easiest herbs to grow, chervil provides
sweet, fragrant leaves for flavouring
throughout the year.**

Chervil (*Anthriscus cerefolium*) is a hardy annual herb in
the *Umbelliferae* family which grows to 30-45 cm [1-1½′]
high and up to 30 cm [1′] in diameter. Its delicately
feathery, bright green leaves make it an attractive plant to
grow, and it does equally well in a garden or container —
indoors or out.

Chervil has often been compared with parsley in both
appearance and taste, but many gourmets find it superior
in both respects as the flavour is slightly more peppery
than parsley, with a hint of anise. It is most often used as a
garnish, but the fresh leaves can be made into soup and,
either fresh or dried, they are a subtle flavouring for
potato dishes, salads, sauces and bouquets garnis.

The curly-leaved chervil is the most popular variety. There
is also a smooth-leaved chervil, but this is not nearly as
strongly flavoured. When ordering your seeds, therefore,
try to obtain the curly type.

Cultivation

Chervil grows best in semi-shady conditions. In full sun the
plant flowers too quickly, which destroys the flavour of the
leaves. It grows in any well-drained soil.

The herb may be sown successively at monthly intervals
from early spring to early summer and again in early
autumn. Sow the seed on top of the soil and rake the surface lightly. Germination takes place within 7 to 10 days.

If you plant more than one row, allow 30 cm [1′] between
each. Thin the seedlings first to 15 cm [6″] and then to 30
cm [1′] apart.

Keep chervil well watered at all times. It needs no special
feeding and it should produce a completely green bed
which requires virtually no weeding.

Harvesting and propagating

The production of flowers in summer impairs the flavour
of the leaves. For this reason the leaves should be clipped
off when the plant reaches its full height, before the

flowers form. If you make successional sowings in the
spring, you will have a steady supply of young chervil
leaves through the summer months. Then, if seeds are
sown again in autumn, the leaves should stay green and be
available for picking throughout winter and spring.

Propagation should always be from fresh seed as it does
not remain viable for more than a short period. If you wish
to propagate your own crop let two or three of the curliest-
leaved plants produce their white umbels of flowers and go
to seed. Gather the seeds when ripe.

Storing the crop

Fresh leaves should be used immediately after picking
because they wither very rapidly. Otherwise they may be
dried. Unlike most herbs, which are simply hung upside
down to dry, chervil dries most successfully with a short,
sharp blast of heat. Put the leaves in a basket or tray and
place this over a low heater at night. By morning, the
leaves should be crisp. Rub them together to a fairly fine
texture and put them into an opaque, airtight container.

Chicory

**A welcome salad in winter and early
spring, chicory is easy to grow. The first season's
leaves are eaten like spinach, while the
inner leaves produced by forcing during
the second season are blanched and
eaten as 'chicons'.**

Chicory is a native of north-western Europe, growing in
meadows and on roadside verges. It has dark green leaves
rather like those of the dandelion; which belongs to the
same plant family. The flowers, also dandelion-like, are
pale blue, 2.5 cm [1″] or more in diameter, and are borne
on tall, branched fibrous stems. Gardeners do not normally see the flower unless they want to obtain the seed.
Improved varieties of wild chicory are much used in
pasture for cows and sheep; and one European variety is

The salad type of chicory is grown for both its heart and leaves, ideal for an early summer vegetable.

cultivated for its roots which, when ground, are added to some blends of coffee.

Chicory is grown primarily for its blanched inner leaves or 'chicons' which provide welcome winter and early spring salad. They can withstand quite severe frosts down to −7°C [20°F] or even lower when fully mature. The leaves will die back in winter, but the roots will remain alive through periods of hard frost.

Sugar-loaf chicory is quite distinct. In autumn it produces a very close head of inwardly curled leaves, rather like Chinese cabbage in appearance, which will withstand moderate frost. Unlike the other varieties, it is not lifted in autumn and forced indoors but remains where it is, providing a very acceptable winter salad, when other salad greens are scarce.

Suitable site and soil

An open site with not too much shade is ideal. The soil should be rich and 60 cm [2'] deep, and not waterlogged. Shallow or stony soils cause the roots to fork. In autumn dig deeply and apply rotted farmyard manure or garden compost so that it is completely absorbed during winter. A week or two before sowing, work in carbonate of lime (chalk) if a soil test shows the soil is at all acid.

Sowing and planting

Sow in early summer in drills 1.5 cm [$\frac{1}{2}$"] deep and 30-38 cm [12-15"] apart, in soil worked to a fine tilth. When the plants are large enough, thin to 23-25 cm [9-10"] between each one.

Do not transplant; the plants should remain where sown for the entire summer. The roots reach their maximum growth in autumn, when the leaves start to die down.

Cultivation

Chicory does best when kept well watered and growing strongly. If the soil has been well manured beforehand, no additional feeding should be necessary. Vigorous growth will smother many of the smaller weeds, but use the hoe to remove larger weeds.

Harvesting the crop

A bonus crop may be taken from some varieties by cooking

Chicory flowers are very striking but will only be seen if the plant is allowed to go to seed.

Chicory
Cichorium intybus (fam. *Compositae*)
Perennial, grown as a **biennial.**
Size: leaves grow to a height of 25-30 cm [10-12"] in the first year (when harvested); chicons (blanched shoots) 12.5-23 cm [5-9"] long.
Climate: cool temperate.
Sowing to harvesting time: 26-29 weeks from sowing to lifting the roots, which are then stored and forced at intervals during winter and spring.
Yield: 12-15 plants, each 125 g [4 oz], per 3 m [10'] row.

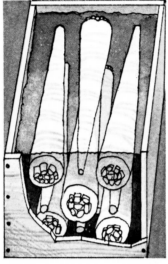

1. *To store chicory roots cut 2.5 cm [1″] above surface. Pull and trim.*

2. *Store roots in moist sand in a box and keep in a cool, dry place.*

3. *To force, cover roots in 23 cm [9″] of moist peat in black plastic bag.*

4. *Inflate bag to keep top and sides off crowns; secure with string or tag.*

5. *Stand in a warm place and open plastic to check progress after 2-3 weeks.*

6. *Block top of hole in and pot and set roots 6.5 cm [2½″] apart.*

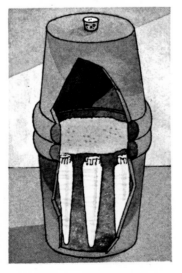

the leaves as spinach. During the summer either take a few leaves from a number of plants, in order not to weaken any one of them, or reserve certain plants for this purpose.

Sugar-loaf chicory will form tightly packed hearts in autumn and may be cut for salad as required. When cutting, remove the soil down to the point where the heart joins the root; this will probably be 2.5 cm [1″] or so below the soil surface. Cut off the heart with a sharp knife, or pull up the plant and trim afterwards. The root of sugar-loaf chicory is not lifted and stored, as with other varieties. Chicory roots may be lifted in autumn and stored in boxes, or they may be left in the soil until shortly before being required for forcing. The former is the more satisfactory method, for roots left in the ground may start to sprout prematurely in mild weather.

Storing

The ideal method of storing is in boxes of moist sand. The roots are lifted and trimmed back to about 20 cm [8″] in length. The leaves are cut off to within 2.5 cm [1″] at the crown, which should have a diameter of about 7.5 cm [3″] at the top. The roots are then placed in closely packed horizontal layers, with moist sand between each layer. The boxes are stored in a cool, dry place free from frost. Any roots left in the ground will produce flower stems in the second year and should be saved only for producing seed. Otherwise consign the plants to the compost heap.

Forcing

About three weeks before the first chicory shoots, or 'chicons', are required for the table, take out the required number of roots and set them upright 5-7.5 cm [2-3″] apart in barrels, tubs, pots or some other container. Fill the container with damp sand or light soil. Quite good results can also be obtained by using moist horticultural peat, or moist potting compost. The crowns of the roots should be 2.5 cm [1″] or so below the surface of the soil.

Put the containers in a reasonably warm outhouse and cover them with boxes, black plastic, sacking or anything else that will keep them completely dark. The roots need a temperature of about 10°C [50°F] to start producing shoots. Give the sand an occasional sprinkling of slightly warmed water to keep it just moist, but on no account overwater.

The chicons will emerge, white and spearlike, and will be ready to cut when about 10 cm [4″] above the surface of the soil. The crowns are below the surface, so pull up the root and cut off the chicon afterwards. The aim is to get a complete chicon, not one that disintegrates into separate leaves as soon as it is touched, and this can be achieved by cutting immediately above the crown. Use the chicons as soon as possible.

A second smaller and poorer crop of chicons may sometimes be taken by replacing the roots in the same container after cutting.

Pests and diseases

Chicory is remarkably free from the pests and diseases which attack other vegetables. The only trouble that is most likely to occur is slugs.

Chinese Cabbage

**This crisp, crunchy cabbage
is more like a cos lettuce
than other cabbages. It can be
eaten either cooked or raw.**

Chinese cabbage, which is also known as Pak-choi, looks far more like spinach beet than a cabbage. A distinctive feature is the thick, white central midrib of the leaves, and a network of prominent white veins, radiating from it, which gives the leaves a beautiful marbled look. Most varieties available have leaves that form a compact conical-shaped heart weighing 1.5 kg [3 lb] or more. In some varieties the leaves tend to form an open rosette rather than a heart. The leaf colour ranges from a very delicate light green to dark green.

The leaves have a crunchy texture and a very delicate flavour, quite unlike that of ordinary cabbage. Very similar is Pe-tsai, or mustard greens, (*Brassica pekinensis*) which resembles a large cos lettuce. It may be grown and used in the same way as Chinese cabbage.

Chinese cabbage is most useful in autumn and early winter when other fresh vegetables, particularly any suitable for salads, are getting scarce. It is very fast growing and is often ready for eating within nine to ten weeks of sowing. One of its drawbacks is that it is by nature a short-day plant, and tends to bolt, or run to seed, rather than forming a heart, if it is sown early in the year when the days are getting longer. For this reason, although it can be sown in a cool temperate climate any time from mid

A freshly-cut 'Pak-Choi'. The plant is ideal for autumn salads when conventional green salads are scarce.

In order to blanch the heart of a Chinese cabbage, tie the leaves with raffia at both the top and bottom.

Chinese cabbage
Brassica chinensis (fam. *Cruciferae*)
Half-hardy annual.
Size: 38-45 cm [15-18″] high and 30-38 cm [12-15″] across.
Climate: temperate.
Sowing to harvesting time: 12-16 weeks.
Yield: 10 plants per 3 m [10′] row.

spring, it is advisable to postpone the first sowing until early summer. For a succession, two subsequent sowings can be made in mid and late summer.

Suitable site and soil

Chinese cabbage does best on a rich soil that retains moisture and is not too acid. It will tolerate light shade. It may be treated as a second crop, sown after an early summer crop, such as early potatoes, broad beans, peas or lettuce, has been cleared. No special soil preparation is necessary — just clear any weeds, and rake down the soil to a fine tilth. Avoid cramping Chinese cabbage. Plant it where the air can circulate freely to help prevent the leaves rotting, as they are prone to do in a prolonged damp autumn.

Sowing

Sow the seed thinly in rows at least 38-60 cm [15-24"] apart. Sowing individual seeds about 2.5 cm [1"] apart is a little more time consuming, but does make thinning later far easier.

If you are sowing in hot dry conditions, make sure the soil is thoroughly moist before sowing. Either water the ground very well beforehand, or draw out the drill, water the drill itself very carefully — a small-spouted can is best for this — until it is almost muddy. Sow the seeds in the drill, and cover them with dry soil from either side of the drill. This dry soil acts as a mulch, prevents the moisture beneath from evaporating, and ensures that the seeds get off to a good start.

Care and development

Chinese cabbage is a plant that needs moisture if it is to grow satisfactorily, so if the weather is very dry, watering may be necessary. An occasional very heavy watering is far more beneficial than intermittent light watering and, after watering, it is best to mulch the soil with a 5-7.5 cm [2-3"] layer of organic matter such as lawn mowings, spent mushroom compost or garden compost. This preserves the moisture in the soil and enables the Chinese cabbage to make steady growth even in a prolonged dry spell.

Start thinning as soon as the seedlings are large enough to handle, thinning in stages until they are 30-38 cm [12-15"] apart, depending on the variety. The only other care necessary is to keep the ground weed-free. The main pests are slugs, flea-beetle and grey mould.

Harvesting

The main season for summer-sown Chinese cabbage is early to mid autumn. After this the quality of plants left in the open ground depends entirely on the weather. In dry, mild weather they can stand in good condition into later winter, but in harsh or wet weather they deteriorate rapidly and may not last beyond late autumn. For this reason it is well worth covering them with cloches in mid autumn to protect them and prolong their useful season.

When required for use Chinese cabbage is usually lifted whole, though it is possible to take off a few leaves at a time, leaving the plants in the ground. Chinese cabbage can either be eaten raw in salads like lettuce or cooked.

Chinese Gooseberry

This hairy red-brown fruit with greenish flesh is larger and juicier than a gooseberry. The taste is slightly tart but it is eaten raw. It contains three to five times the vitamin C of a lemon.

This vigorous vine originated in South East Asia where it is known as the 'Tree of health'; though it is very hardy when dormant, the spring growth and first flowers are frost tender. It will not crop properly in the cooler parts of the temperate zone, as it needs warmth to ripen the fruit. In the Mediterranean climate of the Southern Hemisphere it has been particularly successful. The plant is often grown solely for its decorative appearance. The new leaves are heart-shaped 15-23 cm [6-9"] long and 20 cm [8"] across; there is a cream and yellow variety *aureovariegata,* and a related ornamental species, *A. kolomikta,* has green, cream and pink leaves. The shoots are covered with dense reddish hairs and the flowers are borne in clusters on short stalks from the leaf axils. They appear in late spring and are 4 cm [1½"] across, fragrant, clematis-like and creamy white at first, turning to buff yellow in midsummer. The berries are the size of a hen's egg and contain numerous black seeds. Only female plants bear fruit, but a male plant must be planted with it for pollination.

Suitable site and soil

The plant can be grown successfully in cool temperate

Chinese Gooseberry
Actinidia Chinensis (fam. *Actinidiaceae*) also called kiwi fruit.
Hardy deciduous climbing vine with a cropping life of at least 20 years.
Size: vigorous varieties up to 9 m [30'] long.
Climate: cool to warm temperate.
Planting to harvesting time: 2 years.
Yield: mature vine 4-5 kg [8-10 lb].

Solid support is needed to hold weight of vines. Buy 2.5 m [8'] creosoted posts and insert them 45 cm [1½'] into the ground with a 1.8 m [6'] span across a garden path. Space 3.6 m [12'] apart. On top lay lengthways 4m [13½'] posts about 25 cm [4"] square. Slimmer poles 25 cm × 12 cm [4" × 2"] are fixed securely on top. Run wires lengthways down the structure at 60 cm [2'] intervals. Plant female plant on one side. Train by regular pruning and tying in so it occupies the whole of the top. The male is planted the other side and trained lengthways.

male plant kept pruned

3.6m [12']

1.8m [6']

2.2m [7']

female plant trained over top

wires to support laterals

path

PERGOLA CONSTRUCTION FOR CHINESE GOOSEBERRY

Prune established plants in early winter — above the last bud which bore fruit the previous summer.

Though Chinese gooseberries have 30 times the vitamin C of apple, they are often grown for ornamental use.

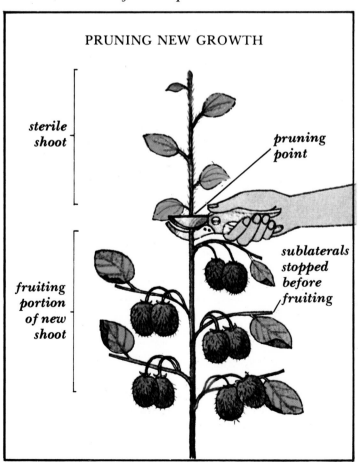

PRUNING NEW GROWTH

sterile shoot

pruning point

fruiting portion of new shoot

sublaterals stopped before fruiting

areas in a sheltered site; a wall facing the midday sun is best as the fruit is late developing and sun into the autumn months is vital for success. Low-lying areas and sites that are exposed to prevailing winds should be avoided. The Chinese gooseberry should be planted against a wall or fence, to which you have fixed supports. A trellis or wires spaced 30 cm [1'] apart are suitable and it will twine around them.

In a warm temperate climate the plant can be grown on a durable arch or pergola. It is slightly less tender than citrus fruit, though it should not be exposed to wind. The pergola should be sufficiently sturdy to support the weight of both stems and fruit. A system of wires, such as that described in BLACKBERRY is also suitable.

Chinese gooseberries thrive on well-drained soil; a deep sandy loam is best as they dislike wet. Add bulky organic manures, garden compost or peat to the site, 12 L [2½ gal] per plant, some weeks before planting.

Cultivation

Though vines can be propagated from seed sown 0.5 cm [¼"] deep under glass in mid spring, this is inadvisable. You will have to wait several years till the plants flower to determine their sex, while varieties do not come true to seed. You will do better to buy rooted cuttings of a plant of each sex from a nursery.

Set the plants 5.5-7.5 m [18-24'] apart depending on variety. Fork 0.5 kg [1 lb] of blood and bone fertilizer into the bottom of the planting hole.

Once growing they require very little attention. On lighter soils a regular supply of water is needed if fruit are to grow to full size, especially during periods of drought. An annual top dressing of rotted farmyard manure or other organic material in late winter is all that is needed to feed the plant.

It is only necessary to prune established plants. This is done in early winter and consists of pruning above the last bud which bore fruit during the preceding summer. In the following spring this too will develop into a branch, which will bear fruit the same year on the first 3-6 buds. The following winter it should be pruned in the same way. If the vines get into too great a tangle, and to keep the centre open, you may prune hard; new shoots will arise along the length of the plant. There is no need to let the male plant grow to the same size as the female. It may be kept hard pruned to 2 m [8'].

Growing under glass

In colder parts of the temperate area, plants are best grown under glass, in potting compost in large containers 30 cm [1'] across, which will help constrict growth. The climber must be given some support, such as a trellis or a string system such as that for cucumbers (*see* CUCUMBER). The female flowers will have to be hand pollinated (by the method described under APRICOT). Give the plants liquid feed at regular intervals during the summer months.

Harvesting and use

After the flowers have set the first fruits begin to appear in midsummer and grow rapidly. Worthwhile crops are produced in about four years, maximum production is reached at about seven, though less vigorous varieties are slower. The fruit should be gathered in late autumn when the leaves begin to fall, and allowed to ripen indoors in a warm room. The fruit can then be kept in the refrigerator for several weeks. To peel the fruit, soak in warm water for a few seconds.

Chives

The hollow green leaves of chives are eaten for their delicate flavour, as an addition to other dishes.

Chives, *Allium schoenoprasum*, are the most delicately flavoured of the onion family, the *Alliaceae*, and unlike the more familiar relatives are not grown for the bulb. Their "grass" is chopped up and added to salad, sauces and cooked dishes or mixed with cream cheese, although the small, bulbous root can also be eaten.

Growing wild across the Northern hemisphere, they will tolerate most soils and conditions, often growing all year round. The purple flower-heads make the plant an attractive edging to the herb or vegetable garden and are very decorative in early summer. Chives can vary in height between 15 cm [6"] and 45 cm [18"], but the small varieties have the best flavour. Giant varieties are more suited to being grown for ornament.

Cultivation

The best site for chives is a warm border with partial shade, but they will grow in most positions. Profuse leaf growth is encouraged by providing a site of medium loam, enriched with leafmould or well-rotted manure. Seed can be sown from early to late spring in the open ground or you can start in early spring with bulbs bought from a local seed merchant or nursery.

Chive flowers make a decorative border but do not allow them to go to seed. Cut off buds to increase foliage.

Chive bulbs should be planted in early spring. Press firmly into prepared ground with the tips at soil level.

Harvest the chives with a pair of scissors. To maintain supply through late summer leave some foliage to grow.

Chives started from seed are sown in shallow drills where the plants will continue growing. When the seedlings are up, thin them to 15 cm [6"] apart, or transplant the sturdier ones to a well enriched bed.

If bulbs are being planted, press them firmly into the soil, 22 cm [9"] apart, with their tips level with the soil surface. They quickly become established and grow into clumps, each having a large number of bulbs at the base. At this stage they should be lifted, preferably by mid spring, split up and replanted. Clumps can also be lifted after the flowering period. Divided, replanted and kept watered, these will provide a good supply of young leaves in late summer. The flowers should not be allowed to go to seed.

Harvesting and maintaining

Cut the foliage with scissors, always leaving some "grass" to continue growing. No winter protection is needed but if foliage is wanted during the off season a cloche, closed at each end, will maintain or encourage fresh growth in late autumn or late winter. A clump can be grown for winter use, in a sunny window box or indoors in 10 cm [4"] pots. Chives need little attention once established in firm, humus-rich soil and if replanted to avoid overcrowding they seldom fall prey to pests and diseases.

Citrus Fruits

**Oranges, lemons, tangerines and grapefruit
are the most common citrus fruits.
Each has a bitter rind enclosing
juicy flesh. Citrus fruits are eaten
raw, used to flavour a variety of
dishes or to make drinks.**

Citrus trees probably originated in south-east Asia, the East Indies and India, and were comparatively slow to reach the Mediterranean. When Columbus took the orange to America it was a relatively new fruit. The best quality fruit is grown in areas with a Mediterranean climate, such as California. Citrus fruit will tolerate very high temperatures — well over 38°C [100°F] — but respond better to regularly alternate cool and warm periods. During the dormant period most will tolerate a certain amount of frost. Below 10°C [50°F] they experience some check in growth, but a sudden frost is disastrous and a slight frost can damage ripening fruit.

Citrus flowers are produced chiefly on new growth, either singly or in clusters in spring. They are about 2 cm [¾"] across and are very fragrant. Lemons, however, flower throughout the year in warm habitats. Pollination is by insects, though fruit is also produced without fertilization. While the fruit is forming, it contains a high percentage of citric acid, which is replaced by sugars as maturity is reached, up to 90% of the eventual juice content. The pulp is contained inside a white pith of varying thickness.

TYPES OF CITRUS

The lemon, *C. limon*, is a small tree or spreading bush which droops more than the other citrus trees. It has irregularly placed branches and stout spines. It is widely grown in areas with a Mediterranean climate, but is intolerant of cold and very sensitive to changes in temperature. Under natural conditions it will blossom almost continuously, though it produces too many flowers for them all to set. The big advantage, however, is that ripe fruit are available throughout the year.

The fruit is greenish to yellow 7.5-12.5 cm [3-5"] long, with a knob at the bottom. The acidity of its fruit is a virtue in the kitchen, where it is often used for flavouring. Though frost has a damaging effect on fruit on the tree, lemons need less heat to ripen than the orange.

The lime, *C. aurantifolia*, another small tree with green fruit up to 4 cm [1½"] wide, is grown instead of the lemon in tropical areas. **The citron,** *C. medica*, is a slightly larger tree, bearing fruit shaped like a lemon or pear which can be up to 20 cm [8"] long. Of this group of acid fruits, the lemon is the best choice for the home gardener.

Citrus fruit
Sweet orange *Citrus sinensis*, sour or Seville orange *C. aurantium*, mandarin, tangerine or naartje *C. reticulata*, lemon *C. limon*, grapefruit *C. paradisi*, lime *C. aurantifolia* (fam. *Rutaceae*)
Nearly hardy evergreen trees with a useful life of 80-100 years and 30-40 years in a pot.
Size: lemons are the smallest at 2.5 m [8'], grapefruit the largest reaching 12 m [40'], oranges grow to 7.5 m [25'], tangerines are smaller 4.5-6 m [15-20'].
Climate: warm temperate and sub-tropical.
Planting to harvesting time: 2 years for lemon and grapefruit, 4 for orange.
Yield: a pot tree will give about 3 dozen fruit, lemons 45-65 kg [100-150 lbs], oranges 65-110 kg [150-250 lb], grapefruit 110-135 kg [250-300 lb].

The sweet orange, *C. sinensis*, makes a round-topped tree with regularly arranged branches and slender spines. It is more resistant to cold than the lemon and nearly hardy. It is the hardiest of all citrus trees except the tangerine. The navel orange has a second, very much smaller fruit inside the peel at the end of the main fruit. The blood orange, *melitensis*, is a variety of the sweet orange with red juice.

The Seville, bitter or sour orange, *C. aurantium*, is similar in appearance to the sweet orange. Though the pulp is sour, it is celebrated as the raw fruit for orange marmalade.

The tangerine (originally tangierine — from Tangiers), mandarin orange or naartje, *C. reticulata*, (syn. *nobilis deliciosa*), grows on rather smaller trees than the orange. The fruit is bright orange or reddish, usually with many seeds but sometimes seedless, and peels very easily. It is the hardiest of the citrus. The clementine is either a variety of tangerine or a cross between tangerine and sweet orange.

The calamondin or Panama orange, *C. mitis*, which fruits when only 60 cm [2'] high, is becoming popular as a house plant. Its tiny fruit are sour and best used for marmalade.

The grapefruit, *C. paradisi*, is an improved form of the shaddock or pummelo, *C. grandis* (syn. *C. maxima*). It grows into a large tree and the fruit on it comes in clusters like grapes, which gives it its name. The tree is very sensitive to cold, especially when young. The peel is yellow and the flesh creamy or pink; the fruit is 15 cm [6"] across. The tangelo and ugli are hybrids with tangerines.

The kumquat, *Fortunella japonica*, is not a true citrus but is a closely related shrub or small tree growing up to 2.5 m [8'] high, with dark glossy leaves and small orange-like fruit 2.5-4 cm [1-1½"] across. They have slightly acid pulp but a sweet spicy peel and as a result are eaten whole, either in syrup or as marmalade. Kumquats have the advantage that they will grow in colder areas than true citrus fruit.

Poncirus trifoliata is much used for citrus root stocks, as it increases their resistance to frost. It has been crossed with the sweet orange to produce **the citrange,** which is hardy in mild parts of the cool temperate area. This tree is also grown for its ornamental appearance, as the fragrant white flowers are up to 6.5 cm [2½"] wide. The fruit, which are orange to yellow, are golf ball size with aromatic and subacid pulp.

CULTIVATION

Citrus fruit are grown outside in warm temperate areas. It is necessary to avoid frost spots when fruit on the tree may be damaged, and some shelter from prevailing winds should be provided, particularly for young trees. In cool temperate areas citrus fruit can be successfully cultivated outdoors in summer, provided they winter indoors away from frost. This characteristic led to a large number of 'orangeries' being built in Northern Europe from the eighteenth century onwards. A minimum of 5° to 7°C [40° to 45°F] should be maintained and sudden change of temperature avoided. The trees should be planted in tubs or pots. Once filled the pots are fairly heavy, so the most convenient, and easiest, way to move them is to have wheels

(Above) Limes grow on small trees. In the tropics they replace lemons for drinks and most kitchen uses.

(Right) Valencia oranges, a popular variety of sweet orange, ripen late and have a long fruiting season.

(Right) Tangerine trees resist cold better than other citrus fruit.

(Below) A lemon tree has spines and a rather straggly, irregular shape.

1. *For seeding, plant single pips 1.5 cm [½"] deep in 7.5 cm [3"] pots.*

2. *Pips produce several seedlings; pick off the less vigorous ones.*

3. *With clay pots, soak in a bucket of water to prepare for potting.*

4. *First put in a layer of broken crocks to a depth of 4 cm [1½"].*

5. *In hot weather the plant should be syringed every evening.*

6. *Regular watering is essential to prevent the roots drying out.*

7. *Empty stale earth, leave root ball and repot with fresh compost.*

9. *As the tree grows, place it in tub with castors. Mulch should be added but the stem left clear.*

10. *The Versailles caisson, with sliding sides, enables the earth to be changed without repotting.*

8. *If tree is pot-bound, stretch out roots and clip back to two-thirds their length with secateurs.*

attached to the bottom of the final container.

Citrus are fairly tolerant as to soil, but it must be deep with good drainage. A light to medium loam that is slightly alkaline is best. Heavy soils will be improved with the addition of manure or garden compost and some coarse sand. In warm areas grass should not be grown under the tree.

Raising citrus fruit from seed

Growing citrus from seed is not such a gamble as it is with other fruit. They produce polyembryonic seeds, which means that more than one plant may grow from each seed. If you discard the least vigorous seedlings, the selected seedlings should come reasonably true to type. Plant lemon or orange seeds 1.5 cm [½″] deep in sandy soil in early spring, singly in 7.5 cm [3″] pots. They need a temperature of 13-15°C [55-60°F] to germinate, which takes about three weeks. Leave the seedlings for two years in these pots then transplant them into 10 cm [4″] pots. In the fourth spring transplant again into a bigger pot.

The main disadvantage of seed sowing is that they are slow to fruit — cropping may be delayed ten years. However, trees raised from seedlings are slightly more hardy than those raised vegetatively, and they are all very long-lived.

Buying a tree

Commercial trees are two to three years old and usually budded on to rootstocks of various types. The sweet orange, *C. sinensis*, gives good trees, cropping well, but is susceptible to root rot. The sour orange, *C. aurantium*, resists this and is good for drought and exposed areas. It has proved the most popular in California but not satisfactory in South Africa. There, the rough-skinned variety of the lemon, *C. limon*, has proved best; this is good for soils with a high sand content. *Poncirus trifoliata* is more hardy than the others and has been used to try to develop a tree that will withstand cold. The type of stock does not much affect the quality of the fruit, so the stock is chosen according to local conditions.

Planting out

Spacing depends on the height of the species chosen. The diameter should be the same as the height; for example the lemon grows to 2.5 m [8′], so you should allow 2.5 m [8′] space.

Many nurseries supply trees in plastic containers, and these may be left a few days before planting if they are watered. Trees with bare roots must be soaked for an hour or so and then planted quickly. The roots of citrus dry very rapidly, and if possible they should never be left without moist wrappings.

Prepare the site about a month in advance by digging in rotted organic matter. Dig a hole 60 cm [2′] deep and wide and plant, firm and water your citrus like other fruit trees (*see* APPLE).

Watering

Roots must not be allowed to dry out. Evergreens are particularly vulnerable to lack of water, and drought while fruit are ripening makes them pithy and juiceless. The trees will benefit from a daily syringe with a fine spray of water in the evening in hot weather.

Feeding

Crops from a mature tree are heavy so this drain on the tree must be made good. Manure or garden compost should be applied twice a year, at the start of the growing season and half way through it, at the rate of four 12 L [2½ gal] buckets a time. Failing this from about the sixth year, give them sulphate of potash at the rate of 30 g per sq m [1 oz per sq yd] and bonemeal at 60 g per sq m [2 oz per sq yd] for the area covered by the tree; the amount will therefore increase with tree size. Where manure is used, give half these quantities.

Citrus trees suffer from deficiency diseases, that is, a lack of the trace elements which are essential to growth. These can be replaced by foliar feeding, so you should seek local advice.

Pruning

Bought trees will have a formed framework so little pruning is required. Pinch out the growing tips of trees grown from seed at three years to keep them bushy. Too crowded or crossing branches are cut out to keep the tree reasonably open. In warm areas it is essential to keep a cover of foliage, as strong sun on the woody parts will cause damage. Water shoots are very strong shoots arising inside the tree, usually on the upperside of the branches, which quickly outgrow the supporting branch and therefore ruin the shape of the tree. These should be removed when young unless they are required to fill a gap. Lemons are pruned more than other citrus fruit, as they are inclined to be straggly, and are prone to water shoot development.

In the greenhouse

In cool temperate areas citrus trees need wintering under glass and can be raised there entirely. The main requirement is for light and for a minimum temperature of about 7° to 10°C [45° to 50°F]. The lemon will stand a night temperature of 4°C [40°F], the orange likes a daytime temperature of 10°C [50°F]. In early to mid spring the temperature should be allowed to rise to 21°C [70°F], and in the summer when the tree may be moved into the garden or patio until early autumn, a temperature of 27°C [80°F] is desirable.

Choose a container with drainage holes and put a layer of drainage material at the bottom. Fill with a good potting compost or equal parts by volume of loam, sharp sand, peat, or leafmould or manure. Add 30 g [1 oz] of bonemeal, or 15 g [½ oz] if you have used manure.

Pot cultivation offers a convenient method of keeping an orange tree small. Use the smallest pot that will take the roots of the new tree. At three years old it may be transplanted into a 25 cm [10″] pot and three years later into a larger one, and so on to a maximum size of 60 cm [2′].

Fresh compost should be given to the tree each year, or at least biennially; the tree is repotted at the end of every winter even when there is no need for change in pot size. Water it, then lay the pot on its side. Do not disturb the

*Before they fruit citrus trees produce fragrant flowers,
like the blossom of the Ruby Red grapefruit shown here.*

compost around the roots, but remove all the rest and replace with new. During this operation any long root curling around the pot can be pruned to two-thirds its length. When the tree has been moved into its final pot or tub, potting on is abandoned, and it is mulched annually with rotted manure or garden compost.

Watering must be regular in summer, though in winter the tree may be allowed to get almost dry. Liquid feed can be given in summer while the fruit is swelling. Syringe the leaves with clear water daily in warm weather and once a week in winter. On warm days when the tree is still under glass, ensure that it is adequately ventilated.

Harvesting

The best quality fruit — and the best to store — is that which reaches a good size before colouring, though oranges may be ripe when green. A steady temperature above 18°C [65°F] is needed. Healthy trees produce very heavy crops of fruit. Except for lemons and limes, most citrus fruit are left on the tree until mature. Fruit are not likely to ripen all at once, and the picking season is therefore spread over many weeks. Though the skin appears tough, it is susceptible to damage and mould will result. Use secateurs to separate the fruit from the tree. Lemons should be stored at 16°C [60°F] until ripe.

Propagation

Semi-ripe cuttings of new sideshoots 7.5-10 cm [3-4″] long can be rooted with the help of a mist propagator or a plastic tent and rooting hormone. They may take in under a month but it could be eight months before they root. Rooted plants may then be potted up and gradually hardened off before planting out about a year after rooting. These cuttings are unlikely to be as vigorous as plants which have been budded from a nursery, or as those produced from seed, and they may be more susceptible to certain diseases.

Pests and diseases

Scale insects, whitefly and greenfly are likely to attack the trees. Canker is a bacterial disease affecting the bark and also producing spots on the leaves, and is subject to governmental regulation in some countries — *see* **CHERRY** for control. Attacks by moths and fruit flies may be severe in some areas, where they are subject to regulation. Inside, scale can be cleared by a soap and water wash.

Collards

SEE CABBAGE

Coriander

**Coriander seeds are used whole or ground
in curries, chutneys and desserts.
Young leaves are used as a garnish,
in salads and for flavouring fish.**

Coriander (*Coriandrum sativum*) is a hardy annual herb 45 cm [1½′] high in the *Umbelliferae* family which is grown mainly for its slightly orange flavoured seeds. Whole, they may be added to rice dishes, curries and chutneys and used in pickling fish. Ground, they are excellent in curry dishes, and go well with roast pork and baked ham. The powder can be sprinkled on custards and used in Eastern pastries, and cakes such as gingerbread. Coriander is one of the flavourings in gin, and may be added to a hot rum toddy.

Before coriander goes to seed, the young leaves may replace parsley as a garnish and be added to salads, curries and fish.

The plant is an attractive bright green with round, upright stems, deeply divided shining leaves and small delicate white flowers, sometimes tinted mauve, which appear in early summer. These are borne in umbels of five to ten flower stalks, springing from a common point like the ribs of an inside-out umbrella. Before the seeds are ripe in late summer the plant develops a disagreeable smell. The name coriander comes from the Greek *koris* meaning a bug — its odour was thought to be like that of bed bugs. As they ripen this disappears and they become pleasantly aromatic.

Cultivation

Coriander is extremely easy to grow and, although it prefers light, warm, rich soil, it will grow almost anywhere. Propagation is from seed, which is rather slow to germinate. It can be sown in drills 1.5 cm [½″] deep and 30 cm [1′] either in early autumn or in mid spring. It can also be sown under glass in early spring in a temperature of 15°C [60°F] for planting out in late spring. When the seedlings are established, thin so that the plants are 20-23 cm [8-9″] apart. All that is needed in the way of care is to keep them free of weeds and, for the best results, to water when the weather is very dry and warm.

Harvesting and storing

Classically, coriander is reaped with a sickle, but for small quantities secateurs or shears will do. The seeds tend to fall the moment they become ripe, so watch out from the beginning of late summer and harvest them quickly when they turn beige. Tie the seed-heads in bunches and dry them in a warm, dark, airy place over sheets of paper to catch the seeds. Store in opaque, airtight jars.

Corn
SEE SWEET CORN

Corn Salad

This extremely hardy plant grows well in a dry, sandy soil and will provide a welcome supply of salad during the winter months.

Corn salad is at its best at the blank and bleak end of the salad calendar — mid to late winter. The slightly earthy taste of its 7.5 cm [3′] long leaves is reminiscent of cos lettuce and dandelion, and is much esteemed by epicures. It is also known as lamb's lettuce, possibly because the height of its season coincides with lambing, possibly because sheep, especially in Europe, enjoy huge quantities of the wild plant while grazing. It can be grown for picking at any time of the year, but the best time for a first sowing is in late summer, with two or three successional sowings up to mid autumn. In cooler climates, sowings can begin in midsummer. These sowings will provide a supply of corn salad in winter, when other salad crops are not usually available in the garden and are expensive to buy.

Suitable site and soil

Choose soil which has been well cultivated, and preferably enriched for a previous summer vegetable crop. A sandy soil suits these plants especially well. Corn salad makes most of its growth when the amount of daylight is decreasing, so a sunny spot is vital to maintain progress.

Cultivation

Make shallow drills 15 cm [6″] apart and sow the seeds 1.5 cm [½″] deep. Thinning is not essential but for a tidier row thin the plants to 15 cm [6″] apart. Although corn salad is fully hardy — it can withstand the most severe winter — you can keep its leaves fresher during hard weather by cloching plants from late autumn onwards. If cloches are not available, straw, hay or bracken drawn up over the plants will achieve the same results. Birds and slugs are the only pest, when plants are young.

Harvesting

Ideas on how to harvest corn salad differ. Some prefer to cut whole plants, as with lettuce, but it is probably wiser to pluck tender young leaves from different plants as they grow, just as you would gather spinach or kale. Make sure, however, that you do not take too many leaves from each plant — no more than two or three — otherwise you may weaken it beyond recovery. Wash the leaves well to remove any soil or grit, and use as soon as possible after harvesting.

If you do not like the slightly bitter taste of corn salad, you can partially blanch the plants to create a milder flavour. Do this by placing boxes or plant pots over them for a few days.

Protect young plants from birds, and from slugs after rain.

Corn Salad
Valerianella locusta (fam. *Valerianaceae*) also known as lamb's lettuce.
Hardy annual.
Size: grows to 15-23 cm [6-9″] high.
Climate: cool temperate.
Sowing to harvesting time: 5-6 months.
Yield: about 20 plants per 3 m [10′] row.

Courgette
SEE ZUCCHINI

Crabapple

Crabapples produce a tart fruit, about 2.5 cm [1″] across, which make excellent jelly and preserves.

The crabapple, *Malus sylvestris (Rosaceae),* makes a fine ornamental tree, rivalling the ornamental cherries when covered with blossom in mid and late spring, and covered with yellow, red or orange fruit in autumn. They are longer lived than other apple trees. Though standards are common, crabapples are available on the same dwarfing rootstocks as other apples. They are often planted in the ornamental section of the garden where they are useful as a pollinator for other apples. Not all apples are edible. For cultivation *see* APPLE.

Cress

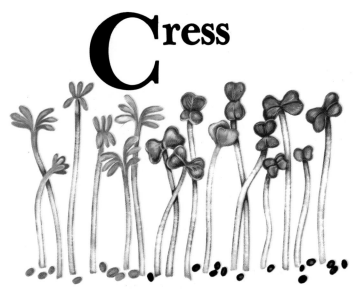

Common cress (left) shown with mustard (right), land cress and watercress are all peppery little plants, easily grown for use in the kitchen.

The name cress is used rather loosely for a variety of salad plants, most of which belong to the mustard group of the *Cruciferae* plant family.

The three main types of cress are similar for culinary purposes, but are grown in different conditions, so the gardener may choose the one which is best suited to the available space and situation. Common cress is grown indoors in trays, land cress, is a hardy, year-round outdoor crop, and watercress is grown in a pure natural stream, a flooded bed or a container of fresh water.

COMMON CRESS

Common cress (*Lepidium sativum*), which is also known as garden cress or pepper cress, is often grown as part of 'mustard and cress'. It is the seedling stage of a plant which is a native of Iran; the adult plant, which grows to about 45 cm [1½], has small white flowers. There is also Golden or Australian Cress, which is shorter, grows more slowly and is a yellowish colour.

Cultivation

Common cress is best grown indoors at the times of year when other salad plants are rare.

It is essential to sow fresh seed. It is not satisfactory to grow common cress outdoors in the open ground because it is easily beaten down by rain or overhead watering, and it readily becomes soiled. Seed which is more than a year old will germinate at different rates, and the younger seedlings will be choked by the older ones.

If you want to grow it with mustard, cress should be sown three days before to be ready for cutting at the same time. Quantities of mustard and cress required at any one time are not great; a standard seed tray 35 x 20 x 5 cm [14 x 8 x 2″] will hold a crop of about 125 g [4 oz].

For a succession, sow the seed once a week, allowing 8 days to cutting in autumn and spring, 7 days in summer and 11 days in winter. 15 g [½ oz] of cress seed will fill a standard seed tray in autumn and spring; in winter 20 g [¾ oz] will be needed. Half fill a 5 cm [2″] deep container with either a standard potting compost thoroughly watered, or with peat soaked in a liquid fertilizer. The growing medium needs to be well watered beforehand as watering during growth can result in damping-off, or rotting.

Sow the seed evenly and thickly on the surface, press it lightly into the growing medium and cover with a black plastic sheet, or glass and brown paper. The temperature should be 10°C [50°F] at night, rising to 18°C [65°F] maximum during the day.

Germination will occur about four days after sowing, when the covering should be removed and the seedlings given a good light and kept in the same temperature as when sown. The atmosphere should be moist.

Harvesting

Cress can be cut when just over 0.5 cm [2″] high, doing the cutting 0.5 cm [¼″] above soil level. It should be used quickly once it is ready.

LAND CRESS

Land cress, *Barbarea praecox*, which is also known as

1. *Cress grown with mustard should be sown three days before. Keep the box covered until after germination.*

2. *Mustard and cress seedlings can be harvested with a pair of scissors, two to three weeks after sowing.*

1. *Thin land cress out to about 20 cm [8"] apart.*

2. *Pick only the outer leaves at first, but when these become tough, take the larger central ones instead.*

3. *Remove flowering stems to encourage new leaves.*

yellow cress, bank cress, early winter cress and American cress, is one of the few herbs or salad plants which can be grown outdoors for eating all around the year, including winter, in cool temperate regions. It is exceptionally resistant to cold weather. Land cress used to be very popular as winter salad and is well worth re-introducing into the herb garden. Although a perennial, it is usually treated as an annual, with a succession of sowings each year throughout spring and summer.

A compact plant, it forms a rosette of lobed leaves, several inches in diameter and about 15 cm [6"] high. If allowed to seed, it will send up flowering stalks 30 cm [1'] or more high, bearing small white flowers.

Cultivation

Land cress is easy to grow, makes only small demands on space and has the great advantage that it thrives in the shady, damp corners most other plants will not tolerate. It should be planted in a damp border shaded from the direct rays of the summer sun. The cress is also an excellent crop to grow in tubs or boxes in a shady part of a patio.

Land cress thrives in a rich, moist soil. Add generous applications of well-rotted animal manure or garden compost. A top layer of organic matter helps to retain moisture within the soil.

First sowings can be made in early spring, as soon as hard frosts are over, with a succession of sowings at three-week intervals throughout the summer. Sowings can be continued right into late summer for winter use.

Sow in drills — shallow furrows — about 0.5 cm [$\frac{1}{4}$"] deep, the rows being 30 cm [1'] apart. After a few weeks, when the plants are large enough to handle, either thin to about 20 cm [8"] apart or transplant into rows with 20 cm [8"] between the plants. The thinnings are good to eat too.

Watering is as important in spring as in the height of summer for, without it, the seeds can take a long time to germinate and there is the danger of weeds taking over. Weeding is not easy as cress seedlings are very similar to those of several common weeds. Sow the seed in marked rows, so that at least the space between the rows can be kept clear of weeds in the early stages by hoeing.

Harvesting and aftercare

One of the attractions of land cress is that you only need pick a few leaves at a time. Under favourable conditions, the first pickings can be made about eight weeks after sowing. At first, pick only the outer leaves, allowing the centre to continue producing new ones. Later, when the outer leaves tend to toughen and discolour, pick the larger

Common cress must be eaten soon after it is harvested but curly cress is more resilient which makes it good for garnishing. Both are grown in exactly the same way.

Prepare the watercress bed with peat and soil. Flood it and, when drained, broadcast but do not cover the seed.

A watercress bed should be in a partly shaded place and must be kept moist. Sow in mid spring or late summer.

of the central ones. The leaves, at their best, will be deep green and succulent. Keep pinching back; do not allow the cress to get too lanky. Removing flowering stems will encourage the continued production of leaves. Picking can go on indefinitely if the plants are well watered and growing vigorously.

If the plot of ground is required for another crop, simply dig in what remains of the cress plants. They make excellent green manure for conditioning the soil.

Plants which are being kept through the winter need complete protection only in severe weather. Then the cloches or frames in which they are being over-wintered may need to be covered with sacking during extremely severe spells of hard frost. This should, however, be removed during the day because the plants need light. A little ventilation may also be given on all but the coldest days. During winter, watering should not be necessary, but be sure the soil is moist.

When spring arrives, remove the protective coverings and fork around the plants, mulching with a little compost or rotted farmyard manure if available, and sprinkle with a general fertilizer.

Pests and diseases

The only pests likely to give trouble are snails and slugs.

WATERCRESS

Watercress is *Nasturtium officinale*, a hardy annual. There are two types: green watercress, which is best for summer supplies, and brown, best for winter and spring.

Cultivation

You must be very careful about the water in which you grow watercress. Never plant it in a garden pool. If you have access to a natural stream you can sow along the bank about 15 cm [6″] above the water line, but you must be sure the water is free from pollution. It is best grown in a permanently moist and partially shaded position from seed sown in mid spring or late summer.

Dig the soil deeply and incorporate moisture-holding peat or other organic material. The surface of the bed should be about 2.5 cm [1″] or so below that of the surrounding soil. Firm and rake the bed and flood it with fresh water. When the water has drained away broadcast the seed. Do not cover it with soil. Seedlings will be ready to eat from about two weeks after sowing. Watercress bought from a grocer may be used as cuttings. Some have roots already but if not they will easily develop roots if you stand them in a glass of water. Watercress may also be grown in pots or clay pans stood in shallow containers of fresh water, well shaded, or in a container sunk in the ground.

Cucumber

**Cucumbers are a very refreshing salad
crop, because of their high water content.
The small, rough-skinned varieties
called gherkins are used for pickling.**

A tropical trailing or climbing plant of Asiatic origin, the
cucumber was known to the Romans. It is an important
commercial crop, and one that is well-worth cultivating in
the garden. With a little care it is not a difficult crop to
grow well.

There are two basic sorts of cucumbers; the first is the long
smooth skinned variety about 20-38 cm [12-15"] in length,
often known as frame cucumbers in cool temperate areas,
because there they need a frame or greenhouse. These are
grown as climbers so that the fruit can hang down.

Ridge varieties, which include those used as gherkins for
pickling, are short, about 12 cm [5"], with knobbly or
spiny skin. They get their name because they are grown
prostrate on ridges out of doors, though they need cloche
protection in colder areas.

The new Japanese outdoor varieties are long and slim, like
the greenhouse kinds, and can be trained to grow vertically.

Apple cucumbers have round fruit the size of a small apple
with a pale yellowish white skin and are of good quality.
Another trailing variety, they are generally regarded as
more digestible than green-fruited varieties. They can be
grown in pots or boxes in a greenhouse, in a frame or outside in sheltered parts of cool temperate areas.

Wild cucumbers bear separate male and female flowers on

Cucumber
Cucumis sativus (fam. *Cucurbitacae*)
Tender plant, grown as an annual, trailing or
climbing.
Size: controlled to 2.5 m [8'] in the greenhouse and
1.2 m [4'] square in a frame or the open.
Climate: warm temperate.
Sowing to harvesting time: 10-14 weeks.
Yield: greenhouse cucumbers 20 fruits per plant,
ridge cucumbers 25.

---

the same plant. This is also true of the outdoor ridge types,
which must be pollinated to produce crops. Indoor
cucumbers, on the other hand, are parthenocarpic, that is
they can bear fruit without pollination. The unfertilized
fruit are superior for cropping purposes, and so care is
taken to prevent pollination.

GROWING UNDER GLASS
If you cannot raise your own seed, you can buy plants from
a nursery. Choose short stocky plants, dark green in colour
with three or four true leaves and their seed leaves still intact, which have been kept indoors by the stockist.

Sowing
The best way to raise the seedlings is in a propagator or in
a warm greenhouse, at an absolute minimum night-time
temperature of 15°C [60°F], but 18° to 25°C [65° to 75°F] is
safer. It is vital that the seeds germinate quickly. Seeds
sometimes show considerable variation: select only plump,
clean ones and discard those which are flat or discoloured.
Sow the seeds singly in late winter or very early spring in
6-7.5 cm [2½-3"] plastic pots, containing seed compost or
soil-less compost to within 1.25 cm [½"] of the top of the
pot. Do not use old soil because it has not been sterilized.
Place the seeds on edge, about 1.25 cm [½"] deep, and firm
the whole surface. Water the compost and then cover the
pot with black plastic or a sheet of glass and brown paper.
The seeds should germinate within two, or at most three,
days at the highest temperatures. Remove the covering
and place the plants in a light position in the greenhouse.
In a temperature of at least 15°C [60°F], growth should be
rapid.

Making a hotbed
Put down a layer of fresh manure 45 cm [1½'] wide and 15
cm [6"] deep to produce heat for the plants. This should be
spread out in the open beforehand and turned over occasionally for a few days to allow the excess nitrogen to be
given off as ammonia. Another way of producing heat is to
use a 60 cm [2'] thick layer of straw, firmed down,
sprinkled with sulphate of ammonia, and saturated with
water. On top put a layer 30 cm [1'] deep and 60 cm [2']
wide, of good loamy soil. This is now ready for cucumbers.

Planting
When the pots are full of roots and two to four leaves have
expanded, nip out the growing point and plant the
cucumbers in 23 cm [9"] pots or in boxes containing potting compost, or in a hotbed.

Training
Carry out cordon training of cucumbers on roughly the
same principle as that used for tomatoes. Space the plants
45 cm [1½'] apart. Erect two wires, the top one about 2.1
m [7'] above ground level, the basal one running along the
surface of the bed, both about 30 cm [1'] from the outside
glass. Tie a string for each plant on to the wires so that it

*(Right) The long smooth-skinned cucumber is grown as
a climber, needing a greenhouse in cool temperate areas.*

runs vertically and tie the leading shoot to this at intervals. Remove all sideshoots up to a height of 38 cm [15″] from the base of plant; beyond this, stop any sideshoots at the one- or two-leaf stage, depending on where the fruit is developing. Continue the operations of tying the plant to the string, stopping sideshoots and removing unwanted flowers beyond the second leaf, until the leading shoot has reached the top wire, when it is tied in and stopped.

Cucumbers may also be trained like melons in the greenhouse (*see* MELON).

Care and development

The cucumber must be given plenty of moisture at all times; its fruits have the highest water content of all vegetables. Never allow the compost in the pots, boxes or beds to become dry, especially in hot dry weather. The atmosphere in the greenhouse should be very humid; damp down two or three times a day in hot weather, although ventilation must also be provided. A drip or trickle irrigation system can be of considerable help.

It is difficult to lay down hard and fast rules regarding feeding. When the fruit start to swell apply a compound fertilizer, but not earlier. Apply this about once every two weeks, following the directions on a proprietary compound.

Preventing pollination

Varieties are available which produce only female flowers, but these require slightly higher greenhouse temperatures. Where ordinary varieties are grown, it is usual to remove male flowers to prevent pollination. It is easy to recognize males, because they do not bear miniature cucumbers behind the petals, as do the females. Some growers fix fine gauze over ventilation openings in order to exclude insects. If these do manage to enter and pollinate the female flowers, the resulting fruit will be swollen-ended, bitter-tasting and full of seeds.

Growing cucumbers in a frame

Where a greenhouse is not available, cucumbers can be grown successfully in a cold frame which must have a stout wooden, brick or concrete base to retain warmth. Plant the cucumbers in late spring in the centre of the frame in a hotbed, made in the way described earlier. If you have no hotbed, delay planting to early summer.

Keep the frame closed, except for the occasional ventilation on warm days. When the weather becomes warmer, it may be left open throughout the day.

Pinch out the growing tip of the plants in the same way as was recommended for greenhouse plants, when four or five leaves have been formed on each plant. Subsequently shoots will be produced in the axils (joints) of these leaves and you should select four and train each one towards a corner of the frame.

Carry out watering, feeding and pinching out sub-sideshoots as described earlier.

GROWING OUTDOORS

Ridge cucumbers may be sown outdoors in a mild climate, or under cloches, in a sunny sheltered position.

Dig a generous helping of garden compost, leaf mould or rotted farmyard manure into a trench 30 cm [1′] deep and the same width, and cover with the excavated soil, mounding it up into a low ridge. Alternatively, dig the organic matter into holes 90 cm [3′] apart and 30 cm [1′] deep by 30 cm [1′] square, again finishing of with a low mound. If organic material is not available, use a general fertilizer at the rate of 60 g per sq m [2 oz per sq yd], forked into the top few centimetres of soil two weeks or so before sowing.

Sow the seed in late spring in the open, two weeks or so earlier under cloches. Sow a group of three seeds on the mounds or 90 cm [3′] apart on the long ridges, and thin to one plant in due course.

Allow the plants to grow about six leaves and then remove the growing tip. The sideshoots that are produced as a result are trained out singly and evenly, stopping those which have produced fruit at the seventh leaf, and the further shoots if needed to restrain the plant.

Pollination is by insects, but if you want to make doubly sure fruit will set you can pollinate them by the method described in melon (*see* MELON).

In dry weather frequent watering will be necessary around the plants, being careful not to wet the stems. Liquid feeding should be started when the fruit begins to swell, and continued at two-weekly intervals.

A framework must be erected to support Japanese varieties, so that the fruit can hang down. Buy 2.2 m [7½′] poles and insert them so that they are 1.8 m [6′] above the ground and 1.8 m [6′] apart. Run wires between them and attach netting with a 20 cm [8″] mesh. Plant the cucumbers singly 30 cm [1′] apart and train them upward, pinching out the leaders when the top of the net has been reached. Stop sideshoots, as previously described.

HARVESTING AND PROTECTION

Greenhouse cucumbers will start to crop in late spring or early summer, and should be cut when about 30-35 cm [12-15″] long. They will continue cropping until autumn. Ridge cucumbers which have been sown under cloches should begin to crop in late summer and slightly later if sown outdoors. The first frosts will end the crop, as the plants will be killed. All cucumbers should be harvested before they reach full size and turn yellow, as this impairs the flavour. Early harvesting also helps to encourage the production of more fruit.

Pests and diseases

The most common pest of cucumbers is the red spider mite which can destroy the plant. Whitefly and greenfly are also dangerous, the latter because it can carry virus and distorts the fruit by its feeding. Biological controls are available for whitefly and red spider mite, or usual insecticide control can be applied. When you use an insecticide on cucumbers, make sure you choose one that will not damage the plants; the *Cucurbitaceae* family are rather sensitive to spray.

To avoid cucumber mosaic as far as possible use virus-free seeds for propagation, and avoid contaminating healthy plants with knives or fingers infected from diseased plants,

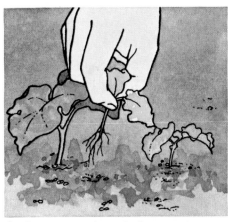

1. To prepare ridge cucumber bed, dig garden compost into straight trench and cover with soil ridge.

2. Sow cucumbers in late spring. When first leaves have developed thin to one seedling per group.

3. Train out sideshoots singly and evenly. Protect cucumbers from the soil by placing a tile under them.

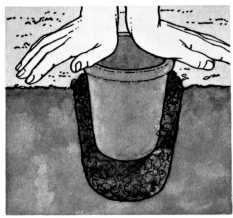

1. To plant: dig hole the size of pot, fill with moist peat, press in empty pot and twist clear.

2. To remove cucumber from pot turn upside down and, holding soil, tap out on table edge.

3. Put cucumber plant into hole made by empty pot and water it with warm water, 15-20° C [60-70° F].

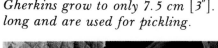

Gherkins grow to only 7.5 cm [3"]. long and are used for pickling.

The larger yellow flowers of the ridge cucumber are male. The smaller female ones quickly develop young cucumber fruits behind them.

when trimming plants. Affected plants should be cleared and burned as soon as seen and the remaining plants treated for greenfly.

Sometimes the young cucumbers wither from the tip and die when only 5 cm [2′] or so long. This is usually due to overwatering. To rectify this condition, the soil should not be watered for a few days, the plants should be sprayed overhead daily, and old stems removed. Then give a mulch and start watering again.

Collar-rot is generally caused by excessive damp close to the stem and results in a complete plant wilting and dying. A mixture of 10 parts lime, 3 parts sulphur and 1 part copper sulphate should be applied around the stem. A mulch of well-moistened peat applied afterwards close around the stem will induce new roots to grow above the diseased area, but if the plant is too far gone, it is best destroyed.

Cucumber leaf blotch *(Cercospora melonis)* is a fungal disease which may be serious and require spraying and even soil sterilization. Powdery mildew may also occur.

Damson

Smaller than the plum, oval and dark-
skinned with yellow flesh,
damsons are usually cooked, when they
produce a delicious red juice.
They can be regarded as a cold weather plum.

The damson, *Prunus damascena*, is a member of the plum family and closely related to the sourer and smaller bullace, *P. insititia*. They are late-ripening, in early autumn. The fruit is 2.5 cm [1″] long, with mealy rather juiceless flesh, but develops a peculiarly rich flavour when cooked. They are excellent for bottling and jam, can be made into a stiff fruit paste known as 'butter' or 'cheese', and into wine. When really ripe they can be eaten raw.

Grown as standards or half-standards, they make small trees, from 3.6-4.5 m [12-15′] high. Damsons are very hardy, and in the colder parts of temperate areas may be a

better choice than the early flowering plums. They crop abundantly in thin soil, provided there is excessive rainfall. In some colder areas they are grown as a hedge to provide shelter from the wind. Though they are not evergreen, they retain their foliage through the autumn, and the branches interlock to form an effective and productive windbreak. They are cultivated in the same way as plums *(see* PLUM).

Dill

A herb with a distinctive flavour, dill
is chiefly used in pickles. Both seeds
and leaves are used for flavouring.

Dill *(Anethum graveolens)* is a very spindly annual of the *Umbelliferae* family. It is often used in Scandinavian and Russian fish dishes and for pickling cucumbers, but it is also successful on potatoes, tomatoes, beans and peas. The seeds are good with cooked brassicas and in salad dressings. Dill is said to have digestive properties and babies may be given dill water to relieve gripe.

Its feathery green leaves grow on a single stem about 60-90 cm [2-3′] high and it produces large yellow flower heads from mid to late summer, from which seeds are freely produced.

Cultivation

Dill will grow in ordinary soil in an open sunny aspect, either grouped in a border or in a row. Prepare the site by deep digging to allow unimpeded tap root growth.

Sow the seeds outside during mid spring not more than 0.5 cm [¼″] deep and as thinly as possible. Germination takes about 10-14 days. The seedlings emerge with a pair of narrow leaflets, often with the seed shell affixed to one, with the curled growth bud in the middle. Once the seedlings are large enough to handle, thin them to 10 cm [4″] apart. As they develop continue to thin until the plants are approximately 23 cm [9″] apart — use the thinnings fresh, or dry them. Firm the remaining plants well.

Unless the weather is very dry, watering is not necessary. The area should be kept weed free and in windy areas the plants should be supported with twigs when they reach about 60 cm [2'].

Harvesting and growing a winter crop

Leaves should be harvested when as immature as possible, before the flower buds show about eight weeks after sowing. When seeds are desired the first flower-heads should be left on, otherwise remove the flower-heads to encourage further leaf growth. Allow the seeds to ripen until they are dark brown and harvest them in early autumn. Then hang them in a warm dark position, over paper, until they are dry.

During mid autumn sow seeds in 7.5 cm [3"] pots in a warm greenhouse or indoors if you want dill for winter use. Transplant carefully into larger pots when the plants are 15 cm [6"] tall. Keep the plants away from direct sunlight and radiators, water regularly and support with sticks.

Pests and diseases

During a dry season greenfly attack dill and badly infested plants should be burned. Spray the remainder frequently with pure soapy water. Do not use insecticides, which could damage the plant and the flavour.

Eggplant

Harvested young and cooked properly eggplants provide a delicious and versatile vegetable and an important ingredient of Arab, Near East, Indian and Mediterranean dishes.

The eggplant or aubergine is native to southern and eastern Asia, where it is one of the earliest known cultivated vegetables. The fruit of the most common type of eggplant has a purple, shiny skin and creamy white flesh with a high water content. There are also varieties which bear white, red or even yellow fruit. The shape of the fruit varies according to variety, from roughly egg-shaped and squat to the more usual, elongated pear shape. One variety, the snake eggplant, has fruit which is very long, thin and curled at the end. Sizes also vary — from about 5 cm [2"] to 30 cm [1'].

The plant is too delicate to survive exposure to temperatures below about 10°C [50°F], but apart from this can succeed almost anywhere if protected by cloches or a greenhouse.

Although eggplants need plenty of sunlight and warmth to succeed, the protection and care given the plant is rewarded by a crop which is far superior in taste to the eggplants sold in shops and markets.

Suitable site and soil

Even in Mediterranean and sub-tropical climates eggplants require a very sunny aspect. In cooler temperate areas grow them in a greenhouse or under cloches on a sunny site, though in the mildest areas they may be tried outdoors against a sunny wall.

The soil must be fertile and well drained. Dig it over and enrich with well-rotted manure or garden compost some weeks before sowing or setting out plants.

Sowing and thinning

A minimum soil temperature of 23°C [75°F] is the ideal for good, even germination — sow from mid to late spring, when danger of frost is past. Sow seeds at stations 75 cm [30"] apart, at a depth of 2.5 cm [1"]. The seed should germinate and sprout after about 7-14 days.

Care and development

Pinch out the growing point of plants when they are about 15 cm [6"] high. This will encourage the plants to produce sideshoots bearing mauve flowers which are self-pollinating. The fruit will mature within 10-14 weeks from this stage.

Keep plants well supplied with water. Lawn mowings or straw may be spread around the plants when they are growing well to prevent moisture evaporation. Use a proprietary tomato fertilizer at the manufacturer's recommended rates if the soil is not very fertile, even after preparatory improvement. Use a hoe to keep down weeds around the plants. The mulch will also restrain weed growth.

Eggplant
Solanum melongena (fam. *Solanaceae*) also known as aubergine, eggfruit or guinea squash.
Perennial, but cultivated as **half-hardy annual.**
Size: reaches an average height of 90 cm [3'].
Climate: temperate to tropical.
Sowing to harvesting time: about 16-23 weeks, depending on warmth and intensity of sunlight.
Yield: 4 plants per 3 m [10'] row, 4-5 fruits per plant.

1. *Sow seeds in seed tray filled with seed compost. When seedlings are 5 cm [2″] tall prick off singly into 7.5 cm [3″] pots leaving no stem showing above the soil.*

2. *Move to 15 cm [6″] pots when smaller pots are full. Always put stake in first.*

3. *Move to larger pot for fruiting. Pinch growing point out at 15 cm [6″].*

4. *With cloches, remove plants from pots and set at 60 cm [2′] intervals.*

5. *Spray with warm water twice daily, especially the underside of foliage.*

(Above left) Peat-filled plastic bags have proved very successful for growing eggplants in the open. Planting should take place in early summer.

(Left) Eggplants vary greatly in size, shape and colour. The largest here is 'Black Beauty', the commonest variety.

If your plants are bearing heavy crops and are exposed to wind they may need staking. Set a cane close to the plant and tie it on loosely. If cloches are used, these must allow adequate headroom for the plants. They may be removed entirely if the summer is a very hot one, otherwise remove them during the day to ensure good ventilation and replace them at night.

Harvesting the crop

Eggplant fruit are ready for picking when they are about 15 cm [6″] long and have stopped swelling. You can test this by pressing the fruit gently with a thumb. If an indentation remains, swelling has stopped. If the imprint disappears, the fruit is still swelling. The fruit should have a good deep colour and a bright, shiny skin. The stem is sometimes prickly, so wear gloves and use shears to cut off the fruit.

Once they are ripe, eggplant fruit must be harvested promptly, or the gloss on the skin begins to disappear and seeds develop inside the flesh, which makes the fruit less palatable. Length of harvest is about 6-8 weeks, through late summer.

Growing under glass

Seeds may be sown in a heated greenhouse from late winter to mid spring; in an unheated greenhouse or outdoors in a glass frame from mid to late spring, after the last frost. Sow seeds 2.5 cm [1″] apart in seed trays, or in small pots filled with seed compost suitable for tomatoes, with two or three seeds to each 7.5 cm [3″] or 9 cm [3½″] pot at a depth of 1.5 cm [½″].

Keep trays or pots fairly moist and ensure that the temperature does not fall below 10°C [50°F]. A propagator will keep the pots warm in an outdoors frame. Transfer small seedlings from the trays to one per 7.5 [3″] or 9 cm [3½″] pot and thin pot-sown seedlings. Stop the young plants at 15 cm [6″] high, by removing the growing tip.

When greenhouse-raised plants are from 15-20 cm [6-8″] high, remove plants from the pots and set out at 60 cm [2′] intervals in the greenhouse border, or in the garden frames at this stage if you prefer to start them indoors. Weed regularly and ensure ventilation is good.

Growing in pots, tubs and containers

Eggplants are excellent plants to grow in containers where space is limited. One plant should produce from four to six fruit.

Sow as directed for **growing under glass.** Transfer seedlings from the small pots to 15 cm [6″] pots and finally to 25 cm [10″] pots. Keep in a greenhouse or indoors in a sunny spot and stand outdoors in warm weather. They can be kept on a patio all the time if it is warm and sunny.

Plants in pots need feeding when the first fruit are swelling, and from then on until the last fruit have reached full size. Feed as directed under **care and development.**

Pests and diseases

Avoid planting eggplants in soil where either tomatoes or potatoes, which belong to the same family, have been growing in the previous two or three years. Lack of crop rotation can lead to wilt diseases. Other pests common to the family include greenfly, red spider mite (especially under glass) and potato beetle. Under glass, slugs can attack seedlings and grey mould (*botrytis cinerea*) will affect flowers and fruit if the ventilation is bad.

Endive

Endive can be sown for both summer and winter use, and is delicious either raw or cooked. There are two different types — the curled, or staghorn, varieties and the round-leaved, or Batavian, varieties.

Endive is unfamiliar to many amateur gardeners. It has a bitter taste if not properly blanched — much of the endive offered for sale has been insufficiently blanched by the grower or has lost most of its blanch during the journey to the market. When properly treated, however, endive is a delicious vegetable and one that is quite easy to grow.

Neither of the two types of endive is entirely hardy, though the stronger-tasting Batavian varieties will tolerate the sort of light frost that would ruin the last of the summer lettuces. Cloche or frame cultivation, however, will ensure survival of both sorts of endive through moderate frosts. The curly-leaved varieties can be sown in mid spring if a crop is wanted in summer, but usually they are sown in early summer for an autumn crop. The tougher Batavian

---

Endive
Cichorium endivia (fam. *Compositae*)
Half-hardy annual, resistant to light frosts.
Size: 12.5-20 cm [5-8″] tall; 30-38 cm [12-15″] wide.
Climate: cool temperate.
Sowing to harvesting time: 2-3 months in summer, longer in winter.
Yield: about 10 plants per 3 m [10′] row.

To blanch endive, place inverted pot over plant. Plug up drainage holes.

If growing endive under cloches, cover them with black plastic sheeting.

The Batavian varieties are the tougher type of endive.

Curly leaved endives are more often sown for harvest in the autumn, but may be sown earlier for summer salads.

types are sown in midsummer so that they mature in late autumn and early winter.

Suitable site and soil

Soil which is light and well-drained is ideal for endives. Of all vegetables, endive appreciates a humus-enriched soil more than any other, although it can be grown, with more effort, on heavier land. In spring, work in handfuls of peat or leafmould on ground that was manured for a previous vegetable crop. Mix fertilizer into the soil about a week before sowing — hoof and horn meal at 60 g per sq m [2 oz per sq yd].

Sowing and transplanting

Do not sow all the seed at once, otherwise there will be a glut of seedlings and, inevitably, many will die. Draw V-shaped drills, spaced about 38 cm [15"] from each other, and sow the seed thinly, barely 1.5 cm [½"] deep. As endive thrives in firm soil, tread the drills or compact them with the back of a spade after sowing. Germination should occur about three days later; if it takes appreciably longer, it is better to resow, as the crop will otherwise be very likely to run to seed. Early thinnings can be transplanted, but it is worth noting that, like lettuces, the later that young endive plants are disturbed the greater the risk of failure when replanting. Plants need to be finally sited 30 cm [1'] apart.

Cultivation

Endive toughens rapidly if its roots are allowed to become dry. It may also bolt if transplanted without receiving plenty of water, so select a plot in dappled sunlight, free from gusty winds, preferably facing north or east, and water the plants liberally, especially during hot, dry periods. On light soil, keep the plants mulched with materials such as peat or garden compost during hot weather to retain all possible moisture. About halfway towards maturity, the plants can be given a weak solution of liquid fertilizer or manure water every 7 - 10 days.

Blanching

Blanching can be carried out only when the plants are absolutely dry, otherwise they are likely to rot. Cloche cultivation is essential for later-sown plants, once the weather starts to deteriorate in autumn. By late autumn the crinkled leaves of the staghorns will quickly suffer if not housed under cloches or a portable frame. It is pointless to begin the blanching process if the endive's foliage is coated with water. The cardinal rule is to cloche first and blanch later.

Blanching itself presents no problems. If you wish to whiten only the heart or centre leaves of your endives, simply place a saucer or plate over the top of each plant — this plan works well with the flatter, frilled varieties — and leave them for between two and three weeks under the cloches. Winter-maturing endives will need to be kept in the dark for twice as long. The most convenient method of blanching the inner leaves of Batavian varieties requires only lengths of raffia or some rubber bands. Gather the outside leaves together and tie them at the top to exclude the light from the centre of plants. In about a month the process should be complete.

A simple method for blanching whole plants is to cover them with clay pots, remembering to plug the drainage hole at the bottom so that the plants are in total darkness. If the plants are under cover, it is possible to cover the whole cloche or frame with black plastic sheeting and blanch them this way. Another good method is to lift some plants whole, put them into a box of soil, closely packed, and place the box in a dark cellar until they are blanched. By using these methods and by sowing in succession, it will be possible to have endive available to eat for most of the winter.

Whatever plan appeals to you, always cut the plants as soon as blanching is complete. Failure to do this could lead to heart rot.

Pests and diseases

Caterpillars and slugs may cause damage to the leaves, and you should watch out for mildew.

Fennel

**The swollen, blanched basal stems
are served as a vegetable, raw or braised.
The feathery aniseed-flavoured
leaves are used for flavouring like
the herb fennel.**

Florence fennel is a vegetable that was almost unknown outside Italy and the south of France until recently, when it was 'discovered' by holiday-makers. It is a variety of the common fennel, *Foeniculum vulgare*, which was valued by the Romans as a medicinal and culinary herb, the main difference, apart from the bulbous base, being the height — it is not so tall as common fennel. The haze of feathery, thread-like, blue-green leaves, and the golden-yellow flowers make it both a decorative and useful plant.

Suitable site and soil

As Florence fennel needs plenty of warmth at all times, it should be given a sunny, sheltered position, preferably against a wall. Soil should be well drained and fertile; add well-rotted farm manure or garden compost in the winter before planting at about a 10 L [2 gal] bucket per 5 sq m [6 sq yd] and mix it in thoroughly. Add lime as required, if a soil test shows the pH to be at all acid, applying at least 6 weeks after farm manure, never at the same time.

A light sandy soil which has been bulked up with lavish applications of organic matter will do very well, but a heavy clay is likely to give disappointing results.

Sowing and planting

It is vital that the seed-bed has several inches of fine-textured soil, and if there is any doubt about this, the addition of a 7.5 [3″] layer of seed compost is advisable. Two to three weeks before sowing, put cloches on the seed bed to warm up the soil, and about a week before sowing, mix a general compound fertilizer into the surface at the rate of about 30 g per sq m [1 oz per sq yd]. Lightly water the seed bed the day before sowing if no rain has occurred. Sow the seed thinly in mid to late spring, 0.5 cm [¼″] deep in drills 30 cm [1′] apart, and cover with soil. Protect with cloches during cold weather, especially at night, and thin the young plants to 20 cm [8″] apart.

Care and development

The plants should be kept well watered throughout the season, especially during dry weather, and a mulch of spent hops, peat, garden compost or a black plastic sheet will retain soil moisture; black plastic is particularly useful as it helps to warm up the soil. Keep the weeds down as required, and feed the plants when the base starts to thicken, overlap widely and swell, with 60 g per sq m [2 oz per sq yd] of a general fertilizer, applied when the soil is moist.

Blanching

Blanching makes the bulbous base more tender and removes any bitter taste; it is started when the base is about the size of an egg. Draw up the soil around the lower part of the stem to about three-quarters of its height.

Harvesting and storing the crop

Florence fennel is harvested about one month after starting to blanch, from mid summer onward, depending on the time of sowing. The leaves can be cut and used for

---

Florence fennel
Foeniculum vulgare dulce (fam. *Umbelliferae*) also known as Florentine fennel, finocchio, sweet fennel
Hardy annual.
Size: grows to about 60 cm [2′] tall.
Climate: warm temperate.
Sowing to harvesting time: about 18 weeks.
Yield: 15 plants per 3 m [10′] row.

The blanched, bulbous stem of Florence fennel is eaten raw or braised but does not keep long unless frozen.

flavouring from the time of flowering, or just before this. Unless it is put into a deep freeze, the bulbous base of Florence fennel cannot be stored for very long, however the leaves can be dried in the same way as herbs, though they are not likely to be as aromatic as the fresh foliage. If late sowings were made, crops which were intended to mature in late autumn and early winter should be protected against frost with bracken or straw.

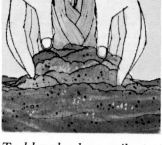

Black plastic sheets keep soil warm and moisture in.

To blanch, draw soil up round base when egg-sized.

Fennel

Fennel is grown for its leaf stalks and seeds which are often used to complement fish.

Fennel (*Foeniculum vulgare*) is a very handsome, upright perennial herb with branching, hollow stems. Fresh or dried, the leaves are used as a flavouring, or in a sauce, to accompany fish. An infusion made from the leaves is soothing to inflamed or strained eyes, and fennel tea is famous for suppressing hunger in weight-watchers. The seeds may also be used with fish, or in the same ways as dill seeds.

The fine, thread-like, dark green leaves have a licorice flavour. The plant grows about 1.5-1.8 m [5-6'] high and 60 cm [2'] across and from midsummer to early autumn bears yellow umbels of flowers which produce a large quantity of seeds. It will cross-pollinate easily with dill, so should never be grown near it, as plants grown from the resultant seed will not have a distinctive flavour of either.

Cultivation

Choose a sunny position at the back of a border, since the

The sprays of the herb golden fennel are attractive and aromatic. They are used fresh or dried for flavouring.

plants grow so tall. Fennel will grow in any good, well drained, deep soil. Fork the growing area well to break up the subsoil, incorporating peat or well-rotted compost.

Sow the seeds outside in mid spring 0.5 cm [¼"] deep, in rows 45 cm [1½'] apart. Germination will take 2-3 weeks. When the seedlings have produced a central, feathery leaf, thin to 45-60 cm [1½-2'] apart.

Harvesting and aftercare

Water regularly and well until the plants are established and keep the rows free from weeds. In exposed areas, stake the plant. After four to six weeks the young leaves may be harvested until the flower buds show. If seeds are not required the heads should be removed to encourage leaf growth. When seeds are required leave the first flowers on. They will start to appear from midsummer. Harvest when the seeds start to turn brown. Hang the seed-heads over paper in a dry place and store them in an air-tight container after they have dropped.

The top growth will die down in autumn, but unless the winter is severely cold, the plants will survive then sprout again the following spring. Otherwise, for winter use, you can remove the flower stems and divide the roots in early autumn. Put into pots and keep them indoors or under glass.

Fig

This brown or purplish, pear-shaped fruit is peeled for its delicious pink interior, and is best eaten raw straight off the tree. There are also greenish-yellow varieties with white flesh. Figs grown in the garden are almost seedless.

The family *Ficus* includes the well-known rubber plant *Ficus elastica*. The fruiting species *carica* is one of the oldest fruits known, mentioned in the Bible. Originating in western Asia, it is widely cultivated in the Mediterranean. The fruit does not transport well, so commercial figs are usually dried and are full of seeds, but the garden varieties are relatively seedless. Figs contain 50% sugar when dried, while syrup of figs is well known as a laxative.

Botanically the fig is a curiosity because there are no visible flowers; the buds swell to develop straight into the fruit. The fruit is actually made up of a collection of many flowers within the skin and some varieties require pollination, but the Adriatic fig is self-fertile. The fruit is about 5 cm [2"] long, while leaves may be from 10-20 cm [4-8"] long and are hand-shaped with three or five lobes.

Figs can stand quite low temperatures — probably as low as 11°C [52°F] — when dormant, provided the temperature drops slowly. A sudden big drop will do more damage. Any frost when growth has started will cause serious damage. Frost-damaged wood may be cut to the ground but the tree will re-establish itself again by means of suckers.

If planted in good soil, growth will be rank and soft so, to get the ripe wood that bears fruit, it is necessary to restrict root growth.

In warm climates with a short period of dormancy, three crops will ripen. In sheltered parts of cool temperate areas one crop will ripen if it gets plenty of summer sun. In a greenhouse two crops will be secured, but for three extra heat, up to 27°C [80°F], will be needed in late winter. This is not advised as it may be at the expense of the following year's crop.

Suitable site and soil

In sheltered parts of cool temperate areas, trees can be trained against a wall facing the midday sun. Ideally, the wall should be 2 m [8'] high and at least 4.5 m [15'] across. If lower, it should be at least 5 m [18'] across. In a warm corner, for instance the angle of two walls, a bush will succeed. Figs like well-drained chalky soil; a medium to light loam with some sand is suitable. If the soil is at all acid add enough lime so that a soil test gives a pH of 7-7.5. Then fill in with soil, putting the topsoil back last. About two weeks before planting, add 60 g [2 oz] of bone meal and mix in well.

Planting

To restrict the root development, dig a hole at least 1 m [3'] square and the same depth. Line the sides with brick

---

Fig
Ficus carica (fam. *Moraceae*)
Hardy deciduous tree growing to 9 m [30'] in a natural state, but confined as a bush to 3-3.6 m high by 2.5 m wide [10-12' x 8'] or 3 x 4.5 m [10' x 15'] as a fan. Fig trees have a very long life, up to several centuries.
Climate: warm temperate.
Yield: a 1.2 m [4'] pot-grown tree will produce 2 dozen fruit, an outdoor tree or indoor fan 6 kg [13 lb] of fruit for a first crop and half that for a second.

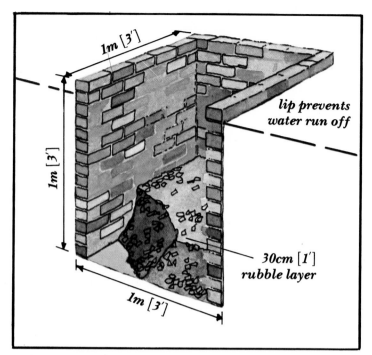

1m [3']

1m [3']

1m [3']

lip prevents
water run off

30cm [1']
rubble layer

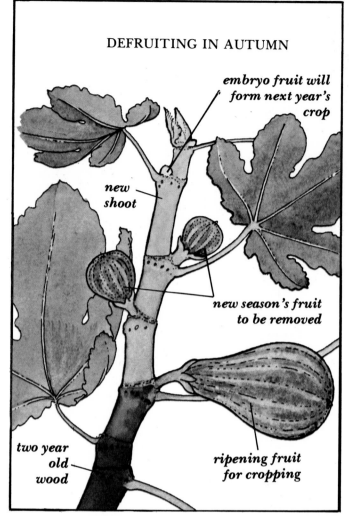

DEFRUITING IN AUTUMN

embryo fruit will
form next year's
crop

new
shoot

new season's fruit
to be removed

two year
old
wood

ripening fruit
for cropping

The roots of the fig tree must be confined, otherwise it grows too large and will not fruit. Rather than root pruning, prepare a walled pit like this before planting.

In the autumn when harvesting the ripe figs on a tree outdoors, also pick any other fruit which is already recognizable as a fig. Only the embryo buds at the very tips of the shoots will survive and ripen next year.

(Below) In cool areas fig trees can be fan-trained on a sunny wall, where they will be protected and crop well.

or concrete and put a 30 cm [1′] layer of broken brick or rubble at the bottom for drainage. If you do not do this, you will have to prune the roots regularly.

Trees are best planted in early spring. Those from nurseries are usually two years old and container grown. Plant like other fruit trees (*see* APPLE), spreading out the roots and firming the soil thoroughly after replacing. Watering is particularly important against a wall. A mulch of rotted manure or moist peat will help retain moisture.

Care and development

Little watering is required until growth starts, then a good soaking every four days or so, increasing to every other day in the height of summer until the fruit is nearly ripe, will be necessary for fully grown trees. After the first year, feed with a good balanced fertilizer at the rate of 60 g per sq m [2 oz per sq yd] of the area to which the roots extend, in early spring. If the drainage is too good, a second feed will be required in early summer. Mulching in late spring, or after the second feed if needed, with rotted manure or garden compost will help to retain moisture.

A fan can be developed along the same lines as a peach (*see* PEACH). Train young shoots up and along the wall as they develop, pinching out any not required. Extension growth is always from terminal buds, so as many ripe one- and two-year-old shoots with undamaged tips as possible should be tied in. Therefore, two or three of the oldest bare branches on each side of the fan can be shortened in winter to a suitably placed dormant bud at a joint, and new growth will appear from the cut-back shoot, lower down, in spring.

Disbudding the fruit

The fig bears its fruit at the tips of the shoots and simultaneously carries fruit singly or in pairs, at different stages of development on one and two-year-old wood. Out-of-doors in a cool temperate climate only fruit which has been started the year before has a chance of ripening.

During the summer fruit is formed in the axils of the new leaves, but those lower down the stem become too large and tender to pass undamaged through the winter; fruit which can be discerned as such in autumn is best removed. This stimulates the production of the embryo fruit at the very tip of the shoots; these will survive the winter to ripen in late summer or autumn the following year.

In the greenhouse

If the house gets plenty of sun, and artificial heat can be supplied in late winter, two crops can be obtained in the year, ripening in early summer and early to mid autumn. The temperature should be increased to 13-15°C [55-60°F] in late winter, soil watering should be started, and the house kept humid as the new leaves start to unfold, by damping down and syringing the foliage daily.

As with outdoor figs, the root growth should be restricted and similar soil provided. The tree should be watered moderately until growth is fully under way, and then as for outdoor plants, though in really hot summer weather twice daily waterings may be needed. When the first crop of

There are many varieties of common fig; colours range from dark purple or black to a pale greenish white.

GROWING FIGS IN POTS

Fig trees are well suited to pot growing; root restriction helps crops.

Mound up earth, spread roots and use trowel to firm soil between them.

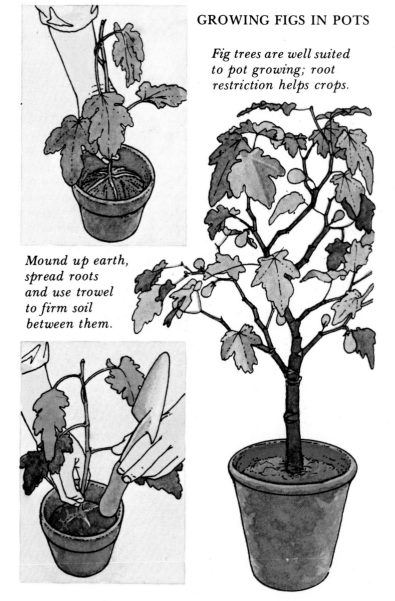

fruit starts to colour, give about half as much water until the crop is picked. Topdress with rotted manure or garden compost in early spring, and feed every week with a liquid fertilizer when the fruit starts to swell. Prune as for outdoor trees, but do not remove the well-developed figs as these will provide the autumn crop. In winter keep the tree moist.

Pot growing

Pot grown trees can be used outdoors or in the greenhouse. A 25-30 cm [10-12"] pot is large enough and will support a bush of about 1.5 m [5'] and with good crops. As the roots cannot spread, a richer compost can be used. Planting the tree is as shown in the diagrams, while for repotting and root pruning instructions, *see* CITRUS FRUIT. Water and feed like a greenhouse tree. In early autumn pinch out the growing tips at six to eight leaves to ensure new wood gets ripe before dormancy.

Ideally, trees should be repotted each autumn, trimming the roots to leave 2.5 cm [1"] or so between them and the pot wall, and using the same size pot. Alternatively in the second year as much compost as possible can be removed from the top and replaced with a fresh supply.

Little water is required while the trees are dormant, but regular and frequent watering will be needed once they start growing.

If a crop is large or if watering has leached out fertilizer, topdressing will be required about early summer, as well as the spring feed. You can add further compost around the edge of the pot, leaving a hole around the trunk, or feed with a balanced fertilizer at the rate of 30 g [1 oz] per pot, with a second application three weeks later.

Harvesting

The flavour does not develop until full ripeness, when the fruit droops and cracks slightly, usually producing a small drop of moisture at the eye. Ripe fruit are very soft and thin-skinned. Handle them by the stalk only to avoid bruising.

Propagation

Figs can be increased by cuttings of short jointed shoots about 30 cm [1'] long with three buds of wood from the previous year at the bottom. Insert half the shoot into a peat/sand mixture in early spring, preferably with bottom heat. They root readily and will be ready to pot up in early summer.

In early summer, strong young shoots can be layered by pegging into the soil with the tip turned up and exposed (*see* BLACKBERRY). They should have rooted enough to plant in the autumn.

Pests and diseases

In warmer climates, figs can be seriously infected with virus spotting of the leaves, but in cooler areas this is never serious. The most common pest is scale; as soon as this is seen, spray with malathion, with a second spray two weeks later. Red spider mite is another pest and, in the greenhouse, airless and humid conditions may lead to canker. Affected branches should be cut off and burnt.

French Beans

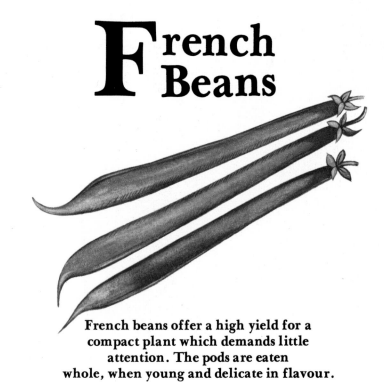

French beans offer a high yield for a compact plant which demands little attention. The pods are eaten whole, when young and delicate in flavour.

Originating in South America, these beans were popularized by the French. Called kidney beans in some countries, in others this refers to a specific type.

French beans are an ideal crop for a small area. Most varieties are of dwarf or bush type which, when grown 23 cm [9"] apart in rows, form a dense canopy of large leaves beneath which the bean pods, 7.5-12 cm [3-5"] long, hang. There are, however, a few climbing varieties which need the support of poles. The flowers are typically leguminous, or butterfly-like, and are usually white, red or pink. The pods are long, rather slender and with an almost circular cross-section. They should be picked while still young and tender and cooked whole.

Of the many varieties of French beans some of the most interesting are those which have pods of different colours from the ordinary green. One of the most popular has wax-skinned yellow pods and is known as a waxpod. There are also mottled red and white and indigo blue pod types.

Other well-known varieties belonging to the same bean species are haricots and flageolets, known in the United States as French horticultural beans. Treatment of the crops up to harvest is exactly the same as for other varieties, but flageolets are picked when the beans are fully formed in the pods, although the pods are still soft and

(Right) The most common varieties of French bean have tapering green pods; flowers are white, red or pink.

French bean
Phaseolus vulgaris (fam. *Leguminosae*) also known as snap bean and string bean.
Size: 15-20 cm [6-10"] high, 10-15 cm [4-6"] across.
Climate: warm temperate
Sowing to harvesting time: 8-11 weeks.
Yield: 1-1.3 kg [2-3 lb] per 3 m [10'] row.

green. Haricot beans are harvested when the seeds are fully ripe and have dried in their pods. Both flageolet and haricot beans are grown for their seeds alone, the pods being discarded. Both are, more exclusively than ordinary French beans, vegetables of warm temperate climates, which require longer, warmer summers than is normal in cool temperate countries.

Suitable site and soil

French beans do best in a sunny situation. They will grow in almost any soil, but prefer one that is not too heavy. A heavy soil can be lightened by working in peat, garden compost or coarse sand. They like plenty of nourishment, so you should add garden compost, farmyard manure or chemical fertilizers.

Sowing

Sow outdoors in late spring, after all danger from frost is past. French beans cannot tolerate even slight frost when young. They also need reasonable warmth — about 16°C [60°F] — in the soil to germinate.

In cool temperate climates gardeners often acquire more growing time and produce earlier crops by starting the beans under cloches. There are, in fact, three alternative programmes for sowing French beans: 1. sow outdoors in rows 30 cm [1'] apart, after the last frost date, at a depth of 5 cm [2"]; 2. sow under cloches about the date of the last expected frost, at a depth of about 2.5 cm [1"]; 3. sow in boxes or pots in a greenhouse, four to six weeks before the last expected frost date.

Planting

The bean plants brought on indoors should be transplanted outdoors after the last frost date. Those under cloches may also be transplanted, though the more usual plan is to remove the cloches when no further frosts are expected. When transplanting, keep a ball of soil around the roots and water well.

After the first sowing or transplanting, sow a succession of crops, about one per month, until about a month after midsummer.

Care and development

French beans need to be well fed and well watered. The watering should be frequent so that the plants never experience a check to their growth. You should hoe frequently, not only to keep weeds under control but also to keep the soil broken up. In dry weather some soils, especially if watered by hose or watering-can, form a crust which, if undisturbed, will considerably decrease the yield. Small doses of liquid manure can be given but take care to keep this clear of the foliage.

The dwarf varieties of French beans do not normally require any support, except when they are grown in a position exposed to strong winds. A few short twiggy sticks can then help to prop them up. The climbing varieties need the support of tall rods or canes around which they will twine in the same way as runner beans. Erect one rod or cane per plant; these should be about 2 m [6½'] high after they have been pushed well into the ground. The framework consists of a line of pairs of rods or canes strad-

Given a sunny site and plenty of food and water, beans will produce a harvest within three months of sowing.

When cooked, the tender, stringless pods of this climbing variety change from purple to green.

Among less well-known types of bean are the wax-pod varieties with yellow pods and black seeds.

French bean

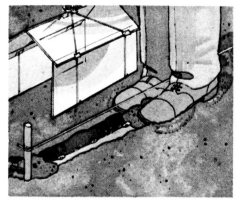

Sow seed 2.5 cm [1"] deep and firm with feet. Protect with cloches.

Use short twigs to support dwarf varieties against strong winds.

Regular weeding with an onion hoe also helps keep the soil loose.

When flowers appear, spray plants to encourage pod formation.

Mulch with garden compost or peat to keep the soil moist.

Harvest with scissors, as pulling by hand can uproot the whole plant.

OBTAINING HARICOT BEANS

Lift plants when pods are yellow and hang up to dry in an airy room.

The beans can be shelled when the leaves are shrivelled and brittle. Store the dried beans in glass jars with loose-fitting lids.

Spread the shelled beans on trays and dry in a well-ventilated room. Pale green haricot beans fresh from the pod turn cream when dried.

dling the axis of the row, not less than 50 cm [1½'] apart at soil level.

Harvesting

The beans are ready for picking from 8 to 11 weeks after sowing. Once the pods have started to form, check them every day, for they mature very quickly. On no account allow them to stay on the plant too long. Test a pod by snapping it across the middle. If just right, it should break cleanly and show no stringy fibres. The beans inside the pod will not have expanded to their full size.

When picking, do so carefully, using the nails of thumb and fingers, or cut the beans from the plants with scissors or a knife. Do not pull them off forcibly or the whole plant, which is shallow-rooted, is likely to come out of the ground. Once picking has begun, continue daily.

French beans are best eaten fresh and cooked on the day of picking. They are also excellent for deep freezing. Apart from that, however, they do not store well.

Aftercare

It is possible to harvest a second smaller crop from the same plants. Apply a light dressing of a compound chemical fertilizer at an approximate rate of 60 g per sq m [2 oz per sq yd] to the soil, a hand's width away from the plants, and hoe in well. Water generously.

Late-sown crops may not produce their pods before the threat of autumn frosts, in which case cover the rows with cloches to prolong the harvesting season to the beginning of winter. When cropping is over, cut off the dead or dying foliage but leave the roots in the ground. As with all leguminous crops, French beans will increase the nitrogen-content of the soil as they decay, to the benefit of subsequent nitrogen-hungry plants, such as brassicas, in a crop rotation system.

Pests and diseases

Two measures should be taken as soon as the beans are sown outdoors. One is to protect them by a network of black cotton or a nylon-meshed net, to ward off birds which scratch up the seedling plants as fast as they emerge. The other is to sprinkle slug bait around the rows. Slugs attack the swelling bean seed even before the first shoot has emerged and then eat the young foliage.

As slugs are particularly fond of the young pods, they are most likely to eat the pods in contact with the ground, so use twigs to prevent the plants being blown over.

Anthracnose of French beans *(Colletotrichum lindemuthianum)* is a fungus disease. Characterized by blackish-brown spots on foliage and pods, it is fostered by cool, wet summers. Usually the disease is seed-borne, and reputable merchants ensure that their seed is free from it, but it can develop on unburied vegetable debris.

Fusarium wilt, which results in bean plants wilting and decaying, is another fungus disease caused by a lack of proper crop rotation. Other diseases which may occur are grey mould *(Botrytis cinerea)* and *Rhizoctonia* — little can be done once an attack has developed, but proprietary chemicals can be worked into the soil, just before sowing or transplanting, as a precaution.

Garlic

The garlic bulb has a powerful aroma. One of the most distinctive and popular of all flavourings, garlic is an essential ingredient in many international dishes.

Garlic, *Allium sativum*, a member of the onion family *Alliaceae,* is a perennial herb grown as an annual for the cloves contained inside the bulb. A clove or two of garlic gives an intense flavour and aroma to an enormous variety of dishes, many associated with the Mediterranean. Garlic can be crushed or finely chopped before it is added to dishes, but often it is enough to just cut the bulb in half and rub it around the inside of the cooking or serving dish. In folklore it was a charm against evil — thought to absorb and overpower anything unclean.

Garlic is thought to have come from central Asia, from where it spread to the Mediterranean. The Romans were probably the first to introduce garlic to other parts of Europe, and today it grows virtually everywhere. Because it is so simple to grow and easy to store, garlic presents welcome relief to the busy gardener and encouragement to the beginner.

The bulb is covered in several layers of papery white skin and contains up to 20 cloves concentrically arranged inside and each wrapped. Garlic bulbs average 4-7.5 cm [1½-3"] in both diameter and height though bulbs 20 cm [8"] wide are not unknown. A clove of garlic, roughly 2 cm [¾"] long, is rounded on one side, flat on the other and pointed at the top.

Cultivation

If you have a bulb of fresh garlic at hand, simply plant the cloves from that. Otherwise, order cloves from your seedsman. Plant garlic in mid autumn; if severe frosts are unlikely, in early or mid spring, in a sunny window box or the herb section of the garden. Garlic likes a rich, sandy loam, and it is a good idea to mix in rotted garden compost some weeks before planting and an application of 60 g per sq m [2 oz per sq yd] of bonemeal a week or so before planting.

Rake the surface down finely and place the clove about

5 cm [2″] deep, base down and tip pointing upward, so that there is 2.5 cm [1″] of soil on top of the tip. Allow 15 cm [6″] between each clove and 30 cm [1′] between the rows if you plant more than one. You will get the best results if you use the largest cloves from the outside of the bulb, particularly if you plant in autumn. If planted in autumn, give a mid spring dressing of 15 g per sq m [½ oz per sq yd] of sulphate of ammonia and another in early summer of a potash-high fertilizer. For spring-sown bulbs, only give the potash dressing.

Hoe weeds out as they appear. Garlic is rarely prey to pests or diseases which trouble the onion family.

Harvesting and storing

Garlic produces leaves, and, like other members of the onion family, a white or red-tinted flower or a leafless stem 30 cm [1′] or more tall. When the leaves begin to wither and turn yellow, usually from late summer to early autumn, dig the bulbs out of the soil carefully with a fork; do not pull. After lifting, let the bulbs dry in the sun for a few days, covering them at night to protect them from dew. When completely dry, clean off any soil and loose skins and take the bulbs inside to a frost-free shed or room. Bunch the bulbs together by tying the stems with raffia or string and then set out in trays, or string the bulbs for hanging on the wall by braiding or plaiting them, weaving the tops with the string. They will last a year or more.

rough knobbly or prickly surfaces, and should be picked when young. They are pickled in boiling vinegar after being soaked in brine.

Wild gherkins, *Cucumis anguria* (fam. *Cucurbitaceae*) are weeds of the damp regions of the West Indies and of tropical and sub-tropical America. They have deeply five-lobed leaves and small fruits, 2.5-7.5 cm [1-3″] long, with prickly surfaces. The immature fruits are used for pickling, mainly in the United States.

For cultivation *see* CUCUMBER.

Good King Henry

Good King Henry is a very hardy perennial vegetable, valued in old English kitchens for its nutritious spinach-like leaves. The stems can be blanched like asparagus.

Although Good King Henry is cultivated as a vegetable, it is the medicinal herb called mercury when found growing wild. A member of the goosefoot family *Chenopodium,* it is distinguished by its name from 'Bad Henry' the weed, *Mercurialis annua.* The leaves have a characteristic triangular shape, and the green flowers have extraordinarily long stigmas. The natural habitat includes large areas of Europe, Asia, and North America.

Gherkin

Gherkins belong to the cucumber family. The small rough-skinned fruits make a very tasty pickle.

'Gherkin' is the Slavonic name for cucumber. Some small varieties of ridge cucumber, *Cucumis sativus* (fam. *Cucurbitaceae*) are known as gherkins when pickled. They are usually thick, small to medium-sized cucumbers, with

---

Good King Henry
Chenopodium bonus-henricus
(fam. *Chenopodiaceae*) also known as mercury, Lincolnshire spinach, poor man's asparagus.
Hardy perennial.
Size: grows to 30-60 cm [1-2′] tall.
Climate: cool temperate.
Sowing to harvesting time: 4 months.
Yield: 2.3 kg [5 lb] per 3 m [10′] row per season.

The vegetable does best in a rich, well-manured soil; although it will tolerate a poor, dry soil, the yield should not be expected to be nearly so high per plant.

Cultivation and harvesting

If propagating from seed, sow outside in mid spring. You may also sow indoors in trays for transplanting out when the soil is more easily worked. Spring temperatures of about 15°C [60°F] give the best chances of speedy germination. Place the young plants well apart, or sprinkle the seeds and later thin to about 25 cm [10"].

Since Good King Henry is a semi-wild herb, it needs less treatment than most food crops. Nevertheless, it will benefit from feeds of diluted liquid fertilizer and frequent watering during the summer on light, well-drained soils.

Take the broad, triangular green leaves in summer, without stripping a whole plant, and use in a similar way to spinach. The firm, fleshy shoots that grow from the leaf axils can also be eaten — these bear young green leaves and end in embryo flower buds. They can be used like sprouting broccoli, or like asparagus, if they are first blanched. Cut back the stems in late autumn and cover the roots with bracken or straw. The covering provides protection and blanches the shoots for use in spring. Stop cutting shoots after early summer to allow the plant to build itself up again, as for asparagus. Once you have raised a crop of Good King Henry from seed, propagate by planting pieces of the base of the stem with roots attached.

Triangular green leaves and unusually long stigmas are the distinctive characteristics of this semi-wild herb.

Deservedly popular, the fruit of the red gooseberry are excellent for cooking, canning and bottling.

Gooseberry

The familiar gooseberry is hairy and yellowish green, although there are creamy and reddish pink varieties. The flesh is juicy with many pips.

Native to Europe, the gooseberry is closely related to currants. The bush is encouraged to grow on a single short stem like a miniature tree and is very spiny. Gooseberries are the earliest of the soft fruit to crop at the beginning of the summer. There are a a good many varieties differing in size and colour. All are suitable for eating raw when really ripe, for cooking and jam making, though for bottling and canning some are particularly suitable.

The Worcesterberry is thought to be a cross between a gooseberry and a blackcurrant. The bush is tall like a blackcurrant but spiny with dark gooseberry-like fruit.

Suitable site and soil

Shelter from frost and cold spring winds is important. The flowers appear in mid spring and are very susceptible to frost, while wind prevents helpful pollinating insects from doing their work, and means that the fruit set is poor. Make sure you do not plant in frost pockets.

Gooseberries like a medium textured, well-drained loamy soil which retains summer moisture. They are more fussy than other bush fruits; light soils do not suit them, and only certain varieties do well on clay. They make deep 'sinker' roots in clay soil and a mass of fibrous, food-absorbing roots in the top few centimetres.

Planting

Gooseberries can be grown as bushes, cordons and standards. Cordons may be single or double stemmed, carrying fruiting spurs, and are often trained against wires or fences. A standard is supplied on a 1.5 m [5′] high stem with the head already formed.

Autumn is the best planting time but any time during the winter when the soil is workable is satisfactory. Bushes are usually sold as two or three-year old plants and are planted 1.5 m [5′] apart. Cordons are planted at about 30 cm [1′] apart if they are single and 75 cm [2½′] if they are double.

Prepare the site by eliminating all perennial weeds. Then dig garden compost into the top 23 cm [9″] at about one barrowload per 9-11 sq m [10-12 sq yd] before planting. Holes must be big enough to take the roots in comfort, and firm planting, to the same depth that the bush was in the nursery, is essential. The surface should be left lightly scuffed; if it is trodden, rain may lie in puddles.

Plants usually arrive from the nursery already pruned to the third bud from the base of each branch. If this has not been done, you should do it immediately after planting.

Cordons must be supported by a bamboo cane driven in behind them, to which they are tied and trained, and standards will also need staking.

Feeding and mulching

Mulch annually in spring with a barrowload of garden

---

compost or rotted farm manure per 9-11 sq m [10-12 sq yd]. This conserves soil moisture, provides a permanent supply of essential organic matter, and suppresses annual weeds. There is firm evidence that the root mass is greater by some 20-30% under a mulch than under bare soil, which means bigger and more productive bushes. Any perennial weeds that appear are more easily pulled out from mulched soil.

With organic cultivation little fertilizer is normally needed. Sulphate of potash at about 20 g per sq m [¾ oz per sq yd] in late summer should be all that the bushes will require, and not necessarily every year. But this dressing must be given if there are signs of potash deficiency, when leaves will have brown-grey margins and tend to curl downward.

Pruning

Bushes will consist of 10-12 main branches eventually, grown from a single short stem 15-23 cm [6-9″] long. On these, fruiting spurs will be formed by routine pruning. The main branches are cut back hard in the early years, to buds on the lower surfaces if the growth is upward, or to upper surface buds if the habit is drooping. The object of this is encourage strong branch extensions with an open centre, in order to build up a sturdy framework capable of producing many side shoots for fruit spur formation. In the second, third and possibly fourth years, the shoots chosen to form the main framework should be cut back in winter by about one half to two-thirds, to encourage strong growth. In the third and subsequent years, the side shoots are cut back in late summer to just above the fifth leaf, and again in winter, to the third leaf, from the base of the shoot.

The tips of the main branches are also pruned in winter cutting back the new growth to leave about 10 cm [4″] of it. This method induces fruit spurs along the branches, and results in really large berries. Cordons and standards are spur pruned in exactly the same way. Bushes fruit on the previous season's growth.

A simpler system allows the berries to form directly on the main branches instead of on induced spurs. Branches are left to fruit for two or three years and are then cut out completely. This encourages new shoots to grow from the top of the leg, as replacements. Fewer sideshoots appear with this method; those that do are ignored if they are short, or just snipped back if long. The right sequence gives branches in fruit and new ones taking over, ensuring a steady continuity of crop. Congestion must be avoided; allow a hand's span between fruiting branches and always remove weak branches, and any which are crossing or crowding the centre.

Harvesting and propagation

Varieties in general can be picked over early in the season for cooking purposes. This encourages maximum development of the main crop if it is done systematically, to leave retained berries evenly spaced.

New bushes are propagated from the new shoots in early to mid autumn. Well ripened lengths about 23 cm [9″] long, have all buds removed except for the top four and are

---

> **Gooseberry**
> *Ribes grossularia* (fam. *Grossulariaceae*)
> **Hardy deciduous bush** with a cropping life of up to 15 years.
> **Size:** 1 m [3′] high and 1.2-1.5 m [4-5′] wide.
> **Climate:** cool to warm temperate.
> **Planting to harvesting time:** 2-3 years.
> **Yield:** 3-6 kg [6-12 lb] per bush.

(*Above*) Three or four gooseberry bushes should produce enough fruit for the average family.

(*Left*) Standards have the variety grafted on to the rootstock; the wooden supports on either side hold up the branches.

(*Right*) To propagate, remove all but top four buds. Put in fine soil trench in early to mid autumn with all the buds clear of the ground.

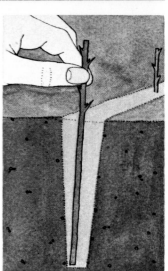

PRUNING THE GOOSEBERRY BUSH

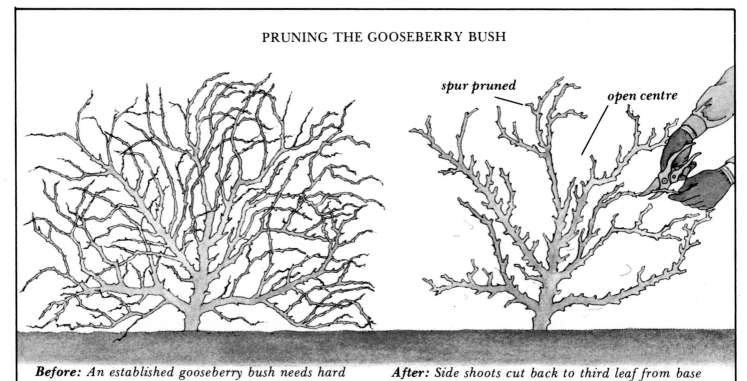

spur pruned

open centre

Before: An established gooseberry bush needs hard pruning in winter, as well as a lighter summer one.

After: Side shoots cut back to third leaf from base and new growth at tips of main branches shortened.

inserted some 15 cm [6"] apart, with all the buds above ground, into friable soil. The following winter the young bushes should be ready to transplant into their permanent quarter. Layers can also be used, in summer, and these root very readily.

Pests and diseases

The principal fungus disease is American gooseberry mildew. This shows as a dense, white powdery fungus on the under surface of leaves, and on shoots in spring and later on berries. On the shoots it becomes brown and felty. Cut out infected shoots as soon as seen, back to healthy growth, and spray with dinocap or a systemic fungicide, repeating as the makers instruct. Remove infected berries and take particular care to prune out felted shoots in winter, and burn them.

European gooseberry mildew shows as white patches also, but on the upper surface of leaves. Treat as for American mildew, and collect up fallen laves, on which it can over winter.

Gooseberry sawfly caterpillars can strip bushes of every leaf, and three generations may occur in a season, the first in mid spring. They are easily controlled with liquid derris sprayed thoroughly all over the bushes as soon as the newly hatched caterpillars are seen. Hand picking maybe sufficient. Other pests are greenfly, capsids, red spider mite and birds. If birds have pecked out the winter buds, attacked branches should be cut back to the first strong bud which still remains and is suitably placed. Occasionally die-back of shoots will occur and this must be removed.

Grape

These luscious creamy white, green or black fruit may be eaten raw as dessert, pressed for their juice (which is fermented for wine) or dried to make raisins, sultanas or currants.

The grape vine is one of the oldest fruit-bearing plants. Records show it was known to the Egyptians. It appears to be native to Southern Russia, near the Black Sea. Carried by conquering Greeks and Romans, it has spread to most temperate regions of the world.

Vines climb by means of coiling, forked tendrils produced opposite two out of every three leaves. The leaves grow on long stalks and are hand-shaped with toothed edges, 7.5-23 cm [3-9"] long. When the vine is kept short by pruning, it develops a stout stem. The fruit is creamy white, or green, both classified as white, or dark red to blue-black with a blue bloom. Flesh is always greenish; it is the inclusion of the dark skin that gives red wine its colour.

The genus includes about 60 species, most of them native to America. The fox grape, *V. labrusca*, and the muscadine, *V. rotundifolia*, both produce fruit with a musky flavour. When American vines were first introduced into Europe, they brought with them the aphid *Phylloxera vitifoliae* causing devastation. Resistant American rootstocks were then imported and in many countries, though not in Britain, *vinifera* is grown on *Phylloxera* resistant roots. Happily *vinifera* was introduced into California, where it is now the main wine grape, without problems.

Vinifera grapes need cool winters and long dry summers with plenty of sun for successful ripening of the wood and to convert the acid in the fruit into sugar. The vine is hardier than the fig; it can stand moderate amounts of frost in a dormant state, down to $-12°C$ [$10°F$], but spring frosts occurring after growth has started will kill the shoots. Nor does it like humid summers, though the related American varieties *V. labrusca* and *V. rotundifolia* withstand humidity better.

Grapes are grouped by the uses to which they are put. There are about 8000 varieties of grape and the juice of all of them can be fermented but only a few are selected for growing for wine. Dessert grapes need to have a high sugar content and low acidity. Wine grapes need a balance of acidity and sugar, and in addition need some individuality to lend character to the resulting wine.

The grapes used for wine making can be divided into four main groups. The wines called white burgundy and

> **Grape**
> Most important is *Vitis vinifera* (fam. *Vitaceae*) but also American varieties from *V. labrusca, V. rotundifolia,* and *V. vulpina.*
> **Deciduous vine,** with a long life of several centuries.
> **Size:** growing to 27 m [60'] in the wild, but in cultivation kept to 3.5-5 m [12-16'] by the long rod method, and 1.5 m [5'] wide by 1.2 m [4'] high by the double Guyot method.
> **Climate:** warm temperate to sub-tropical.
> **Planting to harvesting time:** 2 years.
> **Yield:** one long rod will give 10-12 bunches of dessert grapes indoors; the double Guyot will give 2.5-5 kg [5-10 lb] of fruit per plant and this will yield up to 3 L [6 pt] of wine. Grapes on a wall may yield up to 90 kg [200 lb] of fruit.

(Facing page) 'Black Hamburg' grapes in a cold house.

(Left) A fine crop growing on part of established vine.

champagne, named for districts in France, are both made from the same small yellowish green fruit, the Chardonnay or Pineau Blanc. Pineau Noir is a purplish black grape, and makes a rich heavy red wine called burgundy, named for the French town. This has proved popular in California. The claret grape is Cabernet, which is bluish black and produces the light red wine of Bordeaux in France; the grape is another that has been a success in America. White wine grapes are often grouped together as Riesling grapes, and give us the wine known in Britain as hock.
Raisins are black wine grapes dried in the sun for a month, therefore varieties for this purpose must mature early. Sultanas are smaller, from white grapes, and usually seedless. Currants are the smallest of all and come from smaller, black fruited varieties. Grapes can also be made into jam and jellies.

Suitable site and soil
Grapes can be grown successfully out-of-doors in cool temperate areas, provided you choose suitable varieties. In colder parts they are best grown on a wall facing the mid-day sun. They can be grown on a specially erected wire fence, preferably on a gentle slope, running from north to south, or on fences, house porches or walls. If they are trained on low wires, they can be given the protection of cloches. Grapes are very suitable for the greenhouse and the finest dessert grapes are greenhouse grown. In warm temperate areas they can also be trained on pergolas (*see* diagram in CHINESE GOOSEBERRY).
Grapes will thrive on a wide range of soils, but a deep medium textured loam, preferably over a chalk or gravel subsoil, is the ideal. Add lime if need be to bring the pH level up to about 6.0-6.5.

GROWING BY THE PERMANENT ROD METHOD
For growing in the greenhouse, for pillars and pergolas outdoors, the permanent rod and spur system is generally preferred. By this method one stem is allowed to extend to the full length of the space to be filled, and gradually thickens, while pruning maintains a constant supply of fruiting spurs. For walls a variant of the permanent rod, trained to fit the available space with more horizontal wood, is best. When ordering plants, specify a stem or cane about 1.8 m [6'] long, in pots.

Suitable greenhouse sites
Grapes may be grown in a very small greenhouse. The roots may either be planted in a well-prepared border within the house, or be planted outside. The rod or cane is then passed through a prepared hole in the wall, to fruit under glass (*see* diagram). In a small house, the rod is passed through the end wall, goes upright as high as the ridge and then passes horizontally along the length of the ridge of the house, some 45 cm [1½'] below the glass.

(Left) Riesling grapes are grown for making white wine.

In a three-quarter span or full span house the rods are trained from the floor up under the sloping glass to within 45 cm [1½'] of the ridge. Plant two vines 1.2-1.5 m [4-5'] apart and let each one bear one rod. If each vine bears two rods, then plant 1.8-2.1 m [6-7'] apart. In a lean-to house, used for other plants (but not tomatoes or cucumbers), plant one vine for each 3m [10'] and train horizontally with spur pruning.

Wire the glass horizontally at 30 cm [1'] intervals by screwing vine eyes (long spikes with eyeholes) into the greenhouse framework and threading wires through them. They should be 45 cm [1½'] from the glass. These wires support the main rod and eventually take a lot of weight.

Planting in the greenhouse

Good drainage is essential to vines. In the greenhouse border you will do best to dig out the soil to 75cm [2½'] depth and fill the bottom 15-23 cm [6-9"] with rubble. Return the soil, mixing with it two 12 L [2½ gal] buckets of rotted manure and 125 g [4 oz] of bonemeal per plant.

Training a permanent rod

The best time to plant is late autumn. Spread the roots out well, plant at the same depth as in the pot, and water each vine well after planting. Stake with a 1.8 m [6'] cane to each plant. Once established, vines grow vigorously and should fill the space by summer's end.

After planting, cut the stem back hard to about 30 cm [1'] and tie to the cane. In spring, choose the strongest shoot for the main rod and tie this in vertically removing any other sideshoots.

When sideshoots start to develop on the main rod, allow them to grow to 45-60 cm [18-24"] long, then stop them just above a leaf and tie them in. They should be spaced alternately on each side of the stem, with about 45 cm [1½'] between two on the same side. Rub out others.

Sub-sideshoots are pinched back, just above the first leaf. The tip of the main rod is removed when it reaches the second wire from the top or if it has begun to get straggly and thin. When this has been done, all sideshoots can be allowed to grow naturally from then until the end of the season. Remove tendrils and the embryo flower buds constantly.

Early in the second winter, cut the main rod back one half to one third, and sideshoots to one or two buds, beginning the formation of the spur.

During the second spring and summer, a new shoot will grow at the end of the main rod and this is again treated as a leader, and stopped at the second wire from the top. Sideshoots are treated as before, but if the vine is growing strongly, it can be allowed to set fruit, but only two or three bunches. In the third winter, prune the new growth of the leader by about half, and sideshoots to one or two buds.

Thereafter routine pruning of the established vine is as follows: in early winter, cut any new growth at the end of the rod, and the sideshoots, back to one or two buds. In spring: remove shoots when about 2.5 cm [1"] long so as to leave one at the tip of the rod, and one on each spur. In early summer, stop all sideshoots at just above the second

leaf beyond the bunch, or at the sixth leaf if there is no bunch, and tie in. Pinch out sub sideshoots at one leaf and remove all tendrils constantly.

Outdoors on a pergola in cooler climates the leader may not be ripe enough to go through the winter so each winter cut it to mature dark brown wood and train on the leading shoot to form the rod.

Spur thinning in old vines

Vines can bleed copiously through pruning wounds if cuts are made when they are not completely dormant. Early winter is the best time to prune. Spurs become gnarled after some years but should still continue to produce shoots. Any overcrowding ones can be cut out.

Feeding and watering

In late winter, whether the vine is rooted inside the greenhouse or outside, rake off all the old mulch. Dress the soil surface at the rate of 0.5 kg per sq m [1 lb per sq yd] with either a proprietary vine fertilizer, or half this quantity of a good general fertilizer. Fork this in lightly, then mulch if possible with half-rotted manure. If the grape is rooted inside the house or against a wall, start in early spring to soak the border with water at about 10 L per 100 sq cm [2 gal per sq ft].

On completion of thinning in early to midsummer, commence regular feeding. Start with a proprietary vine fertilizer at 250 g per sq m [½ lb per sq yd], and follow this at two week intervals with a liquid fertilizer at the rate of 12 L [2½ gal] per vine, until colour appears in the berries.

Ventilation and syringing in the greenhouse

The vine is perfectly hardy after leaf fall; for the best results it should be subjected to a few weeks' exposure to wintry weather, with the ventilators fully open.

Late winter is a good time to encourage the vine into new growth by closing all ventilators and syringing the rods mid morning and again in the afternoon.

If the house contains more tender varieties, some artificial heat to 5°C [40°F] is desirable from late winter until the end of spring, when it should rise to 15°C [60°F]. While pollination is taking place in early summer, you should try to maintain a minimum night temperature of 10°C [50°F] for all varieties. During the growing period commence ventilation before the temperature exceeds 19°C [65°F].

Aiding pollination in the greenhouse

As soon as the vines commence flowering, producing a delicious scent, in late spring, open the ventilators for longer periods, but do not lower the temperature unduly. When the buds begin to break, a moist atmosphere is necessary; cease to syringe the vine but keep its surroundings moist. Until setting is complete, leave a crack of ventilation open at night.

With free setting grape varieties (they form fruit from flowers with ease), a smart tap with the side of the hand to each rod at midday will disperse pollen. But with Muscats and shy setters, cup the dry palm of the hand around each bunch and gently stroke downward towards the tip. After setting, remove dead flowers by syringeing.

PLANTING VINES OUTSIDE GREENHOUSE

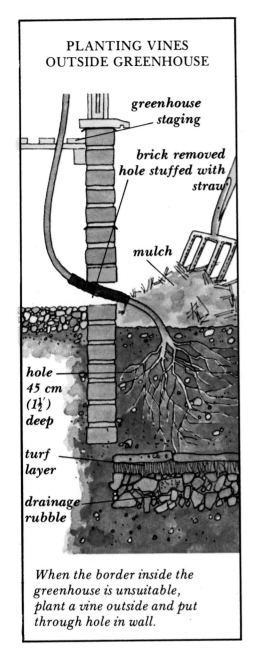

greenhouse staging

brick removed hole stuffed with straw

mulch

hole 45 cm (1½') deep

turf layer

drainage rubble

When the border inside the greenhouse is unsuitable, plant a vine outside and put through hole in wall.

TRAINING IN THE GREENHOUSE

Grapes can be grown in a small greenhouse. Train the rod upright as high as the ridge and then pass horizontally along the length of the house, 45 cm [1½'] below the glass.

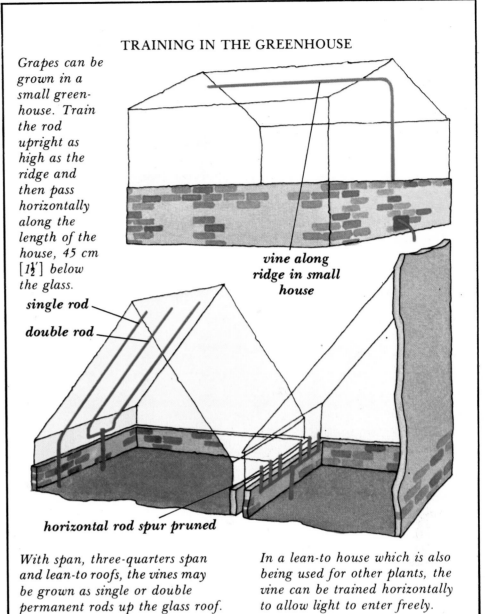

vine along ridge in small house

single rod

double rod

horizontal rod spur pruned

With span, three-quarters span and lean-to roofs, the vines may be grown as single or double permanent rods up the glass roof.

In a lean-to house which is also being used for other plants, the vine can be trained horizontally to allow light to enter freely.

SPUR PRUNING OF PERMANENT RODS

Pull down laterals and tie in to horizontal wires. Prune two leaves after the grape bunch and prune sideshoots to one leaf.

Prune each spur to two buds, from each of which a lateral will grow.

Grape thinning

Vines should not be allowed to bear heavy crops till after their fifth year. Dessert grapes (but not wine grapes) are thinned to improve appearance and quality. First reduce the number of bunches. A strong rod of 4.5-4.8 m [15-16'] should be allowed to bear 10-12 bunches.

Do not touch berries as this destroys the bloom. Use a forked twig or piece of wire about 15 cm [6"] long to manipulate that portion of the bunch being thinned. Use a sharp pair of pointed scissors carefully; avoid pricking and spoiling other berries while removing those not required.

Loop a piece of raffia under the first fruit stalk of each bunch to be retained and tie it to the wire above. This will take some of the weight off the bunch stalk. It will also raise the 'shoulders' of the bunch slightly. You do not need to thin much in this portion of the bunch. Seedless berries are distinguished by their diminutive size and should be cut out first. For all varieties which set freely you should remove at least 50% of the berries (*see* diagram).

GROWING BY THE DOUBLE GUYOT METHOD

Plant outdoors in mid autumn or early spring. Buy rooted cuttings and allow three years before cropping.

Erecting training wires

Buy stout posts 2.1 m [7'] long, creosote the bottom only, and drive them in spaced 2.7 m [9'] apart for every two vines you plan to grow, leaving 1.8 m [6'] above ground. If you plan to have two rows, allow 1.5 m [5'] between them. To these attach a single 2.5 mm [⅛"] gauge wire 38 cm [15"] above the ground, then run double wires at 75 cm [2½'] above the ground and another pair of double wires 1.2 m [4'] above the ground. At 1.8 m [6'] run a single wire from the tops of the posts to support a net.

Planting outdoors

Space vines 1.2 m [4'] apart. A few weeks before planting dig a hole 60 cm [2'] deep and 90 cm [3'] square. Break up the bottom and return the soil, mixing rotted manure or

PRUNING FOR A DOUBLE GUYOT

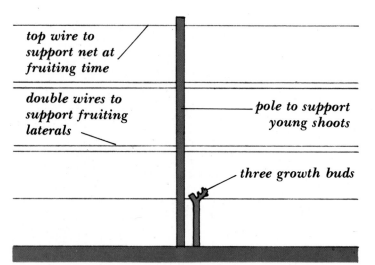

top wire to support net at fruiting time

double wires to support fruiting laterals

pole to support young shoots

three growth buds

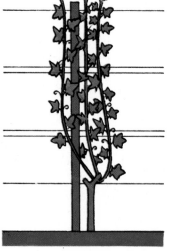

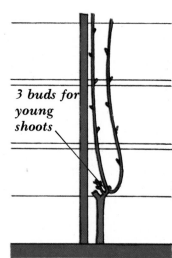

3 buds for young shoots

1. For a double Guyot system the vine is pruned back to three buds just after planting in autumn or spring.

2. Next season these will produce three good shoots.

3. Second winter, prune best two to 75 cm [2½'].

4. When the sap starts rising, pull down the two shoots to the bottom wire. The third has three good buds.

5. Select six to eight laterals per vine and support between twin wires. Tie replacement shoots vertically.

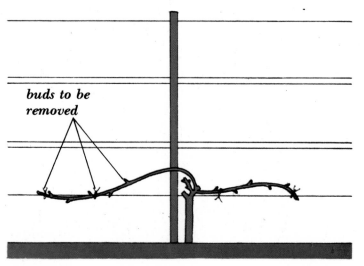

buds to be removed

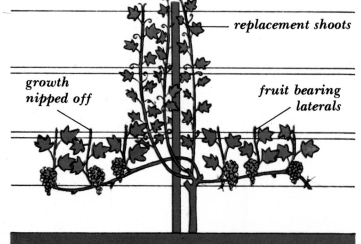

replacement shoots

growth nipped off

fruit bearing laterals

garden compost with it at the rate of a 12 L [2½ gal] bucket — add bonemeal or fish, blood and bone fertilizer at the rate of 125 g [4 oz] per plant.

Set the plant in position, spread out the roots, and cover them with topsoil, drawing the plant up so that the eventual soil mark will be the same that it was in the pot. Firm by treading, water with a bucketful per vine and finish by mulching, preferably with rotted stable manure.

Training by the double Guyot method

Dr Jules Guyot evolved a method in the 1850s whereby the rod bearing the fruiting laterals is completely cut out at the end of each year. New shoots are encouraged by pruning and then selected and kept growing throughout the year to replace the old fruiting rods.

After planting, cut the stem down to three good buds. The following season these will sprout to produce three strong shoots. Two of the best of these are shortened to about 75 cm [2½'] in early winter, and then, in early spring when the

sap rises, they are tied to the bottom wire, right and left. The third shoot is shortened to three good buds from which three replacement shoots will develop for the following season. Any other shoots which still remain are removed. During the year, shoots developing as replacements are trained vertically. Tie a 1.8 m [6'] bamboo cane to the wires straight up behind the vine and loosely tie on replacement shoots at 15 cm [6"] intervals.

During the summer, fruiting sideshoots will form along the two one-year-old shoots which you have tied along the bottom wire. Train these sideshoots perpendicularly and support them between the first pair of wires at 75 cm [2½'] above the ground and then again when they reach the wires 1.2 m [4'] above the ground. In the first year six to eight laterals per vine are selected and the remainder are removed by cutting close to the horizontal rod.

Regulation and pruning

In their first cropping year, it is wise to allow not more

Siegerrebe, reddish-brown when ripe, is excellent for both wine and dessert.

USING CLOCHES WITH THE SINGLE GUYOT

Grow only one replacement rod. Cover fruiting rod after fruit sets. Leave cloche ends open.

THINNING GRAPE BUNCHES FOR DESSERT FRUIT

shoulders supported by raffia

Bunches should be this sparse after thinning. Do not touch the fruit.

Black grapes from St. Jeannet in the south of France, grown on the Guyot system. The vines must be in their fifth year before carrying a heavy crop.

VINE PROPAGATION

bud

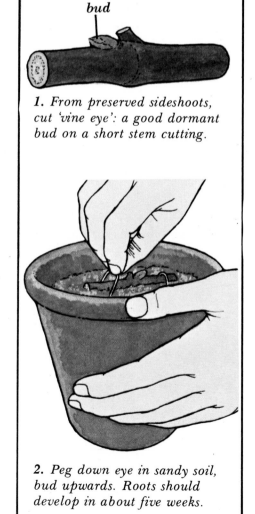

1. *From preserved sideshoots, cut 'vine eye': a good dormant bud on a short stem cutting.*

2. *Peg down eye in sandy soil, bud upwards. Roots should develop in about five weeks.*

than one bunch of grapes per sideshoot; remove the surplus flower buds at an early stage. Pollination is by insects. Allow the sideshoots to grow to the top pair of wires, attach them and then pinch out the growing points. After this, sub sideshoots will rapidly develop on each of the perpendicular sideshoots. Cut off each one after their first leaf. In the second year the number of bunches may be doubled to two per lateral, and increased again later on.

In the early winter, the horizontal rods are cut back to the main stem. The best pair of replacement shoots are shortened to 75 cm [2½']. Do not, however, bring them down now to the horizontal wires. Delay this for another two months until the sap is rising. The third shoot is shortened to three buds, for the new replacement shoots.

HARVESTING AND PROPAGATION

A dark tinge with black grapes and a slightly transparent appearance in white grapes are the signs of approaching ripening. In the greenhouse reduce humidity by ceasing to dampen the floor and surroundings, and increase ventilation by day, permitting some at night. Keep a good canopy of foliage over black grapes to improve berry colour, but expose white grapes to all available light, avoiding direct sunshine. Taste for ripeness and cut with 5 cm [2"] of lateral on each side of the shank.

Propagation

The most rapid method of raising young vines is from vine buds or 'eyes'. When you prune at the beginning of winter, preserve selected sideshoots by heeling them into the soil out-of-doors. Then in late winter cut chosen dormant buds with 2.5 cm [1"] of stem on each side. Peg these short lengths down flat with a bit of wire in sandy soil in a 9 cm [3½"] pot, with the bud pointing upwards. Place them in a moist atmosphere, with plenty of warmth in a propagator with a bottom heat of 21°C [70°F]. A strong shoot should develop in five weeks; pot on into a 15 cm [6"] pot.

For outdoor vines, the usual method is to take cuttings. Make cuttings with three dormant buds on them from the shoots pruned off in early winter and put them in sandy soil immediately, three to a 20 cm [8"] pot, kept in the greenhouse in cooler temperate areas.

PESTS AND DISEASES

In the greenhouse, mildew (*Uncinula necatrix*) causes the most trouble of the fungus diseases, while red spider mite, greenfly, scale insects, mealy bug and vine weevil are the most likely of the insect pests to attack. Vine weevil is a tiny black, beetle-like pest, 0.8 cm [⅓"] long, which feeds on the leaves at night, biting semi-circular holes in the edges. The larvae are stout white maggots 1.5 cm [½"] long, attacking the young, fleshy feeding roots. Control by working g-BHC into soil and dusting it into hiding places. The aphid *Phylloxera vitifoliae* infests the roots, producing galls on them, and also attacks the leaves, but to a lesser extent. If its presence is suspected, it must be reported to the relevant government department.

When the stalks of the berries dry up before ripening, this is a condition called shanking. It can be caused by over-cropping, or any severe check in growth. Another

physiological trouble is scalding, in which one side of the berry becomes sunken, dry and wrinkled. It is caused by sun shining onto moisture on the berry, and ventilation must be increased, starting earlier in the day. Outdoor grapes are most likely to be infected with mildew and grey mould (*Botrytis cinerea*), causing most trouble in wet summers and autumns. Net against birds and wasps.

Greengage

**Greengage is a type of plum, with a distinctive honey flavour.
The typical greengage is named for its scented green flesh, but some are gold fleshed.**

The greengage, *Prunus italica,* is named after Sir Thomas Gage who reintroduced it to England in the eighteenth century. Fruit come reasonably true to seed and they have been interbred with other plums. There are two types of gage: the transparent gage which has a transparent skin when ripe, and the old English gage, with a thicker skin. Skins are green or yellow, sometimes red spotted.

They grow on sturdy bushes or small trees 3.7 m [12'] high. Like other plums, they need a lot of moisture and a climate with short springs and hot summers.

For cultivation *see* PLUM.

Gumbo

SEE **OKRA**

Hamburg Parsley

A variety of the familiar herb, Hamburg parsley is grown for its thick, off-white parsnip-like roots, which taste rather like celeriac. The leaves can also be used for flavouring.

Hamburg parsley originated in central Europe, and was introduced from Germany, hence its name. The roots can be eaten raw or cooked.

Suitable site and soil
Hamburg parsley can tolerate a good deal of shade, so it is a useful plant to grow where other crops will not thrive.
The soil should have been manured for a previous crop; failing this, work in well-rotted garden compost, or a general fertilizer at the rate of 125 g per sq m [4 oz per sq yd]. Fresh manure should not be used, because it would cause the roots to fork, as with other root vegetables. The soil must be dug thoroughly, and all stones removed.

Sowing, thinning and cultivation
Sow in early spring, putting seeds into drills 1.5 cm [½"] deep and 30 cm [1'] apart. Thin seedlings to 23 cm [9"] apart.
As long as the weather is reasonably warm and the soil is kept moist, the seeds should germinate within 10-14 days, but the process can be very slow, sometimes taking several weeks. It is a good idea to sow lettuce or radish between the parsley drills to mark their position; this also makes maximum use of the land. The salad crop will be ready to lift in early summer, leaving the root crop to mature for

Hamburg parsley
Petroselinum crispum tuberosum (fam. *Umbelliferae*), also known as turnip-rooted parsley.
Hardy biennial grown as an **annual.**
Size: grows to 30-60 cm [1-2'] tall; roots 17.5-20 cm [7-8"] long and 7.5 cm [3"] thick.
Climate: cool to warm temperate.
Sowing to harvesting time: 9 months.
Yield: 4.5 kg [10 lb] per 3 m [10'] row.

(Above) The foliage of Hamburg parsley remains through the winter and can be used like parsley for flavouring.

1. Sow Hamburg parsley during the early spring, with a lettuce or radish catch crop to avoid wasting space.

2. Harvest Hamburg parsley in late autumn or winter when the roots are fully developed. Store like parsnips.

pulling later in the year. To have Hamburg parsley ready for pulling in spring, sow in the previous summer.
Hoe to remove weeds and water the plants generously.

Harvesting and storing the crop
Harvest spring-sown Hamburg parsley in late autumn and winter when the roots are fully grown — 17.5-20 cm [7-8″] long. In contrast to those of most root vegetables, the largest roots are the best-tasting.
The roots may be left in the ground to be dug as required. The foliage remains throughout the winter and can be used, like that of the herb, for flavouring. If there is a possibility that the ground in winter may be frozen too hard to dig, lift some of the roots in late autumn and store as for parsnips. Reject any roots that have been damaged by pests, disease or bruising.

Horseradish

Horseradish roots have a pungent peppery flavour. The distinctive tang of horseradish sauce is a favourite accompaniment to beef and fish.

Native to Europe, the horseradish plant *(Armoracia rusticana)* is a member of the *Cruciferae* family. A perennial herb, it bears large, glossy, spoon-shaped leaves and small white flowers which appear in early summer. The plant grows up to 60 cm [2′] tall with lower leaves as long, and it is cultivated for its fleshy roots. The roots, freshly grated are used in cooking.
A hardy perennial, horseradish will grow anywhere, and after dying away in winter it will take over more ground each season if it is left to itself. If the plant is allowed to run rampant it produces wispy, elongated roots.

Cultivation
Choose a small section of well-drained ground in full sun.

The long pungent roots of horseradish can be fitted well into a crop rotation plan, as they are lifted annually.

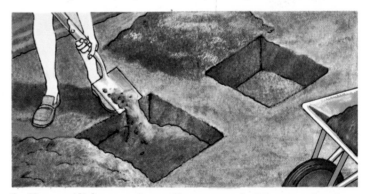

1. Horseradishes need a well-excavated site, to a depth of 60 cm [2′], as the tap root is exceptionally long.

2. Plant the roots 15 cm [6″] deep, so that the top is just below soil level, at a spacing of 45 cm [1½′] apart.

Each plant needs 1 sq m [1 sq yd], dug to a depth of about 60 cm [2′] for really good roots — it produces very large tap roots. A deep, rich loam is ideal, so plenty of well rotted manure, garden compost or leafmould should be added. It pays to be generous to the horseradish because other crops will benefit when they are moved to the site. Avoid using fresh manure as it will cause the roots to fork. Roots for planting should be about 20 cm [8″] long, with a bud. These should be obtained at a nursery or taken from some already established plant in late autumn or early winter. Plant the roots 45 cm [1½′] apart and 15 cm [6″] deep. Roots planted at this time will produce new shoots by spring. The only attention a horseradish bed needs is to keep it neat by removing dead leaves.

Harvesting and propagation

When the leaves are growing strongly, by late spring, there should be roots to dig near the surface which can be harvested without disturbing the whole plant.

The roots are more pungent when freshly dug and lose their essential flavour when dried, but it is usually possible to dig them throughout the year.

To get really plump roots and keep horseradish under control, lift the whole plant in early spring the following year. Divide for replanting in a new bed and keep the thicker roots for grating, packing them in moist sand or peat if they are not immediately required.

Kale

An exceptionally hardy plant, kale can be grown successfully even in poor soil. It makes an excellent alternative to cabbage, cooked and eaten in the same way.

There are four types of kale: the moss-leaved or Scotch kale, the most popular, grown for its parsley-like leaves; the plain-leaved type, even hardier, and grown for its

shoots, produced in winter and early spring; rape kale, one variety of which is well named Hungry Gap, as it provides shoots in late spring, when vegetables are at a premium, and fourthly, a new race of hybrid kales which are grown both for their leaves and spears, like sprouting broccoli. The name borecole refers only to the moss curled varieties. Kale is the supreme stand-in for producing winter greens and is hardy so will stand severe frost.

Suitable site and soil

There are few places in the garden where kale will not thrive, although plants grown in the open tend to be stronger and stockier than those grown in shade, and the tall varieties may be blown over on sites exposed to the wind. Kale does best in a rich soil but will grow almost anywhere, in either acid or alkaline soils. Use soil that was manured for a previous crop.

Sowing, thinning and transplanting

Few gardeners want kale for harvesting at any time other than the colder months of the year. In order to obtain the main crop then, sow seed from mid to late spring.

Sowing to germination takes 7-12 days and the temperature for germination can vary between 4 and 35°C [40 and 95°F]. Sow the seed thinly in drills 1.5 cm [½″] deep and 23 cm [9″] apart, and transplant firmly when 4 or 5 leaves are present, at a spacing of 45-60 cm [1½-2′]. Put the plants in up to the lowest true leaf.

The rape kales, which are harvested from mid to late spring, are sown between late spring and midsummer, where they are to crop. Drills should be 45 cm [1½′] apart, and the young plants are thinned to the same spacing.

Harvesting and cultivation

Most varieties have loose crowns rather than the tight hearts found in cabbages. These crowns are cut first, and then, in the case of kales grown mainly for their leaves, the youngest leaves are removed, from the top downwards. This stimulates the production of side-shoots.

Little attention is required after transplanting or sowing, except to keep the plants well watered in dry weather and to control weeds with the hoe. Earth the plants up to their basal leaves in autumn.

Aftercare

By the end of winter, the stalks will be almost as woody as young trees. The surplus foliage may be put on the compost heap, but the stalks would take so long to rot that they

---

Kale
Brassica oleracea acephala (fam. *Cruciferae*)
Also known as borecole.
Hardy perennial, grown as an **annual.**
Size: up to 45 cm [1½′] across; height from 30 cm [1′] for dwarf varieties to 120 cm [4′] for tall varieties.
Climate: cool temperate.
Sowing to harvesting time: 36-52 weeks.
Yield: 0.5-0.75 kg [1-1½ lb] per plant.

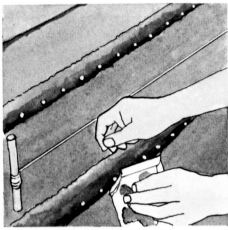

1. *Sow kale thinly in late spring or early summer in shallow drills.*

2. *When five leaves have developed, transplant firmly up to lowest leaf.*

3. *In autumn, earth up the plants to basal leaves with a draw hoe.*

4. *On leaf and spear varieties, harvest loose crowns in the spring.*

5. *Without crowns, sideshoots will develop; pick these like broccoli.*

6. *Store kale by immersing whole head in frequently changed water.*

Moss-leaved or Scotch kale variety is grown solely for its leaves.

A blue-green curly variety: kale is an excellent source of winter greens. All varieties can withstand harder frost than other brassicas.

are best burnt — after drying — or else put in a place where, covered with soil or debris, they can be allowed ample time to decay.

Pests and diseases
These are the same as those of cabbage, flea beetles being the chief menace, but kales have some resistance to clubroot and cabbage root fly.

Kohlrabi

Kohlrabi belongs to the cabbage family, but actually looks more like a turnip. The swollen stem is the part which is eaten and makes a delicious, nutty flavoured vegetable.

Kohlrabi is said to have been brought to western Europe by the Crusaders. Although it is usually classified as a root vegetable, the edible part is really the stem, swollen to bulbous dimensions. There are two varieties — 'white' (actually pale green in colour) and 'purple'. Both have white flesh and there is little to choose between them. The quality of this vegetable depends largely on quick,

1. *Lime in winter; do not manure at the same time.*

2. *Sow in shallow drills; outdoors, from mid spring.*

3. *Thin seedlings as soon as large enough to handle. Leave one at each station.*

4. *Lift roots of 5 cm [2″] first. Leave alternate roots to grow larger.*

(Opposite) Mature kohlrabi and (below) young plants.

Kohlrabi
Brassica oleracea caulorapa (fam. *Cruciferae),*
also known as turnip-rooted cabbage.
Biennial grown as an **annual.**
Size: the swollen stem (the edible part of the plant) should be allowed to reach a diameter of not more than about 7.5 cm [3″]; the plant grows to a height of 12-20 cm [5-8″].
Climate: cool temperate.
Sowing to harvesting time: 9-11 weeks.
Yield: 20 'globes', each about 200 g [7-8 oz], per 3 m [10′] row.

unchecked growth, and it is not suitable for storing, except when deep-frozen. If left in the ground it may become too large to be edible.

Suitable site and soil

The site should be sunny. Kohlrabi grows best in a fertile loam, although it can be grown in most soils. The better the soil, the quicker the growth and therefore the more succulent the vegetable, but do not grow kohlrabi in freshly manured soil; use one which has been manured for a previous year's crop. Check the soil for acidity with a pH test and apply lime if necessary.

Cultivation

Sow outdoors in mid spring; successive sowings can be made up to early summer. For an early crop, sow under cloches or in frames or greenhouses 4-6 weeks earlier. Transplant about a week after the last frost date.

Sown about 1.5 cm [½"] deep in drills 38-45 cm [15-18"] apart. Transplant to rows about the same distance apart, with 10-15 cm [4-6"] between the plants in each row. Be careful not to insert the plants too deeply in the soil when transplanting, or the 'globe' will form below the surface. Alternatively, sow the seeds thinly where they are to mature and thin them to 15 cm [6"] apart.

It is essential to keep the plants growing without a check. Keep them well-watered, and hoe frequently, not only to suppress weeds but also to loosen soil around plants.

Harvesting and aftercare

Pull up the plants as soon as a moderate-sized globe has formed — 7.5 cm [3"] diameter is about the maximum; 5 cm [2"] is better. If left to grow bigger, the globe will be woody inside. When harvested young, the globes may simply be scrubbed and cooked whole; older specimens should be peeled. Cut off the roots and leaves. For deep-freezing, blanch whole if young, peel and dice if older.

Kohlrabi produces a small amount of waste material — this can be added to the compost heap. For future use of the plot, remember that kohlrabi is a brassica and avoid following on with other brassicas.

Pest and diseases

The pests most likely to occur are turnip-flea beetle (*see* TURNIP), and clubroot if kohlrabi are grown in acid soil.

Lamb's Lettuce

SEE CORN SALAD

Leek

One of the finest of all vegetables, the leek is easy to grow. The blanched bases of the leaves make a tasty fresh vegetable in the depth of winter. The leaf tops may be used for soup.

Although some of the finest leeks are cultivated in Scotland, their connection with Wales and St. David goes back to the sixth century when the Welsh wore them as distinguishing badges in their battles with the Saxons. 'Leek' is in fact derived from the Saxon word for a plant.

Suitable site and soil

Leeks do best in moist, light soil that has been heavily manured for a previous crop, or one which was treated with garden compost or leafmould the winter before planting. Apart from this, the choice of situation in the vegetable plot may be influenced by the fact that leeks are generally left in the ground to be dug up as required throughout the winter, and can occupy the site for over 12 months. If you use a strict rotation system you should bear this in mind, unless you have reserved a plot for semi-permanent crops like asparagus and artichokes, and there is some free space there for your leeks.

Sowing and thinning

Sow the seed outdoors in early spring in a well-prepared nursery bed. Sow thinly (about 100 seeds to the metre) in drills about 0.5 cm [¼"] deep, and cover with fine soil. Germination should take 14-21 days, and thinning should

---

Leek
Allium ampeloprasum porrum (fam. *Alliaceae*)
Hardy biennial.
Size: Leaves to 30 cm [1'] long; bulbs 7.5-15 cm [3-6"] long and up to 11 cm [4½"] in diameter ('pot' varieties), 15-30 cm [6-12"] long and 5 cm [2"] in diameter ('long' varieties).
Climate: temperate.
Sowing to harvesting time: about 23 weeks.
Yield: 10-12 plants per 3 m [10'[row.

1. *By midsummer, leeks should be transplanted. Lift carefully with fork.*

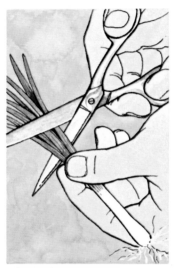

2. *Before replanting, trim tips of leaves to avoid excessive drooping.*

3. *Also trim roots back to within 2.5 cm [1"] of base to improve rooting.*

4. *Make holes for leeks vertical and wider at the top; use a thick dibber.*

5. *After planting leeks, fill holes with water and leave standing upright.*

6. *A blanching method: tie black plastic round stem up to base of leaves.*

7. *Then draw up soil from between rows using a draw hoe. Repeat as necessary.*

8. *Harvest the leeks when wanted; always lift with a fork, the largest first.*

9. *To heel in, dig narrow trench in cool place and place leeks on one side.*

10. *Cover the leeks with soil up to the leaves and then firm down with feet.*

ALTERNATIVE BLANCHING METHOD

1. *Fix paper collar like this soon after planting.*

2. *Later use 30 cm [1'] by 10 cm [4"] drain pipe.*

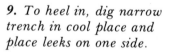

begin as soon as possible, when the plants are not more than thin green shoots, about 6 weeks from sowing. Thin moderately the first time, as some of the plants may die, and then thin again when all seems to be going well, to end up with plants about 10 cm [4″] apart.

Transplanting

By midsummer, when they are about as thick as pencils, the leeks will be ready for transplanting to the permanent bed. Manuring the permanent bed has already been mentioned. Water the seedbed the day before lifting if the soil is dry. You may simply plant the leeks in shallow drills, like cabbages, but it is really not more trouble to adopt the popular method of planting them in holes.

Make the holes with a thick dibber to a depth of 15 cm [6″] spaced about 23 cm [9″] apart, with 30 cm [1′] between the rows. Make sure that the holes are vertical, and move the dibber about from side to side to enlarge them at the top. Cut back the roots to within 2.5 cm [1″] of their origin, trim off the tips of the leaves to a length of about 10 cm [4″]. Then simply lower the young leeks into the holes, and gently fill the holes with water, leaving the plants standing upright. Sufficient soil will be washed in to support the plants. As you hoe the rows from time to time the holes will gradually fill up with soil.

Leeks grown in this way will not be completely blanched, but the pale green portion seems to impart the best flavour to a soup. If you prefer to eat your leeks thoroughly blanched, however, this can be done quite easily, as described later.

Another way of growing leeks, used mainly by gardeners growing their plants for exhibition, is to plant them 25 cm [10″] apart in a trench. This should have been excavated to a depth of about 30 cm [1′], and if there is more than one trench, they should be about 60 cm [2′] apart. Into the bottom of each trench, dig about 7.5 cm [3″] of well-rotted manure or garden compost and cover it with about 15 cm [6″] of the topsoil. Shape the remaining topsoil into flat-topped ridges between the rows, upon which a catch-crop of lettuce, for example, can be grown before the soil is required for earthing up the growing leeks. In the now fairly shallow trench, carefully plant the leeks, perfectly upright, with a trowel.

Care and development

Water the transplanted seedlings generously until they are well established. Soon after planting give them liquid manure. If the pre-planting application of organic matter was in short supply, nitrate of soda, nitro-chalk or sulphate of ammonia may be applied at the rate of 10 g per metre [⅓ oz per yd] about 5 weeks after planting; alternatively, apply twice this amount of soot along the row when the plants are well established.

Blanching

Begin the process of blanching in early to mid autumn.

Harvesting leeks. When siting the plants remember that they may remain in the ground through the winter. Place accordingly for easier harvesting.

This is usually done by earthing up the stems. To ensure that soil does not get into the stems, 'collars' are secured around them up to the base of the leaves. Various materials can be used for the collar; lengths sawn from plastic piping or, at virtually no cost at all, pieces of strong brown paper secured with string or rubber bands. The latter will need support from bamboo canes. If necessary, the collar can also be made from short lengths of clay drainpipe; this is about the right size and will remain stable, even in strong winds.

Attach the collars before carrying out the earthing up process. To do this, draw up the soil from between the rows with a draw hoe. As the plants grow, draw up more soil, fitting on another collar above the first one.

Harvesting the crop

Leeks may be harvested from late autumn to mid spring. As mentioned earlier, they are generally left where they grow until they are wanted. The only problem likely to arise is when the soil is frozen too hard for a fork to be driven into it. Never try dragging leeks out of the ground by brute force; you will be left with a slimy handful of leaves and a ruined plant. Lift them with a fork, taking the largest leeks first, leaving the smaller ones in the ground to grow.

If the plot is needed before all the leeks are consumed, however, they may be dug up and 'heeled in': lay them on their sides in a shallow trench in a cool place with their tops projecting above the ground, and cover them with soil, ready to dig up for cooking.

Sowing under glass

To grow early leeks, for harvesting in early autumn, sow under glass in mid to late winter. Leek seeds, although small, are not too small to handle singly, and they should be sown about 2.5 cm [1″] apart in a seed tray containing a standard seed compost.

About six weeks after sowing, the tray may be moved into a closed cold frame for the seedlings to be gradually hardened off. Later prick them out into another frame at about 20 cm [8″] apart. Provided that the weather is not unduly harsh for the time of year, the leeks will be ready for planting by mid spring.

Pests and diseases

These are generally the same as for onions, although leeks are usually free of troubles. There are, however, one or two diseases which are specific to leeks and can be a nuisance. Rust can cause trouble, especially when the autumn and winter are mild. Older leaves show orange-yellow powdery spots, and later turn yellow, dying in a severe attack. Remove badly infected plants, and possible weed hosts, and spray regularly with zineb if the attack is very bad.

White tip is a fungus disease appearing from late summer through the winter. The leaf tips die back, other parts of the leaves and stems show white patches and growth is greatly checked. Badly affected plants should be removed and destroyed, and the plants sprayed fortnightly with a copper fungicide, until white patches disappear.

Lemon Verbena

**Lovely lilac flowers
and a delicate fragrance make verbena
a favourite in herb gardens.
Its lemony flavouring, without
the lemon's acidity, is useful
in all kinds of cookery.**

Lemon verbena (*Aloysia triphylla*) is a member of the *Verbenaceae* family and is often confused with vervain (*Verbena officinalis*) which is very different and bitter tasting. The leaves of lemon verbena are dried for lemon flavouring, used to make a refreshing tea and to scent soaps and cosmetics. They can also be used fresh in salads and fruit drinks in summer. It is a deciduous, aromatic shrub, native to Chile and Peru but easily cultivated in cool temperate areas. On a sunny wall it will grow up to 1.8 m [6'] high, bearing small lilac flowers and fragrant leaves for harvesting in late summer.

Lemon verbena is also an excellent choice for container growing. Any large tub or similar container is suitable

Cultivation

The most suitable site is by a sunny wall, but any sunny position which is reasonably sheltered is adequate. Lemon verbena prefers a light, well-drained soil. If the soil is heavy, improve it by working in coarse sand. If you are growing the plant in a tub or other container, use a standard potting compost.

Lemon verbena is started from plants bought at the nursery. Usually one will be sufficient for domestic use. Plant out in late spring. Be sure the roots are well watered while the plant establishes itself; a mulch of garden compost or leafmould over the root area will offset the dryness common to plants grown by a wall or fence.

After young shoots begin to grow, a light pruning can be given in early summer to cut out any dead wood and shorten some of the shoots to keep the shrub a good shape. Lemon verbena will survive mild winters in a sheltered position, but in frosty areas it is advisable to protect the roots and lower stem with canvas or sacking on a light frame. Do not allow the covering to become soggy — it needs to be frost-proof and dry. In areas where winters are

(Right) The beautiful, lilac flowers and fragrant leaves of the lemon verbena plant will thrive on a sunny wall.

very severe it is better to grow lemon verbena in a tub and take it indoors or into the greenhouse in autumn.

Harvesting and propagation

Leaves may be clipped off in late summer. Tie them in bunches and hang to dry, then powder them and store the powder in an air-tight jar or container to preserve its flavour and aroma.

Once the shrub is established it can be propagated by cuttings taken from new shoots in early summer.

Lettuce

**The most popular salad green, lettuce
is easily grown and has a high
all-year-round yield. Its leaves
also make a delicious soup.**

Lettuce is reputed to have reached us from the East Indies; it was introduced into England in the sixteenth century, and was known in the gardens of Hampton Court in the time of Henry VIII.

There are three main types: 'cabbage' lettuce, the taller and snappier 'cos' and the frizzy-headed 'loose-leaf'. The latter is harvested by picking single leaves, not by pulling

Lettuce
Lactuca sativa (fam. *Compositae*)
Half-hardy annual.
Size: between 23 and 38 cm [9 and 15"] wide.
Climate: temperate.
Sowing to harvesting time: 8-14 weeks.
Yield: 9-12 heads, each, on average, 340 g [12 oz], per 3 m [10'] row.

(Above) Butterhead lettuces being grown under cloches. Butterheads are cabbage types. They are soft and round and usually grow very quickly.

Crisp heart varieties are slower maturing and usually more heat- and bolt-resistant than butterhead types.

The 'loose-leaf' varieties are very popular in America and Australia. This type has a high vitamin content.

the whole plant, and can be useful for garnishing. The 'cabbage' variety can further be divided into 'butterheads' with tender, butter-coloured hearts and 'crispheads', which are crisper and have hearts that blanch to white instead. Numerous dwarf varieties of lettuce are available. Lettuce has been much hybridized in the last fifteen years or so, and there are all sorts of varieties available now, for growing at particular periods of the year. Catalogues will specify which varieties are suitable for which season. When growing out of season, in particular, it is important to choose the varieties which have been bred specially for that particular purpose, say, early spring cropping, or heated greenhouse winter cropping.

Suitable site and soil
Lettuce prefers a moist but well-drained soil, well dug. Well broken down clay soils produce very good plants, but so will sandy or gravelly ones, provided they are bulked well with organic matter. To ensure good water retention without sogginess, incorporate well-rotted manure or garden compost at the rate of 6 kg [13 lb] per sq m [1 sq yd]. Lettuces are 90 per cent water and there must be water in the soil in sufficient amounts for them to grow fast and form well. Poor and ill-prepared soil will produce floppy leaves and failure to heart up.

Summer lettuce
Sowing outdoors can start in early spring with the first of a succession of fortnightly sowings designed to maintain a supply of lettuce until the autumn. Suitable lettuces are the cabbage, cos or American type.

A mechanical routine of successful sowings does not, however, guarantee an uninterrupted supply of prime lettuces. Except in a steadily favourable climate there are likely to be times when sowing is checked; alternatively, when the weather becomes hot the crop engages in a race to see which plant can bolt first. However, the new summer lettuces are much less likely to bolt in hot weather, provided they never run short of water. Sowing several different kinds of seed will give varied germination and development. Many gardeners think that their own seeds, saved from year to year, produce the best plants.

Pelleted seeds are available too, but these will take longer to germinate and will not produce seedlings suitable for transplanting. However transplanting is really only satisfactory early in the season. Later on, such plants are very liable to bolt, and lettuces are best thinned. The seeds, which are rather fine, should be sown fairly thinly in short shallow drills about 1.5 cm [½"] deep and 30 cm [1'] apart. Sow about one seed per 1.5 cm [½"]. The seed should germinate in about 4-12 days and thinning should be carried out as soon as the first pair of true leaves have formed. Aim for a spacing of one plant at every 23-30 cm [9-12"] depending on the size of the variety. If the thinnings are required as transplants, lever them gently out with a spatula and handle only the leaves with the finger and thumb. Lower the transplants into prepared holes, then firm them down and water them well to ensure that the rootlets make good contact with the soil. When planting, do not plant too high otherwise they will not heart. Too low planting can mean infection of the lower leaves with grey mould; damp encourages fungus disease. The neck of the plant should be exactly at soil level.

Autumn and winter cropping
Besides summer lettuces which are in season from late spring until late summer, it is possible to crop them later in the year. These will be the cabbage or cos types. Seed is sown in midsummer, in succession, until the middle of late summer. The earlier sowings are thinned, the later ones transplanted towards the end of early autumn, into a frame or covered with cloches or a plastic tunnel. The later ones will be slow to grow and may not be ready by early winter, but with protection should stand the winter, and will certainly be ready in early spring.

Late winter and early to late spring crops
Lettuce for this period (mainly cabbage types) are sown in early to mid autumn outdoors under cloches or in a frame or a plastic tunnel, and thinned a month later. They are kept protected all through winter, and a particularly good variety for this is Winter Density, a cos-like and nutty-flavoured lettuce. It is also possible to sow in late winter, with protection, thin two or three times, and harvest in late spring; plenty of ventilation will be needed on warm days as the spring develops.

Winter lettuce
It is also possible to obtain lettuce (cabbage types) from early winter to early spring but only with the help of a heated greenhouse. Successive sowings are made from early to late autumn in seed trays, pricking out the seedlings into boxes, and then planting in cropping positions when the first pair of true leaves is fully developed. Temperature from sowing to planting out should be 10-15°C [50-60°F], and 15°C [60°F] for three weeks after planting. Thereafter it should be kept at 10-13°C [50-55°F]. Remember that in very cold, mid winter spells, it may be very expensive and difficult to maintain this, and it will be cheaper to purchase.

Care and development
Warmth, moisture and a weed-free environment with protection from garden pests are the main principles to bear in mind. If the soil has been well prepared it should be rich in humus to retain moisture adequately. Lettuces must be allowed as much water as their roots require, but they cannot be hurried by overwatering. In hot weather, it can be difficult to keep the soil surface moist and prevent it forming a crust, but mulching will largely overcome this, especially if applied just after rain. Use either rotted organic matter, or strips of black plastic.

Hoe frequently between rows and plants, which will kill the weeds before their roots are big enough to compete with the crop.

If cos lettuces are being grown, blanching will increase their crispness. This is simply done by applying a tie of raffia or a rubber band around the thickest part of the lettuce as it approaches maturity. About a week later a further tie is made higher up.

1. *Start outdoors in early spring, sowing thinly in shallow drills.*

2. *Thin when two leaves are showing. Handle only leaves if transplanting.*

3. *Put the transplants in prepared holes; firm down and water well.*

4. *Sow some lettuce every two weeks until the autumn to maintain supply.*

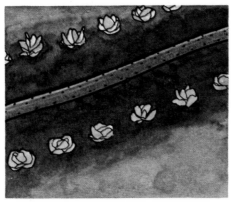

5. *Keep soil moist; a trickle hose is ideal as water seeps out slowly.*

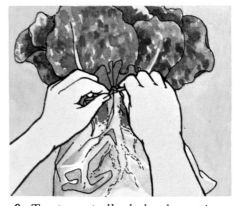

6. *Mulch to keep soil moist, using plastic strips with holes cut.*

7. *To blanch cos lettuce tie around middle; tie top about a week later.*
10. *To catch crop, sow lettuce between rows of peas, running north to south to avoid any shading.*

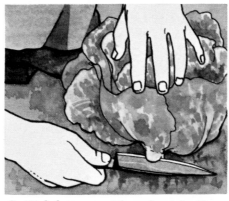

8. *Pick lettuce with a sharp knife, cutting just above lowest leaves.*
11. *For late winter and spring crops, sow winter lettuce during the autumn under tunnels or cloches.*

9. *To store, pull whole plant, tie plastic bag round roots and chill.*
12. *Cold frames can also be used; sow in late winter for late spring harvest; ensure good ventilation.*

A tall, crisp, cos lettuce. Both cos and cabbage types should be cut as soon as their hearts feel quite solid.

Container growing

Town dwellers can grow a few lettuces in 15 cm [6"] pots, provided they are not shaded in any way. Keep them well watered and protect them from direct sunlight at the sides, by a piece of board, or they will become baked solid.

Harvesting

Harvest lettuces as soon as they are at their best and fully-hearted, for their quality will fall off very rapidly the moment the centre begins to show a point. Cut the heads with a sharp knife, just above the lowest leaves. It is better to grow a few more lettuces rather than to wait until they are as large as possible.

Pests and diseases

Lettuce are somewhat prone to troubles: grey mould (*Botrytis cinerea*) slugs, leatherjackets and root aphids are the most common, but they may also be infested by green-fly, carriers of disease, mildew and eelworm. Root aphids are especially a problem when the weather is dry, as their feeding on the roots reduces the supply of moisture within the lettuce even further. Eelworms (nematodes) are microscopic creatures which also attack the roots, producing small knobs on them and weakening the plants severely. Destroy any plants affected by them and leave the ground left free from lettuce for four to five years.

Lima Bean

**Grown for their tasty
ripe seeds, Lima beans need
a warm climate
for successful cultivation.**

The Lima bean is similar to the French (or snap) bean, but is less hardy. It is widely cultivated in the United States and other countries with a warm temperate or sub-tropical climate, but the summers in cool temperate countries, such as Britain, are usually too short to grow it successfully.

There are two basic types — bush and climbing (or pole) Lima beans, and several varieties of each, ranging from small-seeded Limas, also known as butter beans, to large-seeded 'potato beans'. Although the small-seeded types can be picked when young and tender and cooked whole, like French (snap) beans, Limas are normally grown for their ripe seeds, often dried for keeping.

Suitable site and soil

Choose a sunny site, sheltered from high winds. In selecting a site for pole varieties, remember that they grow to 1.8 m [6'] high and will shade any crops planted along side. Allow ample space, 75-90 cm [2½-3'] between rows for pole varieties, and 60-75 cm [2-2½'] for bush varieties. Lima beans need a light, warm soil that is sandy but well-manured. To ensure that the plants grow vigorously from the start, work in a compound fertilizer (with a low nitrogen content) at a rate of about 100 g per sq m [3-4 oz per sq yd] seven to ten days before sowing. A dressing of organic manure is also helpful, but dig this in well beforehand, preferably during winter.

Sowing and planting

In warm climates, sow outdoors about four weeks after the last frost date. In cooler climates, sow under protection about two weeks after the last expected frost date, in preparation for transplanting. Protection can be under cloches, in greenhouses or in frames (preferably heated, in order to make maximum use of summer weather). The temperature for germination should be 15° to 30°C [60° to 85°F]. Transplant plants grown under glass about four weeks after the last frost date, but keep them covered with cloches for about five weeks in case of unseasonal temperatures or chill winds.

Allow 7.5-15 cm [3-6"] between plants of the bush type in each row and 15-25 cm [6-10"] between plants of the pole types. The space between the rows should be 60-75 cm [2-2½'] for bush types, and 75-90 cm [2½-3'] for pole types. Alternatively, with pole types, insert the poles first, hammering them firmly into the ground to a depth of 45 cm [1½']. Sow seeds or plant seedlings around them. The poles should be 1.8 m [6'] high above the ground. Any tall support will do, but the ideal is a stout pole with a 'T'-shaped crosspiece on top; tie strings from the ends of the

---

Lima bean
Phaseolus lunatus (or *limensis*) (fam. *Leguminosae*), also known as butter bean and Madagascar bean.
Size: plants of the bush type grow to about 7.5-15 cm [3-6"] in diameter and 15-30 cm [6-12"] in height; plants of the climbing type reach a slightly greater diameter and a height of about 2 m [6½'].
Climate: warm temperate to sub-tropical.
Sowing to harvesting time: 12-15 weeks.
Yield: 20-30 plants, each bearing about 60 g [2 oz] of beans, per 3 m [10'] row.

1. *In cool climates sow seeds in greenhouse pots.*

2. *Transplant to cloches outside after three weeks.*

3. *Fertilize on moist soil avoiding plant leaves.*

4. *Shell beans by beating the pods with a stick.*

Young lima bean plants do not need too much attention, but must be hoed regularly to prevent a crust forming on the soil. Water the bed frequently but not to excess.

5. *Put the shelled beans on sacking and dry in sun.*

In tubs grow three plants; twine each up own string.

crosspiece to the base of the pole. The beans will then hang straight downwards and be easy to pick. Short, twiggy sticks help to prevent the bush types from being blown over.

Sow the seed at a depth of 2.5-4 cm [1-1½"]. The sowing to germination period is 7-12 days.

Cultivation

Little is required apart from keeping the plot well-hoed and well-watered. At all costs, avoid letting a crust form over the soil surface; frequent hoeing will take care of this. Water frequently to keep the soil moist, but do not over-water. On poorer soils, an application of the same fertilizer as used earlier in the season, at the rate of 60-90 g per sq m [2-3 oz per sq yd] will be beneficial. Apply it in strips alongside the rows, preferably when the soil is moist, about 15 cm [6"] from the plants, and hoe it in.

Harvesting

If you want the beans when they are still green for cooking whole, pick the pods when they are young and succulent. If more mature beans are wanted, leave them on the plants for as long as possible, but pick the pods before they turn yellow, and shell them. Pick frequently to prolong the production of pods. When picking, snap the pods carefully from their stems or cut them off with scissors; careless pulling may uproot the bush plants. Finish picking about a week before the date of the earliest expected frost.

Storing and aftercare

Dry the shelled beans in the sun, and then store them in sacks kept in a dry place or in sealed jars. They are good vegetables for deep freezing.

The first frost will destroy what remains of the plants after harvest. Put the debris on the compost heap, but dig in the roots as they will increase the nitrogen content of the soil. Strip the poles of old vines and store in a dry place for use the following year.

Container growing

Lima beans are good subjects for growing in boxes, barrels and other containers, provided there is sufficient depth of soil — not less than 45 cm [1½']. Insert a central pole and grow several Lima bean plants twining up it; you may grow flowers around the edge of the barrel, and suspend hanging baskets from the ends of the crosspieces. These beans may also be grown in plastic sacks filled with potting compost, either in the open or under glass.

Pests and diseases

Protect the seedlings against birds with cloches, nets or twigs laid on the ground. Support bush types with twiggy sticks to prevent them from being blown over, also to stop beans trailing on the ground and being eaten by slugs. Diseases are mostly the result of wrong treatment, such as over-watering, which gives fungus diseases their chance, while inadequate nutrition may result in poor crops and premature death.

See also FRENCH BEANS and RUNNER BEANS.

Loganberry

This long red berry resembles the raspberry in appearance, but is bigger and has a tarter flavour.

The loganberry originated in California in the 1880s, in the garden of Judge Logan. It is believed to be the result of a cross between the American blackberry *R. ursinus* and a raspberry. The loganberry is a vigorous grower and, like the blackberry, it fruits on canes produced the previous year. It has proved to be the most successful and best known of all the crosses between blackberries and raspberries. The fruit is long, up to 5 cm [2"], and remains quite acid until fully ripe. It cooks and freezes well, and can be eaten raw when really ripe.

The canes are winter hardy, provided they have stopped growing and are hardened off before low temperatures start. Fruiting laterals may be damaged in spring by a sudden sharp frost after a period of mild weather. Flowers are usually late enough to escape frost damage. Loganberries are self-fertile and attractive to bees. A thornless variety has now been produced which is easier to handle.

Another hybrid Californian berry is the **boysenberry.** Raised in the 1930s, its origin is unknown, usually classed with loganberries. It is now grown in many parts of the world because it will crop in dry conditions and will stand heat better than the blackberry, which is a cool climate fruit. When fully ripe the fruit is almost black, it is almost seedless and the long berries have a good flavour. Its cultivation is like that of the loganberry.

The **youngberry** was raised by a Mr Young in the United

> **Loganberry**
> *Rubus loganbaccus* (fam. *Rosaceae*)
> **Hardy perennial cane,** usually prickly, with a cropping life of about 15 years.
> **Size:** 1.75 m [5½'] high up to 4 m [13'] when trained.
> **Climate:** cool temperate.
> **Planting to harvesting:** 2 years.
> **Yield:** 2-8 kg [4-16 lb] per plant.

States in the 1920s and is another berry for warm temperate conditions. It is thought to be a cross between two dewberries. The fruit is large, round and almost black when ripe, with a raspberry flavour.

The **veitchberry** is a very useful cool climate berry, which was introduced in 1902, and should be grown more; it is a cross between an autumn-fruiting raspberry variety and a blackberry. The berries are large, red to black, and in season from time the raspberries end until late summer.

The **wineberry,** *Rubus phoenicolasius*, originated in Japan. The berries are light orange-red and subacid in flavour and follow the raspberry in season. They grow on arching stems thickly covered with red bristles and without prickles. They can be tied in like loganberries, are trouble free, and are sometimes grown just for their appearance.

Much hybridisation was carried out in the early part of the twentieth century and other crosses between blackberries, raspberries, and loganberries are: the lowberry or King's acre berry, whose fruit are like long black loganberries, the phenomenal berry and the newberry, very like the loganberry, and the laxtonberry with berries like very large round raspberries.

Suitable site and soil

The loganberry can be grown in partial shade under trees, and on walls, but it performs better in sunny sites where young canes grow and mature properly. Avoid frost pockets, and see that plants are sheltered from winds which may damage young leaves or fruiting laterals.

The soil must be capable of holding good reserves of water. Lighty sandy loams to heavy loams are all suitable but heavy clays must have generous quantities of rotted organic matter added to them. Avoid planting in sites previously occupied by loganberries, blackberries or raspberries. Remove all perennial weeds and dig the site well two weeks before planting, adding garden compost or well rotted manure, at 12 L [2½ gal] bucket per sq m [yd].

Preparing to plant

If they are available, always buy one-year-old plants which are certified disease-free, and buy from a reputable nurseryman. Field-grown plants are normally planted in late autumn or the spring when still virtually dormant. If conditions are very wet when plants arrive, it is better to put them into containers, using a good soil or potting compost, to await weather improvement.

Loganberries should be spaced about 3 m [10'] apart but 1 m [3'] more or less may be allowed, depending on rainfall and soil, and the vigour of the variety selected.

Erecting training wires

It is best to erect posts before planting. Posts 2.3 m [7½'] long should be driven into the ground at about 45 cm [1½'] intervals between the plant sites, with one at each end of the row. End posts need to be substantial and well supported (*see* diagrams in BLACKBERRY). For loganberries, galvanized wires are stretched tightly along the row at heights of 1 m [3'], 1.3 m [4½'] and 1.8 m [6']. You may delay erecting wires for one year by putting a post at

Loganberries are grown in cool temperate climates. This is a thornless variety which makes handling much easier.

The youngberry, developed in the United States, is a warm temperate berry. It turns almost black when ripe.

SINGLE POLE CULTIVATION

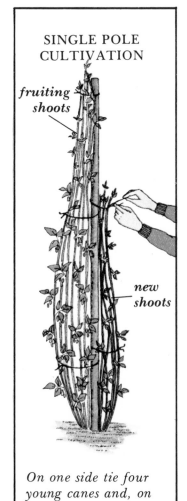

fruiting shoots

new shoots

On one side tie four young canes and, on the other, five or six fruiting canes.

(Above) The boysenberry suited to warm climates, has a good flavour and is practically seedless. It crops in dry conditions.

(Right) To propagate, use tip layering: peg young cane down to soil with tip buried in small hole. Sever in late winter and move to permanent site.

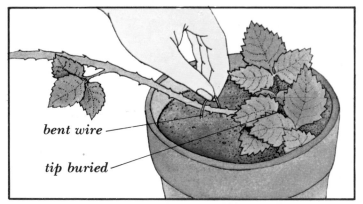

bent wire

tip buried

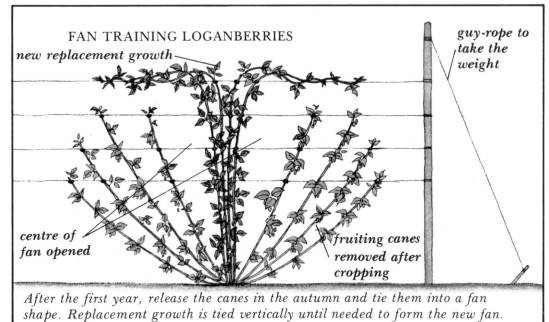

FAN TRAINING LOGANBERRIES

new replacement growth

guy-rope to take the weight

centre of fan opened

fruiting canes removed after cropping

After the first year, release the canes in the autumn and tie them into a fan shape. Replacement growth is tied vertically until needed to form the new fan.

each station, giving support until the following winter.

Planting and training

When planting, the roots of the young loganberries should be well spread out in the planting hole and covered with selected loose friable soil. Canes should be planted at the same depth that they were in the nursery. If the canes are longer than 30 cm [1'] cut them back.

A mulch is essential and this should be applied after planting, but before growth starts in the spring and the soil begins to dry out. Almost any organic matter is suitable, lawn mowings, sawdust, garden compost or well rotted manure. Very little fertilizer is needed at this time but on the lighter sandy soils an application of sulphate of potash at 75 g per sq m [2½ oz per sq yd] is often beneficial.

The first year after planting the young canes should be tied in once they have reached manageable lengths. Initially it may be easier to bundle the canes together, giving them a post for support, and to leave the erection of posts and wires to the following spring.

The object of training is to make fruiting canes accessible and to keep the new young canes out of the way, but growing in a good light. This may be done by growing the canes straight up a pole (as has been suggested for first year plants), by bundling the canes along two bottom wires in opposite directions leaving the third top wire free for the year's new growth, or by fan training.

If young canes have been tied up to a post in their first year, release them in the autumn and, wearing a stout pair of gloves for protection against prickles, tie them into the fan shape (*see* diagram) leaving the top wire clear, as well as the centre of the fan over the roots. In the course of the year as new shoots grow, these are trained and tied in vertically and then along the top wire.

After fruiting, old canes are cut to the ground, and the young canes are released and tied into the pattern. Some selection of young canes is possible during the growing season and unwanted material should be cut out.

Care and development

To ensure the proper development of the fruit and growth of young canes, the soil should not be allowed to get too dry during the fruiting season. Once the young canes have reached the right length, no further watering is necessary as canes must be matured and hardened off before winter.

A biennial application of sulphate of potash 75 g per sq m [2½ oz per sq yd] may be necessary on light soils. If the production of young cane is not sufficient, then an application of sulphate of ammonia or similar fertilizer at 75 g per sq m [2½ oz per sq yd] may stimulate new growth.

The loganberry has an unlimited life as long as it remains free from disease. But, because it stays in the same site for a long term, it is likely to become smothered with perennial weeds so control of weeds is essential from the start.

Harvesting and propagation

The fruit of the loganberry ripens over a period of weeks starting in midsummer. Constant picking over benefits the later fruit. The fruit should be picked when quite dry, otherwise it quickly becomes mouldy. The fruit does not pull off the plug, like a raspberry, but is picked with it.

The easiest way to propagate the loganberry is by tip layering. A young cane is bent down to the soil and its tip buried in a shallow hole and covered with soil. A bud or buds grow from near the end of the buried part, to lengthen into shoots, and roots are produced below ground. In late winter the new plant is severed from the parent and put in its permanent position.

Pest and diseases

The majority of pests and diseases which attack loganberries are the same as for the raspberry and blackberry (*see* RASPBERRY and BLACKBERRY).

Lovage

**This relative of the wild celery is
very similar in taste and smell.
Its name comes from its
past popularity for use in love potions.**

Lovage (*Levisticum officinale*) is a member of the *Umbelliferae* family. A handsome, hardy perennial, native to the Mediterranean, it often grows up to 1.8 m [6'] high with an almost equally wide bush span. The leaves (either fresh or dried) and the stems can be used to add a celery flavour to casseroles, stews and soups made with the stronger tasting meats and fish. Lovage leaves or stems may be added to sauces, and the stems and seeds can be used in the same way as celery and its seeds.

Cultivation

Lovage thrives in a rich, moist soil. Damp peat or leaf-mould forked into a dry soil will help to retain natural moisture. A certain amount of sunshine is necessary, but shade during part of the day suits lovage very well.

Sow the seed in a tray when it is just ripe, in early autumn, as it is viable for only a short time. Keep it dark and in a temperature of about 4° to 10°C [40° to 50°F] when ger-

Celery-flavoured lovage is a most useful cooking herb.

mination should start 14-21 days later. Prick out seedlings when large enough to handle into boxes. Transfer to permanent position 1-1.2 m [3-4'] apart, the next spring. Lovage is a thirsty plant and needs extra water at the roots when dry. In very exposed places staking may be necessary.

Harvesting and propagation
Young leaves may be clipped off the plant sparingly from late spring. Yellow-green flower heads bloom in mid-summer, producing seeds for harvest in late summer. The freshly harvested seed, sown thinly in boxes under glass, will be ready for planting outdoors the following spring. Spring sowing is also possible, but germination then is less certain. Lovage can also be propagated by lifting and dividing the roots in late summer, making sure that each has a bud on it; plant 5 cm [2"] below the soil.

Mange-tout

SEE **PEA**

Marjoram

**Marjoram has a sweet and unusual
aroma that makes it a favourite in
the traditional herb garden.**

Marjoram is the name given to several species of the *Labiatae* family — all of them are *Origanum*. *O. vulgare*

Wild marjoram or oregano, a favourite Italian herb. The leaves are best harvested just before the plant flowers.

161

is commonly called oregano or wild marjoram; it is native to Europe including the United Kingdom where it grows in the chalk downs. It is a bushy, perennial plant, growing to about 75 cm [2½'], which has light red flowers in summer and loses its leaves in winter. Its grey-green leaves are particularly pungent in flavour and aroma. There is a form with yellow leaves called 'aureum'. Oregano is a favourite Italian herb, used in pizza and other savoury dishes.

O. onites is pot marjoram, also a hardy perennial, which grows to about 15 cm [6"] tall, but tends to lie on the ground, the shoots producing roots at the leaf joints. The purple flowers appear in late summer on stems 60 cm [2'] tall. It can cover a space at least 30 cm [1'] square, and is the one most often potted and grown indoors through the winter.

O. majorana is sweet or knotted marjoram, more delicate and treated as a hardy annual in cool temperate climates, though in warmer climates it is perennial. It reaches only about 20 cm [8"] high, with rounded grey leaves, and several minute flowers coming from rounded buds or knot-like growths on the stems. Marjoram is used to flavour soups and stews and is particularly good with lamb. The leaves, either fresh or dried, are used sparingly to add a distinctive flavour, particularly in meat stuffings and omelettes.

Cultivation

A native of southern Europe, all marjoram prefers a light, well drained soil in full sun. If the site is on clay soil this must be opened up by working in sand or wood ashes. An application of hydrated lime is also helpful if the soil is acid.

Pot marjoram and wild marjoram can be grown in the same way, from seed sown thinly outdoors in early to mid spring, in drills 2 cm [¾"] deep, and 20 cm [8"] apart, or in seed trays with protection, with a fine covering of peat or silver sand. Germination will take 14-21 days and the plants can be put into their permanent places when three true leaves have formed, about 30 cm [1'] apart for pot marjoram, slightly more for wild marjoram. Keep the young plants well weeded, and well supplied with water in dry weather, though older plants are not so sensitive to drying out.

Pot marjoram can be lifted in early autumn and potted up for winter use. Plants are first cut back by about two thirds before they begin to die down, then potted in a standard potting compost when they show signs of fresh life and taken indoors to a light and not too warm position. Wild marjoram will lose its leaves in autumn and will survive all but really cold weather, when it should be protected with mulches and cloches. Both can also be propagated by division in spring or autumn.

Sweet marjoram is best sown in a seed tray in mid spring, using a seed compost, in a temperature of about 15°C [60°F]. It will therefore be best in a propagator under glass or indoors. Germination, which will take about 8-12 days, should be followed by pricking out the seedlings 5 cm [2"] apart each way, finally planting out in late spring or early summer, with about 15 cm [6"] between plants. They are slow to grow to begin with, and need shade until well established. Hoeing and weeding are important.

Harvesting and aftercare

From a spring sowing, leaves are ready for harvesting just before the plants flower in late summer. They should be dried and stored in an airtight opaque container. There may be another crop of leaves before the winter. After the best leaves have been taken from pot marjoram the plant may be left to grow for the following season. Sweet marjoram seldom survives cold weather, so the remains of the plant should be dug up and added to the compost heap.

Marrow

Best harvested before they reach their maximum size, late summer marrows make a pleasant hot vegetable dish.

One of the hardiest of the large and varied cucurbit family, which also includes cucumbers and melons, the vegetable marrow is classed with squashes, which have to be cooked. There is considerable confusion in the use of names. In the United States marrows are considered as one of the summer squashes; in Britain the term marrow often includes varieties which might be called squashes. The French baby marrow, 7.5-10 cm [3-4"] in size, is known as courgette or zucchini (*see* ZUCCHINI) and is specially grown for eating small.

Marrows have long been popular in the cool temperate regions of Europe although they may have originated in North America. Watery in consistency and bland in flavour, they are usually served with a highly spiced addition — either with a sauce or a stuffing or with ginger. Their delicate flavour deteriorates as they grow in size.

The plant has the trailing habit, bristly stems and leaves of other cucurbits. Marrows are divided into two groups.

A marrow plant of the bush variety; three or four of these will produce enough to supply the average family.

1. *In cool temperate areas, start marrows under glass in early spring. To avoid root damage while planting out, sow seeds singly in well-watered peat pots.*

2. *Having hardened the seedlings off in a cold frame, plant out at the beginning of summer in a low mound. Protect with cloches and space bushes 60 cm [2'] apart.*

3. *Make a small trough around the mound and fill it up with water.*

4. *The seedlings are very prone to slug attack, so spread slug bait on mound.*

5. *With trailing varieties of marrow, the stems should be trained as they grow. To do this, insert stakes on either side of the stems at 60 cm [2'] intervals.*

The trailing variety will produce 2-3 m [7-10'] stems if unchecked, but is usually confined by pruning to about 1.2 m [4']. The bush marrow is so-called because it has a truncated main stem: occupying about 60 cm [2'], it is more suitable for the small garden. Three or four plants of either type will be adequate for most households.

The most commonly grown form of marrow has attractive pale cream and dark green bold stripes, and is long, rather than round, but there are other varieties; fruits can be the same shape but creamy white. Other shapes, which may be listed in catalogues under marrow, are covered in the article on squashes (*see* SQUASH).

Marrow
Cucurbita pepo ovifera (fam. *Cucurbitaceae*), one of the summer squashes, and sometimes referred to by this name in the United States.
Half-hardy annual.
Size: fruit at its best at about 25 cm [10″] long, but will grow to 1 m [3'], plant kept by pruning to 1.2 m [4'] square.
Climate: cool to warm temperate.
Sowing to harvesting time: 12-14 weeks.
Yield: varies according to size cut — 5-6 marrows per plant, average weight of 1.5 kg [3 lb] each.

Suitable site and soil
Marrows were formerly grown on the rubbish heap as a suitable site, before scientific composting became widely practised. As they took up a lot of space and needed plenty of humus, this seemed a neat solution. Nowadays, however, marrows are normally grown in open ground. The marrow needs full sunshine and plenty of water.
At the time of sowing, prepare the eventual site. Dig a hole to a spade's depth and 30 cm [1'] square at each station, keeping the top soil separate. Put in a bucket of well-rotted manure or garden compost. Return most of the dug out soil, and ridge up the topsoil around the hole, so that a depression is formed in the centre. When this is filled with

6. *If trailing stems do not grow sideshoots, tips should be pinched off.*

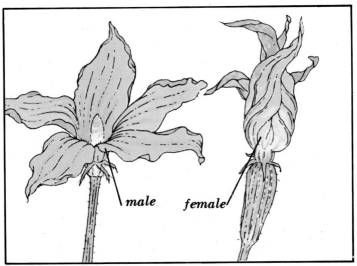

7. *Marrows have male (left) and female (right) flowers. Pollination can usually be left to insects, but for early crops, hand pollinate. Pick off unwanted males.*

8. *Small-fruited trailing varieties are best suited to being trained upwards.*

9. *To harvest the marrows cut them free where they lie then lift gently.*

10. *To keep marrows over winter, hang in nets in cool but frost-free place.*

The cream and green striped marrow is one of the most common varieties. For the best flavour pick the fruits when young and tender — this also encourages new fruit.

water, it will percolate down to the spongy material beneath, where the roots will absorb it after planting. Alternatively, prepare a slight mound on which to plant the marrow, surrounded by a moat-like trench into which water can be poured whenever needed.

Sowing and planting out

Outdoor sowing must be delayed until late spring and seeds and seedlings protected against any threat of frost by inverting flower pots over them. Sow them two to a station, on edge, not flat, and 2.5 cm [1″] deep. Subsequently remove the weaker seedlings by cutting the stem at soil level, so as not to disturb roots of the seedling retained.

In cool temperate areas the marrow is only half hardy and therefore it must be sown under glass in the early spring. Sow at the same depth singly in 7.5 cm [3″] pots of a standard seed compost. A temperature of 10°C [50°F] is needed for germination, which can be supplied in the greenhouse, glazed porch or cold frame. Germination takes from 5-14 days, depending on temperature. Harden off and plant out when all frost is past.

Many gardeners buy seedlings; look for springy stems and upright seedlings of good colour. Space the trailing varieties 1.2 m [4′] and the bush varieties 60 cm [2′] apart.

Training marrows

The tips of the stems of the trailing varieties can be pinched out if they do not produce sideshoots. Any side shoots should be stopped at the seventh leaf to keep them under control, if required. These trailing stems can be trained by inserting short stakes into the soil on either side of the stems at intervals of 60 cm [2′].

Another method, specially suited to the smaller varieties of marrow, whose fruit are the same size and shape of a grapefruit, is to grow them up a 'wigwam'.

Pollination

In general marrow pollination can be left to insects, but to make sure of obtaining the earliest marrows, hand pollinate. If other cucurbits, such as cucumbers, melons and squashes, are grown in the vicinity, you must take steps to prevent insects carrying pollen between the different species. Pollination must only be by hand. Cover the marrows with muslin bags as soon as the flowers begin to open to make sure of this.

Female flowers have an embryonic marrow behind their yellow petals, and a cluster of squat yellow lobes. Male flowers have a prominent central core, bearing yellow pollen. Pick the male flower in the evening and strip off the petals as described in melon pollination (*see* MELON). If male flowers open before the females, hold them back by cutting them and placing them in water until the females are open.

When fruit has set the petals will quickly fall off and the fruit will begin to swell.

Recently there has been some consternation about cross-fertilization between marrows, and ornamental gourds and other wild members of the cucurbit family. The fear is that the marrow will become bitter and even poisonous if this occurs. However, this cross-fertilization will only affect the seed, therefore make sure you buy your seed from a reputable seed merchant. If you grow ornamental gourds in the garden as well as marrows, do not use any seed which you may have saved from your own marrows.

Care and development

Plants increase in size rapidly, and watering must ensure that the soil never dries out, particularly in hot weather. Other care consists of giving a feed of liquid manure when watering from time to time, and hoeing to prevent encroaching weeds.

Harvesting and storing

Cutting begins in late summer. Marrows are best eaten when no more than 25 cm [10″] long, and when the thumb-nail will pierce the skin easily. At one time gardeners aimed at producing marrows of enormous size, by such means as feeding them with milk, but with size the flavour deteriorates and the flesh becomes drier.

Cutting them young stimulates the production of more fruit. Since the marrow is prodigal in the quantity of fruit it bears, and the baby ones have a better flavour, you may prefer to grown them as zucchini only. For winter storage, conserves and pickling, you can let a few marrows grow to become larger. It is better to reserve a few plants specially for this purpose.

Marrows harvested at the end of the season in autumn will store right through winter under cool, dry conditions away from frost, and with the minimum contact with the wall, floor and one another. Slatted shelves in a dry outhouse or cellar are ideal, or they can be hung out of the way individually in nets.

Pests and diseases

Slugs are very fond of the seedlings. Greenfly may attack and spread virus diseases. Mildew and grey mould (*Botrytis cinerea*) may occur, also collar rot (*see* CUCUMBER). Fruit rotting from the tip is due to bad fertilization, or infection of the flower remnants by grey mould, in low temperatures.

Melon

Melons are one of the most refreshing warm weather fruits. The different kinds vary greatly in size with white, green, pink or orange flesh.

Both sweet and watermelons are annual plants, producing tendrils, though the watermelon is a climber rather than a trailer. In a frame or outdoors in a vegetable plot, melons are kept low and allowed to grow along the ground. In the greenhouse they are trained upwards and need support in the form of wires and strings, or a supporting vertical net. They are warm climate plants, and generally require a temperature in excess of 19°C [65°F] rising to 32°C [90°F] or more in summer.

The watermelon, *Citrullus vulgaris*, comes from tropical and southern Africa and, because it requires even higher temperatures, it is difficult to grow even in greenhouses in cool temperate areas. It is a hairy plant with leaves often deeply toothed and lobed. The rind of the fruit is hard but not durable; the flesh is usually pink to red but may be green or yellow. Ripe fruit contains up to 97% water and has little flavour: they are chiefly eaten for refreshment. Each fruit contains numerous seeds, usually dark, up to 1.5 cm [½″] long. They are oily and nutritious and are eaten salted. Big water melons can weigh up to 6.7 kg [15 lb] but there are also smaller varieties around 4.5 kg [10 lb], with a better flavour.

Melon
Varieties of *Cucumis melo* (fam. *Cucurbitaceae*) for sweet fleshed melons, *Citrullus vulgaris* the watermelon.
Half-hardy trailing or climbing **annuals.**
Size: 30-45 cm [1′-1½′] high, 1 m [3′] across, up to 1.5 m [5′] long; up to 1.8 m [6′] high grown in the greenhouse.
Climate: warm temperate to sub-tropical.
Sowing to harvesting time: 4 months.
Yield: 6 good quality fruit, depending on variety per 3 m [10′] row. In a frame 2-6 fruit, in a greenhouse 2 fruit per plant.

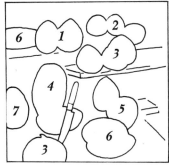

There are many different varieties of melon, which interbreed readily, so it is impossible to classify them in precise groups. The varieties illustrated here are:

1. Crenshaw melon
2. Musk or netted melon
3. and 7. Casaba melon
4. Watermelon
5. Honeydew melon
6. Christmas melon

(Below) Watermelons need much more heat than other types and are hard to grow even in greenhouses in cool temperate areas.

(Below right) Climbing melons must have their fruit supported with nets.

Sweet melons, *Cumumis melo*, have soft, hairy, ridged stems with leaves varying according to variety, but generally rounded with wavy serrated edges. From Asia and Africa, the rind, size and appearance of the fruit is very variable. Slender white seeds are contained in a fibrous centre.

Melons interbreed so readily that it is difficult to make precise botanical classifications. The group with hard skins and white or green flesh, without a strong aroma, is called Winter melon. Honeydew is included in this family. Skins may be yellow or dark green, smooth or slightly corrugated, but there are no ridges or suggestion of a netted pattern. These melons ripen late, can be stored for about a month, and are a warm climate melon.

Netted melons are so-called for the appearance of the skin which has a raised pattern, generally lighter in colour. Some also have grooved skins and some do not. The interior may be green or salmon-orange and they are also called musk melons for their aromatic flavour. In the United States it is common to refer to the orange-fleshed melons of this group as 'cantaloupes' even though botanically they are not in the cantaloupe family. Netted melons are the most popular for growing in greenhouses in cool temperate areas, but can be grown outside in warm climates.

The cantaloupe group of melons is distinguished because they tolerate cooler temperatures than the other groups and can therefore be grown in frames or under cloches without additional heat. Originally a warty melon from Italy, where it acquired its name, the group now embraces a wide variety of size and colour. Some of them are more like netted melons, most of them have orange flesh — the tiny Charantais melon is in this group. The small Ogen or Ha-ogen, bred in Israel, belongs to this group and has yellow skin with green stripes and green flesh.

BASIC STEPS IN MELON GROWING

Melons like a warm sheltered site in full sun. In a Mediterranean climate they may be grown outside, in cool temperate areas they must be grown either in cold frames (or under cloches) or in the greenhouse, according to variety.

The basic steps are described below. These apply to all melons, whichever your choice of site. A fertile well-drained soil is suitable.

Soil preparation

One month before planting prepare the site by digging one spit (spade's depth) deep and add rotted organic matter at the rate of 2.5-5 kg [5-10 lb] per sq m [yd], depending on the condition of the soil. Do not use heavily nitrogenous fertilizer if manure is not available, or stem and leaf

1. *Tip out the plant.*

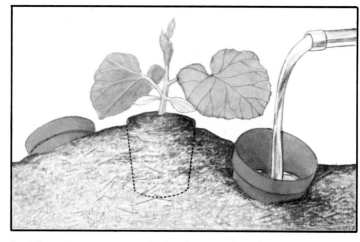

2. *Plant it on a mound. Sunken pots assist watering.*

3. *Pinch out tip to help flowers form.*

4. *Lateral shoots are trained symmetrically. Each will then bear one fruit, and all will develop evenly.*

single female flower

double male flower

growth will be at the expense of fruiting. If you are growing in a fixed frame, do not neglect to dig over the bottom thoroughly before fertilizing.

Sowing

Melons can be sown outdoors in late spring in warm temperate areas, protecting them with inverted pots. In cool temperate areas, seeds should be sown singly in 7.5 cm [3"] pots in mid spring under glass. If sowing is carried out too early in cool temperate areas, the plants will have to remain too long in their pots, where they will become starved, and they may never recover from this check in growth. More seeds should be sown than are required, as not all of them may germinate. The seeds should be placed on edge in a good seed compost which has a loam base, and about 2 cm [¾"] deep.

Germination takes place more readily in a fairly high temperature — 21°C [70°F]. To maintain this in cool areas, a greenhouse or heated propagation frame is required. If neither of these is available, an airing cupboard may be used, but germination will be longer and, as soon as it takes place, the seedlings must be moved to a light place with a fairly congenial temperature of about 15° to 18°C [60° to 65°F].

Young melon seedlings need careful watering, making sure that the soil never dries out, but also avoiding overwatering. They must not be deprived of nutrients either — if the leaves start to look yellow add a little liquid fertilizer to the water if you cannot plant for a few days.

Planting out

Before planting, the soil should be drawn up into a low mound for each plant, making the soil firm. Small flower pots may be inserted one either side of the mound for watering. Water is subsequently poured into the pots and reaches the roots while avoiding the stem.

Water the seedling a little before moving it; the soil ball should be moist. Knock the plant out of the pot carefully, placing your hand across the top and holding the stem between the base of two fingers, before you reverse it. Tap the bottom of the pot till the soil ball loosens.

Plant at the same level on the mound as it was formerly at in the pot. Indeed it is better to be too high than too low. This is important in order to ensure that water cannot collect round the base of the main stem and cause canker. Make the soil firm around the roots.

Watering

Frequent watering is required as the plants grow,

Melons are lifted off the soil as they swell. Ripeness is indicated by smell and tiny hair cracks on the fruit.

Strip the petals off a male flower.
Insert core into female flower to transfer the pollen.

especially in periods of hot weather. Melons need lots of water and should on no account be allowed to dry out. In hot weather this will mean giving each plant a 12 L [2½ gal] bucket every day.

Overhead watering must be avoided during the time the plants are in flower until such time as they have set and swelling has begun.

In warmer climates a strip of black plastic 60 cm [2'] wide can be used to reduce water loss through evaporation. This is best applied at the time of planting, with a hole cut for the insertion of each young plant.

Training

Plants grown on the ground are trained by moving the young growths gently into the chosen direction and pegging behind a leaf with a small stick or piece of bent wire so that it holds its position. A balance of growth in each direction is desirable.

For training climbing plants, see the Greenhouse section.

Pruning

Pruning is done in two stages. The first phase is to encourage the formation of flowers. The second phase is to remove unwanted shoots after the fruit have set (formed fruit from the flower), so that all the plant's energy goes into producing fruit of a good size.

Encouraging flowers to form: To obtain early flowers, some cutting back is necessary. Count four adult leaves from the base and then pinch out the growing point immediately above the fourth leaf. Normally this results in the production of a side growth from the axil of each leaf. Two of these should be selected — one from each side of the plant, preferably the strongest. They should then be encouraged to grow in opposite directions and each allowed to bear one fruit. The other two side growths are pinched out. If you want to grow more than two melons you can retain all four side growths and allow each to bear one fruit.

This pruning should encourage the production of female flowers. If however none appear, it must be repeated. Again remove the growing point beyond the fourth or fifth leaf. Side growths will again appear, and normally these will bear female flowers.

Reducing plant size: When the fruit has set and you have decided which ones are to be retained, the sideshoots should also be stopped, at the first leaf beyond the fruit. Sub sideshoots can be pinched out either after two leaves or, if growth is becoming congested, where they originate from the main sideshoot. The removal of surplus growths should be done regularly, every few days if possible, to avoid the growth checking that would occur if all of them were removed at the same time.

Pollination

The male flowers grow two or three in a group and have a prominent central core. The female flowers have a flattish centre and a small round swelling just behind the flower where it joins the stalk; they grow singly. Out-of-doors pollination will be by insects but under glass or plastic it must be by hand, and all the flowers must be pollinated at the same time, preferably just before noon.

Remove the male flower by its stem and divest it of its petals. Then shake the powdery central core into the centre of the fully open female flower.

You will do best to pollinate several flowers, if available, on either side of the plant. Out-of-doors melons set first by insects will swell quickly and leave behind those pollinated at a later date. When they have set and start to swell, four which are developing at the same pace on separate shoots may finally be selected. Other flowers are then pinched out. You must choose at this point whether you want two fruit of superior quality — in which case retain only two — or more but smaller fruit.

Care of swelling fruit

Feeding: Applications of liquid fertilizer at the manufacturer's recommended strength should be used to help improve fruit size; an average might be 9 L [2 gal] of feed per three plants once a week.

Support of the fruit: Melons grown on the ground should be lifted off the soil by placing an inverted flower pot, a tile, slate or piece of board underneath. The support of melons grown under glass is covered in the Greenhouse section.

HALF HARDY MELONS

The cantaloupe group of melons tolerate cooler temperatures than other melons. They can be grown out-of-doors in cooler climates provided they have the protection of frames, cloches or a plastic tunnel. A sunny site is needed preferably facing the midday sun, and sheltered from wind.

Growing melons in a frame

A frame averaging between 125 cm x 125 cm [4' x 4'] and 150 cm x 75 cm [5' x 2½'], with an opening light, will hold one or two melons. For a small quantity of high quality fruit, a pair of melons can be planted at diagonal corners. Melons grow luxuriantly and, if you choose this method, you will have to prune back the growth continuously after the fruit sets to keep the plants in reasonable bounds.

If you would prefer to grow a larger number of smaller and less perfect fruit, one melon can be planted in the middle of the back of the frame. This allows room for the side growths to spread out naturally.

Make a low mound in the chosen spot ready for planting. After the melons have been planted, the light may be closed for a few days, unless the weather is very hot when a little ventilation should be provided during the hottest part of the day. In very hot weather some shade should be given by painting the glass of the light or cloche with a proprietary shading paint.

Growing melons under cloches or plastic

Dome cloches are too small to allow proper development of the plant, which needs at least 1 sq m [1 sq yd]. A succession of barn-type cloches or a 45 cm [1½'] high plastic tunnel may be used.

The melons should be planted 125 cm [4'] apart, The glass or plastic tunnel is then erected over the plants so that the

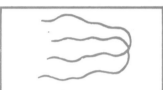 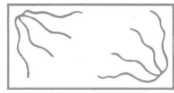

With a frame, cantaloupes can be grown outdoors in cool areas. There are two alternative lay-outs: for a large number of small fruits, put one plant at the back of the frame, or for fewer, more perfect fruit plant two, kept heavily pruned back, in opposite corners.

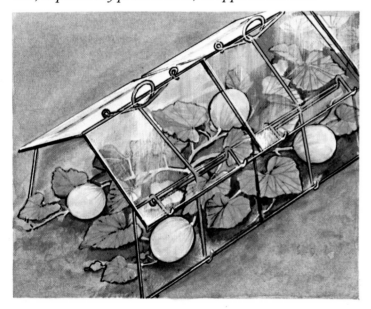

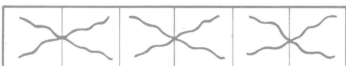

Cantaloupe melons may also be protected by barn-type cloches or plastic tunnels. Enough space must be left under these for proper plant development. Plant the melons 125 cm [4'] apart and then put the cloches over them. Train out four laterals per plant as shown in the plan, and stop them when they reach the frame limits.

first melon in the row is sited 60 m [2'] from the entrance and all the melons are trained equally in both directions down the tunnel.

After planting, the ends of the tunnel are closed off with panes of glass or, if plastic, knotted round a stake. These may be opened up for ventilation. Shade may be given in hot weather as for frames.

Always remember to hand pollinate if plants are grown under glass or any container of this sort; the insects obviously cannot reach the flowers. Also keep the plants well watered, especially when the weather is dry.

GREENHOUSE MELONS

In cool temperate climates the best melons are produced in the greenhouse, where the temperature can be kept above 15°C [60°F] at night, with a rise of 22°C [40°F] or more by day. Watermelons should only be attempted here.

Sowing and planting

Plants are best sown and grown in 6.5-7.5 cm [2½-3"] pots. Before sowing, knock a large hole in the pot base. As the plant grows it is placed, still in its pot, in position and allowed to root through into the bed. The stem is raised up, and this greatly reduces the risk of canker disease, as only the bed beneath is watered.

Melons require a fertile loam; the soil should be prepared as described for cucumber (*see* CUCUMBER). A hotbed of that type is also suitable. Put down a layer of fresh manure 45 cm [1½'] wide and 7.5 cm [3"] deep, to produce heat for the plants. This should be spread out in the open beforehand and turned over occasionally for a few days to allow the excess nitrogen to be given off as ammonia. Another way of producing heat is to use a 60 cm [2'] thick layer of straw, firmed down, sprinkled with sulphate of ammonia, and saturated with water. On top, put a layer 30 cm [1'] deep and 60 cm [2'] wide, of good, loamy soil. This will now be ready for melons. Remember, however, that too much manure will encourage overluxuriant growth at the expense of fruit.

Place the melon pots 45 cm [1½'] apart on the bed, and up to 60 cm [2'] apart for more vigorous varieties.

Erecting training wires

Melons under glass are generally trained on wires fixed to a metal or timber support, which follows the angle of the greenhouse roof, 30-35 cm [12-14"] away from the glass. In a span roofed house the training wires should be about 23 cm [9"] apart and form an inverted V.

A more modern method is to fix 20 cm [8"] mesh wire netting to the apex of the house and again to a wire running 15 cm [6"] above the bed, with a supporting wire in the middle. A small cane is provided to support the plant until it reaches the bottom wire.

Care and development

The main shoot will grow upward, and should be stopped soon after planting when about 10-15 cm [4-6"] tall, and two sideshoots allowed to grow, one on each side of the main stem, up the netting, to which they are tied as required. They are stopped only if sub sideshoots are not

171

being produced. Each plant can be allowed to produce two to four fruits, two being the more usual number. Male flowers are produced about a week before the female, which can be identified by the embryo fruit behind the flower. As soon as the flowers have set, and the fruits are beginning to swell, you should stop the sideshoots at the first leaf beyond the fruit. At the same time, remove any fruits other than the chosen ones, while they are still young. The sub sideshoots should be thinned by stopping or removing them when still young to obtain a good, even leaf cover, without swamping the fruit by excess production. This should be done little and often to avoid any check to growth

Water the plants frequently, especially when the weather is hot and dry. Hand pollination will also be necessary if you are growing your melons in the greenhouse. Applications of liquid fertilizer should be applied as described under Basic Steps.

Like cucumbers, melon roots may appear on the surface · and should be covered with a light dressing of soil.

Ventilation

Ventilators should be opened when the temperature reaches 27°C [80°F]. Towards the end of the day they should be closed to retain heat for the night. Plants should be syringed with water in the early morning in hot weather, and the house and border damped down once or twice in the morning and early afternoon to maintain a humid atmosphere.

While the melons are in flower, more air should be admitted until the fruit have set. When ripening commences ventilation should be increased again and both syringing and watering should be reduced. The fruit flavour will improve with exposure to the sun, so tuck a few leaves aside.

Supporting the ripening fruit

Melons swell rapidly, especially in hot weather, and soon need support, otherwise their stems would break. Choose a square of about 5 cm [2"] mesh netting, large enough to encompass the expected size of your variety. Loop one string through each end and tie each to the wire above. Check from time to time that the net is not constricting the fruit and preventing its development.

HARVESTING AND PROTECTION

When a melon is approaching ripeness, hair cracks appear round the stalk where it joins the fruit. It begins to change colour and soften at the blossom end — test this by pressing with a finger. Also at this time, the characteristic aroma becomes more perceptible. Reduce watering considerably and stop feeding.

It is not necessary to wait for complete ripeness before harvesting the fruit — you can do this when deep cracks around the stalk indicate that separation is near.

If placed in a warm dry place for a few days, complete ripening will take place. Melons can be stored in a refrigerator; this will delay ripening for several days or so. Most types of melon should be eaten at room temperature, as chilling tends to reduce their delicate flavour.

Pests and diseases

Canker or collar rot may occur at the base of the main stem (*see* CUCUMBER). Red spider mite, wilt, greenfly, grey mould (*Botrytis cinerea*) and virus are also troubles which can attack melons.

Melons are sensitive to some chemicals, so check before you spray.

Mint

Mint is one of the oldest cultivated herbs, mentioned in the Bible and long valued for its refreshing fragrance and flavour.

Mint is the name given to several *Mentha* species of the *Labiatae* family. A hardy perennial, mint usually grows to about 30 cm [1'] high but may reach up to 60 cm [2'], depending on variety and situation. *M.* x *spicata*, (the x indicates a cross-bred species) common mint or spearmint, is the most familiar type; *M.* x *villosa*, Bowles' mint or applemint, is the next best type for culinary purposes with its woolly leaves and rich flavour; this variety has flowers in pink spikes and is taller at 75 cm [2½']. Of the many other species, eau de cologne mint, *M* x *piperita* (from which peppermint is derived) is particularly attractive in a herb garden for its aroma and pretty purple-tinged foliage. Pineapple mint. *M.* x *suaveolens variegata*, is interesting to grow for its surprisingly genuine pineapple-like fragrance, and woolly leaves which are cream variegated round the margins. Pennyroyal, *M. pulegium*, used to be grown in former times; its popular name was fleabane because it was thought to drive away bugs.

Mint leaves are traditionally used in a sauce for roast lamb or cooked with new potatoes and peas to add to their

Spearmint is the most popular of the mints for cooking. Best used when young and freshly picked, this is the basis of the traditional mint sauce to accompany lamb.

Mint can thrive in pots, provided leafmould or peat is added to the soil and the plant is kept well watered.

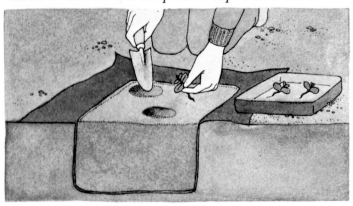

To restrict spreading roots, line 30 cm [1'] deep hole with black plastic sheeting. Plant 30 cm [1'] apart.

1. Propagating mint. Cut pieces of rooting runners.

2. Plant 7 cm [3"] long runners 5 cm [2"] deep.

flavour. Fresh or dried, the leaves also make a delicate and invigorating tea. Fresh leaves may be used in salads, sandwiches and cool summer drinks. Eau de cologne mint is an ingredient of Chartreuse liqueur and peppermint, *M. x piperita,* is widely used in confectionery.

Cultivation

Mint can be erratic in habit. It usually has a tendency to send out underground runners which encroach on the territory of other plants. It can also disappear entirely from the garden or revert to a very coarse flavour. Both problems arise from leaving mint in one site for too long. To keep plants healthy and under control they should be replanted in a different site every three years. The site may be in either full sun or partial shade, as long as the root run is kept cool and damp. Rich, moist leafmould or peat provides an excellent base, worked well into the soil.

To prevent the plants from spreading, dig a hole 30 cm [1'] deep, and line it with black plastic sheeting; then return the soil, adding leaf mould or peat, and plant your mint.

If the space is limited mint can be grown in tubs, where the roots will be restricted, but it will need to be kept well watered. Soil for tubs should be prepared as for the open ground, with the addition of rich, light loam, or a good potting compost can be used.

All mint varieties are started from plants obtained at a nursery and planted 30 cm [1'] apart or propagated by detaching pieces of rooting runners from an established plant and laying these in drills 5 cm [2"] deep. Either method can be done any time from spring onwards during the growing season.

Keep the plants watered until new growth appears. Any weeds that appear must be scrupulously eliminated; if they get a hold it is difficult to untangle them from the mint. Mint grows rapidly and will provide plenty of fresh leaves during summer. If the top cluster of leaves is removed first, this will encourage the stems to branch. Topdress with manure in spring or after the first cutting.

During the summer mint can also be started from seed sown in boxes or a seedbed, but the plants will not be ready until the next season.

Harvesting

Harvesting leaves for drying is done just before the plant is ready to flower in late summer. Tie the leaves in bunches and hang up to dry, rub them to a powder and store in airtight containers.

The season for fresh mint can be extended by lifting some roots before the first frost and planting in a frame or greenhouse, where they will continue growing during winter. Plants left outdoors will die down during winter and begin a new growth in spring, but cloche protection should be given if the weather is severe. Pineapple mint is the most delicate and will not survive cold, wet conditions.

Mint can be attacked by greenfly and the fungus disease rust, which shows as powdery brown-red patches and spots on the undersurface of the leaves. The plants can be severely weakened, and such plants are best lifted and destroyed. New plants should be put in a different place.

Mulberry

Mulberries look rather similar to blackberries. The mulberry tree lives for several centuries and produces large quantities of fruit.

The black mulberry, *Morus nigra,* is the only one commonly planted for its fruit, although there are several species of mulberry. The white mulberry *M. alba* is chiefly used for feeding silk worms, and as a rootstock for the black; its berries are edible, light red at maturity and, sweet but insipid. It is rather taller at 12-18 m [40-60′]. Black mulberries are very dark red and can be eaten raw if left on the tree to get really ripe, but they have a sub-acid flavour and are usually picked for pies, jam, wine and for steeping in gin. The red juice stains all it touches. The fruit is a botanical curiosity, being formed from unisexual flowers the calyx of which swells to form the berry.

The tree is comparatively small and very attractive when planted in a lawn. It can be grown as a bush with a short trunk, when it forms a spreading rounded specimen, or as a standard. The branches are crooked and when the tree becomes increasingly gnarled in old age, the limbs need to be supported on posts.

The tree is slightly tender, and needs shelter in cooler parts of the cold temperate area. Deep, rich, well-drained but moisture retentive soil is the ideal.

If the young tree has long thick roots, the planting hole must be big enough to accommodate these; the brittle roots must not be damaged or cut, as they will bleed. Planting is like other deciduous fruit trees, except that the best time to plant is in early spring.

No special formative pruning is needed, but only the

Mulberry
Morus nigra (fam. *Moraceae*)
Hardy deciduous tree with a useful life of several centuries.
Size: height 6-9 m [20-30′] and the same across.
Climate: temperate to sub-tropical.
Planting to harvesting time: about 8 years.
Yield: mature tree 150 kg [350 lb].

Given the right climate and soil conditions, the black mulberry tree will bear fruit for hundreds of years.

The branches are crooked and, as the tree becomes increasingly gnarled with old age, have to be supported by posts. Lower branches are sometimes removed from very old and droopy trees.

When ripe, mulberries are very dark red. To remove any that have not dropped off, cover the ground and shake the branches with care as the brittle wood breaks easily.

routine removal of dead wood and the thinning out of crowded shoots and branches in winter. Even so, it should be kept to a minimum as the tree will bleed considerably from wounds.

Berries for dessert should be left to ripen on the tree. Spread a sheet on the ground and they will fall when ripe, mostly in late summer. Shake the tree carefully — the wood is brittle and liable to break.

Only canker attacks the mulberry and this is rarely important enough to need treatment. Protection against birds will be needed, as they are very fond of the fruit.

Mushroom

One of our most popular foods, mushrooms are different in character, shape and method of culture from other vegetables, but with a little care they are easy to grow.

Man has known of mushrooms since he first began to eat vegetables. They grow wild all over the earth wherever the conditions are right for them — from China and Japan to the Americas, Europe and England. The cultivated mushroom is a close relative of the common field mushroom *Agaricus campestris*.

The entire growth above ground is edible, consisting of

Mushroom
Agaricus bisporus (fam. *Agaricaceae*)
Size: a capped fungus, 7.5 cm [3″] in height; caps vary from about 2.5 cm [1″] across for 'button' mushrooms to 10 cm [4″] for mature ones.
Climate: temperate, if grown outdoors, but most mushrooms are grown in artificial conditions.
Planting to harvesting time: 8-10 weeks; the harvest then continues for 11-12 weeks longer.
Yield: 0.5-1 kg [1-2 lb] per 900 sq cm [1 sq yd].

---

white, creamy or brownish caps with brown gills beneath and brownish stalks. They give a high yield and can be grown all the year round in properly prepared ground.

The natural method of propagation is by spores, which correspond to the seeds of green plants. Under suitable conditions the spores develop into long, white, thread-like filaments known as mycelium or spawn. Mushrooms can be used whole or chopped and eaten raw in salads or cooked by almost any method.

Suitable site and compost

The site can range from the floors of cellars and sheds to an open field, but most commercially grown mushrooms are grown in specially prepared beds in dark places. Mushrooms can also be grown in the garden. Start to prepare the site at least three weeks before planting. Stack strawy horse manure about 1.2 m [4′] high, and water it as you do this, if it is at all dry, so that it is moist but not really wet. It will then heat up and begin to ferment, when the temperature should be in the region of 65°C [150°F]. Turn it to ensure that it all rots and does not dry out, doing this four or five times, at intervals of about four days. By the end of about three weeks, the compost should be brown, crumbly and moist, and it should no longer smell of ammonia. It will now have a temperature of about 27°C [80°F] and is ready for use. Commercial growers often add gypsum, at the rate of 12.6 kg per tonne [28 lb per ton] of manure — during the first turn — to prevent the finished produce from being sticky.

When horse manure is unavailable you can use as a substitute either ready-made mushroom compost or home-made compost. The latter is made with the aid of an activator. A proprietary brand of this chemical can be bought from your seedsman or garden shops. Specific instructions will be provided, but the general principle is simple. Make a heap with alternate layers of straw and activator and then follow the same procedure outlined for manure. This heap must also be kept moist but not soaking.

An easier method is to grow the mushrooms in a field or lawn. Simply remove a piece of turf and place the spawn beneath it. This is a more chancy method, but it can sometimes produce successful results. Plant around mid-summer for a crop in early autumn.

Spawning and casing

The spawn, generally shaped into fibrous blocks (though now also available in granular form) is available from seedsmen.

For the spawning of your mushrooms you need air temperatures of 12-14°C [54-58°F]. These conditions are, of course, more easily maintained within a building than outdoors.

In buildings, flat or ridge-shaped beds can be made against a wall. The compost should be well packed to a depth of 20-30 cm [8-12″]. After being placed in position the temperature of the compost will rise to about 38°C [100°F] and will then gradually fall. Keep it moderately well watered during this process — when squeezed, the compost should feel damp but should not drip water.

1. *Making suitable compost. Stack manure and straw. Spray with water to promote fermentation; do not soak.*

2. *Use a fork to turn the heap four or five times every four days to ensure it all rots and stays moist.*

GROWING MUSHROOMS IN A BED

3. *Test the temperature of the compost with a soil thermometer. Plant spawn when temperature falls to 21°C [70°F]*

4. *Break walnut-sized pieces of spawn from the cake and plant them 2.5 cm [1″] deep and 30 cm [12″] apart.*

5. *If using grain spawn, scatter it on the surface. Do not water, but cover box with black plastic to keep the compost moist.*

6. *Prepare 'casing' by thoroughly mixing moist peat and gypsum together, in a ratio of three to one by volume.*

7. *Ten days after the white threads of mycelium appear, spread the casing lightly over the compost at a depth of 2.5 cm [1″].*

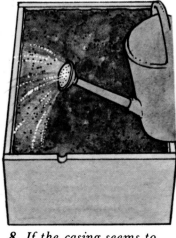

8. *If the casing seems to be drying out, water sparingly using can with a fine rose. Always keep the box well ventilated.*

9. *Pull mushrooms from the compost with a twist of the hand; do not cut. Fill the holes left with some of the casing.*

Plastic buckets of compost and pre-sown spawn are available from garden centres and are easy to grow.

1. *To grow mushrooms in the grass outdoors, first lift a section of turf.*

2. *Using a small fork (but not a hand fork) loosen the exposed soil.*

3. *Scatter grain spawn on the surface, replace the turf and firm lightly.*

4. *Midsummer-sown seed should produce a first 'flush' in early autumn.*

The white-capped mushroom is the most popular variety, but brown-capped mushrooms resist disease much better.

After a few days the temperature will fall to 21°C [70°F]. This is the correct moment to insert the spawn.

Break the cake into fragments about the size of a walnut and insert pieces about 2.5 cm [1″] deep in the compost, at a spacing of 25-30 cm [10-12″] in each direction.

After a few days or so, the mushroom mycelium will be seen spreading like fine, white thread through the compost. Leave it for a further 10 days, then cover with a 'casing' of soil. This will help to retain the heat of the bed and to conserve moisture. A rich, fine, loamy soil is ideal, and if it has been sterilized, so much the better. Cover the compost to a depth of 2.5-4 cm [1-1½″]. Alternatively the casing can consist of a mixture of moist peat and gypsum, in a ratio of three to one by volume.

Care and development

The mushrooms should appear after about two to three weeks, according to temperature. From this point until harvesting should take only a few days, again depending on temperature. During this period water sparingly and only if the casing seems to be drying out. The water so applied should not be sufficient to penetrate to the compost beneath. The bed temperature should not be allowed to rise above 21°C [70°F] for more than brief periods, or the mycelium will be damaged. Keep the beds well ventilated, but avoid draughts. Moderate frosts will not harm outdoor beds.

Harvesting and aftercare

When ready for picking, twist out each mushroom or break it off from a cluster. Mushrooms ripen in large numbers, in 'spates' or 'flushes'. When the first flush is over remove any dead stems and fill in the holes in the compost. Water generously, although not to saturation. A second flush should appear in about 10 days. This pattern should continue for about three months.

When the last mushrooms have been gathered, the compost should be cleared from the bed. On no account use it for mushrooms again, although it makes excellent manure for other crops. Give frames, boxes or other casing a thorough disinfecting to remove any trace of insects or infection. You should limewash walls and scrub floors.

Pests and diseases

The main troubles of mushrooms are the larvae of mushroom flies, mites, springtails and slugs, and such fungal diseases as bubbles and the plaster moulds.

Fly maggots, mites and springtails can be dealt with by mixing BHC dust with the compost when bringing it in before spawning. Bubbles or mushroom disease (*Mycogone perniciosa*) results in clusters of mushrooms growing into an undifferentiated mass, smelling unpleasant and covered in white mould. Provided the manure reached a high enough temperature when breaking down, and the casing soil was sterilized, there should be no trouble with this, otherwise all affected mushrooms should be destroyed, and the bed sprayed with a copper compound between each flush.

The plaster moulds make the casing look as though it has been covered in white powder, turning brown later in the case of brown plaster mould. Again, properly produced compost will kill this disease; otherwise take off the surface of the compost before casing.

Mustard Greens

SEE CHINESE CABBAGE

Nasturtium

Nasturtiums are frequently grown for their beautiful flowers alone, but the plant is valuable in many ways as a herb.

The common nasturtium (*Tropaeolum majus*) of the *Tropaeolaceae* family is available in many hybrids, but the original garden variety has single flowers and will trail vigorously over the ground or climb to a length of about 1.8 m [6']. Although nasturtiums are a hardy annual, wherever they have grown they will appear the next year from their own scattered seed. The leaves are similar in taste to watercress. The flower petals can be added to salads and the green seed is useful for pickling as a substitute for capers.

Cultivation
Nasturtiums are native to South America and grow in dry, hot places. It is usually recommended to grow them on poor soil to encourage flowers rather than leaf growth, but

the flowers are not as important if the plant is being grown as a herb. If the soil is very rich, however, the leaves will be oversized and the stems will grow long and coarse, making them less suitable for salads. If the ground you are planting them in has been well enriched for previous crops it will have to be slightly impoverished by replacing some of the soil with stonier ground.

The situation should be in full sun. Seed is sown in late spring 2.5 cm [1"] deep and 30 cm [1'] apart. Germination takes about ten days. The plants grow rapidly and do not need attention, apart from keeping them within bounds. If support is provided the plant will climb by curling their leaf stems around it. Blackfly is sometimes troublesome.

Harvesting and aftercare
Leaves may be pulled from the plants as they are required. Nasturtiums flower from early summer onwards, until the first frost, and become rampant and leafy towards the end of their life. You can start cutting back the stems from midsummer. Towards the end of summer when they have died, the sprawling trailers must be cut back quite severely and all foliage should be removed to the compost heap.

There will usually be a multitude of seeds on the ground at the end of summer. If these are gathered up and stored for sowing the following year, as well as for pickling, you will have a more orderly display of plants than if you leave them on the ground to become a forest of seedlings.

Nectarine

This delicious stone fruit is a 'fuzzless' peach, with the same flesh and taste, but the smooth skin of a plum. It is closely related to the peach.

The nectarine (*Prunus persica nectarina*) is closely related to the peach, so much so that stones from one fruit may grow into the tree of the other and sports (single deviations) may appear on trees of the other.

The fruit are smooth-skinned peaches, rather smaller than

the peach and with a richer flavour. The plum-like skins may be red or yellow and there are both yellow and white fleshed varieties. More than 50 varieties are known.

Like the peach, nectarines grow into small trees, and the nectarine is even more tender than the peach, the least hardy of deciduous fruit trees. It requires a sheltered site and in mild parts of the cool temperate area is usually grown against a wall facing the midday sun. In cooler parts it should not be attempted. Like peaches, nectarines may be grown in unheated greenhouses.

For cultivation *see* PEACH.

1. *New Zealand spinach is best grown in lime-rich soil. If the soil is acid apply lime in the autumn.*

2. *Soak the seeds well, just before sowing. This softens the casing which speeds germination.*

New Zealand Spinach

Unlike true spinach, which is a short-lived plant, New Zealand spinach continues throughout the summer, and supplies a succulent mild-flavoured green vegetable in hot weather.

Although intoduced into Britain from New Zealand in the late eighteenth century, New Zealand spinach is thought to have originally come from South America or Japan. It is a trailing plant and requires ample space; if this is not supplied, it will invade the territory of other garden crops

> **New Zealand spinach**
> *Tetragonia expansa* (fam. *Aizoaceae*)
> **Half hardy annual.**
> **Size:** a low-growing trailing plant, which will spread over 1 sq m [1 sq yd] or more.
> **Climate:** temperate to warm and sub-tropical.
> **Sowing to harvesting time:** 7-8 weeks.
> **Yield:** almost unlimited; the more you pick, the more you have.

3. *Summer heat makes spinach bolt, but New Zealand spinach will continue to produce tender young leaves.*

Young New Zealand spinach grows slowly and must be clear of weeds. It should also be protected from frost.

and tend to smother them. It has the great advantage over ordinary spinach that it will not bolt in hot weather.

Suitable site and soil

Choose an open, sunny site. New Zealand spinach likes soil fairly rich in lime, so it does particuarly well on chalk or limestone subsoils; avoid acid soils or lime them well before growing, at a rate determined by the result of a soil test. Although it appreciates a good, well-manured, deep soil it can flourish on comparatively poor ground.

Sowing and planting

The one problem with this plant, which is otherwise easy to grow, is that its seeds have a very hard casing, making germination slow. It is well worthwhile soaking them in water just before sowing — ideally three or four hours in warm water followed by 24 hours in cold water. They should then germinate quite quickly, and an outdoor sowing in late spring should start to produce a harvest of leaves within seven or eight weeks.

New Zealand spinach is much less resistant to cold than the drought, especially when young, and should not be exposed to frost. It may therefore be worthwhile to bring on some plants in a greenhouse or under cloches. Sow two or three seeds in a 7.5-10 cm [3-4″] pot, during mid spring, up to a month before the last frost date.

When sowing outdoors or transplanting young plants outdoors, allow 60 cm [2′] between each plant and at least 90 cm [3′] between rows; even a spacing as wide as this may not be enough. It is as well to find a border or spare plot where the plant can spread to its full extent. To allow for the proportion of seeds that may fail to germinate, sow two or three seeds together and thin out the weakest if they all happen to grow.

Care and development

During the early stages keep the hoe moving around the plants. New Zealand spinach is rather a slow starter and can quickly become crowded out by weeds. As it grows, it becomes able to take care of itself and will smother weed growth. The plants will benefit from watering, especially in the early stages, but later on they can, if necessary, survive prolonged drought and high temperatures. No feeding is necessary.

If the plants are growing in a garden with limited space, their spreading habits may be kept in check by pinching out the tips and snipping off the longer shoots.

Harvesting the crop

Pick the succulent young leaves, and keep picking them. Leave the older, coarser leaves. If the harvest begins seven or eight weeks after sowing, it can continue right through the summer until frost destroys the crop. When cooking, treat the leaves as spinach. They can also be deep-frozen.

Aftercare

When frost has killed the plants, dig them up and consign the remnants to the compost heap. By this time, however, they will have scattered seed over the plot, for next year's harvest. It is therefore a good plan to reserve a plot

permanently (or, at least, for several years) for New Zealand spinach, letting it perpetuate itself. Otherwise the young spinach plants will grow as weeds and have to be dealt with accordingly.

Container growing

New Zealand spinach is quite suitable for container growing; the plant will soon hide a tub, box or barrel with its mass of trailing green shoots and attractive leaves.

Pest and diseases

Apart from the danger of damage by slugs in the early stages, this is a trouble-free crop.

Okra

The long, finger-shaped young pods of the okra plant are among the more unusual vegetables. Although the plants need warmth and care, okra pods can be used to produce many exotic dishes.

Okra is a native of tropical Africa, but has spread to such tropical zones as the West Indies, the southern states of America and Asia, where it is now a common ingredient in many of these countries' dishes. Okra is closely related to the hibiscus cotton plants. Although tropical in origin, it

---

Okra
Hibiscus esculentus (fam. *Malvaceae*),
also known as ladies' fingers, gumbo or bamya.
Tender annual.
Size: the bushy plants grow to about 1.2-1.8 m [4-6′] high. The edible pods range from 7.5-20 cm [3-8″] long, depending on variety.
Climate: warm temperate to sub-tropical.
Sowing to harvesting time: 8-16 weeks.
Yield: 5-8 plants per 3 m [10′] row.

1. *In cool temperate areas, sow in peat pots in a heated greenhouse.*

2. *Transplant into greenhouse bed, 38 cm [15"] apart. Keep soil moist.*

3. *In warmer areas, transplant to a sunny outdoor site under cloches.*

Okra pods ready for harvesting. Pick these delicately flavoured pods when they are still immature, as they become too fibrous to digest when ripe.

4. *If sites are not well sheltered, tie plants to canes for support.*

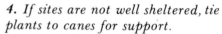

5. *Use scissors to cut pods whilst they are still young and tender.*

can be grown in warm temperate climates, but it may need some protection and artificial heat since it requires temperatures of 24° to 27°C [75° to 80°F]. The plant is stout and can grow to more than 1.8 m [6′] in its native tropics. The leaves are large, often 30 cm [1′] across with three to five lobes and with toothed edges. The flowers are yellow with the same dark red spots at the base of each petal as the ornamental hibiscus. The edible parts are the long, grooved, dark green, spear-shaped pods, which range in size from 7.5-20 cm [3-8″] depending on which variety is grown.

The pods should be picked when young and tender and either steamed, fried in batter, used in casseroles, or as an ingredient in such dishes as vegetable curry and gumbo.

Cultivation

For most temperate areas this is a vegetable for the greenhouse. Grow it in good potting compost or in beds prepared with a heavy application of well-rotted garden compost. In warmer climates where okra can grow outdoors, choose an open, sunny site, sheltered from high winds. A rich, loamy soil is ideal.

In a climate with a long, warm summer, but cool winter, okra may be started under glass, either in peat pots or in greenhouse beds. Sow in spring, with a temperature of 15° to 27°C [60° to 80°F]. Transplant to a sheltered but sunny outdoor site with the protection of cloches where necessary to warm the soil.

In cool temperate climates, grow okra entirely indoors, in a heated greenhouse. Sow in peat pots or in a greenhouse bed in spring and transplant the seedlings about 38 cm [15″] apart, either into a greenhouse plot, or singly into 25-30 cm [10-12″] pots. Use a good potting compost and keep the plants well watered, but not overmoist. Insert supporting stakes before planting. The time from sowing to germination will be 7-25 days, depending on the temperature, which must be between 15° and 36°C [60° and 97°F].

For outdoor crops in warm climates, sow 0.5-1.5 cm [¼-½″] deep in rows 90 cm [3′] apart. Thin or transplant to a spacing of about 38-60 cm [15-24″] between plants. Keep the okra moist but not overwatered. Hoe very carefully between plants to eliminate weeds, especially in the early stages of growth after planting out. In a less sheltered site, the plants may need to be supported with canes or poles.

Harvesting and aftercare

Begin picking the pods when they are very young and tender and the seeds inside are soft and half-grown. If they are left too long before harvesting, the seeds will become hard and the vegetable unpalatable when cooked.

Picked regularly, a succession of new, immature pods can be harvested for several weeks. Harvest with care so that the roots of the plant are not disturbed; it is better to cut off the pods rather than pull them off.

When the plants have finished bearing new pods, pull them up and add them to the compost heap.

Pests and diseases

Water daily and spray leaves to keep down red spider mite.

Okra may be attacked by the other common greenhouse pests slugs and mildew. Outdoors it is usually trouble-free, but may attract leaf and stem-eating caterpillars. In climates where cotton is grown okra may suffer the same pests and diseases, since it is a member of the same plant family.

Onion

The different kinds of onion are among the most indispensable of all vegetables; they are delicious raw, and can be cooked in many ways. A major advantage is that they can be grown on the same site year after year.

One of the oldest of all cultivated vegetables, the onion is thought to have originated in Central Asia, although it was well known in ancient Egypt. During this long period the species has split into a number of different types, some of which are now regarded as separate species or varieties. The Welsh onion, for instance, is scientifically known as *Allium fistulosum*; the tree or Egyptian onion as *Allium*

Onion
Allium cepa and *A. fistulosum* (fam. *Alliaceae*)
Hardy biennial cultivated as an **annual.**
Size: average diameter of onion bulb 5-10 cm [2-4″], although much larger ones can be grown. Spring onions, 15-30 cm [6-12″] high with negligible diameter. Shallots 2-5 cm [¾-2″] in diameter.
Climate: temperate to sub-tropical.
Sowing to harvesting time: 14-23 weeks for bulb onions; 42-56 days for spring onions.
Yield: For onions, 20 bulbs, each about 125 g [4 oz], per 3 m [10′] row; for shallots, 15 plants, each bearing about 250 g [8 oz] of bulbs.

cepa proliferum; the shallot as *Allium cepa aggregatum*.
The gardener has to deal with seven main types of onion. They are:

a. A main crop of bulb onions, sown in spring and harvested in autumn.

b. An autumn-sown crop, grown for harvesting as bulbs in the following autumn.

c. Onion 'sets' — these are small bulbs planted in spring for quick growth.

d. Salad or spring onions, also known as scallions, which are sown either in spring or autumn for pulling when young and green, for salads.

e. Pickling onions, which are a quick-growing type, sown in spring and harvested in summer, the small bulbs being used for pickling.

f. Shallots, planted in spring as bulbs; some sideshoots are used as spring onions while others are left to grow into bulbs which are harvested in late summer.

g. Perennial onions, such as the tree and Welsh onion.

Suitable site and soil

Onions do best in a sunny, open site. They can be grown in the same plot for years, but they are also useful for fitting into a crop rotation, as, for example, providing a break from brassicas.

Onions need a firm, loamy, fertile soil. They prefer a light soil to a heavy one, and any acidity should be corrected by applications of lime at a rate based on the result of a soil test. Any organic plant food (farmyard manure or garden compost) should be dug into the soil several months before sowing (e.g. in autumn for plots that are to bear a spring-sown crop). A compound fertilizer may also be applied, just before sowing, and worked well into the soil.

SOWING AND PLANTING

All types of onion need a firm, compact seed-bed of fine soil. The sequences are sown as follows:

The spring-sown maincrop

Sow outdoors as early in spring as soil conditions will permit, in drills 1.5 cm [½"] deep and 30-45 cm [1-1½'] apart. Sow fairly thickly — about 10-20 seeds per 30 cm [1'] row — because the thinnings can be used as salad onions. Germination temperatures range from 2° to 35°C [36° to 95°F], and the period from sowing to germination, on average, is 14-21 days. Thin the young plants in two stages to a final distance of 15 cm [6"] apart.

As with most vegetables, an advantage can be gained in spring by sowing under cloches. These sowings can be made up to 8 weeks earlier than those in the open. The extra weeks are particularly useful with onions, as the plants need a long growing period.

Many gardeners also achieve a flying start by planting onion 'sets'. These are small onion bulbs which have had their growth arrested in the previous autumn. Most are imported from sub-tropical zones for planting in temperate climates in spring. Plant them in rows 30 cm [1'] apart with the bulbs 15 cm [6"] apart in each row. Set them in the soil with the 'neck' at the top of each bulb just visible above the surface.

Onion sets and onions sown under cloches have two main advantages over later-sown crops. In the first place, they grow quickly and make much of their growth while the soil is still moist from the winter rains, thus avoiding a severe check at a critical stage during a summer drought. The other is that they are also sufficiently well grown to resist the attacks of the onion fly, which is active in late spring and summer.

Autumn sowing

Sowing in autumn gives the same results as sowing under cloches or planting sets. The bulbs from this sowing should be ready for harvesting a month or so earlier than those from a spring sowing. The seed should be sown in early autumn, to give the plants time to attain a reasonable size — about 15 cm [6"] in height — before the onset of winter frosts. The seed should be sown rather more thickly than in spring, to allow for casualties. Onions are hardy but not completely so, and a severe winter will cause damage. It is important to select the correct varieties, bred for autumn sowing. Onion plants bought from nurserymen for transplanting in spring should also be of the autumn varieties.

In recent years a new range of Japanese onions has been introduced. These are sown in late summer and will continue growing right through a mild or moderately mild winter, to produce bulbs by midsummer of the following year. When grown successfully, they should fill the gap between the using of the last stored onions from the previous year and the availability of the new crop. So far they have not been fully tested in all climatic zones.

Sowing salad onions

For salad onions, both autumn and spring sowings are feasible, the onions from the autumn sowings filling the gap until those from the spring sowings are available. For spring-sown salad crops, use a quick-growing variety. A succession of sowings may be made throughout the summer. Alternatively, the thinnings of any variety may be used in salads, and pickling varieties are generally sown with this dual purpose in mind.

CARE AND DEVELOPMENT

The manner of their growth — with tall, thin, hollow leaves — makes onions a crop particularly susceptible to weed competition. Hoe the soil frequently but shallowly to avoid loosening the compact soil around the onion roots. Hand-weeding will almost certainly be necessary. Water well throughout the growing season to avoid any check in growth, which can result in bulges in the bulbs, or in thick necks and thin bulbs.

Examine onion sets a week or two after planting, as they tend to rise out of the soil and may travel several centimetres [inches] from the place where they were planted. If this has happened, press the sets back into the soil. They may also have been pulled out of the soil by birds.

During the growing period the plants may be fed with either liquid manure at regular intervals until midsummer, or applications of a nitrogenous fertilizer,

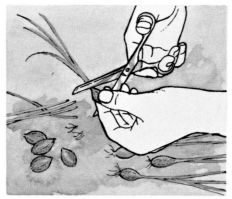

1. *Before planting onion sets, cut off any leaves that may be present.*

2. *Plant sets in shallow drills by mid spring, with 'necks' uppermost.*

3. *Check sets after a week or two and press back sets that have moved.*

1. *To seed, rake bed to light tilth; tread down when soil is not sticky.*

2. *Sow seed fairly thickly in drill. Then just cover seed and firm down.*

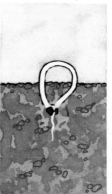

3. *The tips feed from the seed. Do not disturb; they straighten later.*

4. *Thin the onion rows twice; second thinnings can be used for salads.*

5. *Weed regularly; close to onions hand-weed to avoid loosening soil.*

6. *In late summer, bend leaves over to expose bulbs to light and air.*

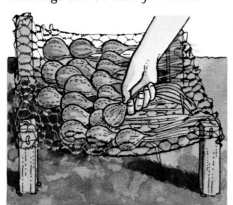

7. *To harvest, lift bulbs carefully; dry above ground in dry, sunny spot.*

8. *In wet weather, bulbs can be dried on the floor of a cold frame.*

9. *When thoroughly dry, the bulbs can be kept in slatted bottom trays.*

such as nitrate of soda, at the rate of about 60 g per sq m [2 oz per sq yd] in late spring and early summer, the latter being hoed in.

When the bulbs are ripening, as indicated by the yellowing and dying back of the leaves, discontinue any watering or feeding and bend over the tops, if they have not already bent over naturally, to expose the neck of each bulb to the sun and so hasten its ripening. The ripening process may last for four or five weeks with large bulbs.

Harvesting the crop

Salad onions may be pulled at any time when large enough, but if the thinnings of crops intended for bulbs are being used for salad, be careful to firm the soil around the remaining plants.

Bulb onions will be ready for harvesting throughout the summer and autumn, according to the time sown. The earliest are the new Japanese varieties which should be mature around midsummer. Japanese onions are for immediate use; most other varieties can be used at once or can be stored. In stormy weather it is as well to discourage a second growth period after ripening has started, as the onions will not store well. Lift them gently with a fork and allow the bulbs to lie flat on the ground. Turn them now and again, to ensure even ripening, but in a wet season lift them on to a platform raised above ground level, allowing the circulation of air beneath it. A tray of small-mesh wire-netting is ideal. This can be moved into a shed to complete ripening, if rain persists.

Storing the crop

Bulb onions are normally grown for storing and use throughout autumn and winter. Being biennial plants, they will start to produce green shoots and, if allowed to, flowerheads in the following spring.

Bulbs for storing should be perfectly healthy and quite dry. Discard any that are not. The conventional and probably the best method of storing is to tie each bulb to a length of rope suspended from the roof of a shed or outhouse, arranging them spirally around the rope. They can, alternatively, be stored on trays of wire netting, or suspended in rope or nylon nets or placed on wooden shelves, though it is best to have air circulating all around them. The shed in which they spend the winter should be dry, airy, and frost proof. If conditions in the kitchen are suitable for storage, a rope of onion can look attractive.

Aftercare

The onion is among the most economical of plants in its production of foliage. By the time the bulb has ripened there is very little left of other parts of the plant. Consign any dead leaves to the compost heap, if they are free from pests and disease; otherwise, burn them.

OTHER TYPES OF ONION

There are a number of other types of onion, the best known of which is the shallot.

Shallots

These are grown as described for onion sets but produce a

(Above) Only hang onions outside in warm, dry weather.
(Left) Three stages in onion cultivation, plus shallots.

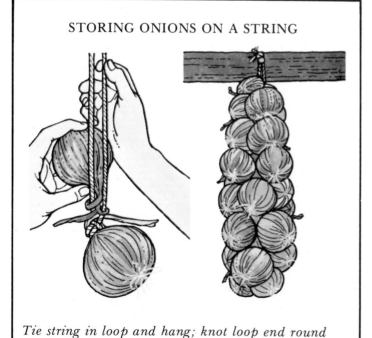

STORING ONIONS ON A STRING

Tie string in loop and hang; knot loop end round bottom onion shoot; twist on subsequent shoots.

Egyptian tree onions in fact come from Canada. Plant in summer or autumn for a crop the following year. The bulbs form at the ends of the stalks instead of flowers.

Spring or salad onions may be sown in autumn, spring and in succession through the summer. Those planted in autumn will fill in till the spring crop comes through.

cluster of small bulbs instead of expanding to form a single large one. These too are sometimes called scallions, like spring or salad onions. The shallot used to be regarded as a distinct species but is now considered to be merely an aberrant form of the ordinary onion. Shallot bulbs are planted in spring, about 20 cm [8″] apart in rows 38 cm [15″] wide, with the tips just protruding above the surface of the soil. Planting should be as early in spring as possible, preferably several weeks before the last frost date. Soil and site are as for onions; avoid a heavy, acid or wet soil.

The shallot plants will soon start to produce sideshoots. Some of these can be pulled for use as salad onions (their flavour is rather mild), while the rest are left to form bulbs about the size of the one originally planted — about 2.5 cm [1″] wide. During the growth period, keep the bed free from weeds by using the hoe and provide just enough water to keep the plants growing; be careful not to over-water. The bulbs will start to ripen soon after midsummer. Scrape back the soil to allow the sun to shine on them. The foliage will soon yellow and die. Lift the bulbs carefully and dry them as for onions. Store on a shelf or tray in a dry, airy place. Shallots should keep right through the winter, and their culinary uses are similar to those of

onions, although shallots have a more subtle flavour.

Welsh onions
These are a perennial type of onion, with the botanical name of *Allium fistulosum*. They grow in clusters or clumps and produce masses of thickened stems, like those of large salad onions, rather than bulbs. They are used primarily for salads, though they can play a role as a flavouring agent in cooked dishes. In the second year they run to flower and seed and so can be regarded as a biennial. They can best be propagated by dividing the clumps and transplanting individual plants, rather than by seed. Welsh onions are also known as stone-leeks, onion leeks, and Japanese bunching onions; the last name could be misleading, as they are quite distinct from the Japanese varieties of autumn-sown onions already referred too.

Ever-ready onions
Further confusion may be caused by the fact that there is a sub-species of the common onion (with the botanical name of *Allium cepa perutile*) which is also known as the Welsh onion, though more properly as the ever—ready onion. This, too, grows in clumps, from which small bulbs may be split off for propagation. Each individual bulb will, if

Ever-ready onions are hardy perennials, standing up to frost very well. They grow in clumps and a single bulb will produce a clump within a year if planted in spring.

Shallots are an aberrant form of ordinary onions. They produce a clump of small bulbs rather than a single big one. Stored like onions they should keep through winter.

planted in spring, form a clump within a year. It is very hardy and will produce green shoots for salad or flavouring right through a moderately mild winter. Though grown primarily for salad, it can also be used in cooked dishes.

Potato onions

The potato onion, seldom seen nowadays, is a less hardy plant and growing it in cool temperate climates is a risky proposition. From bulbs planted in mid winter or soon afterwards it should produce a bunch of small bulbs, about 2.5 cm [1″] in diameter, soon after midsummer. It is grown primarily for the sake of these bulbs, which have a mild flavour. When growing, it responds to occasional feeding with liquid manure and should never be kept short of water. They are cooked like maincrop onions.

Tree onions

In spite of its name, the tree or Egyptian onion originated in Canada. From a planting in summer or autumn it will produce a crop of small bulbs, or 'bulbils', in the following summer and thereafter each year, for the plant is a perennial. The bulbils are produced, however, not on or under the soil but in the flower-head cluster, instead of

flowers. As the flower-stalks may grow to a height of 90-120 cm [3-4′] or even more, it is usually necessary to support them by canes. Unlike several of the less common types of onion, tree onions have a very strong flavour and should be used sparingly. They can also be used for pickling.

Pickling onions

Onions sown specifically for pickling belong to a group of varieties that produce small, silvery-skinned bulbs. They grow quickly, producing a crop ready for harvest soon after midsummer from a mid-spring sowing. Sow in a light, thin soil. Small bulbs of other varieties of onion are, however, also suitable for pickling.

Container growing

There is no difficulty about growing onions of any variety in containers, and they have the advantage that they require a smaller depth of soil than many other vegetables. The unusual varieties are often of most interest for container growing, particularly the tree onion, which is quite an imposing plant.

Container grown onions need plenty of sunshine, so position them on a sunny patio or similar place. Make sure

189

that the plants are well watered, but also that they have adequate drainage to prevent waterloging.

Pests and diseases

The most troublesome pest is the onion fly, the larvae of which tunnel into the plant tissues from late spring onwards. Control them by diazinon granules in late spring or early summer. Successive generations will emerge during the summer if the first is not dealt with, resulting in intermittent attacks. Young onions are particularly susceptible and, if onion fly is prevalent, it may be as well to stop pulling young plants for salad. Very early sowing will ensure that thinning is done before the onion fly is about to attack the plants.

Stem and bulb eelworms may also affect onions. If the leaves are distorted, and their bases swollen, suspect eelworm. There is no really effective chemical control, and an attack is normally a sign of neglect of a proper rotation and a lack of garden hygiene, allowing the pest to build up to dangerous levels. Destroy any infected plants and make sure that you grow onions in a different place in the garden in future.

White rot sometimes builds up in crops of salad onions in hot, dry summers. The leaves become yellow and the bases of the bulbs are covered with a white or grey fungus. It can be combated by dusting the soil at sowing time with calomel dust, but the best control is to keep onions away from any affected plot for at least eight years. Welsh onions are not affected, and some varieties of common onions are more resistant than others. The variety White Lisbon, on the other hand, is particularly susceptible to the disease.

Other common troubles may be the fungal diseases, mildew, neck rot and smut, the bacterial soft rot, and the virus yellow dwarf. Neck rot is a storage rot occurring when bulbs have been insuffiently ripened or are stored in damp stuffy conditions. Smut shows as sooty spots and patches on the leaves, and can kill seedlings. There is no chemical control; rest the soil as long as possible, destroy the affected plants as soon as you spot them, and be extremely careful not to spread the contaminated soil about the garden to ensure against any further attack.

Yellow dwarf results in stunted stems, and yellow-streaked leaves. It occurs mainly in America, but the disease shallot virus yellows is very similar to yellow dwarf and is found in the United Kingdom.

Oregano

SEE **MARJORAM**

Parsley

Parsley is the most familiar of herbs, widely popular as a garnish for many dishes and a rich source of vitamin C.

Parsley (*Petroselinum crispum*) is a member of the *Umbelliferae* family, grown extensively for its curled clusters of leaves. Finely chopped, the fresh leaves feature in many recipes, particularly parsley sauce, casseroles and stews. Sprigs of leaves are used to garnish fish, strong meat dishes and boiled vegetables. The plant is biennial and, if left to grow for a second year, the thin tap roots can be cooked as well. There is a moss-curled variety, more suitable for garnishing, and a French variety, which has more flavour for use in cooking. The plant grows about 30 cm [1′] high and 15 cm [6″] wide and produces small yellow-green flower heads in early to midsummer of the second year.

Cultivation

Parsley prefers a position in full sun, but a partially shaded site is acceptable. For garden cultivation it should be grown in soil enriched with well-rotted garden compost. This will help to retain moisture, which is very necessary, for parsley bolts when the roots become dry. For this reason, it will do well in a well-broken down clay soil, in which water is retained.

Sift the topsoil to make a fine, firm surface. Sow the seed thinly 0.5 cm [¼″] deep in rows 30 cm [1′] apart and barely cover it by pressing a thin layer of peat or silver sand over it, then water using a fine rose on the watering can. Parsley has a reputation for slow germination. Delay sowing until the soil is beginning to warm up in mid to late spring and there should be no difficulty in obtaining seedlings within two weeks, otherwise they may take as long as five weeks.

Keep the seedbed watered and watch for signs of germination after two weeks. If there are no seedlings in eight weeks, make another sowing. Once the seedlings have appeared keep the seedbed weeded. When the plants have produced two true leaves, you may thin them to 15 cm [6″] apart and transplant the thinnings to 30 cm [1′] apart.

Parsley sown in spring will supply leaves for cutting from

For a good crop, thin parsley well, as it is intolerant of overcrowding. Prevent bolting by regular watering.

midsummer until the following early spring, when it will start to produce flower stems instead of leaves. However, if a fresh supply is sown in midsummer, this will supply leaves from early autumn until the following midsummer, so that a continuous supply should be possible. The midsummer sowing will germinate in a few days, due to the increased warmth of the soil and air. Cloches placed over the plants in winter will keep them clean and enable picking during snowy weather.

Parsley may be attacked while young by greenfly and carrot-fly (*see* CARROT).

1. Cover seed with a very thin layer of peat and water with a fine spray.

2. Cover thinnings' roots with soil to avoid drying out during transplanting.

3. Sheets of glass placed either end of a cloche will protect from winds.

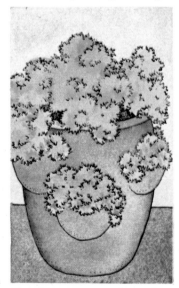

Parsley sown or planted in a special 'parsley pot' can be very attractive.

Parsnip

Parsnips are one of the easiest vegetables to grow and need only the minimum of attention to produce excellent results.

The wild form of the parsnip occurs commonly throughout northern Europe, and in its taste and smell it is still recognizably the ancestor of the root now cultivated. Breeding and selection have enlarged the root and eliminated its tendency towards woodiness. There are three types of cultivated parsnip: short rooted and conical shaped; medium length, and blunt ended or tapered; and

---

Parsnip
Pastinaca sativa (fam. *Umbelliferae*)
Hardy biennial.
Size: root to 45 cm [1½′].
Climate: cool temperate.
Sowing to harvesting time: 28 weeks.
Yield: about 14 parsnips, each weighing on average 450 g [1 lb], per 3m [10′] row.

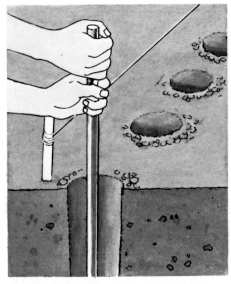

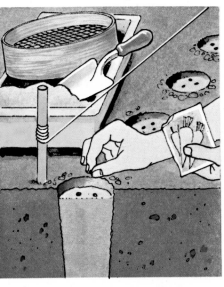

1. *Work the iron rod to and fro in the soil to make a conical hole 75 cm deep and 15 cm wide at the top.*

2. *Almost fill holes with sifted soil, space 3 or 4 seeds in each and cover to a depth of 2 cm [¾″].*

3. *Thin out when the seedlings have two seed leaves and one true leaf.*

If growing in rows, choose a site manured for a previous crop; dig a trench to a depth of 50 cm [20″].

One of the hardiest vegetables, parsnips require a minimum of attention. Their sweet-tasting roots can be roasted, boiled or made into wine.

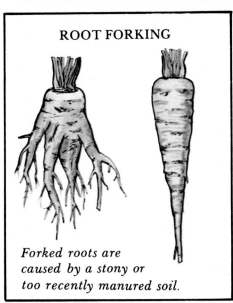

ROOT FORKING

Forked roots are caused by a stony or too recently manured soil.

long, with tapering ends, grown mainly for exhibition. Freshly dug, this hardy root vegetable has a slightly sweet flavour and is excellent roasted or braised.

Suitable site and soil

An open, sunny site is preferred, but parsnips will grow in a lightly shaded plot. Growing the long variety involves quite a lot of soil preparation and it may present problems with certain soils, such as those where a chalk subsoil that must not be disturbed comes too close to the surface. In this case shortened varieties are available.

All parsnips like rich soil, but if this has been recently manured the roots will be rank and inclined to fork. It is best to grow them on a site that was manured for a previous crop. Stones in the soil are another cause of forking and these should be removed.

A family of 4-5 will need a 9-10 m [30-33′] row, or its equivalent in several rows, which will produce up to 40 roots in a year. If there is more than one row, they should be 30-38 cm [12-15″] apart. Each row must be trenched to a depth of about 50 cm [20″] for the long type, and if there are many stones to be removed from the ground it may be best to resort to a method used for producing exhibition parsnips. Drive a 1 m [3′] long iron rod into the ground to about threequarters of its length to make holes 23 cm [9″] apart. Work the iron rod to and fro to produce a deep, conical hole about 10-15 cm [4-6″] wide at the top. Fill the hole with sifted soil in readiness for sowing. The parsnip will grow straight downwards.

If the soil is markedly acid it should have lime added in autumn or winter to make it almost neutral (pH 6.5); use a soil-testing kit. Ten days before sowing, it is advisable to apply a mixture of 4 parts superphosphate, and 1 each of sulphate of ammonia and sulphate of potash at the rate of 100 g per sq m [3½ oz per sq yd].

Sowing and planting

Parsnip seed does not keep well, so sow really fresh seed as early in spring as conditions will allow. Long, steady growth is the rule with parsnips, but there is no point in sowing in hard frost or sodden soil, only to have the seeds rot. Assume that germination will be poor and sow 3 or 4 seeds at every station. If the trench method is used this will be in a drill, and seeds should be sown 23 cm [9″] apart and covered with soil to a depth of 2 cm [¾″]. With the proposed crowbar holes, nearly full of sifted soil, space 3 or 4 seeds in each and cover them to a depth of 2 cm [¾″].

Germination will take 21-28 days and maturity should be attained in 28 weeks, though the short-rooted kinds may be ready in less time. During this time weeds will get well ahead of the parsnips, so weed carefully. You may also sow a quick-growing crop of lettuce or radish between the rows or stations; it will also mark the position of parsnip seeds.

Cultivation

Thin the seedlings so that only the strongest remains at each station. Keep the rows clear of weeds by hoeing regularly, taking good care not to damage the crowns of the roots. Some watering may be necessary, especially in the early stages, before the roots have gone deep.

Harvesting and aftercare

Parsnips sown in early spring should start to be available in mid autumn. They will still be improving, however, and will improve still further when the frosts come. By the following spring, the flavour will begin to fall off. It is usual to leave them in the ground and dig them up as they are needed. Obviously this is not possible in ground that is rock-hard with frost, so take the precaution of lifting some of the crop in late autumn, cutting the tops off to the shoulder, and storing them like carrots, in layers covered with a little dry sand, soil, or ashes in an airy frost-proof store. The discarded leaves make good compost heap material.

Pests and diseases

The main insect pests of parsnips are carrot fly and celery fly. For treatment *see* CARROT and CELERY. The cause of the reddish-brown patches of canker, so often found on parsnips, especially the shoulders, has not yet been discovered, but dark brown, or black cankers are caused sometimes by disease, and sometimes by growing conditions. Cracking as a result of rain after dry weather allows fungal infections to take hold — so do injuries caused by the carrot fly. Cold wet weather and badly-drained soil encourage cankering. In such conditions, spray the soil with zineb regularly from late summer to lifting. Avonresister is a canker-resistant variety.

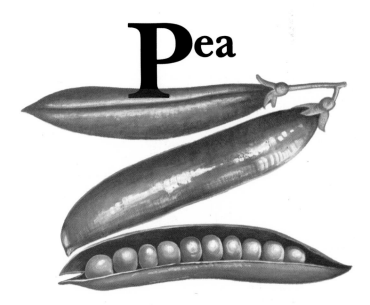

Pea

One of the earliest summer crops, fresh, tender peas are among the most delicious garden vegetables. They are only suitable for a cool temperate climate.

Peas may well be the oldest cultivated vegetable crop in the world; even before they were cultivated, they were gathered from the wild. They probably originated in Asia, the Near East and southern Europe.

As is only natural after such a long history as a garden crop, very many varieties of peas have been evolved. There are early, maincrop and late varieties; peas that climb almost as high as a man and dwarf peas that need no support and may be grown under cloches; the small-seeded and succulent petit pois; mangetout or sugar peas, with edible pods; asparagus peas (*see* ASPARAGUS PEA) and purple-podded peas. All peas are, however, a cool-temperate crop. Trying to grow them in warm-temperate zones invites problems, as most of them will stop producing pods when the temperature rises above about 20°C [70°F].

Suitable site and soil

Choose an open, sunny site, but one sheltered from high winds. Allow plenty of space and remember that the taller varieties will shade other crops grown alongside them.

Peas are rather fastidious about soil. Acid soil is unsuitable, the ideal being at a pH of 7.0; carry out a soil test and correct by an application of lime in the winter before sowing if necessary.

Peas also like a rich soil, but not one recently enriched by applications of manure; it is better to sow them in soils well manured for a previous crop. Poor soils can benefit from chemical fertilizers containing superphosphate and potash, but use nitrogenous fertilizers very cautiously, because the pea plant can extract nitrogen from the air for itself, and excess of nitrogen leads to lush leaf growth at the expense of the pods. Peas need plenty of water and thrive in a reasonably heavy soil which retains moisture, although it must not become waterlogged.

Sowing

Peas are sown where they are to remain for their entire lives because they are deep-rooted and do not usually transplant satisfactorily.

The normal time for sowing maincrop peas is from mid to late spring, for harvesting between midsummer and early autumn, but by using different varieties and giving the plants protection from frost you can extend the season considerably. Early varieties can be sown from late winter to early spring under tall cloches, and harvested from early summer to midsummer. They can also be sown in early summer, covered with cloches in early autumn and picked from early to mid-autumn; or sown under cloches in mid to late autumn for harvesting the following spring. Prepare a shallow drill 15-23 cm [6-9"] wide, and sow the

---

Pea

Pisum sativum (fam. *Leguminosae*)

Hardy annual.

Size: height varies according to variety, ranging from 30 cm [1'] to 1.8 m [6']; pods range from 7.5 cm [3"] to 15 cm [6"] long.

Climate: cool temperate.

Sowing to harvesting time: 9-13 weeks.

Yield: 40 plants per 3 m [10'] row, each bearing up to ¼ kg [½ lb] of peas.

---

seed 7.5 cm [3"] deep in two rows with 7.5 cm [3"] between them. Sow at the rate of 6-10 seeds per 30 cm [1']. Allow a space of 45-60 cm [1½-2'] between each drill. The temperature range for germination is 4° to 29°C [39° to 84°F] and the peas should take between 6 and 15 days to germinate.

Two types of seed

There are two types of pea seed, round and wrinkled. The wrinkled-seeded, or 'marrowfat', varieties are splendid succulent peas but hold too much moisture for autumn sowing. Peas sown in autumn must be of round-seeded varieties, several of which are very hardy. In districts where winters are moderate, they can be sown in the open; elsewhere they should be protected by cloches. It is as well to sow autumn peas rather more thickly than with spring-sown crops, scattering them along the flat drill rather than planting each seed separately; this allows for some mortality. After a mild winter, autumn-sown peas will probably produce a crop several weeks earlier than those sown in early spring. A severe winter, however, may check them to such an extent that they offer no advantage, producing at the same time as the spring-sown ones.

Spring-sown peas

Spring-sown peas are divided into three main groups: first early varieties, second earlies (also called early maincrop or mid-season varieties) and maincrops. The division is made according to the time the varieties take to grow. From sowings in early spring, first early varieties will produce peas fit to gather in 11 or 12 weeks. Second earlies sown at the same time will need 12-13 weeks, while maincrop varieties will require 13-14 weeks. It would be possible, therefore, to provide a succession of pickings by sowing varieties of the three groups in the same week. Alternatively, you can follow the usual practice and make a succession of sowings, starting with the earlies and proceeding to the second earlies and maincrop. You can also gain time by protecting the first sowing of earlies from frosts by means of cloches.

Peas do not transplant satisfactorily, but they can be grown in peat pots or in seed-trays with slide-out bottoms, as the important point is not to disturb the roots when transplanting. Nevertheless, the operation is unnecessary, as a rule, and may end in failure; it is wiser to sow peas in their permanent quarters.

Late peas

In general, although there are few exceptions, early varieties of peas tend to be dwarf and the maincrop ones taller and bushier. For the latest crops of all, use early dwarf varieties, for two reasons. One is that they will mature more quickly and so be ready for harvesting before the onset of frost; the other is that, if necessary, they can be protected in their late stages by cloches. Successful crops of late peas may often be taken from plots from which early potatoes have been dug.

Choose early dwarf varieties of pea for the latest crop of all, as they should mature before the onset of frost.

Succulent garden peas, ready for harvesting. Pick about 3 weeks after flowering, when the pods have filled out.

The pods of the mange-tout or sugar pea have a crisp and crunchy texture and sweet flavour. Cook them whole.

1. *To dress seeds against pests, soak in paraffin then dust with red lead.*

2. *Sow first early varieties under tall cloches, in double rows 7 cm [3″] apart and 5 cm [2″] deep. Allow 10 seeds per 30 cm [1′]. Protect at either end with a mousetrap.*

3. *Sow maincrop peas without protection, following the method for early types.*

4. *Protect young plants from birds with pea-guards of fine mesh netting, 12 cm [5″] high and 20 cm [8″] wide.*

5. *Remove weeds by hand to avoid damaging roots.*

6. *Support growing dwarf peas with twiggy sticks.*

Cultivation

One of the main hazards in growing peas is that pests attack the plants in their early stages. Many inexperienced gardeners who sow good seed in well-prepared soil finish up with half a crop, or less. Mice are the chief culprits. They eat the germinating peas and will quickly clear a row. A sensible precaution is to dress the pea seeds with a repellent or poisonous substance before sowing. Paraffin and red lead are the traditional dressings. The peas can be dipped in paraffin and then dusted with red lead or they can be shaken up in a tin containing both substances. Alternatively, use proprietary repellants or mouse traps; if using the latter take precautions against pets, birds or other creatures being injured.

The other prime pests at the early stages are birds. Protect the plants with pea-guards, which are half-cylinders of small-mesh wire netting for placing over the peas, obtainable from most garden centres. An alternative is to construct entanglements of black cotton; even twiggy sticks placed flat on the ground will act as a deterrent. Protection is necessary for only a week or so for, once they have emerged, the plants grow quickly.

Peas require frequent attention throughout their lives.

Remove weeds by regular hoeing. Be careful, however, when pulling out weeds growing very close to the peas; the pea-roots may come out as well or be damaged.

Peas need ample moisture and require frequent watering during droughts. A mulch will help, consisting of garden compost, lawn trimmings, peat (unless the soil is acid) or well-rotted strawy manure. Apply this as near as possible to the base of the plants, where it will not only supply nutrients and help to retain moisture but will also smother some of the weeds.

Unlike beans, which climb by twining themselves around a support, peas grasp the support with their tendrils. They therefore need twiggy sticks or netting, both of which give them plenty of tendril-holds. With dwarf varieties, the sticks need be only small twigs, 45 cm [1½′] or so high. Even with taller varieties it is useful to help the young plants with short twigs in the early stages. Pea-sticks of the traditional type are now difficult to obtain and therefore expensive, so that many gardeners use, as an alternative, a trellis consisting of plastic mesh stretched between poles.

If the peas are sown in well-prepared, well-manured soil, little additional feeding should be necessary during the growth period. In poorer soils they will benefit from an ap-

Taller varieties can be supported on a trellis 125 cm [4'] high, made of chicken wire with a 5 cm [2"] mesh. Support trellis with nails hammered into wooden stakes.

Use scissors to harvest ripe pods, as picking by hand can pull the entire plant out of the ground.

After harvest, clear the site. Remove bits of pea haulm from netting and store it for future use.

plication of a compound fertilizer that is low on nitrogen and high on phosphates and potash. Apply this at a rate of 90-125 g per sq m [3-4 oz per sq yd].

Harvesting and aftercare

Garden peas are usually grown for eating when they are fresh and green. If allowed to become ripe and hard, they lose much of their flavour. Usually, they are ready for harvesting about 3 weeks after flowering. Harvest when the pods have filled out and are firm to the touch although, during a drought, some pods will fail to fill completely, and it is better to pick too early than too late. Cut the pods from the plants rather than picking them, or you may pull up the whole plant.

Two harvests per plant may be expected. The first is the main one; the second consists of pods which are later to mature and are usually not of the same quality as the first.

With early varieties it is sometimes possible to pick a few early pods a few days in advance of the main picking. Before cooking or deep-freezing, shell the peas.

There are, however, a number of varieties in which the

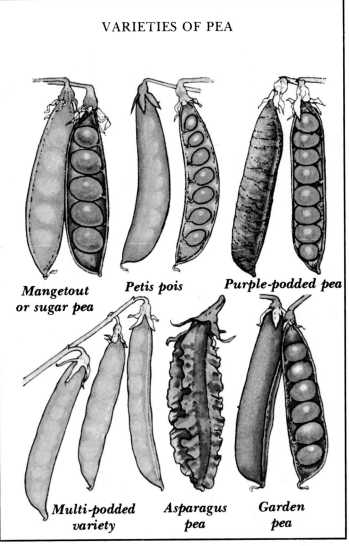

VARIETIES OF PEA

Mangetout or sugar pea

Petis pois

Purple-podded pea

Multi-podded variety

Asparagus pea

Garden pea

pods are eaten with the peas in them. The best known of these is the **mange-tout** or **sugar pea** of which there are two main types — a dwarf sugar pea and a tall one, up to 1.5 m [5'] high, grown largely in France, where it is known as the mange-tout. Both are late varieties, producing an abundance of pods in late summer, and both need a warm, sunny summer. The pods are stringless and are best steamed, having been gathered when they are young.

Petit pois produce an abundance of very small, sweet tasting peas. Pick immediately the pods have filled and steam them whole. After cooking, the peas will fall out of the pods, which are then discarded. The **purple-podded pea** also has small pods but the peas are shelled in the normal way and the deep purple pods discarded. This is a tall pea, growing to a height of 1.5 m [5'], and it continues to bear pods for an unusually long period, allowing a succession of pickings. Peas of many varieties can be dried and stored for winter use. They are also one of the most successful vegetables for the freezer.

There is no point is trying to retain the plants after the pods have been removed. Clear the site and use it for another crop immediately; brassicas are a good choice.

The pea haulm should be incorporated in the compost heap, unless there was a bad attack of pea moth, but the roots, which are rich in nitrogen, can be left in the ground to benefit the following brassicas.

Pests and diseases

Peas are subject to several pests and diseases. One of the most troublesome pests of later crops are the larvae of the pea moth *(Laspeyresia nigricana)*. These have white bodies and black heads and look like maggots. Their prevalence is one reason for gardeners concentrating on the early crops, which are seldom attacked. Treatment consists of spraying with derris or fenitrothion about 7-10 days after flowering to catch the maggots just after they hatch, but before they get into the pod. The plants should be thoroughly wetted.

Pea thrips *(Kakothrips robustus)* are sometimes numerous enough to cause damage, especially in dry seasons. Symptoms are silvery mottled patches on the pods and leaves, which later turn brown. Treat the plants with resmethrin or derris, applied just after the flowers have set.

Pea weevil *(Sitona lineatus)* may attack the plants by eating regularly notched holes in the edges of the leaves. The larvae feed on the roots. Adults are greyish beetles 0.5 cm [¼"] long, and are controlled by spraying with derris.

Other pests may be greenfly, pea and bean seed beetles, and birds attacking the pods to get at the peas.

Occasionally such diseases as mildew, grey mould and black root may occur. For the last named remove the entire plant, and also any leguminous weeds.

Peach

This delectable white or yellow-fleshed fruit has a felted skin. It grows on small trees and is therefore well suited to a garden with limited space.

Despite its name, *Prunus persica,* the peach originated in China. It was probably brought to Persia along the trade routes and was introduced from there to Europe by the conquering Greeks and Romans. It reached a high standard of cultivation in France in the seventeenth and eighteenth centuries. A member of the *Prunus* genus

which also includes plums, cherries and apricots, peaches are the earliest of all to flower.

Widely grown in areas with a Mediterranean climate, in cool temperate areas it needs the shelter of a wall facing the midday sun. In colder parts peaches are best grown in a greenhouse. Though the tree is quite hardy, the blossom is liable to be damaged by frost.

Like other deciduous trees, they need a dormant period and their cultivation is only possible where there is winter cold. The ideal conditions are a cold, dry winter so that the tree remains dormant, followed by a warm, frost-free spring and a hot summer.

Peaches may be divided into groups by the colour of the flesh. White has the best flavour and the tree is hardier in a cold climate. The yellow-fleshed peach needs a warm climate, but is popular for canning.

Nectarines are a sport (naturally occurring variant) of peaches, with the smooth red or yellow skin of plums. The trees are less hardy and do not succeed as bushes in cool temperate areas.

CULTIVATION

The peach can be grown in the open in favourable areas, but in cool temperate areas it is best grown on a sunny wall. Shelter for blossom is particularly important. The peach can be grown outdoors as a half standard, or standard, but a two- to three-year-old bush is generally most satisfactory. Against a wall or under glass it is grown as a fan. In cooler areas plant early fruiting varieties. If a peach stone is planted, a tree will result, but it will not come true to variety and is slow to reach bearing.

Soil preparation and planting the tree

The ideal soil is a medium to heavy well drained limey loam, not less than 60 m [2'] deep, though the peach is tolerant of a wide range of soils.

Dig thoroughly and deeply several weeks before planting over an area of 2 sq m [yd] and add one barrowload of garden compost or manure. Then about a week before, fork into the top 23 cm [9"], 125 g [4 oz] of a balanced fertilizer, and the same amount of dried blood.

In poor greenhouse soil or near a wall, a month before planting, excavate a hole, 1.8 m × 1 m × 75 cm [6' × 3' × 2½'] deep. Where soil drainage is poor, lay a tile drain 1 m [3'] deep and cover it with 15 cm [6"] layer of lumpy chalk.

Peach
Prunus persica (fam. *Rosaceae*)
Hardy deciduous tree, often short lived.
Size: bush trees 2.6 × 2.6 m [12' × 12'], fan trained tree 2.5 × 5 m [8' × 16'].
Climate: temperate.
Planting to harvesting time: 2-3 years, depending on whether the tree is 2 or 3 years old when planted.
Yield: 22 kg [50 lb] for a fan, 36-44 kg [80-100 lb] or more for a bush.

Add one part by volume of old lime, bricks and sand mortar to 10 parts of returning soil. Two weeks before planting to each cubic m [yd] add 5 kg [10 lb] good general fertilizer, 2.5 kg [5 lb] coarse sterilized bonemeal and 2.5 kg [5 lb] dried blood, and thoroughly mix in.

Late autumn, when the soil is still warm, is the best planting time. The root system must not be allowed to dry out or be exposed to frost. A fan tree should be planted 23 cm [9"] away from the wall and inclined towards it. A bush is planted like other fruit trees (*see* APPLE).

Feeding, watering and pollination

Generous feeding is necessary. Each spring topdress with a balanced compound fertilizer at 90 g per sq m [3 oz per sq yd]. Mulch with manure, or other bulky organic material. Once the fruit have started to swell give proprietary liquid feed every 7 to 10 days, but stop when the fruit begins to colour.

The soil at the base of a wall facing the sun can become very dry which will cause poor fruit set and excessive fruitlet drop. Water thoroughly and deeply whenever there is drought, at blossom time and when the stone is developing.

The peach is self-fertile but flowers very early, so hand pollination is usually necessary (*see* diagram and instructions in APRICOT) as is protection of the blossom.

Training and pruning a bush

The pruning of a peach bush to form it is the same as for an apple (*see* APPLE), except that a peach should have more branches in the centre. Peach trees begin to droop under the weight of fruit and in later years more upright branches from near the centre will be trained to replace those which have become too low. Alternatively, cut drooping branches back to suitably placed vertical shoots. Very little pruning is needed. In early spring cut out any winter die-back to a healthy bud. As far as possible avoid making large pruning cuts because of the disease risk. After cropping encourage new fruiting shoots evenly over the tree by cutting back to a stub about a quarter of the fruited sideshoots.

TRAINING A FAN

A wall 2.4-5 m [8-16'] is needed with wires spaced 15 cm [6"] or two brick courses apart, and held 10 cm [4"] away from the wall by lead wall eyes. The bottom wire is erected 30 cm [1'] above the soil level.

Training a fan tree from a maiden

If you wish to train a fan yourself, buy a one-year-old (maiden) tree, and in late winter cut it down to 60 cm [2'] from the ground to a good bud, checking that there are at least two good buds below this.

In the first summer, several shoots will result. Choose two good ones, one on each side to make your left and right branches. These should be 23-30 cm [9-12"] above the ground. Rub out all other growth on the main stem. When the sideshoots are about 45 cm [1½'] long, tie them to two long bamboo canes with soft string, and tie the canes to the wires at an angle of 45° to the ground, so that they are

at an angle of 90° to each other. If one shoot grows more strongly, it should be temporarily lowered, which slows growth, until the other has caught up with it. The main stem should be carefully cut out immediately above the upper of the two branches, and the wound made smooth.

In late winter the two side branches are then shortened to a bud 30-45 cm [1-1½'] from the main stem. During the following summer an extension shoot will grow from each of these buds and will eventually be tied in. Growth will be made along the length of the branches. Select two on the upper side of each branch and one on the bottom and tie them to the wires to help build a framework. Prune out all other shoots.

In later winter, the third the tree has spent in your garden, cut back these eight branches to a triple bud (consisting of flower and growth buds) so as to leave 30-45 cm [1-1½'] of ripened wood. If the wall is large and you plan to have a large framework, you can continue this summer and winter schedule for another year, otherwise pruning is adjusted to stimulating fruit production.

Formative pruning

If you have bought a three-year-old fan, it will be partly trained, and should have about 15-18 shoots. Prune in late winter, at bud break, and shorten the previous summer's growth on all the shoots by a quarter to an upward pointing bud. This will stimulate the topmost bud and those behind to produce more shoots, some of which can be tied in during the late spring to fruit next year.

Train on each leading shoot and select others growing parallel with the wall and tie them in. Rub out any shoots growing directly towards or away from the wall.

Pruning an established fan

The peach flowers only on the wood made in the previous summer and therefore is pruned on a replacement system. After sideshoots have cropped, they are cut out and new growth is tied in. But since the peach can produce one or two fruit buds and one shoot bud from a single point, a good deal of thinning has to be done.

Rubbing out in spring: At blossom time or just after the flowers fade, deal with the newly produced shoots, which will be about 1.5 cm [½"] in length. Rub out altogether those growing directly towards the wall. Those growing directly away from the wall should be pinched back to one leaf.

Now turn to the blossom-bearing sideshoots which grew last year. There will nearly always be a new shoot growing near the base on such a shoot, or nearby, and this new shoot is left to grow as a replacement. The end bud on the fruiting shoot is also allowed to produce a shoot. The remaining new shoots are rubbed out, except any produced at the same point as the fruit. These are stopped at one leaf. Do this in three stages at intervals of about ten days. At this stage you should also cut out any winter die-back to a healthy bud, and protect the cut with bitumen tree paint if large.

Pinching back and tying in: Tie in the young shoots in spring and summer while they are still flexible. They must

Tender nectarines are excellent pot plants. Their small, smooth-skinned fruit are either red or yellow with a blush, and very richly flavoured.

(Right) A fan-trained peach showing a good crop of ripe fruit. The plastic net will catch any fruit that fall.

Nectarines produce beautiful pink blossom. They do best in warm areas.

PRUNING A FREE-STANDING BUSH

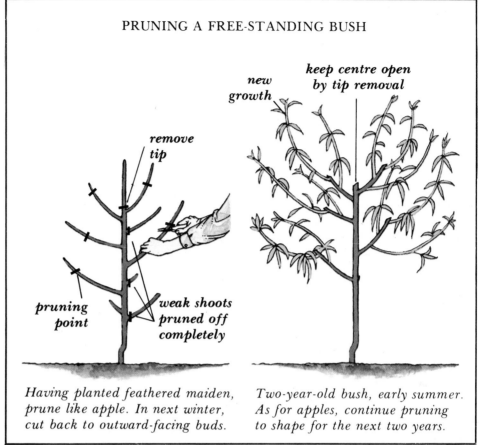

remove tip

new growth

keep centre open by tip removal

pruning point

weak shoots pruned off completely

Having planted feathered maiden, prune like apple. In next winter, cut back to outward-facing buds.

Two-year-old bush, early summer. As for apples, continue pruning to shape for the next two years.

not overlap but should radiate out like the spokes of a wheel. Check that the shoots carrying fruit are securely tied. Pinch back the replacement shoots to six leaves, and stop the new shoot at the end of the fruit-bearing shoot in the same way. At the centre of the framework, where the branches converge, young shoots will need to be pinched back fairly short to about six leaves.

Pruning after cropping
Prune after cropping to lessen the disease risk. Cut out the fruit-bearing laterals back to the replacement shoots. Tie in the new growths and renew any ties where constriction is taking place. The fan should present a neat, flat appearance well secured against winter.

When the tree has filled its space, prune the leaders like a sideshoot, back to the replacement shoot. It is safer, but more difficult, to prune in late summer. In an area where disease is not prevalent, it will be easier to prune in winter, when the leaves are off.

Peaches and nectarines under glass
In cool climates peaches and in particular nectarines are successful under glass, away from frost. If heat is available the season is extended by forcing, and by growing the late varieties.

Heated or unheated, a greenhouse should be 3.7 m [12'] long and 2.2 m [7½'] to the ridge. A lean-to should be the same length and ideally slightly higher at 2.5 m [8½'], with a wall facing the midday sun. The fan follows the sloping roof line in a span house, supported by horizontal wires erected 38 cm [15"] away from the glass. In a lean-to the fan is grown on the back wall.

TRAINING A FAN TREE FROM A MAIDEN: FIRST YEAR

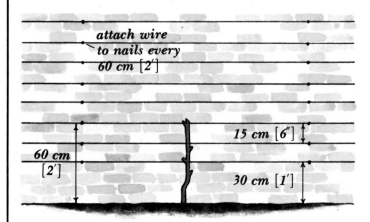

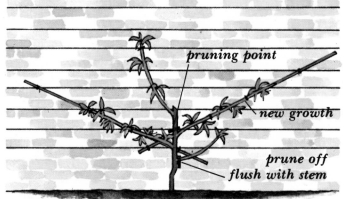

In late winter of first year, when buds on cleared maidens are starting to break, prune to good bud, leaving two other buds for left and right branches.

Young peach in summer of first year, just before it is pruned to remove the leader. The sideshoots have been tied to long bamboo canes placed at 45°.

TRAINING A FAN TREE FROM A MAIDEN: SECOND YEAR

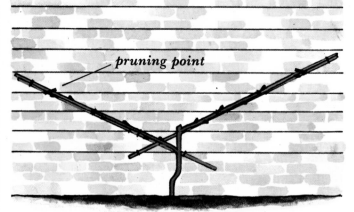

Peach tree in second winter. Before pruning, again wait until the buds are beginning to break. Cut two sideshoots back to bud 30-45 cm [1'-1½'] from stem.

In second summer, select two vertical shoots on the upper side of each of the branches and one shoot on the underside of each. Cut back all others to base.

Take care over feeding, watering, ventilation and pollination. More rigorous control of tree size is necessary by rubbing out and pinching back. A daily syringe from mid spring until the fruit begins to ripen keeps down the risk of red spider mite.

At the end of the season, the fan should be untied, and subsequently retied, with the lower shoots about 7.5 cm [3″] apart. The glass should be cleaned and the tree sprayed with a winter wash of 4% tar oil to clean up any scale insects and the overwintering eggs of aphids. The border soil is lightly pricked over and the top 2.5 cm [1″] renewed afterwards. Fertilize and mulch as before.

CARE OF THE FRUIT
Overcropping will result in small fruit and will reduce the following year's crop. Start thinning when the peaches are

the size of peas, but wait until after the natural fruitlet drop is over before completing the task. First remove undersized fruit and then thin out peaches 23 cm [9″] and nectarines to 15 cm [6″] apart.

Drape a 2 cm [¾″] mesh net over ripening fruit to protect them against birds. If wasps are troublesome, each fruit can be enclosed in a bag or an old nylon stocking.

Early varieties start to ripen in midsummer and cropping can continue for two months. Fruit is ripe when the flesh feels soft to finger pressure at the stalk end. The flavour and colour can be improved by tying back some of the foliage a little before this for peaches, but not nectarines as they sunscald.

Pests and diseases
The commonest and most serious trouble of peach trees is

TRAINING A PEACH FAN: THIRD YEAR

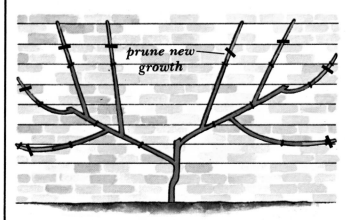

prune new growth

In the late winter of third year, prune back the eight branches to a triple bud (flower and growth buds), leaving 30-45 cm [1′-1½′] of ripened wood.

TRAINING A PEACH FAN: FOURTH YEAR

Unless wall to be covered is very big, after the third year pruning should aim to stimulate the fruit with branches tied in and evenly spaced.

PRUNING ESTABLISHED FANS

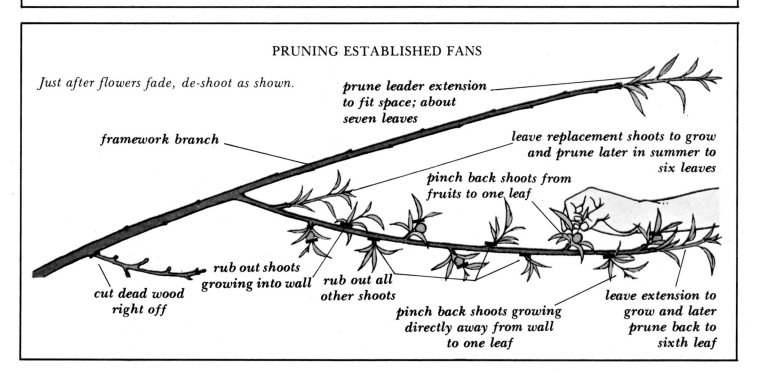

Just after flowers fade, de-shoot as shown.

prune leader extension to fit space; about seven leaves

framework branch

leave replacement shoots to grow and prune later in summer to six leaves

pinch back shoots from fruits to one leaf

rub out shoots growing into wall

rub out all other shoots

cut dead wood right off

pinch back shoots growing directly away from wall to one leaf

leave extension to grow and later prune back to sixth leaf

the fungus disease peach leaf curl, *Taphrina deformans.* The leaves become puckered and curled downwards in early spring, and are pale green or yellowish. The discoloured areas later become reddish and thickened, and develop white bloom as the sporing stage is reached. Defoliation occurs early, and new growth is severely stunted, though new leaves are often produced late in the season. Affected leaves should be destroyed as soon as seen and the tree sprayed at leaf fall with a spray of copper lime-sulphur, repeating in late winter and again two weeks later.

Other pests and diseases of peaches can be bacterial canker *(see* CHERRY) and silver leaf *(see* PLUM), both of them requiring the removal of affected branches. Brown rot, greenfly, red spider mite, scale and mildew may also attack, the last three especially on greenhouse trees.

Pear

One of the most delectable tree fruit, dessert pears are best home grown, because of the short period when they are in perfect eating condition.

Native to Europe and western Asia, pears have been cultivated since early times. They need a warm temperate climate, moist conditions and a rich soil to reach per-

---

Pear
Pyrus communis (fam. *Rosaceae*)
Hardy deciduous tree with a life of 60-200 years.
Size: on quince rootstock 3.7 m [12′] high, 2.7 m [9′] wide.
Climate: cool to warm temperate.
Planting to harvesting time: 5 years.
Yield: mature bush tree 50 kg [120 lb] fruit, dwarf pyramid 7 kg [15 lb], espalier 23 kg [50 lb].

---

fection. The trees are longer lived than apples and retain their fruit-bearing powers longer.

Most pears need a pollinator nearby flowering at the same time, to set fruit. White pear flowers appear in early to mid spring before the apple. The fruit has a gritty texture until ripe. Both shape and colour vary according to variety, from long to round and from green to yellow, red-flushed or russet-coated.

Pears can be divided into three groups. Cooking pears are not acid, but lack flavour; slow cooking with sugar enhances this. They are, however, prolific and store well. Often hardier than dessert pears, in colder parts of the cool temperate area they are likely to be more successful. Dessert pears are softer in texture with a strong scent. Pears can also be pressed for juice which is fermented to make perry. Except for those living in the coldest part of the temperate zones, home gardeners will do best to plant dessert varieties, as these will cook and bottle equally well when picked before complete ripeness.

Pears grown commercially are mostly open centred bushes, and this is the easiest method for the amateur and gives the highest yield in suitable conditions. However, pears train very readily. The dwarf pyramid or central leader tree follows the natural shape and is space saving and convenient to pick. In cool areas where shelter is required, it is worthwhile training an espalier.

Suitable site and soil

In colder parts of cool temperature areas grow only the hardier types of cooking pears, the protection of a wall or fence being essential for good quality fruit. Shelter for blossom is essential, but avoid frost pockets.

Strong winds at spring flowering prevent insects from pollinating, and strip tender young leaves from the tree, as well as severely browning the older leaves during the growing season. In autumn, winds may cause premature fall of leaves and, in particular, large well-grown fruit.

The best soil is deep, well drained, rather heavy and slightly acid. It should have at least 60 cm [2′] of rooting depth. Ideally is should have enough clay to ensure plenty of moisture during the growing season and enough sand and grit to allow for good drainage.

Buying your tree

Unless you choose a self-fertile pear you must plant two trees to ensure pollination. A pear on quince rootstock produces a bush rather than a tree, compact, fruitful and ideal for small gardens. Quince is the most dwarfing and quickest to bear, but some popular varieties such as Williams' Bon Chrétien (called Bartlett in the United States) do not unite properly with quince when grafted. They must therefore be double grafted by the nursery before purchase with an intervening compatible variety to prevent a future break at the union.

Buy two- or three-year-old trees, certified disease free if possible, trained as an open centred bush or espalier, unless you wish to train your own tree.

Williams' Bon Chrétien, or Bartlett, a popular variety of pear which must be double grafted to quince A stock.

Louise Bonne pears are a very old variety; they ripen in late autumn and are heavy croppers in warmer areas.

Pears are an ideal bush for the small garden; grafted onto quince A rootstock, they never grow too big.

Pyramid pruning enhances the natural shape of the tree. Branches are tied down here to encourage wide angles.

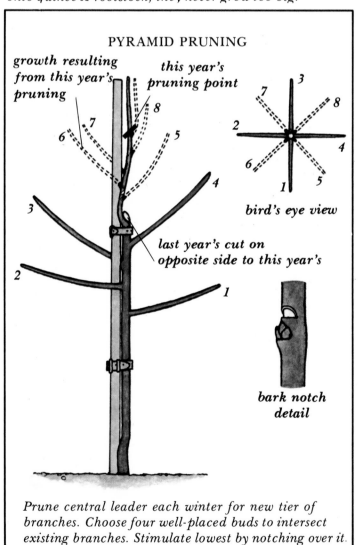

PYRAMID PRUNING

growth resulting from this year's pruning

this year's pruning point

last year's cut on opposite side to this year's

bird's eye view

bark notch detail

Prune central leader each winter for new tier of branches. Choose four well-placed buds to intersect existing branches. Stimulate lowest by notching over it.

Planting the tree

Prepare the soil in advance by breaking up the subsoil and incorporating well rotted manure. Correct the pH level if it is below 6 by liming, and work in a general compound fertilizer about two weeks before planting. Autumn planted trees establish the best. Heel in the tree if necessary. Plant, stake and mulch as in apple (*see* APPLE).

Take care to keep the union of the scion with the rootstock at least 7.5 cm [3"] above soil level. If the scion roots, the pear will quickly dominate the quince roots and a vigorous, unfruitful tree will result.

Bush trees should be spaced 3-3.7 m [10-12'] apart, pyramids can be as close as 1.8 m [6']. A pear on a wall should be allowed 2 m [8'] height and 3.7 m [12'] width. More should be allowed for Quince A and vigorous scions. Take care to spread out the roots so that they occupy the maximum amount of soil from which to draw water and nutrients. If soil texture is poor, perhaps after building operations, it is wise to use old potting compost as the immediate covering for roots to ensure a good start.

Fertilizers and care

The pear responds more than any other fruit to bulky organic matter. It needs plenty of summer moisture and high levels of nitrogen. This should be supplemented by an application in early spring each year of general compound fertilizer at the rate of 60 g per sq m [2 oz per sq yd]. This helps to maintain full cropping.

In extreme cases of poor growth, spray the foliage with urea-based proprietary feeds; this might be at three intervals of two weeks, from petal fall in late spring.

If the tree is excessively vigorous then both pruning and manuring should be reduced. The growth of a mature tree may further be modified by growing grass under it.

Trees planted against walls are particularly susceptible to lack of moisture, so pay attention to watering.

Pruning an open centred bush

The initial pruning to shape an open centred bush is the same as that of apples (*see* APPLE), with two important differences. Pears, if correctly pruned, carry their fruit on spurs close to the main branches and therefore more main branches can be allowed for each tree, say twelve where eight would be more suitable for apples. Secondly pear branches in the young tree are naturally slender and the result can be a drooping tree. To counteract this, continue to prune the leading shoots on the main branches back by one third or a half, according to vigour, until the trees approach their allotted height and spread. This will be when they are about eight years old, when leader pruning should cease.

There are four good reasons for pruning back the leaders: to strengthen the branch, to encourage more side growth, to remove deformed or diseased wood and to remove a branch growing in an undesirable direction. If none of these apply, then leader pruning should cease.

Pears bear fruit on short spurs, which are freely produced on two year and older wood, though some are tipbearers, including many weeping pears. These should be pruned little and then to an upward pointing bud.

Training and pruning a pyramid

Pyramids grow with a strong central leader. From this the cropping branches grow away at wide angles with one tier occupying up to 30 cm [1'] of trunk. The resulting tree is compact and very efficient at fruit bearing.

In early formative years, prune the central leader during the winter to produce one more tier of branches each year. In summer prune the branches and sideshoots.

Each winter for about five years cut the new upward growth from the central leader back to about 23 cm [9"]. Always make the cut to a bud on the opposite side of the tree to that on which the previous year's cut was made. This helps to keep the vertical stem straighter. The top bud will grow upwards and thus continue the central stem. The second bud would probably also grow upward, challenging the leader, so it is best to rub this out altogether (nick them off neatly with your thumb). The next two buds will probably also grow out to make good branches. Two more buds will perhaps also grow if you stimulate them by cutting away a half-moon of bark above the bud. Select the buds which will produce the best eventual tree shape, using your discretion. The chosen buds should be evenly spaced round the stem and, if possible, should point towards the gaps between branches on the tier below. Do not retain a bud immediately above an existing branch but aim for even spacing both up and around. Rub out all unwanted buds.

In summer prune the branches. Start when the new growth has begun to mature and the shoots are becoming stiff and woody and brown at the base. Disregarding the cluster of leaves at the base of the new growth, count five or six leaves and cut beyond a downward pointing one.

From late midsummer when the sideshoots along the branches begin to mature and are 30 cm [1'] long and woody at the base, cut to the third leaf beyond the basal cluster. This helps to build up strong spurs, close to the main branches. Where there has been growth from a sideshoot pruned in previous years, prune back to the first leaf beyond the basal cluster. Spread out the work over a period of 3 to 4 weeks. If in winter you find there has been further growth from any of these summer cuts, prune it back to the first bud.

Restrict the final height of the pyramid to about 2.1 m [7'], by switching pruning from winter to late spring just after new growth has begun. Cut the new central vertical growth by half to reduce the vigour of resulting growth. In following springs cut the new central leader growth to 1.5 cm [½"]. When branch leaders reach the length of those in the tier below deal with them in the same way.

Training and planting an espalier

The espalier is trained on a wall, fence or specially erected wires with horizontal branches in pairs on either side of the central stem. Nurseries usually sell two- and three-tier espaliers but if you train your own you can fill your own space.

Wire your wall with the lowest wire 30 cm [1'] from the ground and additional wires for each tier at intervals of about 30 cm [1']. A horizontal space 4.2 m [14'] is best. To train your own espalier, buy a maiden and, immediately after planting, cut the single stem down to a strong-looking bud about 5 cm [2″] higher than the lowest wire. This will produce vertical growth. Below this top bud choose two more buds, on opposite sides of the stem which will produce shoots growing in the direction of the support wire. Rub out any other buds and if, in spring, growth starts from any buds further down, rub this out. The top and second buds are likely to grow strongly. To stimulate the third bud, cut a notch of bark from just above it.

As growth develops, tie the shoot from the top bud to the vertical cane with soft string, fastening the cane in turn to the horizontal wires. As they become long enough, tie the shoots from the next two buds to canes fastened to the wires at an angle of 45°. Thus, the two lower shoots will be at an angle of 90° to each other. Try to keep the two

growing equally strongly so that they are the same length; slightly lower one cane to slow down growth and raise the other a little to increase growth.

In autumn unfasten the two side canes and bring them down to the horizontal and secure to the bottom wire. In winter prune the vertical shoot to a good bud about 5 cm [2″] above the second wire (this will make your new vertical) and proceed as in the first winter choosing two more buds to fill the second wire. Continue in this way until the required number of tiers has been formed but with the last tier allow only two shoots to grow, one on either side. Prune the branches of the espalier just as if they were cordons: in summer cut the side growths as they mature to the third leaf beyond the basal cluster, and cut shoots from laterals that were pruned previously to one leaf beyond the

TRAINING AN ESPALIER FROM A MAIDEN

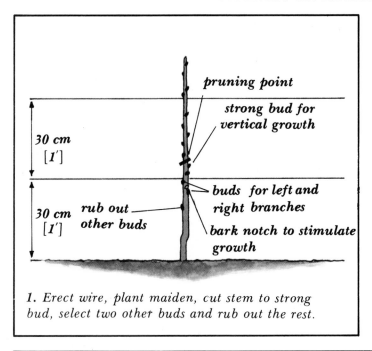

pruning point

strong bud for vertical growth

30 cm [1′]

30 cm [1′]   *rub out other buds*

buds for left and right branches

bark notch to stimulate growth

1. Erect wire, plant maiden, cut stem to strong bud, select two other buds and rub out the rest.

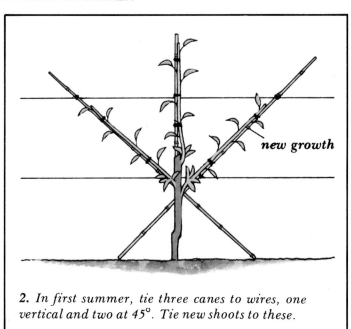

new growth

2. In first summer, tie three canes to wires, one vertical and two at 45°. Tie new shoots to these.

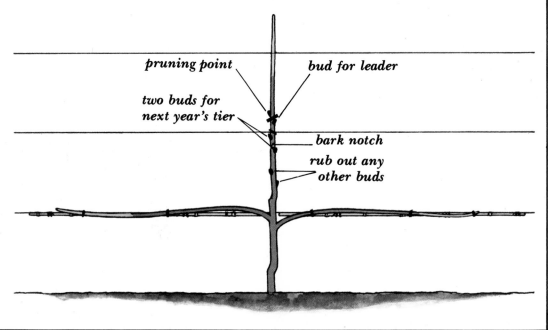

3. In autumn undo the two side canes, lower them to the horizontal and fasten to bottom wire, one on each side. In second winter same procedure is followed to produce second tier: cut back stem to a bud just above the second wire, choose two more buds for second tier, fix their shoots to 45° canes in second summer moving down in autumn. Repeat this procedure up to the last tier but then stop the stem and leave only the pair of buds for the top tier.

pruning point

bud for leader

two buds for next year's tier

bark notch

rub out any other buds

cluster at the twig base as shown in the diagram below.

Spur and fruit thinning

Pears make spurs more readily than apples and as the tree gets older the spurs become overcrowded, therefore spur thinning is beneficial.

The tree that is not growing sufficiently needs stimulation, provided by a harder winter prune and better manuring. The more frequent case is the tree growing too vigorously — all shoots and little fruit. Therefore prune lightly or not at all in winter and prune assiduously in summer. You can tie down the most vigorous sideshoots instead of cutting them out, so that they incline to the horizontal, which encourages them to produce fruit buds. This is particularly true of espaliers which incline to produce strong vertical growths from the horizontal arms.

In cool temperate areas all the fruit that set may be crop-ped. In warmer areas oversetting may occur, and then the fruit should be thinned out to about 15 cm [6″] apart.

Harvesting and storing

Picking starts in late midsummer and lasts for about three months. The early varieties can be picked and eaten as soon as they are ripe on the tree. This will be when the fruit parts readily from the spur when gently lifted to the horizontal. Such varieties have a very short season and deteriorate rapidly if allowed to become overripe, to the extent of rotting the centre. Mid season and late varieties can be picked before ripe for store. Pick before the stalk end changes to yellow. If a sharp tug is needed to get the fruit off, it is not ready for storing. Too early harvesting results in 'sleepy' pears, which shrivel and become soft in the outer flesh before they become sweet. Leave later varieties until frost is expected.

PRUNING ESPALIER LATERALS

pruning point one leaf above basal cluster on sub-sideshoot

pruning point three leaves above basal cluster on sideshoot

basal cluster of leaves

Pear espaliers must be pruned in midsummer. Cut mature laterals growing from horizontal branches back to three leaves above the basal cluster and sideshoots growing from these to one leaf above.

An espalier pear in blossom. Pears flower in early spring and so risk damage from late frost. On cold nights, hang strips of plastic over the blossom.

SPUR PRUNING ON OLD TREES

Pear spurs will become overcrowded in time. Prune oldest and least fruitful ones back to their base.

Pears bruise easily: only store if sound and disease-free. Lay in slatted trays in single layers in cool 7°C [45°F] but moist conditions. Stored fruit may be lightly sprayed with water to maintain a moist atmosphere; too much warmth and dryness also produces sleepy pears. Watch carefully for signs of ripening indicated (in all but russets) by a yellowing skin and a softening of the flesh at the stalk end. Bring into living room temperature before eating.

Pests and diseases

Pears suffer from the same troubles as apples, but to a lesser degree. Scab, mildew, canker and brown rot are the chief fungus diseases. Aphids, sucker, leaf-eating caterpillars, capsid, red spider mite and scale insects are common pests. Birds may attack buds or ripening fruit.

The white maggots of pear midge burrow into the fruitlets which become misshapen, rot and drop to the ground before half grown, where the maggots hibernate. Such fruits should be destroyed and the trees sprayed at white bud stage with fenitrothion. Pear leaf blister mite feeds on the leaves in spring and summer, so that they become blistered. In a bad attack, leaf fall will be considerable. Destroy all infested leaves, after a heavy attack, and spray with lime sulphur the following early spring. A virus disease, stony pit, distorts and dimples fruit with areas of hard woody-type flesh which make it unfit to eat. The fruit is less than the normal size and falls early.

Milder than chillies, but still very 'hot', the fruit of the long red pepper are powdered and used as a spice.

Peppers

Native to tropical America, peppers are now increasingly used both as a vegetable in stews and casseroles and as an ingredient in salads.

The two most common types of pepper are *Capsicum annuum*, which includes the large red and green sweet peppers and *C. frutescens*, which embraces chillies and hot red peppers. *C. annuum* is a narrow, roughly oblong vegetable with a mild, peppery flavour.

Capsicums at different stages of maturity. Do not leave overripe fruit on the plant as this will reduce yields.

(Right) Rich in vitamin C, sweet peppers are delicious stuffed and baked or shredded and eaten raw in salads.

1. *Put the tray on a windowsill to give seedlings plenty of sunlight.*

2. *At the three-leaf stage, prick seedlings out into 7.5 cm [3″] pots.*

3. *Pot on to 12 cm [5″] pots with a richer compost for fruiting outside.*

4. *Harden off in a cold frame prior to moving plants to the open garden.*

5. *Prepare home-made liquid manure; dilute it before feeding the plants.*

6. *Alternatively, buy liquid feed. Always feed when fruits are forming.*

7. *Pinch out the first few flowers by hand to encourage the formation of larger fruit. Keep well watered.*

8. *Prevent infestation by the pest red spider mite by a daily spray of water on undersides of the leaves.*

9. *Sweet red and green peppers can be stored: thread a string through the stalks and hang in a dry place.*

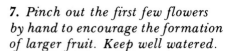

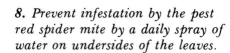

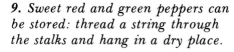

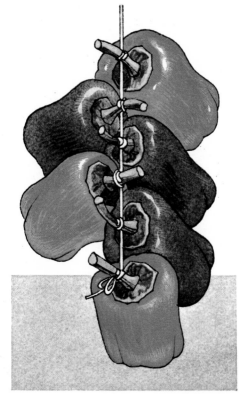

The small tapering fruits, about 2.5-5 cm [1-2″] long of the *C. frutescens* types are renowned for their strong 'hot' flavour, and the paprika made from one of these is much used in Hungarian cooking, especially goulash. Because of their pungency, these peppers are mostly used for flavouring only, often being ground to powder or shredded. Natives of warm climates, peppers are grown as half-hardy annuals in cool climates. The fruits of chilli peppers have to ripen completely before being picked and therefore the plants must be cultivated solely in a heated greenhouse and not moved outdoors. They should never be grown in the same greenhouse as sweet peppers, because of the dangers of cross-pollination between the two species.

Suitable site and soil

Peppers will thrive in any rich, well-worked soil. One method is to use a greenhouse border in which well-rotted manure has been dug in trowel-deep during the winter. Large clay or plastic pots can also be used and in this case any of the standard potting composts is suitable. Alternatively, a plastic bag full of any prepared growing medium, such as that suitable for tomatoes, can be used. Outdoors, a well-drained and fertile loam is preferable. Choose a sunny place.

Sowing and planting out

Sow seeds during early spring in a warm greenhouse or propagator, or a warm room if the climate is cool. They can be sown outdoors (either in the ground or in peat pots) after the last frost, in warm temperate areas.

If being sown indoors, sow seeds in trays, spacing them about 2.5 cm [1″] apart and pushing them just beneath the surface of the compost. A soil temperature of 18°C [65°F] is ideal, but seeds will germinate if it drops a few degrees below this for a short period of time. The first leaves should be showing within 10-24 days of sowing, depending on the temperature.

When the seedlings reach the three-leaf stage, prick each out into a 7.5 cm [3″] pot. Do not allow the plants to become root-bound; as they grow, pot them on to larger pots and into richer compost to encourage the development of good growth. If they are to fruit indoors, use 15 cm [6″] or 17.5 cm [7″] pots; if they are to be moved outdoors to fruit, 12.5 cm [5″] pots will be large enough. Maintain the temperature at between 10° and 16°C [50°

Peppers
Capsicum annuum, C. frutescens (fam. *Solanaceae).*
Also known as capsicum, bell or bullnose pepper, sweet pepper and pimiento; chilli and red pepper.
Perennial, but most culinary capsicums are grown as **half-hardy annuals.**
Size: plants vary in height from 30-90 cm [12-36″]. Fruit of dwarf varieties about 2.5 cm [1″] across; large varieties from 7.5-12.5 cm [3-5″].
Climate: warm temperate to tropical.
Sowing to harvesting time: 20-28 weeks.
Yield: 0.75-1 kg [1½-2 lb] per plant.

---

and 60°F] during this period. Never move these half-hardy plants straight from a warm greenhouse or kitchen window sill into the open garden. If the peppers are to be placed outside when the danger of the last frost has passed, get them accustomed to a lower temperature gradually, preferably by transferring them to a cold frame for a short period, or by giving them the protection of a cloche outdoors while still in their pots.

Where only a small number of plants are being raised and no frame or cloche is available, an easier method is to stand the pots outdoors rather than transplanting from pots into the ground. The pots can be left outside during the day, and returned to the greenhouse or a warm room at night. After one or two weeks the plants can be safely left out permanently.

Young plants which are to be dug into open ground should be set out at the beginning of summer at about 38-60 cm [15-24″] apart, depending on the size of the variety. Always water the soil well before planting, unless it is already fairly moist.

Care and development

The quantity of water which you should give peppers depends on the type of soil in which they are growing, the temperature of the environment and the age of the individual seedlings or plants. If a light soil becomes too dry, even for a very short time, especially during mid-day, the plants will droop. You should provide some form of light shading in the warmest months.

Peppers respond well to liquid feeding once the fruit begins to form and this can be done at ordinary watering times. If soil is very dry, however, soak the ground before using the liquid feed solution according to the manufacturer's instruction. Alternatively, make liquid manure by steeping a bag of rotted manure in a tub of water; use this after diluting it to the colour of straw.

Peppers should not be planted in areas where perennial weeds are persistent. Bindweed and similar weeds must be eliminated and annual weeds can be kept down with a hoe worked between the rows before the roots get a hold on the soil, ensuring the minimum disturbance to the roots.

Canes for support may be necessary for tall varieties, but the dwarf kinds stand up well and do not need sticks.

Artificial pollination is not really necessary as the greenish-white flowers set fruit readily, and may indeed need thinning to get the best-sized peppers. However, a daily light spray of water from a garden syringe may help, at the same time benefiting the leaves which, being thin, tend to dry up more quickly than most. It will also help to ward off attacks of red spider mite.

Harvesting and aftercare

The fruit should be in season from midsummer until early autumn, or late autumn in a good year, coming to an end as the weather becomes colder. The length of the harvesting season depends on the local climate, and can also vary from summer to summer. The fruits should be picked as soon as they are of sufficient size, and the flesh is firm and well filled out. A good quality pepper has a smooth, pleasing shape and an even colour. Green peppers that have been left on the plant will ripen to a rich scarlet, yellowish green or golden yellow colour, depending on the variety. The ripe fruit should be cut from the parent plant with a sharp knife, leaving the other peppers, which develop at different rates, undisturbed. The peppers taste delicious at all stages, but for those who prefer it, the mature red or yellow fruit are somewhat sweeter. Handle peppers carefully, for they bruise easily. The yield from each plant can be as high as 30 fruit in a good season, and two or three plants should provide a steady supply of sweet peppers during summer and early autumn.

To store the fruit, thread a string through the stalks and hang them up in a dry place. Late picked peppers can last until early winter. If picked green, they will gradually change colour until they are red. You should not leave overripe peppers on the plants, because this may reduce yields by draining food reserves.

The plants should not be left in the soil after the last pepper has been picked. For the sake of pest and disease control, it is better to pull up and burn or compost old plants as soon as the days start becoming shorter and colder and the fruiting process has stopped.

Pest and diseases

Greenfly and red spider mite may be troublesome, both indoors and out. In cool conditions grey mould may infect the fruit.

Plum

Plums are the most popular of the stone fruit, and the hardiest in cool areas. Red, blue-black or yellow-skinned, they are delicious raw or cooked.

Plums are related to peaches and cherries but are hardier than both. *Prunus* is the Latin name for plum. Among hardy fruit trees, the European plum, *Prunus domestica,* is second only in importance to the apple. It probably originated in south east Asia and is widely grown throughout Europe, North America and Australia. It is thought to be a hybrid from a wild blackthorn or sloe *(P. spinosa)* with very acid dark purple fruit, and myrobalan or cherry plum *(P. cerasifera),* now widely grown as an ornamental. The latter is chiefly grown for hedging, but it bears a reasonable crop, excellent for jam.

Cooking plums are mainly dark coloured with rather less flesh and a tart flavour. The trees are larger, more vigorous, hardier and heavier and more reliable croppers. Dessert plums have a richer flavour, high sugar content and may be yellow, red, black or purple. Blue plums described as prunes, produce fruit for drying.

In warmer climates the Japanese plum *P. salicina* is successful; this was originally native to China. It blooms very early; fruit have thick skins but lack flavour. *P. americana* is most important of the native American plums.

Damsons, *P. damascena,* produce a smaller and richer fruit on a smaller tree. The old fashioned bullace, *P. insititia,* have soft dark fruit with a sharp flavour; used for cooking they are left on the tree till late autumn for maximum ripeness. Greengages, *P. italica,* have green-toned flesh and crossbreeds with the European plums are usually classed with them.

Suitable site and soil

There is no really dwarfing rootstock, so plums are unsuitable for the small garden unless fan-trained or grown as a pyramid or bush. They can also be standards or half standards. In colder parts of cool temperate areas the choicest dessert fruit may be fan-trained against a wall. Plums bloom early in mid spring when blossom can easily be damaged by frost, so avoid low-lying spots. Shelter is needed from east winds. Shallow or sandy soils, and ill-drained soils and heavy clays should be avoided.

Buying the trees

A few plums are self-fertile, but most require a compatible pollinator flowering at the same time. Plums are grafted or budded on to rootstocks; Myrobalan B gives a large tree, and St. Julien A a slightly smaller one. Buy trees certified as virus disease tested if these are available. Unless you want a standard tree, buy a maiden (one-year-old) or two-year-old.

Some varieties of tree are upright, others have a weeping habit. Droopers are best as standard trees, otherwise the branches will trail on the ground. Victoria makes an umbrella shape and is best on a stem of about 1.2 m [4'].

> **Plum**
> *Prunus domestica* (fam. *Rosaceae*)
> **Hardy** deciduous tree with a useful life of 50 years.
> **Size:** 6-9 m [20-30'].
> **Climate:** cool to warm temperate.
> **Planting to harvesting time:** 4-5 years.
> **Yield:** mature standard or bush tree on St. Julien A rootstock 45-52 kg [100-120 lb], more for more vigorous rootstock, less for a pyramid trained tree. Greengages yield half this figure.

Cooking plums are much hardier than dessert varieties;
The tart fruit is used for pies, preserves and desserts.

Best grown as a small standard tree, damsons bear sweet
oval-shaped fruit which is excellent for home-made jam.

Greengages are highly prized for their flavour. Grown
like plums, they yield only half the quantity of fruit.

To produce high yields, prune plums need a cold winter
followed by a hot, dry summer. Their fruits are dried.

WINTER PRUNING FROM THE SECOND YEAR ON

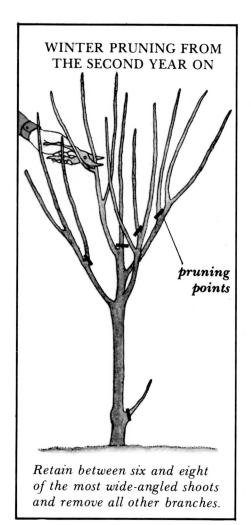

pruning points

Retain between six and eight of the most wide-angled shoots and remove all other branches.

TRAINING A PYRAMID

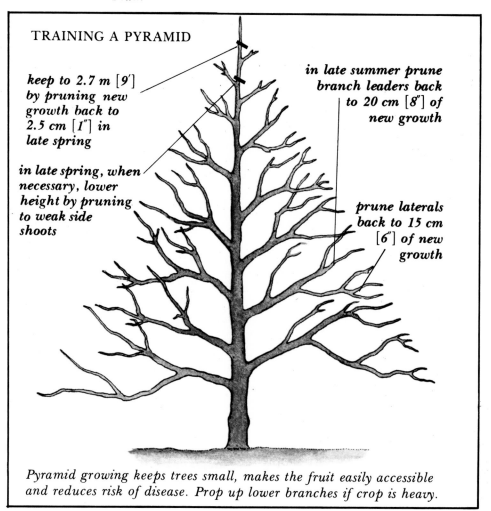

keep to 2.7 m [9'] by pruning new growth back to 2.5 cm [1"] in late spring

in late spring, when necessary, lower height by pruning to weak side shoots

in late summer prune branch leaders back to 20 cm [8"] of new growth

prune laterals back to 15 cm [6"] of new growth

Pyramid growing keeps trees small, makes the fruit easily accessible and reduces risk of disease. Prop up lower branches if crop is heavy.

THINNING THE FRUIT

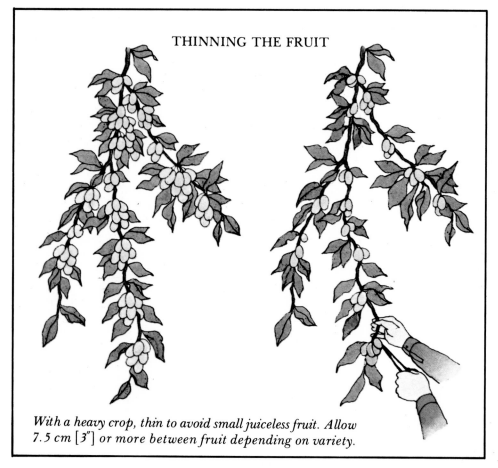

With a heavy crop, thin to avoid small juiceless fruit. Allow 7.5 cm [3"] or more between fruit depending on variety.

SUPPORTING LEADER BRANCHES

Put stake close to the trunk and support the branches with strings attached to its top.

Planting out

With a heavy soil, work in coarse sand before planting, at 3 kg [7 lb] per sq m [yd]. Make well-drained soil more water retentive by mixing in rotted organic matter, half a 12 L [2½ gal] bucket per sq m [yd] four weeks before planting. No lime is needed unless soil gives pH of less than 6.0. Space less vigorous varieties on St. Julien A rootstock 3 m [10']; pyramids and trees on Myrobalan B stock 5.5 m [18']. Plant the tree as for apple (*see* APPLE). Be careful not to injure bark while planting, otherwise bacterial canker may get a hold.

Fertilizing and care

Plums need plenty of nitrogen, and should never run short of potash. A good mulch of rotted farmyard manure or garden compost is especially helpful to young trees, applied in late spring every year. In addition in late winter give 15 g per sq m [½ oz per sq yd]. If organic matter is not available, double this dressing of nitrogen and add 15 g per sq m [½ oz per sq yd] sulphate of potash. Dress an area of soil slightly in excess of that covered by the branches. Water well in very dry weather, and especially for trees trained against walls.

Pruning

For the first two or three years the head of the tree will be pruned to form the main framework. A maiden tree consists of a single straight stem, possibly with a few wispy branches called feathers. After planting the main stem is cut to 15 cm [6"] above the desired height of the lowest branch. Several branches will then grow below this cut. In the following winter choose three or four well-spaced, wide-angled shoots tending to horizontal and remove everything else flush with the stem. Selected shoots are then cut back halfway to an outward facing bud.

In the next summer two or more shoots will grow from each of these cut back branches and in the winter after this six to eight well-spaced shoots should be retained and all vigorous and more upright branches removed.

No tipping is required. Future pruning is only to cut out shoots too close together and diseased and broken branches. The best time to prune established trees to avoid infection is late summer after picking.

Plums tend to produce suckers and these should be removed by pulling out by hand rather than cutting.

Training a plum pyramid

Plum pyramids are smaller and can be grown in a restricted space. Only large-growing varieties are unsuitable. Pyramids are easier to pick and disease is less likely as large wounds and branch breakages are much reduced.

Buy a maiden tree with some feathered growth (side branches). When planting, support the tree with a stout bamboo cane or post standing 1.8-2 m [6-7'] out of the ground. In mid spring cut the main leader to 1.2-1.5 m [4-5'] from ground level. Remove all feather growth up to a height of 30 cm [1'] above the soil, and shorten the remaining feathers to half their length. Tie the leader loosely to the stake to allow growth.

In late summer of the same year, the leading shoot growing from each of the shortened feathers is cut back to 20 cm [8"] and lateral shoots to 15 cm [6"]. The main central leader is gently tied to the stake and is not cut.

In subsequent years the main central leader is cut back in late spring, to within 2.5 cm [1"] of the previous year's growth, and branch leaders and laterals are pruned after midsummer, as they were in the first year. Cut main leader back harder if growing too tall. If very upright shoots grow from the main trunk they should be removed completely as only wide angled laterals will be fruitful.

Wall-trained plums

In cool parts of cool temperate areas, walls provide some protection against spring frost, and reflected heat helps to ripen choice dessert varieties. The wall should be 2.7 m [8'] high for a vigorous variety. The tree should be trained the same shape as peach (*see* PEACH).

Pruning, done mostly in mid to late summer, consists of removing unsuitable shoots, mainly those growing towards or outwards from the wall, and cutting back new sideshoots to about six leaves. In autumn these are further cut to where the fruit buds have formed. In mid spring leading shoots are tipped until the tree has filled its space. After this each leader is cut back in late summer to a weaker side shoot. Choose varieties for fan-training which are naturally inclined to spur. Even so, fan trees will probably need replacing after about 15 years.

Thinning fruit and supporting branches

Plums tend to crop too heavily one year and lightly the next. In a heavy crop the fruit can be small with little flesh. Thin out the fruit to maintain quality and prevent possible branch breakage. Remove diseased, badly shaped and injured fruitlets first. Thin when fruit are swelling and are about one third of their final size after those which have not set have dropped off. Allow 7.5 cm [3"] between any two plums, 10 cm [4"] for larger fruits. Even after thinning weighty branches may need support with a prop (*see* MULBERRY) or drive in an upright stake next to the trunk; branches are then supported by strings attached to the top of the stake.

Harvesting

Trees bear after about five years and cropping is from late midsummer to early autumn. Dessert fruit should be left on the tree until thoroughly ripe. For canning or bottling plums can be picked when fully coloured, for jam when firm and almost ripe. Go over the tree several times picking fruit as it ripens. If they have a bloom pick carefully with finger and thumb – plums bruise easily. Some are easily parted from their stalks, but others need careful picking to avoid removing spur. Plums can be kept a few days if laid out not touching, in a cool place.

Pests and diseases

In many districts, birds are the worst enemies, both when the fruit is on the tree, and in winter when they peck out the blossom buds. Either net the tree, if possible (*see* CHERRY) or spray in winter with bird repellant.

The fungus disease silver leaf, *Stereum purpureum*, is a

The beautiful bloom of a healthy crop. Unlike dessert plums, cookers should be picked before fully ripening.

common complaint of plums, especially the variety Victoria, and is serious and difficult to control. The leaves on one shoot, and then on all shoots, on a branch will become silver on the top surface, and if the branch is cut through, the wood will be irregularly stained purplish brown on one side, if not both. The disease can spread all over a tree and kill it, when purplish leathery sheets or projecting brackets of tissue are produced in layers from the bark, usually in autumn. Disease enters through wounds, such as pruning cuts. When trees are badly silvered all over or have reached this spore-producing stage, they should be destroyed. However, trees can recover, grow and crop if the disease is mild. There is no known cure.

Fruit can be attacked from early summer onwards by the small red caterpillars of the plum fruit moth; spray with derris or fenitrothion in early summer, to control the larvae as they hatch out before they enter the fruit. The creamy white caterpillar of the plum sawfly also feeds on the fruit but much earlier, from the time when they first set. Spray with derris, quassia or fenitrothion but wait until evening when pollinating insects are not about.

Gumming of fruit can be due to injury by capsids or sawfly larvae, or because water supplies have been irregular, especially if the tree is grown against a wall.

Potato

The potato is a versatile and staple food, high in carbohydrate but also containing some essential vitamins. Though widely grown as a farm crop, garden produce tastes best.

Although most potatoes are grown on farms, it is still an important garden crop. Some high-quality varieties are unsuitable for large-scale commercial cultivation; they may not be able to stand transport without injury, they may give a low yield, or serve too specialized a purpose. Early, or 'new' potatoes are also at their best shortly after being dug, and maincrop potatoes grown in the garden usually give a higher yield than with field cultivation.

Suitable site and soil

In a rotation system, potatoes are generally grown to follow roots and to precede the cabbage family, which appreciates the clean, well-turned condition in which this crop leaves the soil. Potatoes are a good choice for a first crop on old pasture that is being taken into cultivation. As a precaution against disease, they must not be grown in the same soil two years in succession. Remember that tomatoes and nightshade weeds are also members of the family *Solanaceae* and can transmit infection. Potatoes are not particular about soil, but on heavy clay soils choose your varieties carefully. Early varieties prefer light land.

The ground should be well dug and treated with rotted manure or garden compost, but not limed. Lime will encourage attacks of scab, while too much nitrogen will produce growth of the 'haulm', or stem, at the expense of tubers. An excess of chloride will give 'soapy' potatoes.

Seaweed, dug into the soil the previous autumn, is an excellent manure. If organic matter is not available, a fertilizer of 2 parts each by weight of superphosphate and sulphate of ammonia with 1 part of sulphate of potash may be applied during preparation at the rate of 40 g per sq m [1⅓ oz per sq yd] of the mixture. The site should be open and not overshadowed by trees, walls or buildings.

Planting the crop

The tubers from which potatoes are grown are dormant ones known as 'sets'. These are obtained from vigorous plants before they are fully mature and exposed for a few days until they have greened. Potato crops are grown from tubers produced on government certified farms. (After the Irish potato famine in the 1840s, breeders worked to develop blight-resistant strains.) Certified sets are often bought every year, but it is considered safe to grow from tubers of your own (undiseased) crop every other year. Sets should be about the size of a hen's egg and look plump and healthy, but a delivery usually contains some larger ones. These may be divided as described later.

If you wish to have potatoes the year round, you will need three varieties: an early, a second early, and a maincrop variety. The earlier the variety, the faster the growth and the lower the yield. Order 2 kg [4½ lb], 5 kg [11 lb] and 2.5 kg [5½ lb] respectively, of each kind per person, if a supply

---

Potato
Solanum tuberosum (fam. *Solanaceae*), known as white or Irish potato where sweet potatoes are also grown.
Half-hardy annual.
Size: tubers average 7 × 6 cm [2¾″ × 2¼″]; height of haulms (stems) about 60 cm [2′].
Climate: cool temperate to sub-tropical.
Planting to harvesting time: 13-17 weeks.
Yield: 3-4 kg [6½-9 lb] per plant.

is to be maintained through the winter and spring, in time to begin sprouting at the end of winter (slightly earlier for early varieties). Allow 20 sq m [24 sq yd] of land for this amount. If you can only grow a more limited number, it is best to sacrifice the maincrop and grow the earlies, which are harvested when potatoes are dearest in the shops.

Put the sets in trays or empty egg-boxes in a light, well-ventilated frost-proof place. This enables growth to begin before it would be wise to plant outside. The wooden fruit trays that have a short leg sticking upwards at each corner for stacking are ideal. Look for the end of the set where the 'eyes' or dormant buds are crowded together — this is the top. Stand them upwards in the trays or egg-boxes and, if there is any risk of frost, spread newspaper over. Chitting, as this process is called, takes about six weeks and is done, not only to get crops earlier, but to get heavier ones.

Plant when the sprouts are 3 cm [1¼″] long, which is usually in early or mid spring. Rub off all except two or three of them with the thumb, removing first the one at the extreme top, then any that are white (if most of them are purplish), and lastly the least promising of any surplus remaining. Large sets can be cut into pieces, each having at least two strong sprouts. Dust the cut faces with flowers of sulphur or plaster of Paris to check loss of moisture; alternatively, bring the exposed surfaces together and cover with a damp cloth until planting. Take great care not to knock off the sprouts.

Potato rows should run north and south so that the plants receive the maximum amount of sunshine and do not shade other crops. The rows should be 50 cm [20″] apart for earlies and 75 cm [30″] apart for the bulkier maincrop plants. This allows room for earthing up later on.

Take out V-shaped furrows from 8 cm [3¼″] deep for a heavy soil to 15 cm [6″] deep for a light one. Never use a dibber for planting because it is liable to leave an air-space underneath the tuber. For improved yield spread a forkful of manure where each set is to go and throw 3 cm [1¼″] of soil over it, so that manure and set will not be in direct contact. Place lawn mowings in and around the drills before filling them in; this will help prevent attacks of the potato scab fungus, which is less likely to bother the potatoes when other organic matter is available. Use small amounts of grass only.

Place each set in position in the drill, top uppermost, 30 cm [1′] apart for earlies and 40 cm [16″] for maincrops, covering each with soil by hand to protect the sprouts from damage when refilling the furrow. Rake the soil level and scatter fertilizer along the row. The earlies should go into sheltered ground at the end of winter, with second earlies and maincrops at monthly intervals.

Care and cultivation

Protection is necessary for all potatoes when there is any risk of frost, as there nearly always is with the earlies. Once the shoots are above the surface, ground or wind-frost will burn them black, causing a 3-week setback. When they are only a few centimetres [inches] high cover them gently with powdery soil, but when they are 7.5-10 cm [3-4″] tall they must be covered with straw or with leafy branches.

Wait until the shoots can be clearly seen before doing any hoeing, and then do not work the hoe too close to them. Start earthing up when the shoots are about 20 cm [8″] high. The haulms of potato plants are jointed, and the tubers arise from underground joints in the haulm. Therefore the more of these there are the more tubers can be formed, hence the practice of earthing up.

Earthing up also keeps the tubers well buried so that they will not turn green through exposure to light — green tubers contain a poisonous substance and are dangerous to eat. Loosen up the soil between the rows and push some up with a draw-hoe on both sides of the haulms several times during the growing period, leaving the top 15 cm [6″] uncovered.

Spray against the fungus disease blight once in mid-summer and again in late summer with Bordeaux or Burgundy mixture. These can protect against blight but not cure it. Any flowers that appear during growth should be nipped off. When growth slows and the haulms turn yellow the tubers mature. If isolated plants show these signs you must suspect disease; cut their tops down and burn them, although the tubers of these plants may be left in the soil until they are of usable size and are harvested.

Harvesting and storing the crop

Early or 'new' potatoes are eaten immature in early summer, when they are no larger than a pullet's egg. Carefully lift one or two to see if they are ready for eating; they can be covered up again if they are not. Some people unearth them by hand, pick the tubers they want, and return the soil to let the rest grow on. Dig up the earlies as you need them day by day, because after they are lifted they quickly lose flavour.

A potato fork is a great asset: its flat, blunt tines miss more tubers and damage fewer than any other tool. Whole potatoes or pieces of tuber remaining in the ground over winter are not only lost, but will be a nuisance growing up among the brassicas the next year, and negate the principle of not growing potatoes in the same soil two years running.

The earlies can go straight into the kitchen as required, but the later crops must be stored. After lifting, let them dry off on the ground for an hour or two, but no longer, before being taken in. Clean off adhering soil by hand, discard any diseased or damaged tubers, and take the opportunity to do any grading required if, for instance, any are required for seed. Store them in the dark or under cover from light in a dry frost- and draught-free storeroom. Bags or boxes will do for storing, but put straw under the bags and take precautions against vermin. The potatoes should be inspected once a month, when rotten ones should be discarded and any sprouts rubbed off.

If supplies are large and accommodation small, one solution is a clamp raised in a dry open situation out of doors on a thick bed of straw. Heap the potatoes on this into a ridge and cover them thickly with more straw, then put some soil on to keep it in place. After 24 hours' drying cover the straw with 15 cm [6″] of soil, obtained by digging a drainage trench all round the clamp. This is then beaten flat with the spade so as to shed rain. Leave ventilation holes at 1 m [1 yd] intervals along the top, pulling up tufts

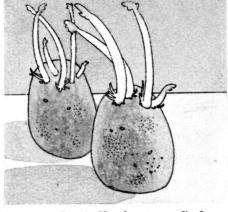

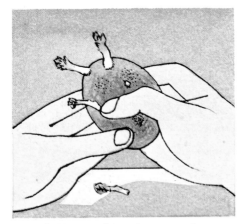

Encourage the tubers to sprout by placing seed potatoes in cardboard egg boxes, with the 'rose' end up.

Long and spindly shoots, unfit for planting, are caused by keeping the sets in too much warmth or darkness.

Rub off any white shoots and any at the extreme top, using your thumb; retain the two most sturdy shoots.

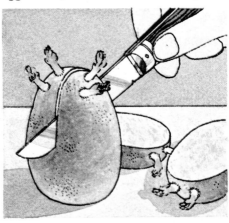

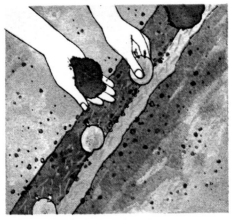

When large tubers are cut, be sure each piece has two shoots. Protect cut surfaces from loss of moisture.

Plant by hand in V-shaped furrows. Use small amounts of lawn mowings to discourage potato scab fungus.

Protect sprouts by crumbling soil over them before raking level. Then scatter fertilizer along the row.

When haulms reach 7.5 cm [3"], they must be covered with straw to give protection against damage by frost.

Begin earthing up when haulms reach 17 cm [7"], to stop exposed tubers going green and protect from blight.

Yellowish leaves indicate the crop is ready. Lift with a potato fork to reduce risk of damage to tubers.

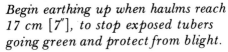

The traditional method of earthing up potato rows encourages more tubers to form and protects them from light, as well as helping keep down weeds.

A high quality second early variety, Craig's Royal prefers a heavy soil.

King Edward is traditionally one of the most popular maincrop varieties.

Leave the crop on the soil for one or two hours to dry before storing.

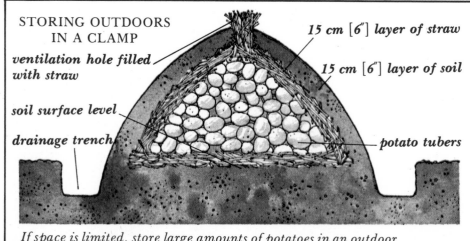

STORING OUTDOORS
IN A CLAMP

ventilation hole filled with straw

soil surface level

drainage trench

15 cm [6″] layer of straw

15 cm [6″] layer of soil

potato tubers

If space is limited, store large amounts of potatoes in an outdoor clamp. Inspect regularly and, if any are rotting, remake the clamp.

of straw from below to keep them open. When removing potatoes, inspect those exposed to view before closing the breach. If many are rotten, you must remake the clamp. Take the haulms away and burn them; do not compost.

Alternative methods of cultivation

It is not essential to earth up potatoes but the traditional method described is still widely favoured. Cultivation time may be cut by planting the tubers individually along the rows with a trowel (without making a trench) and covering the rows with lengths of black plastic sheeting tucked into slits made in the soil, at both its sides and ends, so as to anchor them. When the shoots start to grow and make bumps in the plastic make openings with scissors in the form of plus signs to release them. The opaque sheeting conserves moisture, inhibits weeds, and shields the shallow-grown tubers from light. Harvest the potatoes, after cutting or rolling back the plastic, by lifting them up with a hand fork or potato fork.

Spring supplies of 'new potatoes' can be produced by planting them in warm frames in mid winter, either directly in the soil or in pots, but few gardeners have this much frame accommodation. Half-bury upright sets each in a 20 cm [8″] pot about a third full, and earth them up as they grow. Patio-gardeners sometimes grow three or four earlies in half-wine barrels. Some earlies may be given a good start with cloches, but keep tunnel end closed.

Pests and diseases

Potatoes, unfortunately, can suffer from a good many troubles, but the ones given here are the most likely to occur under garden conditions.

Potato blight *(Phytophthora infestans)* is probably the best known; it is a fungus disease which produces dark brown-black patches on the leaves and stems; infected tubers have sunken areas on the outside which will be found to be brown in the flesh underneath. The disease spreads quickly in warm wet weather and can destroy the top growth completely in midsummer. Protect plants by spraying with Bordeaux mixture or zineb in early midsummer, if the weather warrants it, and repeat as the makers instruct.

Common scab is a superficial fungus disease, affecting the skins of the tubers only, but it makes peeling difficult; line the drills at planting time with small amounts of lawn mowings. Peelings should be destroyed. Wart disease *(Synchytrium endobioticum)* is a fungus disease notifiable in Britain to the governmental department. Affected tubers produce large irregular growths, like cauliflowers, sometimes bigger than the tuber itself, which turns black and rots. The soil is contaminated for up to 16 years. Immune varieties are available, and it should be remembered that recent regulations prohibit the growing of susceptible varieties in some countries.

Black leg is a bacterial trouble which affects the occasional plant in a crop. The stems blacken at soil level, the leaves turn yellow and the haulm withers; tubers rot where they are attached to the stem. Dig up infected plants and destroy them.

Wireworms and black underground slugs can cause much

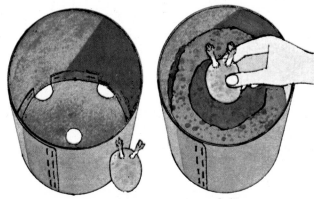

GROWING POTATOES IN CONTAINERS

Plant one seed potato in each 30 cm [1′] container. Use a hand fork to harvest crop.

GROWING UNDER PLASTIC SHEETS

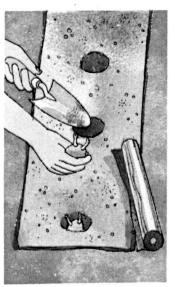

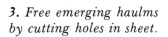

1. Use a trowel to plant tubers in holes along row.

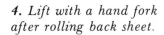

2. Secure plastic sheet in slits dug in the soil.

3. Free emerging haulms by cutting holes in sheet.

4. Lift with a hand fork after rolling back sheet.

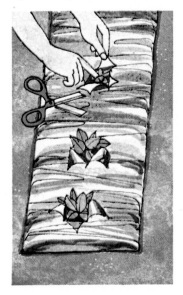

trouble by eating the tubers, especially the latter in wet summers. Little can be done to control slugs beyond ensuring the soil is not of the kind that remains wet, and keeping the garden clear of hiding places for the animals. Early crops are hardly attacked by slugs; some varieties appear to be immune.

Potato root eelworm can be a very serious pest and is likely to occur when potatoes are grown in the same ground every year. Affected plants are stunted and pale green or yellow, and they wilt easily and die when immature. Tuber production will be very small. If eelworms are present, there will be tiny white dots on the roots, just visible without a lens, which later become brown, and which contain 200-600 eggs. Infected plants and tubers should be destroyed, infected soil put down to grass for 8 years.

Colorado beetle (very rare in the UK) is notifiable to the governmental department. The dark red and black larvae feed voraciously on the leaves; the adult beetle is striped black and yellow. Handpick the larvae or spray with fenitrothion.

Greenfly are most serious for spreading virus diseases such as leaf-roll and mosaic, rather than for their feeding on the foliage. Another virus disease is spraing, which produces brown rings in the flesh of the tubers, and is spread by soil-living eelworms.

Hollow heart is a physiological disorder, in which there is a cavity in the centre of the tuber. This happens when wet weather follows a dry spell; it sometimes occurs on too mature tubers.

Pumpkin

Associated with harvest festival and Halloween, the golden round pumpkin can grow to great size, up to 45 kg [100 lb].

There are two sorts of pumpkin: those from *Cucurbita pepo*, which is the same species as marrows and many

squashes, and the Cushaw pumpkin *C. mixta* from Mexico. Both are members of the *Cucurbitaceae* family. Though they are half hardy, they are more tolerant of cool conditions than melons and cucumbers in the same family. They need summer heat to ripen.

Cooked with cinnamon and brown sugar in pumpkin pie, they are an American national dish, although nowadays commercial pumpkin pies are usually made from summer squash. They are also eaten as a savoury.

Pumpkins grow into large hairy plants, and unless trained they can extend as much as 3.7 m [12']. They are best limited to an average of about four fruit a plant. Though the ordinary pumpkin will ripen in a cool temperate climate, *C. mixta* takes about five months to reach maturity and so may best be grown in a cold frame.

Pumpkins must ripen fully on the plant, though frost will spoil them. After cutting, they are left for a week for the skin to harden before storing in a cool place. They should not be eaten overripe. For cultivation *see* SQUASH.

Quince

This unusual fruit is pear-shaped and has an astringent flavour. With addition of sugar in cooking, it makes delicious pies, preserves and jellies.

The quince is probably a native of western Asia and belongs to a genus closely related to *Pyrus,* best known for

Quince
Cydonia vulgaris (fam. *Rosaceae)*
Hardy deciduous tree with a useful life of 100 years.
Size: 4.5-6 m [15-20'] tall by about 3.7 m [12'] wide.
Climate: cool to warm temperate.
Planting to harvesting time: about 8 years per tree.
Yield: 18 kg [40 lb] per tree.

A decorative, slow-growing tree, the quince bears golden fruit which have a strong aroma when ripe.

the pear, and has been reclassified several times.

Quinces make attractive small trees and are self-fertile. In old age they form spreading trees which become contorted. Quince provides the main rootstock for pears.

Cultivation

Quince is propagated by cuttings, suckers or by stooling and is grown on its roots. It only grows really well in warm sheltered sites and moist conditions; a position near a pond is ideal.

Quinces can be grown as half standard trees on a stem of 1.4 m [4½'] but in cool temperate areas they are better grown as bushes on a short leg.

Planting is best done in the autumn and is like that of other fruit trees *(see* APPLE). 3 m [10'] should be allowed between bushes, and twice that distance for standards. On moist fertile soils the quince requires little manuring but, like pears, responds well to surface mulches of rotted manure or garden compost. Weed regularly.

Pruning can be minimal and is confined to the cutting out of overcrowded, unproductive or damaged branches. Long sideshoots are spurred back as for pears *(see* PEAR). Leave fruit on tree until ripe and pick when dry. If stored in cool conditions, fruit will yellow and mature at intervals over three months, when it will still be quite hard. The ripening fruit gives off a pronounced aroma which can adversely affect apples and pears, so store separately.

Radish

An excellent catch crop, the crisp,
tender roots of the summer radish are
usually eaten raw in salads.
Winter or giant radishes can also
be cooked like turnips.

Quick growth and frequent small sowings in a rich, moist soil are the essential requirements for succulent radish roots. The shape and colour of the roots varies according

to type. Those of the salad radish can be red, white or red-and-white, small and round or longer and tapering. The more solid roots of the winter radish can be dark brown or bright red and sometimes weigh up to ½ kg [1 lb].

Suitable site and soil

Sow in a sunny patch of soil which has been well-manured in recent years. A heavy clay soil can be lightened by the addition of peat. If necessary, work this in at sowing time. But in cool countries add the peat early in the winter when digging and allow the frost to break down the clay. In warm countries choose a cooler site.

Sowing and planting out

Seed can be sown under glass from autumn until late winter in the south and directly out of doors from mid spring until autumn. In cool countries the best time to start is during late winter. Seed is sown under glass frames or cloches which can be covered with newspaper or sacks if a frost is expected. If you have no glass protection, for early crops make a first sowing in mid spring and further sowings at two-week intervals for a continuous supply. Winter radishes should be sown in midsummer.

Sprinkle the seeds thinly at 0.5 cm [¼"] depth in neat rows, later thinning to 2.5 cm [1"] spacing for the smaller salad varieties and 15 cm [6"] for winter varieties. With both, allow 15 cm [6"] between rows. Radishes are often intercropped with other vegetables. Their distinctive heart-shaped seed-leaves mark the rows and the roots are soon ready to be pulled for eating, leaving space for the other crop to spread.

Care and development

Moisture is essential. Water regularly in warm areas and during the summer months everywhere. Weeding should not be a problem if the seed is sown in ground which has been well prepared; radishes grow quickly and are ready to pull before any weeds can become established.

Harvesting the crop

The summer radishes are harvested about three to four weeks from sowing, while they are still young. They should be pulled as soon as the root is large enough to use and the plant has a few leaves. When the flowering stem develops the roots become stringy and have a hot, unpalatable flavour. Large winter radishes can be harvested in autumn and stored in damp sand or they may be left outside and pulled when needed.

Radish
Raphanus sativus (fam. *Cruciferae*)
Biennial, usually grown as **annual.**
Size: varies according to type, from thumbnail to forearm length.
Climate: cool to warm temperate.
Sowing to harvesting time: 3-4 weeks for summer varieties; several months for winter varieties.
Yield: 2 kg [4 lb] of summer radishes and 4.5 kg [10 lb] of winter radishes, per 3 m [10'] row.

Sow seed under glass from autumn to late winter. Sprinkle the seed thinly at a depth of 0.5 cm [¼"].

If you expect frost, cover the frame light with sacking or newspapers to protect the seedlings.

Thin the seedlings immediately they are large enough to handle. Thin to about 2.5 cm [1"] apart.

To protect seedlings from birds put wire hoops in ground and cover with fine-mesh netting. Water frequently.

Radishes grown between barn cloches will receive protection and run-off rain from the cloche roof.

Large winter radishes can be pulled in autumn and then stored in a wooden box full of damp sand.

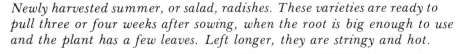

Radishes growing intercropped. The roots are soon ready to harvest, leaving space for the other crop.

Newly harvested summer, or salad, radishes. These varieties are ready to pull three or four weeks after sowing, when the root is big enough to use and the plant has a few leaves. Left longer, they are stringy and hot.

Pests and diseases

Radishes are generally trouble free, especially early spring sown crops. However, if slugs are a nuisance, place half an orange cut-side down to collect slugs or use slug pellets for large crops.

Raspberry

These delicious juicy berries do not transport well, so they are a very worthwhile fruit to grow in the garden, as you will enjoy quality you can never purchase.

The raspberry, *R. idaeus,* grows wild throughout Europe and parts of Asia, and has been cultivated since the sixteenth century. Though red berries predominate, both yellow and white berries are known.

The cane is a cool climate plant, but can be killed off by exposure to very low temperatures. Snow acts as a good protection. Spring frosts can damage fruiting sideshoots and wind may break canes.

Raspberries are self fertile and grow from a perennial stool. The root system can spread over a considerable area. The fruit is round or oblong depending on variety, and up to 3 cm [1¼″] long.

Raspberry

European species derived from *Rubus idaeus* (fam. *Rosaceae*) and in North America in addition from *R. strigosus.*

Hardy perennial prickly cane with a useful life of 12 years.

Size: up to 2.5 m [8′] high untrimmed, kept to about 1.2-1.5 m [4-5′] when fruiting.

Climate: cool temperate.

Yield: up to 3 kg [7 lb] per plant or 15-22 kg [35-49 lb] per 3 m [10′] row.

There are a number of autumn fruiting or everbearing raspberries, which produce fruit on the tips of current season shoots. Fruit quantity may be smaller than that of summer fruiting canes.

Suitable site and soil

Raspberries prefer good light, though they will tolerate a little shade, and a sheltered position in deep, moisture-holding soil. The best soils are deep and well drained, as the roots of the plant are likely to be killed off in very wet soils in winter. Heavy clay soils are not suitable without careful preparation and maintenance. Raspberries will accept more acid conditions than most fruit, though they will suffer from the unavailability of iron in too alkaline a soil, like many other fruits. Avoid planting in sites previously occupied by berries of the same genus and plant as far away as possible from old fruiting canes.

A heavy soil should be prepared well in advance and left open to the weather. If the subsoil is hard and impervious to water, it should be broken up with a fork. Fork in well rotted manure at the rate of a 12 L [2½ gal] bucket per plant. Raspberries will occupy the site for a long time so be particularly careful to remove perennial weeds.

Erecting training wires

The simplest system suited to gardens with limited space is to drive a 2.25 m [7½′] pole 45 cm [1½′] into the ground at each end of the row. In the second autumn erect horizontal wires at 45 cm [1½′], 105 cm [3½′] and 1.2 or 1.5 m [4 or 4½′], depending on vigour of variety, and tie on the new canes singly. For the first year string will be adequate.

Planting out

Buy one year old canes and plant in early autumn or in suitable winter conditions. If very wet or cold, either heel the canes in when they arrive, or wrap the roots in plastic and store them in a cool building.

Spacing is 40 cm [16″] for less vigorous varieties to 60 cm [2′] for the more vigorous.

Care and development

If dry weather occurs when the plants are flowering, watering is essential. Otherwise the new canes, which are growing at the same time, will be small and sparse and next year's crop will be poor.

Weeds, which compete for moisture, must be controlled. Under good conditions raspberries will not require extra fertilizer, but if cane production is inadequate, scatter a nitrogenous fertilizer such as sulphate of ammonia at 75 g per sq m [2½ oz per sq yd]. Alternatively, mulch in mid spring, just before the new shoots start to come through the ground.

Training and pruning

Young canes will grow from below ground; when they reach 25 cm [10″] cut out the old stumps entirely. Apart from provisional support on either side with string or wire, they need not be tied in until the autumn.

Select six canes per stool on the basis of length, removing others. Tie them to the wire by continuous stringing (*see*

TRAINING RASPBERRY CANES

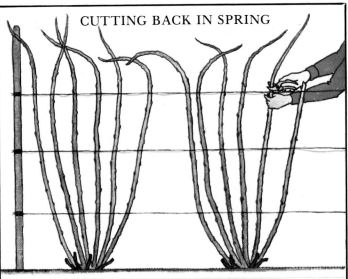

1.4 m [54"]

45 cm [18"]

45 cm [18"]

In autumn cut out old canes and tie in new ones: continuous stringing (below) keeps canes separate.

string

wire

A good crop ripening. A picking season lasts 4-6 weeks.

CUTTING BACK IN SPRING

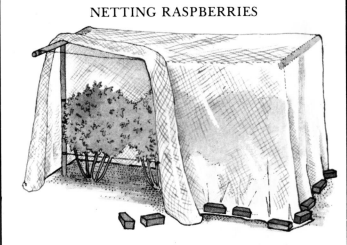

If the canes grow very long, they can be cut back to just above top wire at the beginning of spring.

NETTING RASPBERRIES

To protect fruit from birds, use a homemade cage of netting draped over 'T bars' joined with wires.

PROPAGATION

Usually remove suckers in summer but to propagate leave until autumn, sever and dig up with spade.

Black raspberries are unusual and taste rather like mulberries when fully ripe. Delicious for tarts and jam.

PRUNING BLACK RASPBERRIES

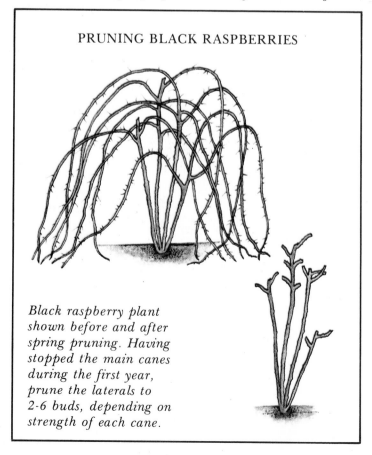

Black raspberry plant shown before and after spring pruning. Having stopped the main canes during the first year, prune the laterals to 2-6 buds, depending on strength of each cane.

diagram) to keep them separated and firm. If the canes are very long, the top 30 or 60 cm [1 or 2′] are usually cut back in early spring of the next year.

Raspberries produce suckers, so all canes not emerging from the stool should be hoed off. Retain only six new canes on each stool, as they must not compete with fruiting canes. After harvesting, remove and burn the old fruiting canes and tie in the young canes for next year.

Growing black raspberries

Newly planted canes of black raspberry varieties are best cut off at ground level after planting. Young canes produced during the first growing year are cut back 50-75 cm [20-30″] high to stimulate side growth. The following spring this is cut back to leave 2-6 buds, depending on the strength of the cane: the stronger shoots can support more buds. Fruiting branches are produced from these buds. It is not necessary to provide support for black raspberries, but they can be tied in for convenience. In the second and subsequent years, the primary canes should be limited to four per stool, preferably by early selection or during the post harvest clean up. Tipping and spurring of laterals continues each year.

Protection, harvesting and propagation

The raspberry is a favourite target for birds and netting is the only satisfactory solution. For traditional raspberry rows, fix a T-piece to each end post so that the horizontal is about 1 m [3′] wide and above the canes. Stretch two wires between the crosspieces and drop net over to cover the canes. This is simpler than constructing a soft fruit cage.

The first varieties to crop can be harvested in early mid-summer; the season lasts for about 4-6 weeks. Autumn fruiting varieties are cropped in early autumn. Pick the fruit over several days, without the centre plug. Constant picking helps the later fruit, and reduces the risk of overripe fruit going rotten and spreading disease.

Red raspberries are normally propagated by rooted suckers removed from cane beds at the end of each growing season. Autumn fruiters are propagated in the same way, but the American black raspberry is propagated by tip layering (*see* LOGANBERRY).

Pests and diseases

Raspberries have pests and diseases in common with the other *Rubus* fruits, loganberry and blackberry. Most serious is the raspberry beetle, *Byturus tomentosus*, the white maggots of which feed on the fruits as they hatch from eggs laid on the blossom. Spray with derris at the start of early summer. *Didymella applanata*, spur blight, is a fungus disease which shows as purple patches on the new canes round the buds; these patches turn silvery grey in winter and the buds die. Cane spot, *Elsinoe veneta*, produces small grey spots with purple edges on the canes, which die back from the tips. In wet seasons, grey mould, *Botrytis cinerea*, will infect the fruit.

Canes infected with the first two diseases should be cut completely out as soon as seen. The rest of the growth should be thinned, as they often cause trouble in crowded plantings, and the remainder sprayed in early spring and once or twice more at intervals of three weeks with a copper or lime-sulphur spray or with the systemic fungicide benomyl. If grey mould has been very troublesome, benomyl can be used when the flowers open and again three weeks later, spraying in the evening only. Greenfly sometimes infest the leaves without doing much damage, but can be serious as they carry the virus diseases mosaic and raspberry dwarfs.

Red and White Currants

An excellent bush fruit in a cool temperate climate, with a high yield of smooth-skinned fruit, the red currant is useful for jams and jellies because of its high pectin content, and makes delicious pies and tarts.

Red currants belong to the same family as the gooseberry and blackcurrant. Most are derived from three principal wild species — *Ribes petraeum,* a native of the mountains of Europe, North Africa and Siberia, *R. rubrum* (the northern red currant) which grows wild across northern Europe and Asia, and *R. sativum,* which is found in Britain and Western Europe.

The white currant can be regarded as a pale-fruited

Red and white currants
Ribes sativum (fam. *Grossulariaceae*)
Hardy deciduous bush with a cropping life of at least 15 years.
Size: bushes grow 1.5 m [5′] high and 1.2 m [4′] wide.
Climate: cool and warm temperate.
Planting to harvesting time: 2 years.
Yield: 3 kg [7 lb] per bush each year.

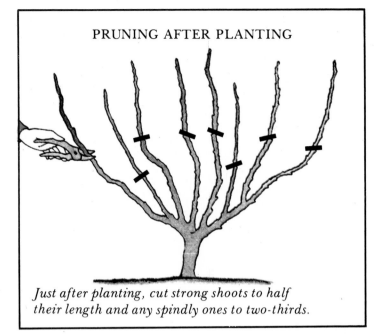

PRUNING AFTER PLANTING

Just after planting, cut strong shoots to half their length and any spindly ones to two-thirds.

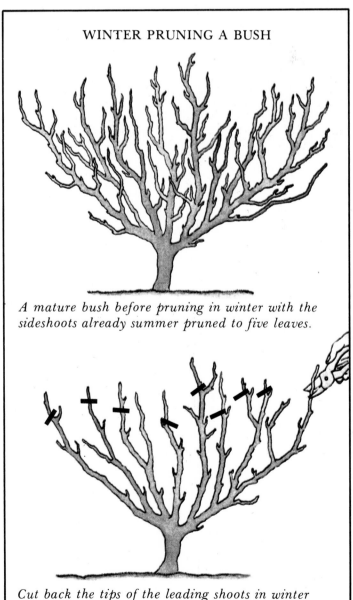

WINTER PRUNING A BUSH

A mature bush before pruning in winter with the sideshoots already summer pruned to five leaves.

Cut back the tips of the leading shoots in winter and prune the sideshoots further back to two buds.

231

Laxton's No 1 growing as a U-cordon; a good cropper with firm berries.

PRUNING RED CURRANTS TRAINED AS CORDONS

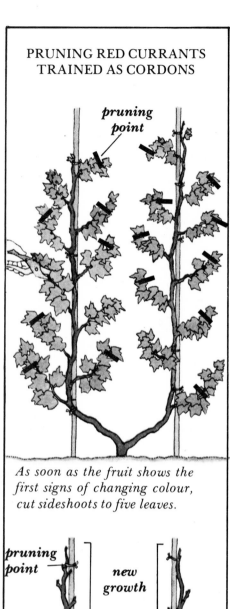

pruning point

As soon as the fruit shows the first signs of changing colour, cut sideshoots to five leaves.

pruning point

new growth

pruning point

In winter cut new extension growth by a third and shorten sideshoots to just two buds

Fruit cages are very important for growing all soft fruits. The crop will be ruined by the birds if left free of protection. Cages are commercially made and come in a variety of sizes. Most are long-lasting — made of steel frames and plastic-coated wire. They are quick to erect and more spacious to work in than a home-made cage. Group soft fruit together to use the cage.

variety of the red. Slightly less vigorous, but with a sweeter fruit, they require the same treatment as redcurrants.

Suitable site and soil
Red currants prefer a sunny position, but will tolerate light partial shade. They should be sheltered from cold winds, both because of pollination, and because the shoots of red currants are easily blown out. The bushes do best on a fairly deep, light, slightly acid soil, which contains sufficient vegetable matter to retain moisture in summer. If this is lacking, dig in a 9 L [2 gal] bucketful of suitably rotted organic material about a month before planting for each plant. Make sure that the site is completely weed free.

Planting
Red currants are usually grown as bushes on a short leg, like miniature trees, but they are extremely amenable to training and may easily be grown as single cordons, U-shaped cordons or double-U-shaped cordons. Cordons may be grown against housewalls or fences where they are easily covered with netting to protect the fruit or buds from birds, or with some thicker material to guard the blossom from late frosts in spring.

Plant as early as possible in the dormant period when the soil works freely. Set the bushes at the same depth as they were in the nursery, as indicated by the soil mark on the stem. Rub off any suckers on the roots, or buds on the 'leg'. Bushes should be spaced 1.5 m [5'] apart each way, single cordons 38 cm [15"] and double-U cordons 90 cm [3'] apart in the row. If planting cordons in rows, leave 1.5 m [5'] between rows. Give cordons support by tying each loosely with soft string to a bamboo cane.

Feeding and mulching
Immediately after planting spread a 5 cm [2"] deep mulch of well-rotted farmyard manure, garden compost or moist peat over the root area to prevent evaporation from the soil if spring and early summer prove to be dry. During the summer water when the soil is dry and weed well.

Dress annually in late spring with rotted farmyard manure. In very light or other soils deficient in potash, give an additional early spring dose of sulphate of potash at the rate of 15 g per sq m [½ oz per sq yd]. Where farmyard manure is unobtainable you can give a proprietary general garden fertilizer according to the maker's directions but remember that red currants do not need much nitrogen and they do need potash.

Pruning
A red currant bush is trained with a leg tall enough to keep the lowest branches well clear of the ground and with branches well spread out so as to expose the centre of the bush to air and sunshine.

Begin immediately after planting by cutting back all the main branches to half their length, making each cut just beyond a bud pointing away from the centre of the bush. Repeat this each winter for two or three years until a framework of sturdy branches has been built up. After that only tip the branch leaders unless harder pruning is necessary to stimulate growth.

Cut back sideshoots along the main branches to just above their fifth leaf during the midsummer weeks and then further cut these back during the winter to the second bud. In the case of cordons cut back the *new* upward extension growth by a third of its length each winter, starting immediately after planting. Where growth has been very vigorous and more than 70 cm [27"] of new wood has been made, cut this new growth back to about 23 cm [9"]. In summer just as the fruit shows the first sign of changing colour, shorten sideshoots to five leaves and then in winter cut these back further, each to its second bud.

Harvesting and propagation
The first small crop can be taken in the second summer after planting, but it is better to wait another year, and let the bush strengthen. Picking can start in early summer and continue, with the right varieties, until late summer.

Do not be in a hurry to pick your crop; red currants are slower to ripen than their rapid colouration suggests. Pick the fruits in complete little bunches or 'strigs', not individually, preferably using scissors. The currants are easily stripped off their stalks after picking, but will keep for a few days longer, where they are still in strigs.

It is very easy to raise new red and white currant bushes from cuttings. Take well-ripened, straight and strong shoots of the current year's growth from healthy bushes in mid autumn. The shoots should be 30-38 cm [12-15"] long after the unripened wood towards the tip has been cut off. Rub off all the growth buds from these shoots except the four uppermost on each cutting. This is to ensure that the new bush will start life with a good, clean leg, free of sideshoots and suckers from below ground.

To make doubly sure of success, press the ends of the cutting (the cut surface only) on to some hormone rooting powder and then immediately plant in a 15 cm [6"] deep slit trench, spacing the cuttings 20 cm [8"] apart. Unless the soil itself is sandy it helps rapid rooting if you first sprinkle a little river sand along the bottom of the planting trench. Return the soil to the trench and press firmly around the cuttings with foot pressure.

See that the cuttings never lack water during the following spring and summer, and that weeds have no chance to choke them. By the winter of the next year the cuttings should have rooted and be ready for transference to their fruiting quarters.

If the plants are to be grown as bushes, prune all the year-old's branches back by half; for single cordons cut back sideshoots to two buds, but leave the main leading shoot unpruned. For a U-cordon choose two opposite sideshoots to form the base of the U and to which you then cut back the central stem; let uprights develop at suitable places.

Pests and diseases
The worst pests in many gardens are birds which peck out the buds in winter and take off the fruit in summer. Wall-trained cordons can be protected by pieces of lightweight small mesh plastic netting, with canes inserted to keep the netting clear of growth. Bushes in the open garden will require some kind of netting cage.

Other pests are capsids and greenfly; the red currant

blister aphid causes the leaves to pucker and produce reddish blisters, and gooseberry sawfly sometimes causes trouble (*see* GOOSEBERRY).

A die-back fungus disease known as coral spot sometimes gives trouble. It derives its name from the tiny coral-red pustules which appear on dead wood. Cut off all dead wood and cut back several inches into healthy tissue. Paint the larger wounds with protective tree paint.

Rhubarb

**No garden should be without rhubarb.
In a small space, it produces
large quantities of stalks, which
are used for dessert in a similar
way to fruit.**

Rhubarb, *Rheum rhaponticum*, is a native of Siberia, the Himalayas and Eastern Asia. Used as a food, it is less than two centuries old, though *Rheum officinale* was formerly used for its medicinal properties. Of hybrid origin, garden rhubarb's reddish stems are used cooked for dessert. The leaves are wide and spade-like and are poisonous. The plant is tolerant of frost and will continually reproduce.

Suitable site and soil

Choose a sheltered, sunny site where it can be undisturbed, since the plant is a perennial. It will not do well in competition with tree or hedge roots or too near other

---

Rhubarb
Rheum rhaponticum (fam. *Polygonaceae*)
Hardy perennial with a useful life of 20 years.
Size: about 45 cm [1½'] high, 1 m [3'] wide.
Climate: cool to warm temperate.
Planting to harvesting time: 18 months.
Yield: 2.8 kg [6 lb] per plant per year, 3 plants per 3 m [10'] row.

---

cultivation. The ideal soil is deep, rich and slightly acid.

As the plant is to stand for a number of years, careful preparation of the site is required. Do this several weeks in advance of planting. Dig deeply to a depth of 45 cm [1½'] eradicating all weeds. The plant is very greedy and manure or garden compost should be worked into the bottom of the hole as well as into the returning soil at the rate of five barrowloads per four sq m [yd]. Two weeks before planting scatter a general purpose compound fertilizer over the surface — 90 g per sq m [3 oz per sq yd].

Planting out

Buy planting crowns in early autumn or spring. A total of six plants should supply most families for many years. Dig the holes large enough to take the roots comfortably, spaced 1 m [3'] apart. Set the plants sufficiently deep for the woody rootstock to be covered, but not the pink growth buds from the centre of the crown. After planting, pull up 5 cm [2"] of soil over the crowns. Make the plants firm and water if the soil is on the dry side.

Rhubarb can also be grown from seed. The initial cost is less but the plants can be variable, and from sowing to harvesting takes longer. Seeds should be sown in mid spring in drills 2.5 cm [1"] deep and 15 cm [6"] apart under a cold frame, or may be sown a month earlier in the heated greenhouse. Prick out when the seedlings have four leaves, into 10 cm [4"] pots for greenhouse-sown seeds, or to a prepared bed in a frame or the open ground with cloches at 15 cm [6"] apart. The following spring discard the weaker plants and transfer the best to permanent beds.

Care and development

In temperate regions rhubarb requires little extra watering, but do not allow the soil to become dry during the summer months. Should any flowering shoots appear, they must be removed before the buds open, otherwise the plants exhaust themselves. Hoe regularly round the stems.

Forcing

Forced rhubarb is desirable early in the season when fruit is scarce. By forcing out-of-doors, pulling dates can be advanced by five weeks. After strongly established plants have been exposed to the first frosts of winter, water them well and cover them in early winter. Plants may be covered individually with the earthenware pots designed for seakale, old barrels, boxes, buckets or oil drums. This forwards growth by keeping off winds and cold, and excludes light. The container should be 60 cm [2'] tall, be completely clean, and have a detachable lid so that you can inspect the crop occasionally. The whole may then be heaped up on the outside with lawn clippings, straw, dead leaves or garden compost.

If rhubarb is brought indoors, the first sticks may be pulled after mid winter. Lift the roots in late autumn and expose them to the weather for a few days, even to frost. Place them on a bed of good soil in the greenhouse or other warm place. The plants may be quite close together and the roots just covered with soil and kept moist. Drape them with black plastic to cut off the light. Screen them from direct heat (such as greenhouse hot pipes) with a

1. Plant rhubarb crowns with roots well covered and buds at soil level.

2. Pull up soil over buds and firm down with feet; water if necessary.

3. Remove any flowering shoots to encourage stem growth next spring.

4. Pull few stems in second spring; grip the stem as low as possible, then twist and pull simultaneously.

A fine crop of rhubarb stems; a clump like this takes three years to grow.

ALTERNATIVE METHODS OF FORCING RHUBARB

1. Cover with a lidded barrel after first frost and pile manure on top.

2. Under heated greenhouse staging, draped with black plastic or sacks.

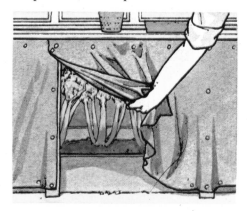

board. A steady temperature of 4° to 10°C [40° to 50°F] is needed until growth is well under way. Then raise to 16°-18°C [60°-65°F], but no higher.

Harvesting, aftercare and propagation

Do not pull any sticks in the first year and only a few in the second. By the third you should have a good-sized clump. Unless you are forcing, pulling begins in mid spring and continues for about two months, but not more, as the plant must be allowed to renew itself. Pull by gripping the leaf stems as low as possible and then twisting and pulling simultaneously. Only take stems whose leaves have fully unfolded. When the season's pulling has finished, topdress the plants heavily with rotted organic matter, making sure that the soil is moist first. Roots from forced plants should be burnt.

When the quality of the sticks begins to deteriorate or to replace rhubarb used for forcing, propagate by division. Lift the clump and divide it with a sharp spade so that each division has one good growth bud. These should then be replanted in their permanent positions.

Pest and diseases

The disease called crown rot, though infrequent, can be quite serious if it occurs. The leaves become a dull grey-green, the stems thin and weak except for the bases, which become swollen. The internal flesh of the crown turns brown, and the crown is easily broken off. There is no remedy and plants should be lifted and destroyed.

Rosemary

A hardy shrub, rosemary is grown mainly for its pleasantly pungent leaves. A favourite herb with lamb, it is equally popular for cosmetic uses.

Rosemary *(Rosmarinus officinalis)* is a member of the *Labiatae* family, a long-lived, evergreen shrub, native of the Mediterranean and often grown for its significance as

(Right) Sweet-scented rosemary is an attractive plant for the shrubbery as well as being a popular flavouring.

the "herb of remembrance". Under favourable conditions it will live 20 years or more and may reach up to 1.8 m [6'] in height, although half this is more usual.

For culinary purposes the distinctive flavour of rosemary enhances roast lamb or duck, whether the leaves are chopped and used for stuffing, or whole sprigs are cooked with the joint. The narrow, fragrant grey-green leaves and blue flowers are popular as a purely decorative shrub.

Cultivation

Rosemary thrives in a sunny, sheltered position. It may be grown either as an individual bush or planted to form a continuous hedge, which is very attractive.

Rosemary does not do well in water-retaining clay soil, so if clay is present it must be broken down to a more open texture by working sandy loam well in. The best soils for it are the light sandy ones, containing a little lime.

Rosemary can be bought as plants from a nursery or easily raised from cuttings. These are taken from young shoots of an established plant in late spring or early summer. They should be about 7.5 cm [3"] long, either cut below a leaf joint or torn off with a 'heel'. Set 3 or 4 in in a 7.5 cm [3"] pot of sandy potting compost, well watered and covered with a clear plastic bag until they root, when they are ready to be planted out. Keep them in a temperature of at least 15°C [60°F] while rooting. Rosemary does not transplant well, so new plants should be placed directly in their permanent positions.

For hedging, space the plants 38 cm [15"] apart and keep them well trimmed by clipping around midsummer each year, after the plants have flowered. This clipping is also important with individually grown bushes. Left to grow unchecked they will develop a bare, woody stem with new growth occurring only at the top of the plant. This is why mature rosemary bushes often have a top-heavy appearance, since they are unable to produce new stems from anything older than one-year-old wood. If you have a rosemary bush which has already become unwieldy, it is more satisfactory to take fresh cuttings from it in late spring or early summer and start again, afterwards clipping annually and allowing only one year's growth to remain. In cool temperate areas it is a good idea to keep one or two pots of rosemary in a greenhouse or on a sunny window sill indoors, in case winter cold kills your outdoor plant. Apart from regular shaping, rosemary does not need any attention once it is growing well. Water when young but, when established, it will survive moderate drought.

Harvesting

Fresh sprigs can be gathered throughout the year. If dried rosemary is desired, the shoots removed by the annual clippings can be dried carefully by tying them tightly into bunches and hanging them in a warm, dry place. Rub the leaves off the stems and store in an air-tight container.

Burning the boughs from old bushes gives a pleasant aroma, so if you have a fireplace you may like to get rid of the waste wood by burning it indoors.

Runner Bean

**Reliable and easy to grow, the
'amateur's vegetable' as the runner bean
is sometimes called, is ornamental as
well as good to eat.**

A vigorous climber, the runner bean is a native of South America. Introduced to England as an ornamental, it did not become popular as a vegetable until the 19th century. Runners are perennials in their sub-tropical homelands, but in cool temperate zones they are tender and susceptible to frost, so they are always grown annually from seed. The gardener can control when the plants appear by the sowing time. In cool climates runner beans may be lost if they break the surface too early, although they can be protected by cloches.

As part of a good rotation plan, runner beans are moved from site to site to follow cabbages or potatoes. Runner beans, like other members of the family *Leguminosae*, possess root bacteria which convert nitrogen gas from the air into nitrogen compounds that can be used by plants, thus enriching the soil for the following crop.

Both climbing and bush runner beans are grown; until the introduction of the natural dwarf in 1961, bushes were produced by pinching out the shoot tops of climbers. The pods of modern bean varieties can attain enormous lengths and will snap clean and tender unless deprived of water as they ripen. The bean pods vary in length and colour, depending upon the variety. One variety has purple leaves, stems, flowers and pods; the pods change to green when

---

Runner bean
Phaseolus coccineus (fam. *Leguminosae*)
Perennial, grown as a **half-hardy annual.**
Size: grows 2-3 m [6½-10′] high, dwarf varieties
30-38 cm [12-15″].
Climate: cool temperate to sub-tropical.
Sowing to harvesting time: 10 weeks from sowing.
Yield: 0.75-1 kg [1½-2 lb] per plant.

*Growing runners on a wigwam frame is amusing and saves
space. Make the frame with a few poles and garden twine.*

(Right) Dwarf runner beans which grow like French beans do not need support and are ideal for use with cloches.

cooked. The flowers are usually red, but some runners have white, pink or red and white flowers. It is thought that the white and pale-coloured flowers are more likely than the red flowers to set reliably and well.

Suitable site and soil

Beans like an open site but it should be as sheltered as possible; in windy or cold conditions pollinating insects do not visit the flowers. Gaps in fences and hedges through which frost is liable to enter should be avoided or blocked off. A row of climbing beans will form a dense wall of foliage at least 2 m [6½'] high. This will shade neighbouring rows of shorter plants on either side for several hours a day, even if the row runs from north to south, so the beans must be sited accordingly, perhaps at the end of the plot, or even against a wall.

The ideal soil is lighter than that for broad beans, but not so light that it will dry out. On such land drainage is likely to be good, so that digging need not be deep. Garden compost or old manure must be incorporated to make the soil moisture retentive. On clay soil deep digging to a depth of 45 cm [1½'] may be necessary to provide better drainage, and compost and manure should be added to keep the soil open. The deeper the soil the better, as the plants produce a great deal of top growth and crop very heavily in a comparatively short time.

Soil in town or industrial districts is often prone to acidity due to pollutants, the use of unripe manure or too much chemical fertilizer. Test the pH of the soil and, if it is moderately acid, add 1 kg [2 lb] carbonate of lime per 3 sq m [yd] but do not overlime.

In the late autumn or winter before sowing, dig a trench 45 cm [1½'] wide and the same depth, and fork well-rotted manure or garden compost into the bottom at the rate of a 9 L [2 gal] bucketful to every 60 cm [2'] length. Then return the topsoil and leave the soil to settle over the winter. About two weeks before sowing, rake superphosphate and sulphate of potash into the top few inches at the rate of 60 g [2 oz] and 30 g [1 oz] per sq m [yd] respectively.

Sowing and planting out

Allow about 10 plants per person if you want to deep freeze some of the crop; otherwise less. This means 1.5 m [5'] of double row for each person.

Seed is generally sown outdoors in late spring, to provide a crop from midsummer to mid autumn. Earlier sowings may be made in early spring, if the locality is mild, to give a crop starting in early summer. Confine early sowings to a few seeds at one end of the row as they may rot if the soil fails to warm up sufficiently. Cloches put over the soil two or three weeks before sowing will warm it, so that germination is helped and, left there, will protect young

(Right) 'Fry', a stringless variety. These types have been developed to make preparation for cooking easier.

(Facing page) Runners produce beautiful scarlet flowers which brighten up the vegetable garden in early summer.

1. On heavy soil, double dig trench using a fork to incorporate manure.

2. Two weeks before sowing, rake in superphosphate and potash.

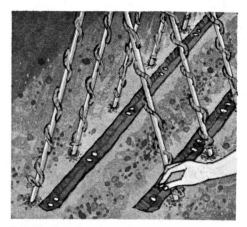

3. Wind twine loosely up canes; sow in deep drills, two seeds per cane.

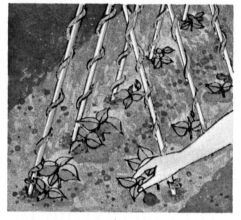

4. As seedlings start growing, cut or pull out the weaker of the two.

5. Wind beans up an inverted V framework held firm by cross-piece.

6. Look out for large yellowy pods in thick foliage and pick them off.

ALTERNATIVE METHODS OF SUPPORTING RUNNER BEANS

Growing on a pole: save space by training one shoot vertically and a second diagonally, four per pole.

Growing on netting: fix the net to stout posts at intervals of 3 m [10'] sunk 1 m [3'] into the ground.

Growing on vertical canes: place stout poles at end of each row with guy ropes and a wire linking canes.

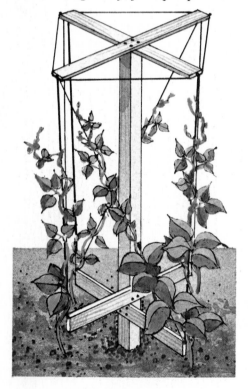

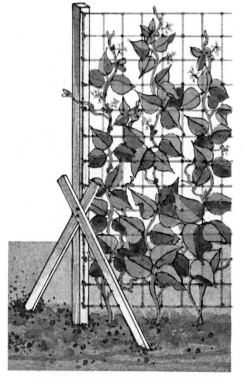

plants from damage until all danger of frost has passed. Draw out a 5 cm [2"] deep drill, water it and sow two seeds every 30 cm [12"] in two lines 25 cm [10"] apart, staggered or not, depending on the method of support used (*see* following). When they begin to develop remove or cut off the top of the weaker seedling.

Method of support

The simplest method is to give each plant one cane or pole, pushing it 45 cm [1½'] into the ground, and allowing a height above ground of 2 m [6½']. A space of 38-45cm [15-18"] should be left between the double lines of supports. Each cane is linked to the next by thin wire or strong twine, and at each end of the row, two much stouter posts are inserted, linked by crosspieces. These posts require additional support from guyropes (*see* diagram in BLACKBERRY). If the row is very long, stouter posts and struts may also be required halfway along it.

One very common method of support is to plant in pairs across a row, with each pole at an angle so that the tops cross at a height of about 1.6 m [5½']. They are tied together at the crotch, and then more poles are laid horizontally along the crotches, overlapping, and bound to one another and to the crotches. This keeps the whole framework rigid. If bamboo canes are used, it is a good idea to twine string up the length of the slippery cane to give the climbing bean stems a better hold.

A third method is to grow the beans up netting, supported between strong posts. These should be 2.5 m [8'] long, hammered 45 cm [1½'] into the soil at each end of the row, and at a spacing of 1.8 m [6'] along it. Two internal struts will be required for each post to take the weight, reaching about 90 cm [3'] up each and being well buried (*see* diagram in BLACKBERRY).

Remember that one cropping plant can weigh anything up to 2 kg [4 lb], and a 3 m [10'] row will be tremendously heavy. A row of beans of this length will present an area of dense foliage of about 6 sq m [7 sq yd] to a summer gale, so it is very important that the supporting framework be soundly constructed. Once a row of beans has collapsed. it cannot be re-erected. It will smother rows of neighbouring vegetables and must be removed immediately after gleaning what proportion, if any, of the crop has ripened and was not damaged in the fall.

If a very small number of beans are to be grown, wigwams of six or seven poles planted in a circle and tied together at the top will be adequate. The beans will do very well, although there will be some crowding when they reach the top. Beans can also be grown in large tubs with strings tied to the top of a central pole, and radiating out to hooks on the perimeter of the tub. A tripod of three canes can also be used in a tub.

There are one or two dwarf runner bean varieties, which have the same habit of growth as the bush French beans. For cultivation *see* FRENCH BEAN.

Care and development

The crop will never be of good quality if the plants are allowed to get at all dry. As their roots penetrate deeply, early preparation of the trench is important. In dry conditions mulching in the early stages will be helpful. Later the shade cast between a double row of beans will conserve the moisture. Always apply mulches to moist soil.

Under normal conditions runners should require no further feeding. But it is important to be fastidious about weeds while the seedlings are developing. Hoe the weeds out while they are still tiny, but with care, as the roots and stems of the young beans are very tender. Once the beans have started to climb and are making plenty of leaf few weeds can compete with them and the plot can be hand-weeded when necessary.

When the first vines start to search for something to climb, tie them loosely with raffia to their own poles. This is important, otherwise the ensuing chaos will be impossible to disentangle and the beans will grow up one another, fighting for light. Once they have been shown their own pole they will stick to it. When they reach the top, pinch them out. Sometimes in dry weather flowers fall off, leaving no tiny beanlet behind. These have failed to set, usually because of lack of moisture deep down in the soil. There may be other reasons for the flowers not setting. In windy or cold conditions, pollinating insects do not visit the flowers. In very hot, dry weather, on the other hand, the flowers droop and close up so that insects cannot enter. Spraying to encourage setting is harmless but ineffective.

Harvesting the crop

Runner beans will be ready for picking in late midsummer. The golden rule is to keep picking. Do not let any beans get too large; 15-20 cm [6-8"] is right for most varieties, though some modern varieties have been known to produce beans 25-30 cm [10-12"] long. Beans that are too old have coarse-textured, unhealthy coloured pods, and the beans inside stand out like gouty finger joints. Such beans are fit only for the compost heap or to use for seeds next year. Care should be taken to remove coarse beans which may have been overlooked amid the dense foliage, as they are a drain on further production.

Pests and diseases

Runner beans generally give little trouble, although halo blight is encouraged by the quite unnecessary practice of soaking the beans before sowing. The disease is bacterial and takes the form of small transparent spots surrounded by a yellow ring. The spots coalesce and dry up and the whole leaf withers. Seedlings may be killed, and older plants wilt completely. Diseased plants should be destroyed as soon as seen. Some varieties are resistant. Blackfly, capsid bugs, slugs attacking the seedlings, and pea and bean seed beetle are also possible, though not of much concern.

Rutabaga

SEE **SWEDE**

Sage

One of the essential herbs, sage used to be a medicinal cure-all. Even today its popularity with rich foods is due as much to its digestive properties as its spicy taste.

Sage *(Salvia officinalis)* is a member of the *Labiatae* family, a hardy, evergreen shrub grown for its grey-green leaves, which are used fresh and dried. One bush is adequate for the average family. The common, violet blue-flowered sage usually grows to about 60 cm [2'] high, with the same diameter. Of the several varieties, common sage is best for cooking — red sage for herbal cures.
Although it is a hardy perennial, even the more robust types of sage will not always survive the winter, so it must be allocated a, dry, sunny, sheltered position.

Cultivation
The soil for sage should be light and well drained but rich in organic matter. On ground that has not been recently cultivated, add good quality garden compost and a handful of bonemeal to each planting site, some weeks before planting. With the exception of broad-leaved, non-flowering sage, most types can be raised from seed in shallow drills in the spring. However, sage is slow to germinate and you will have no herb to cut for over a year. It is more practical to buy a rooted cutting. If a bush is available, and for your own replacements, take cuttings from established plants in late spring or at the end of the growing season, from shoots about 5 cm [2"] long. Each cutting must have a heel or piece of the main stem at its base. Insert the cuttings in moist sand putting 3 to a 8.5 cm [3½"] pot, and keep them moist, covering them with clear plastic sheeting until rooting takes place. Warmth of about 18°-21°C [65°-70°F] is also required. Then transplant to the prepared site, giving the plant at least 60 cm [2'] of room all around.
Pinch out the growing tip of the plant when it is growing strongly. Put a light, firm stake in the centre of the bush when planting for support. The main stem is brittle and, even with support, it may split under the weight of foliage. If this does happen during summer it is often possible to

Common sage has the greatest value in the kitchen, and a bush of this size will supply all the leaves needed.

save the bush by laying the broken stem on the ground and covering it with soil. Kept moist, it will have a chance to produce fresh roots and resume growth. Take cuttings and keep plants in reserve to replace your bush after 3-4 years.

Harvesting
Fresh leaves can be used whenever they are available. Harvesting is done from midsummer onwards, when the leaves should be dried for about a week until they are crisp, and stored in an airtight container.

SCORZONERA AND Salsify

Salsify (above) and scorzonera (below), often called black salsify, are two roots of different genus but they are grown and used in the same way. Their flavour has earned them the name 'vegetable oyster'.

Of these two plants of the family *Compositae*, salsify is the more frequently grown. It has a white, tapering root and

---

Salsify
Tragopogon porrifolius (fam. *Compositae*)
Hardy biennial.
Size: grown primarily for the long narrow tap root, which is up to 30-45 cm [1-1½'] long with a maximum diameter of 5 cm [2"] at the top; also for the young shoots in spring, which are cut when about 15 cm [6"] long. Mature plant grows 1-1.2 m [3-4'] high.
Climate: temperate.
Sowing to harvesting time: 21-27 weeks if roots are left in the ground; young shoot harvested next spring.
Yield: up to 450 g [1 lb] per root.

a delicate unusual flavour, traditionally supposed to resemble that of oysters. Its leaves are narrow and grass-like. A native of northern Europe, it is not difficult to grow and deserves wider attention.

Scorzonera is a native of Spain. Though not of the same genus as salsify, it is very similar to it in both cultivation, appearance and taste. It was introduced to most European countries centuries ago but has never really become popular. It gives a much lower yield than salsify but the flavour is superior. It can also be used as a coffee substitute, like chicory.

The leaves of the scorzonera plant are oblong and end in a point. The thin black roots are the edible part. They are slightly difficult to prepare because they have to be boiled and skinned while still hot; rubbing off the skin rather than peeling is easier. The roots contain inulin, which is found in many other plants of the family *Compositae* (such as the Jerusalem artichoke); a sugar substitute which is used in making bread for diabetics.

Suitable site and soil

Both plants require a deep soil, free from stones. A good, rich loam is ideal, but it should not have been freshly treated with farmyard manure. Both salsify and scorzonera have long roots which should grow straight, and obstacles such as stones, unrotted manure and an impervious subsoil cause them to fork. The crowbar method of making planting holes is ideal (*see* PARSNIP). An open sunny site is best.

Sowing

Sow salsify in mid spring, 1.75-2.5 cm [½-1″] deep, in drills 30 cm [1′] apart. Temperature required for germination is from 4°-21°C [38°-69°F]. Germination takes place in 7-21 days according to temperature. When the plants are large enough to handle thin to about 25 cm [10″] apart.

To ensure straight roots, make a hole 60-90 cm [2-3′] deep with a crowbar and fill to within about 10 cm [4″] of the top with well-rotted garden compost. Add a layer of fine soil to complete the filling of the hole. Plant three or four seeds, thinning to one later.

Alternatively, salsify can be sown in late spring following the usual method to have a crop of roots ready for harvesting from late autumn onwards.

Scorzonera
Scorzonera hispanica (fam. *Compositae*) also called black salsify.
Perennial grown as a **biennial.**
Size: grown primarily for the cylindrical black-skinned root, which is up to 20-45 cm [8-18″] long with a diameter of about 2.5 cm [1″]. The mature plant grows to a height of 1-1.2 m [3-4′].
Climate: temperate.
Sowing to harvesting time: 21-27 weeks. Possible secondary harvest of young shoots.
Yield: about 125 g [4 oz] per root.

Salsify has long, tapering roots with grass-like leaves. The flavour of the roots is said to resemble oysters.

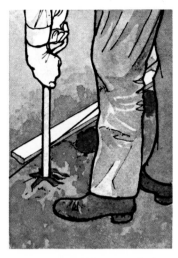

For making planting holes use the crowbar method to ensure deep enough holes.

Fill holes to about 10 cm [4″] below top with well-rotted compost, then soil.

Sow 3 or 4 seeds in each hole. The holes should be about 23 cm [9″] apart.

When the seedlings are large enough, thin them to one at each station.

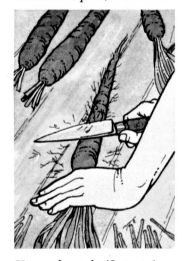

When lifting roots, great care must be taken not to damage them in any way.

Use a sharp knife to trim all the side roots from the main tap roots.

After lifting, store the roots, laying them flat in box of sand. Store the box in a well ventilated, dry place. Alternatively, leave roots in the ground until needed.

PRODUCING BLANCHED SHOOTS OF SALSIFY

In early winter, cut down any remains of foliage to leave about 2.5 cm [1″] of stem above the soil.

To blanch shoots, heap soil around cut stems. Cover the shoots with 18 cm [7″] pots, blocking up the pot drainage holes to prevent light from entering the top of the pot. Make sure the soil is light and powdery.

In early spring, when tips appear through soil, draw soil aside to expose shoots. Cut as required.

Procedure with scorzonera is almost exactly the same, except that the sowing date should be about a month later. Scorzonera is more susceptible than salsify to late frosts and, if checked by them, tends to run to seed.

Cultivation

Keep well hoed and well watered. Both plants are reasonably drought resistant but are liable to bolt in prolonged dry weather. Also, rain after a long drought may cause salsify roots to grow so quickly that they split open. Otherwise, neither crop needs any attention during the growth period.

Harvesting

Both plants are ready for harvesting by mid autumn, although the roots may be left in the ground until needed. If left in the soil the roots will survive a normal winter, but frost will not improve their flavour. To obtain maximum flavour lift them as required for use, taking them straight to the kitchen and using them all before the onset of winter.

Alternatively you can lift and store the roots, laying them flat in boxes of sand and storing these in a dry, well-ventilated place. The hazard in storing is that both roots 'bleed' very easily which loses much of their flavour. For this reason they should be lifted with great care, and even then it may be impossible to avoid some damage.

If you choose a late spring sowing for salsify, the crop will be ready from late autumn onwards.

Most gardeners will want to retain part of their salsify crop for producing a green vegetable in spring. No special treatment is required. For spring greens, cut the shoots when they are about 12-15 cm [5-6″] high. They are then known as chards. They are cooked like asparagus, to which they are at least equal in flavour.

Blanched shoots may be either cooked or used as a salad in late winter or early spring. To produce these, cut down what remains of the foliage in early winter, leaving about 2.5 cm [1″] of stem above the root, and earth up until the top of the plant is covered by about 15 cm [6″] of soil. To keep the soil dry, cover the earthed-up plants with pots of 17.5 cm [7″] diameter, making sure you close up the drainage holes. Cut the resultant blanched shoots in early spring, just as the tips appear at the soil surface, or a little before, drawing aside the soil to search for them. Any blanched shoots not used can be left to grow as greens.

Aftercare

Both the dying foliage and the discarded roots make excellent compost material. There should be no difficulty in clearing the ground of the crop, although broken pieces of root occasionally live and send up shoots in the following year.

The seeds of both species are sometimes difficult to obtain, so it is worthwhile to leave a few plants to flower and go to seed. Both are quite attractive in the garden — salsify bears reddish-purple flowers and scorzonera bright yellow.

Pests and diseases

Like most plants in the family *Compositae*, salsify and scorzonera are virtually free from both pests and diseases. Occasionally both may be infested with a fungus disease, white blister (*Albugo* species), which forms unsightly white patches on the leaves. Treatment consists of cutting off and burning the affected leaves.

Savory

Savory has a strong aromatic scent and a definite digestive effect. It has been most popular in Europe for hundreds of years as a flavouring for all kinds of beans.

There are two species of savory commonly grown: summer savory *(Satureia hortensis)* and winter savory, *S. montana*. Both are members of the *Labiatae* family and they are amongst the oldest of herbs, grown for their small, powerfully scented leaves. Summer savory is annual, grows about 30 cm [1′] high and bears pale lilac flowers, from late summer to autumn. It is tender. Winter savory *(Satureia montana),* is a perennial sub-shrubby form which tastes much the same but is more strongly aromatic and grows to about 38 cm [15″].

Low-growing and compact, savory is ideal grown as a border plant. It is also good for ambitious knot-garden patterns in herb gardens, since it can be clipped to shape and controlled easily. Otherwise, because the scent seems to deter blackfly, it may be planted between rows of broad beans, which are particularly prone to blackfly attack.

The leaves are almost always dried for use in all kinds of recipes including stuffings, stews and as a flavouring for beans. A sprig hung among clothes will keep away moths, and savory leaves ease the sting of insect bites when crushed and rubbed on the skin.

Cultivation

A situation in full sun is best for savory, and there is no need to enrich the soil for it. If, however, the ground is

Both summer and winter savory will grow from seed. They need an open, sunny site. Plants can also be propagated by lifting and dividing the roots for replanting.

heavy clay, it should be broken up with lighter material such as coarse sand or burnt earth from the garden bonfire worked in.

Both summer and winter savory can be raised from seed sown outdoors from mid to late spring, and thinned to a spacing of 15 cm [6″] between plants. Rows should be 60 cm [2′] apart. Seeds should be only just covered, and will germinate in about 10-14 days. Water regularly until the plants are well established, when they can do quite well in dry conditions.

Although winter savory is a perennial it may, like all small herbs, die a natural death, or be killed by severe cold. To start new plants for a reserve supply, take cuttings from small shoots in spring or late summer and root them in sand. Plants can also be propagated by lifting and dividing the roots for replanting, again in spring or late summer. Seed of winter savory can be sown in late summer as well as spring, but it is slow to grow, even if the seed is left uncovered, and cuttings or division will give quicker and much more reliable results.

Harvesting

The annual summer savory will be ready to use within three months from the spring sowing. Harvesting is done just as flowering is about to start and again in mid autumn. Hang up stems with several sprigs on them in bunches in a warm, dark, well-ventilated place until the leaves are sufficiently dry. Then store the leaves in an air-tight container.

Leaves may be taken from winter savory from late spring onwards in the second year but the dried leaves are rather hard, so it is best to keep a pot indoors in winter and use the fresh leaves.

Scallions

SEE **ONION**

Scorzonera

SEE **SALSIFY**

Seakale

**The blanched shoots of this unusual
vegetable, available in early spring,
are a welcome crop at a time when
fresh vegetables are scarce.**

A native of the coasts of western Europe, seakale still grows
wild on British seashores, but is seldom cultivated in gardens today. Its disadvantages are that it takes a long time
to mature from seed and needs blanching. The time factor
can be reduced, however, by planting 'crowns' (root cuttings bearing buds) and blanching is not so difficult as
might be thought. The blanched shoots can be used as a
second vegetable, separately like asparagus, as a basis for
cheese dishes or eaten as a salad.

Suitable site and soil
Seakale, being a seashore plant in its native state, requires
a sandy and fertile soil, well supplied with lime. Heavy soil
should be lightened by the addition of sand and given a
dressing of carbonate of lime if a soil test shows it to be
acid. In winter, dig in farm manure or garden compost at
the rate of 9 L [2 gal] bucketfuls per sq m [per sq yd].
Composted or fresh, wet seaweed is ideal manure. As the
seakale bed is a relatively permanent one, choose a plot
where it will not need to be disturbed for several years. An
open, sunny site is best.

Sowing and planting out
The main difference between sowing and planting is that

Seakale
Crambe maritima (fam. *Cruciferae*)
Hardy perennial.
Size: plants grow to a height of about 45 cm [1½'].
Blanched shoots are cut when they have reached
20-23 cm [8-9"].
Climate: cool temperate.
Sowing to harvesting time: 2 years from sowing
seed; 10 months or more when grown from root crowns.
Yield: about 450 g [1 lb] per plant.

---

*A row of seakale, one section blanched. Unblanched the
flavour is bitter — always blanch for a delicate taste.*

sowing will not produce a harvest for two years, whereas
planted crowns should yield one the following winter.
Using bought-in crowns and taking root cuttings from
these to maintain a stock is the easiest method, as well as
being the quickest. Crowns are planted in early spring,
with a dibber 30 cm [1'] apart, with 38 cm [15"] between
the rows, covering them with a 5 cm [2"] depth of soil. All
the buds should be removed to prevent flowering. If the
seakale is to be 'forced', a slightly wider spacing of plants
and rows is advisable, to obtain stronger plants.

If you are growing from seed, it should be sown in the permanent site, and thinned. Sow seed in early to mid spring
1.5 cm [½"] deep, in drills 38 cm [15"] apart. Germination
takes about 6-12 days. Thin the young plants when large
enough to handle to about 30 cm [1'] apart.

Care and development
Never allow the plants to lack water; water heavily in hot
dry weather, and mulch liberally with organic matter in
late spring, when the soil is moist. Keep the weeds under
control, and topdress in midsummer with agricultural salt
at 30 g per sq m [1 oz per sq yd]. Remove all flowering
stems as soon as they are seen.

Blanching
To blanch outdoors, wait until the foliage has died down
in late autumn, clear it all away, and break up the soil
around the plants lightly with a fork. Cover the required
plants with large flower pots, boxes or buckets, weigh the
covering down with stones or bricks, and surround each
with a cylinder of wire netting to about 7.5 cm [3"] above
the containers, filling in the space with leaves. This protects the plants from much of the cold, and ensures
white stems, ready for cutting the following early spring.
'Forced' seakale is blanched by lifting successively in mid
to late autumn and planting in deep boxes in a dark cellar
or shed. Lift the plants, cut the main root back to about 15
cm [6"], cut off all the side roots, and put them upright in
the containers, 10 cm [4"] apart. Pack them with leafmould, moist peat, potting compost or similar material,
which should be about 23 cm [9"] deep. The crowns should
be just above the surface. Keep the light out completely —
any which gets through will make the shoots bitter — and
keep the soil moist. The temperature to start with should
be about 7°C [45°F], later rising to 13°C [55°F], but no
higher. Shoots will be ready for harvesting in about 7
weeks, if lifted early, and in about 5 for those forced later.

Harvesting the crop
The blanched shoots are ready to be cut when they are
17.5-23 cm [7-9"] long. Scoop the soil away and, using a
sharp knife, cut cleanly where the shoots emerge from the
roots. Cut with about 2.5 cm [1"] of stem attached. The
largest shoots can be removed first and the others taken
when they have grown bigger.

Aftercare and propagation
Do not expect a second crop of shoots. Throw away the
roots that have been used for indoor forcing. Remove
protection from roots that have been forced outdoors, fork

Before planting dig fresh seaweed into the soil, at about 45 cm [18″] depth.

Rub off pointed buds from crowns before planting to prevent them flowering.

Use a metal-tipped dibber to make holes for planting of crowns. Crumble soil into hole around crown covering it with 5 cm [2″] of soil. Pat soil into a small mound.

In midsummer topdress the seakale bed by sprinkling with agricultural salt.

To blanch outdoors, cover emerging plant with a bucket and top with brick.

Invert a bucket over the plant and surround it with wire netting, secured to a post driven into the ground. Fill the intervening space with leaf mould.

FORCING SEAKALE INDOORS

Cut the main roots from the plant, then remove the side root or thong, from main root. The top end of the thong is cut straight and the bottom end slanted, so that you can tell which is which. Bundle and store in moist sand.

To force the crowns, pack them in a wooden box full of moist peat so that top is just showing. Cover.

When seakale is ready for harvesting remove the top growth, cutting off a little of woody crown as well.

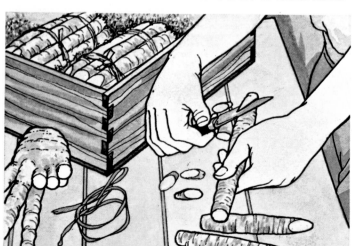

around the plants and topdress with rotted organic matter. Then leave them to grow on naturally.

The seakale bed is a comparatively permanent one. In time, the crowns in the centre will die away and new ones will form around the perimeter. Keep the bed free from weeds, or a vigorous weed-patch will develop, and keep it well fed with mulches of garden compost or manure. When abandoning an old bed, be careful to dig out the roots thoroughly, as every bit left in the soil will grow.

The side roots discarded when lifting the plants for forcing can be used for propagation. Take those of pencil thickness, cut to about 15 cm [6″] long, with the bottom end cut slantwise as a guide to planting the right way up. Store in damp sand or soil until early spring, and then plant about 2.5 cm [1″] deep at the normal spacings.

Growing in containers
Seakale can be grown in deep containers and it is possible to transfer them to a cellar or dark shed in autumn for forcing without disturbing the plants.

Pests and diseases
These are unlikely, but clubroot, violet rot, and black rot may occur. Symptoms of the latter are yellowing of the leaves, and blackening of the internal tissue of the roots. Such plants should be destroyed.

Seakale Beet
SEE **SWISS CHARD**

Shallot
SEE **ONION**

Snap Bean
SEE **FRENCH BEANS**

Snow Pea
SEE **PEA**

Sorrel

Sorrel's slightly bitter leaves are best used to make a very good soup. The leaves can be added to salad, but should be used sparingly because of their tartaric acid content.

Sorrel *(Rumex scutatus)* belongs to the *Polygonaceae* family and is related to rhubarb. The cultivated type is grown for its leaves which are always used fresh, as a substitute for spinach or in small quantities in salad. This is called French sorrel to distinguish it from the wild or common sorrel of Britain, *R. acetosa*. A hardy perennial, French sorrel grows to about 30 cm [1′] high.

Cultivation
Native to the open fields of Britain, wild sorrel prefers sandy soil in full sun. However, lush and rapid supply of leaves should be encouraged for culinary uses, and for this the soil must be moderately rich, especially in nitrates. Well rotted animal manure, particularly poultry manure, will provide nitrogenous material. A good site for sorrel is one where peas or beans have recently been grown, since these leguminous plants leave nitrogen behind in the soil. Sun or shade are equally suitable.

Sorrel can be raised by sowing the seed thinly in shallow drills or by division of established plants. Either method should be done in late spring to provide a good crop of sorrel throughout the summer.

Like spinach, sorrel reduces considerably with cooking; since the quantities of leaves required for soup are usually quoted in kg [lb], it is advisable to allow sufficient room for about 40 plants, unless you wish to use the leaves for flavouring or additions only.

Seedlings must be kept well watered, and when they are large enough to handle they should be thinned to 38 cm [15″] apart. The plants will need further watering if the weather is dry, and if growth is slow, an application of liquid manure will stimulate the formation of leaves. (Liquid manure is made by immersing a bag of animal or poultry manure in a bucket of water and diluting the solution with more water until it is a pale amber colour). Soak the roots with this once a week, after watering them well beforehand.

Harvesting and aftercare

Leaves should be gathered regularly once the plant is established to promote further growth. Sorrel grown in the garden must be kept strictly to its own quarters; it will become a nuisance if flower heads are allowed to develop and disperse seed. Pinch off flower buds as they appear in summer to prevent this, and to encourage leaf production. The plant will die down in autumn and resume growth the following spring.

Soya Bean

Grow this Oriental vegetable for its green beans which contain a higher proportion of protein than any other vegetable.

There are over a thousand varieties of soya bean producing brown, black, green, or yellow pea-like beans or seeds. The plants are generally grown for the high vitamin and protein content of the beans, although oil is also pressed out and used for cooking, salads and making margarine. Soya sauce, used so much in Chinese cooking, is also made from the bean. The world's most grown commercial bean, soya is less often grown in gardens.

In appearance the growing plant is dense and hairy all over, with a trifoliate leaf pattern and short pods; the purple or white flowers are inconspicuous. The species is thought to have originated in south-west Asia, and has long been an important food-plant in China and Japan. In Britain where success depends largely on the weather, late summer needs to be hot for the crop to ripen.

Unlike other beans, the soya bean gets its signal for flowering from the day-length. Most varieties have only a narrow range of day-length in which they will mature properly and produce a satisfactory crop. Each group of varieties is adapted to a different narrow range of latitude.

Suitable site and soil

Choose a sunny patch of soil, preferably sandy and well-drained, which has been manured in early winter. Make sure that every perennial weed has been removed, and the ground raked to a fine tilth before sowing.

Sowing and thinning

In sub-tropical and warm temperate climates sow in spring, 4 cm [1½″] deep at 15-30 cm [6-12″] intervals in rows of 23-60 cm [9-24″] apart.

Germination is straightforward at temperatures between 18° and 21°C [65° and 70°F], the first shoots emerging in 5-10 days. There is no need to thin seedlings as the seeds are large enough to space out at sowing time.

In cool temperate climates sow in late spring or early summer and sow singly indoors in 7.5 cm [3″] pots one week before the last frost is expected, then plant out as above. Seed may also be sown in a warm greenhouse in mid spring for planting out later. Protect with cloches if cold after the young plants have been put out.

In cool temperate climates the main problem in sowing outdoors is germination: a minimum soil temperature of 10°C [50°F] is necessary. Cloches can help here. A high night temperature in midsummer when the plants are flowering is also needed for a successful crop.

Cultivation

Do not hoe too close to plants or you will damage the root system. Mulch with peat after sowing, avoiding line of seeds, to help keep down weeds and retain moisture.

Moisture is essential, since soya beans grow quickly only when there is adequate water around the roots. Provide extra water during an unusually dry season. No staking is necessary for plants up to 50 cm [20″] tall.

Harvesting and storing

A spring-sown crop should be ready for gathering by the

Soya Bean
Glycine max (fam. *Leguminosae*), also known as soybean.
Half-hardy annual.
Size: 40-50 cm [18-20″] tall in warm temperate zones; up to 1.8 m [6′] in sub-tropical zones. Pods 5-7.5 cm [2-3″].
Climate: warm temperate to sub-tropical.
Sowing to harvesting time: 12-16 weeks.
Yield: depends on climate, but 50 pods per plant possible; 3-4 beans per pod.

Sow seed singly in 7.5 cm [3"] pots indoors, one week before last frost.

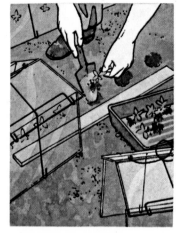

Seedlings do not need any thinning. After planting, protect from any cold.

Make sure there is plenty of water around the roots to ensure quick growth.

Harvest by pulling up the whole plant, removing all the pods at one time.

A vigorous soya bean plant — both bushy and compact.

end of summer. The pods turn from green to dark yellow and should appear swollen with the ripening beans. The best way to harvest is to pull up the whole plant, taking off all the pods at one time. Remove the beans from the pods by soaking the latter in boiling water for five minutes before cracking them in half and squeezing out the contents. The harvesting period can be lengthened by several weeks if a second crop is sown two weeks after the first spring sowing. Store and dry soya beans just as you would haricot beans (*see* FRENCH BEANS).

Pests and diseases

Pests and diseases vary with the country in which the soya bean is being grown. More than one species of the fungus *Fusarium* causes wilting by infecting the roots and one species may be more trouble in one place than in another. This trouble can be avoided by not growing the beans on the same patch two years running. Greenfly can also be a nuisance.

Spinach

Spinach is much richer in protein than other leaf vegetables and has a high vitamin A content. It is easy to grow, but take care not to let summer varieties run to seed.

Spinach grows wild in parts of the East, and it was once cultivated by the Chinese. The Arabs may have brought it to Europe in the tenth century during the occupation of Spain, and it reached England about the middle of the sixteenth century.

There is some confusion over the name spinach, the word often being haphazardly employed for any plant whose leaves are eaten like those of true spinach. 'Perpetual spinach' is the same as 'spinach beet'. 'Seakale spinach', 'Swiss chard', 'silver beet' and 'seakale beet' are one and the same plant; both these plants are beets. 'New Zealand spinach' is neither spinach nor beet; it belongs to the ice-plant family. 'Seakale' is a member of the brassica family, found growing close to the sea. These vegetables are dealt with elsewhere in the book.

True spinach is winter spinach; summer spinach is a variety and there are long-standing types of both. Cultivation is described for summer spinach, with any modifications for winter spinach following. Both make an excellent green vegetable (cooked with little or no water), while the summer variety is the main ingredient of an exquisite summer soup, and with cream cheese makes a superb filling for a *quiche*.

Suitable site and soil

To grow year-round supplies of spinach, you must make up to seven successional sowings in a season, since the rule is to grow enough for a few pickings little and often. The conditions needed for successful growing will change throughout the growing season, with shelter and warmth required for winter spinach and some shade needed for summer spinach during hotter periods. This complicates a rotational cropping plan, so catch-cropping of this fast growing vegetable should be borne in mind. As they need only a few weeks from sowing to gathering, the summer crop can be grown in spaces between other vegetables without interfering with their neighbours. Summer spinach is notorious for bolting, but this can be prevented by using suitable varieties and the right cultivation.

It is a waste of time to sow on dry, poorly-worked soil. The ground should be well dug over and watered, using as much as 10 kg per sq m [22 lb per sq yd] of well-rotted manure if the soil is sandy. At the same time a dressing of a fertilizer containing 12% nitrogen and 6% each of phosphate and potassium should be worked in at a rate of 30 g per sq m [1 oz per sq yd]. No further feeding should then be needed. Similar amounts of garden compost may replace the manure, the idea being not merely to feed the plants but also to keep the moisture content of the soil steady and as high as possible.

Sowing, planting and thinning

The bolt-resistant varieties are best used for the spring sowings. Allow about five plants per person per sowing: that is, a row of about 75 cm [30"]. Make the first sowing under cloches in early spring and keep making successional sowings at the rate of once every two weeks until the end of summer. Make the drills about 5 cm [2"] deep

---

Spinach, summer and winter.
Spinacea oleracea (fam. *Chenopodiaceae*), winter, or prickly (seeded) spinach. *S. oleracea inermis* is the summer or round-seeded spinach.
Hardy annual.
Size: height to 18 cm [7"]; width to 40 cm [16"].
Climate: cool temperate.
Sowing to harvesting time: 6-8 weeks.
Yield: 140 g [5 oz] per plant before it bolts for summer type; 225 g [8 oz] per plant for winter type, 20 plants per 3 m [10'] row.

---

and 30 cm [12"] apart and sow in the bottom of these. The germination rate can be less than 50% so it is advisable to sow one capsule, which contains several seeds, every 7.5 cm [3"] and then thin. Cover the capsules with 2.5 cm [1"] of soil only and firm lightly. The drills can be flooded with water during hot, dry weather, so that the growing plants will not bolt. Germination will take 1-2 weeks, and maturity is attained in 6-10 weeks.

Having been over-sown, the rows will need thinning to leave the best seedlings at a spacing of 15 cm [6"]. As a rule, thinning should be done as early as possible because any delay slows down the development of the favoured plants, resulting in ones which quickly run to seed. The thinnings are often cropped for cooking, though the young plants, when cooked, will not add up to much unless large quantities are being grown.

Cultivation and harvesting

Keep the soil moist, watering whenever necessary, but always bear in mind that spinach hates sudden change and that the object is to keep the moisture content as even as possible. Drills drawn as suggested will contain the water, but use a rose on the can to prevent washing the soil away. Applied mulches are best avoided, but the regular shallow hoeing that should keep the rows clear of weeds will also prevent the soil from caking in hot weather and provide a dust-mulch.

Start to gather the larger leaves as soon as they are big enough to use, taking several from each plant at each picking. Twist the midribs and pull them off outwards, or cut them with scissors to avoid tearing the main stem. Do not strip the plants of leaves, or they will die.

Winter spinach

This variety has prickly seeds instead of the smooth ones of summer spinach. It forms a more spreading plant with more broadly triangular leaves. Make two or three sowings in a fairly sheltered site at the end of summer on soil that is not so rich as that recommended for the summer variety. The sowing procedure for depth and spacing is the same, but moisture is not so critical for winter spinach. Fill the drill completely and indeed, if there is any possibility of the soil becoming soggy it is an advantage to ridge the bed up a little.

Supplies of winter spinach should last through winter until spring provided enough is sown, as this kind does not share the exaggerated tendency of summer spinach to bolt. Nevertheless, pick only the larger leaves.

Though it was thought to be hardier than the summer varieties this has been disproved and the latter are now preferred even for winter use. After harvesting the leaves, the remaining plants of both spinach types should be chopped up with a spade, and then dug back into the soil.

Pests and diseases

Spinach is almost trouble-free, although greenfly and slugs may occasionally occur. Mildew is the commoner disease but the virus spinach blight is more serious. It produces small puckered yellow leaves and is spread by greenfly. Destroy affected plants.

Spinach

1. *Sow seed in the bottom of 5 cm [2"] deep drills, 30 cm [12"] apart.*

2. *Thin rows to leave the best of the seedlings spaced at 15 cm [6"].*

3. *When watering use a rose on can to prevent soil being washed away.*

4. *Spinach takes only a few weeks to grow, ideal for intercropping.*

5. *To harvest leaves, twist midrib, pull outwards or cut with scissors.*

6. *When harvest has ended, chop up plants and dig into soil.*

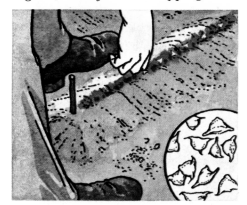

Sow winter spinach in ridged bed to prevent soil from waterlogging.

To protect winter spinach from the frost, pile straw over the plants.

Spinach makes an excellent and very nutritious green vegetable.

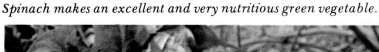

Spinach Beet

Although it resembles spinach in taste, spinach beet is no relation. It produces larger, fleshier leaves, which make excellent winter greens.

Spinach beet is simply a variety of beet that has been bred for leafiness instead of for its root. The whole leaf can be eaten, including the long green stalk. Beet is thought to have been first used as human food on the Mediterranean coast, where it grows well on chalky soils.

The cultivated spinach beet is much hardier than spinach, more stable, has larger, fleshier leaves, and will, unlike spinach, withstand hot weather without bolting. It can be picked for months, even through winter, and will bridge a seasonal gap when there is little else in the way of greens.

Cultivation

Spinach beet prefers a rich but light loamy soil and an open, moist situation; shade is not needed. It is a good crop to follow celery, gaining from the manure incorporated in the soil.

The frequent successional sowings associated with spinach are unnecessary for spinach beet because it continues to produce leaves for a long time. For continuous supplies throughout the year it is enough to sow once in early spring and once in summer.

Sow several rows. Allow 40 cm [16″] between rows, and sow the seeds 2.5 cm [1″] deep, at a spacing of 20-30 cm [8-12″] apart. Germination (which takes 7-14 days) cannot be expected to be much over 50%, so it is usual to sow 3 or 4 seeds at each station and remove all except the best when the seedlings appear. Keep the rows well weeded, and water in dry weather.

Spinach beet
Beta vulgaris cicla (fam. *Chenopodiaceae*)
Also known as perpetual spinach.
Hardy biennial.
Size: edible leaves attain a length of 30 cm [1′].
Climate: cool temperate to sub-tropical.
Sowing to harvesting time: 7-10 weeks.
Yield: 4.5 kg [10 lb] per 3 m [10′] row.

Spinach beet does well on a soil enriched by rotted manure or garden compost dug into the top spit.

Sow seed 2.5 cm [1″] deep, with 40 cm [16″] between each row to allow for future growth.

When thinning, remove all but the best seedlings. Water the remaining plants in dry weather.

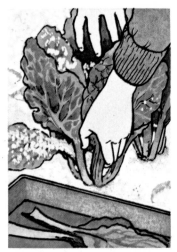

Spinach beet will produce plenty of leaves if the larger ones are picked at fairly regular intervals.

Spinach beet has large, fleshy leaves and will not bolt in heat. It harvests when other vegetables are scarce.

The leaves will be ready 7-10 weeks from sowing. Pick a few of the largest from each plant at regular intervals — partly to have them at their best before they become coarse and tough, and partly because this will stimulate the production of new leaves. The spring-sown beets should overlap the summer-sown ones with the latter carrying on until the following spring.

Pests and diseases

The fungus disease rust will occasionally appear, towards the end of summer. The leaves wilt and develop tiny bumps covered with rust-coloured powder. The treatment is removal of the worst affected leaves and spraying with half-strength Bordeaux mixture every 10 days.

Spring Onion

SEE ONION

Sprouting Broccoli

Sprouting broccoli is grown for its flowering shoots, which are harvested over a period of time. It is hardier than heading broccoli and cauliflowers.

Sprouting broccoli is a brassica of ancient origin, its home

being southern Europe. Broccoli spears are usually obtained from the Calabrese variety, which takes its name from Calabria, the region of southern Italy where it was once extensively grown. The shoots or heads of Calabrese are green; those of the northern sprouting varieties are purple or white.

Sprouting broccoli is closely related to the cauliflower and heading broccoli, or winter cauliflower (*see* BROCCOLI), but instead of forming one large flower head, it produces a number of smaller ones. Each is formed like a miniature cauliflower, with a 'curd' (composed of a tight mass of flower buds) surrounded by small leaves. It seems likely that sprouting broccoli is the older type from which cauliflower and heading broccoli have been developed. Midway between the latter and sprouting broccoli comes a variety once popular in English gardens known as nine star perennial broccoli, or hen and chickens. Once established, this will produce a crop consisting of a small white head in the centre — perhaps 7.5 cm [3″] in diameter — with a profusion of smaller heads around it, for year after year.

Suitable site and soil

The choice of site depends on which type of broccoli you wish to grow. Calabrese will come to harvest during the year in which the seed is sown, and any plot which fits into a proper rotation will do, although ideally they like a sunny, sheltered situation. Early and late sprouting broccoli remain where they were planted throughout the winter and well into the following spring or early summer; while the perennial varieties may be there for four or five years. These should have a site where they are not in the way of other crops, for example, alongside a fence or in a corner of the garden.

Like all brassicas, sprouting broccoli thrives in a rich, fertile soil though it will grow in one manured for a previous crop or even one that has not been treated at all. Preferably, however, work plenty of well-rotted manure in to it, in late autumn or early winter. This must be done early in order to ensure that the soil has time to settle and become really firm before planting. Soil should be one that does not become sodden in winter.

Sowing and planting

Sowing in general resembles that of other brassicas (such as broccoli, cabbage and Brussels sprouts), except that

---

Sprouting broccoli
Brassica oleracea botrytis cymosa (fam. *Cruciferae*)
Includes Calabrese (green sprouting broccoli)
Hardy annual, biennial or perennial.
Size: grows to a height of about 90 cm [3′] although there is great variation in size. Maximum diameter of plant with mature heads about 45 cm [1½′].
Climate: cool to warm temperate.
Sowing to harvesting time: 16 weeks for Calabrese, 40 for other varieties.
Yield: about 9 plants, each yielding up to 1 kg [2 lb] for Calabrese, and about 0.5 kg [½ lb] for other varieties.

Closely related to cauliflower, the northern varieties of sprouting broccoli are either purple or white.

Calabrese, which takes its name from Calabria in Italy, is green; most broccoli varieties originated from this.

sprouting broccoli is so hardy that there is little point in striving for early crops by the use of cloches and frames. Sow in the open from mid to late spring, depending on variety. The seed can be sown either where the plants are to grow or for transplanting later. The latter is probably better, as transplanted plants generally have their roots more deeply set in the soil and are better equipped to deal with the winter.

Sow the seed thinly 1.5 cm [½″] deep. If the plants are not to be transplanted, allow 60-75 cm [2-2½′] between the rows. In the rows either thin as soon as large enough to handle, or transplant, so that there is a space of 60 cm [2′] between plants. The temperature for germination is from 4° to 29° C [40° to 84°F], and the period for germination, from date of sowing, is from 7 to 12 days.

Transplant firmly with care, as described for CABBAGE and other brassicas, retaining a ball of moist soil around the roots of each plant if possible. In dry weather, dig a hole for each plant and flood with water first.

Cultivation

Keep well hoed. A mulch of garden compost or rotted farmyard manure around the plants will aid weed control as well as feeding them and preventing the soil from drying out. At intervals of about a month, starting a month after transplanting, a topdressing of a nitrogenous fertilizer (such as nitro-chalk) at the rate of 30 g per sq m [1 oz per sq yd] will be beneficial. Varieties which have to stand the winter are sometimes earthed up in autumn, the soil being drawn up to a ridge of about 15 cm [6″] round the stem to give these tall plants better anchorage against winds.

Harvesting the crop

From a sowing in mid spring Calabrese will produce a crop of green heads in late summer and early to mid autumn, with a large almost cauliflower-like one in the centre. Cut this large one first when 15-23 cm [6-9″] long, and the plant will continue to produce smaller green heads for several weeks.

The flowering shoots of the other varieties of sprouting broccoli are harvested individually, when about 23 cm [9″] long, removing the top 15 cm [6″] of each shoot by snapping it off. The top few shoots are removed first and this will stimulate the plants to provide more in succession lower down. Always pick while the flower buds are still closed. The harvest starts for these varieties at different times to Calabrese. Early purple and white sprouting broccoli are ready in early spring, sometimes in late winter if the weather is mild; late purple and white varieties in late spring, continuing to early summer, and perennial sprouting broccoli from mid to late spring.

In the kitchen the large heads of Calabrese and the shoots of the others are treated like broccoli or cauliflower. The smaller side-heads of Calabrese, however, may be tied in bundles and cooked like asparagus.

Storing the crop

As all these types of sprouting broccoli, except Calabrese, are perfectly hardy, they may be left in the garden until needed. For deep-freezing sprouting broccoli, other than

1. *Keep a ball of moist soil around the roots and transplant with care, allowing 60 cm [2´] between plants.*

2. *Mulch with garden compost to aid weed control, to prevent the soil drying out and to feed the plants.*

3. *When top-dressing, sprinkle the nitro-chalk evenly around plant in a circle the size of the top growth.*

4. *In autumn earth up the varieties that have to withstand winter to a height of 15 cm [6″] round the stem.*

5. *When harvesting calabrese, cut the main head first, to encourage the growth of smaller, green heads.*

6. *The side shoots are removed next, to stimulate further growth. Always pick while flower buds are closed.*

7. *Harvest the flowering shoots of other varieties individually. Begin with the top shoots, snapping off the first 15 cm [6″] of each one.*

8. *After harvesting a crop of heads from perennial broccoli, feed the plant well with a mulch of either garden compost or farmyard manure.*

9. *After harvest, the tough, woody stems of over-wintering varieties can be burned or put on the compost heap and left to rot for some time.*

Calabrese, trim off the outer leaves and any woody parts and split into small sections or sprigs. Calabrese is ideal for freezing as it is less woody (though stems may need peeling).

Care after harvesting
Consign all debris to the compost heap. The stalks of the over-wintering varieties will be very woody and should be placed where they can rot for some time, or they can be burned. After taking a crop of heads from perennial broccoli, feed the plant well with compost or farmyard manure, mulched or worked in around it.

Pests and diseases
These are the same as for other brassicas (see CABBAGE). Sprouting broccoli is among the hardiest of the group and is likely to experience little trouble once well established, though flea beetles may ravage the seedlings.

Squashes

These sun-loving fruit of varied size, colour and shape contain bland, watery flesh and seeds inside a skin that may be hard or soft.

Squashes
The summer squashes are varieties of *Cucurbita pepo*; *Cucurbita maxima* are winter squashes; *Cucurbita moschata* is also a type of squash (fam. *Cucurbitaceae*)
Half hardy annuals.
Size: sprawling plants, smaller varieties are pruned to 1 m [3'] square, larger ones to 1.8 m [6'] square.
Climate: temperate to sub-tropical.
Sowing to harvesting time: 7-9 weeks for summer squashes, 11-17 weeks for winter squashes.
Yield: extremely variable, 4 or 5 plants of one variety should be ample for a family of 4, according to variety.

Pumpkins belong to the same family as summer squashes. They are used when mature for making sweet spiced pies.

An attractive variety of bush-type summer squash which has a yellow, scallop-edged fruit and milk-white flesh.

(Right) A popular variety, crookneck squash has bright coloured fruits which are best eaten young and tender.

Cover female flowers with muslin bags to avoid the risk of cross-pollination.

Summer squash: cut before skin hardens. Fingernail should puncture it easily.

Store winter squash on slatted shelves in a frost-free, dry place. Handle the fruit with care to avoid bruising.

Trailing varieties can be grown on the ground or on a trellis. In either case, they require plenty of room.

Squash is an American term covering a wide range of vegetables of the *Cucurbitaceae* family. All of them like a warm climate but they may be grown as half-hardy annuals in cool temperate areas.

Squashes are divided into two main groups. Summer squashes, varieties of *C. pepo*, are probably of North American origin and are so called because they do not store. When young they can be eaten with both skin and seeds. Marrows and the young marrows called zucchini (*see* MARROW and ZUCCHINI) belong to this group. There are some exceptions to this rule, as pumpkins, which belong here, have hard skins like winter squashes. This group includes a variety of colours and shapes, including the orange or yellow hookshaped crookneck, the flattish, white, scalloped custard marrow or cymling and straightnecks.

Winter squashes, *C. maxima*, originated in Argentina and require a longer ripening period. The skin is hard (except for the butternut) and unless the squash is baked whole it is removed, together with seeds and stringy portion, before cooking. This group stores successfully, which gives them their name. Included here are the grey-green or orange Hubbard, acorn, turban and smooth yellow butternut.

Most squashes are bland in flavour and require spicing before eating. There are two types, trailing and bushy.

Suitable site and soil

Squashes like a very rich soil; farmyard dungheaps, compost heaps or well manured soil (*see* CUCUMBER) are all suitable. Choose an open, sunny site.

Sowing and planting

To protect early crops from frost in a cool temperate climate, sow in a heated greenhouse in early spring, using trays of compost, or singly in 7.5 cm [3″] peat pots. Sow outdoors in late spring with the protection of cloches. Germination temperature for pumpkins (which may be taken as representative) is 21°-32°C [69°-90°F], and seed should germinate in 5 to 14 days. When transplanting, remember that these trailing plants can cover a lot of space. A pumpkin plant, well rooted in a compost heap, will send out stems 3.6-4.5 m [12-15′] long, though these can be trained to go in the desired direction and surplus growth pruned away. On the other hand, custard marrows are bushy plants and do not require so much space. Plant trailing types 1.8 m [6′] apart and bush types 1 m [3′] apart.

Care and development

All squashes must be kept generously supplied with both water and food. Plants embedded in a compost or manure heap are well provided with nutrients, but require an abundance of water, and this will also keep down greenfly in young plants. Those planted in garden soil, though with an underlying layer of compost or manure, will benefit from a summer mulch. With trailing plants, such as the pumpkin, after one or two fruits have formed, it may be advisable to pinch out the tips of the vines, so that the plant can concentrate on the existing fruits.

Apart from pumpkins, squashes do not require hand pollination (*see* MELON). It is wise, however, to cover the flowers with muslin bags if other cucurbits are grown in the vicinity, to prevent cross pollination by insects.

Harvesting

With summer squashes, which includes custard marrows, cut before they are ripe and use immediately. Your fingernail should easily penetrate the thin skin; if it does not, it is too late. Such plants will then produce a succession of crops over a period of several weeks. Do not store.

Winter squashes should be allowed to ripen on the plant though with these, as with pumpkins and summer squashes, it is common practice to cut the first fruits early for immediate use, then to allow later ones to ripen.

Storing and aftercare

Winter squashes should be allowed to ripen and develop hard, horny shells before cutting. If harvested when the weather is dry, they can be stored in a dry place which has an even temperature and is frost free, for several months. Store on slatted shelves in an outhouse or hang them out of the way individually in nets. After mid winter watch for watery spots indicating decay: if this occurs, use up the rest of the store quickly.

The first frost will kill all foliage and remaining fruit. Clear away and add to the compost heap.

Pests and diseases

Squashes may be subject to the same pests and diseases as melons, but are usually untroubled.

Strawberry

With its mouth-watering red berries and distinctive aroma, the delicious strawberry is the best loved of all summer fruit.

Unlike most fruit, strawberries are produced on a low-growing, herbaceous plant. The cropping life of the plants is short but most of them readily reproduce themselves by means of runners. Botanically the fruit are a curiosity; each consists of a large fleshy receptacle with the seeds (pips) embedded in the surface. They are the quickest cropping of all fruit.

Large modern hybrids derive from a cross in France between two modern American species, *F. chiloensis*, from the Pacific coast, and *F. virginiana* from the east.

Modern strawberries can be divided into three groups — summer-fruiting varieties, perpetuals and alpines. Summer-fruiters are by far the most popular although they generally only crop once in the season. A few varieties may bear a second crop in the autumn if conditions are favourable, or if the first crop has been brought on with cloches or plastic tunnels. All produce runners. Some of the new varieties produce exceptionally large fruit, weighing up to 90 g [3 oz] each.

Perpetual strawberries (or remontants) produce fruit all summer, beginning in midsummer and continuing into autumn. Removing the first trusses of blossom from the plants prevents overlapping with summer-fruiting varieties and ensures a heavier yield from the later flushes. The berries are not as large as those of the summer fruiters. Perpetuals mostly produce only a few runners or none at all, although there is one variety, known as the climbing strawberry, that does bear runners. Botanically speaking, however, this is not a climbing plant, despite its name.

Alpine strawberries are small (thimble sized) but rich in flavour. They can be raised from seed and fruit sometime between early summer and autumn, depending on the age of the plants. Their main disadvantages are their tiny size and the time taken to pick them; they also have few or no runners depending on variety. They freeze well.

Strawberries are susceptible to a number of serious virus diseases. However, stocks have been improved greatly by the introduction of government certification schemes. Buy disease-free certified stock if this is available.

NORMAL OUTDOOR CULTIVATION

Summer-fruiting and perpetual varieties have similar site and soil requirements. Despite their woodland origins, they do best in full sun, ideally on a site that slopes slightly to the south, but need to be in a sheltered position to prevent cold spring winds checking their growth. Choose a site which will not be required for another crop for at least three years. The soil should be well-drained and slightly acid. Soils with a very high lime content are not suitable.

Preparing the bed

Start at least three weeks before planting. Where the

Strawberry
Hybrids of *Fragaria* (fam. *Rosaceae*), derived from *F. chiloensis* and *F. virginiana*.
Hardy perennial herbaceous plant with a cropping life of about 3 years.
Size: 15-30 cm [½-1′] by 15-20 cm [6-8″] high.
Climate: temperate.
Planting to harvesting time: 6-10 months.
Yield: from 115-450 g [¼-1 lb] per plant.

ground has previously been used for vegetables, single digging will be enough. Otherwise, double dig down to the second spit to encourage a good root-run but always keep the topsoil uppermost. Dig in rotted manure or garden compost at about half a garden barrow-load per sq m [sq yd]. This opens up a heavy soil and improves the moisture-retaining capacity of a light one. If neither are available, work in peat or leafmould at the same rate and then scatter and rake in an equal-parts (by weight) mixture of hoof and horn fertilizer, sterilized bonemeal and sulphate of potash at 190 g per sq m [6 oz per sq yd]. After digging, lightly roll or tread down, and then rake level.

Planting

Plant summer-fruiting strawberries in late summer or early autumn. Plant perpetuals in late autumn, only when soil conditions are first class; otherwise wait until spring. You will not lose a crop by waiting.

Plant in crumbly, friable soil; wait if excessive rain has made the bed sticky, or if the soil is dry. Planting strawberries close together increases the yield from the plot as a whole but reduces the yield per plant. However, growing more plants also increases the initial cost. A sensible compromise is to leave 45 cm [1½'] between plants and 75 cm [2½'] between rows, with 23 cm [9"] between plants for compact varieties.

It is important to plant strawberries at just the right depth: if you plant them too deep, the crown rots; if too shallow, the roots may dry out and the plant die. The crown of the plant should be just level with the soil surface.

If the plants come from pots or have been lifted from open ground, make a shallow hole with a little 5 cm [2"] mound in the centre and set each plant on top of the mound, spreading the roots out over and down it to their full extent. If the plants come in peat pots, do not remove them but soak the pots in water for 10 minutes and then plant at once with the rim of the pot (and the crown of the plant) just level with the soil surface. Always plant firmly, then water. Preferably, plant in the evening, but if this is not possible shade plants temporarily from strong sunshine.

Care and development

Water frequently, possibly even every day in the early weeks, if the weather is dry. Once the plants are established, they will probably not need further watering until the berries begin to swell the following summer. In late spring the plants will develop runners: long stems with a plantlet at each joint, which should be cut off at their point of origin as they appear unless they are wanted for propagating.

No feeding is needed as plants come quickly into bearing, but competing weeds should be kept down by light hoeing. Remember that roots are fine and close to the surface.

Cutting off all the blossom on summer-fruiting varieties in their first spring gives more than two seasons' crop the following year, but few gardeners have the patience to wait this long. If planting was later than the beginning of autumn however, it is essential to cut off the first season's blossom. Perpetuals should always have the first blossoms removed to allow them to build up strength for fruiting.

Care of the fruit

To keep the ripening berries off the ground and free from soil splashes, strawberry beds are traditionally covered with barley straw. Wheat straw is harder to obtain and oat straw more likely to carry pests. Try to obtain straw which has been properly thrashed, otherwise any grains left in it will sprout. Do not spread the straw until the weight of the developing berries is pulling them down to the ground, as premature strawing cuts them off from ground warmth, increasing the risk of damage from late spring frosts; frosted flowers which do not set fruit are recognizable by their black 'eyes' in the centre. Spread the straw thickly round each plant, tucking it under the fruit. If straw is unobtainable, special strawberry mats or black plastic strips can be used.

Keep the plastic in place with a few stones and make sure that it slopes evenly away from the plants so that pools of water cannot collect around them. If slugs are likely to be a problem, scatter a few slug pellets around the plant before putting down the fruit protector. The plants may be surrounded with wire collars to hold the fruit trusses clear of the ground.

Protect the crop from birds with lightweight plastic netting spread over the beds. Drive in short posts and run taut wires between them. These can remain in place for the life of the bed. Invert glass jars over the tops of the posts so that the netting will slide without catching, and throw the netting over the plants as the berries develop; mice and squirrels will take them while still small and green. Make sure the netting clears the tops of the plants and can be removed easily for picking.

Harvesting and aftercare

Outdoors, the first strawberries are likely to be ripe between four and six weeks after the blossom opens — sometime in early summer for the main crop. To start with, only a few berries will ripen at a time. These will be the biggest but not the tastiest. The pickings then increase quickly and the plants should be looked over at least every two days. Summer-fruiting varieties usually fruit for three or four weeks, but hot dry weather will shorten the season. Pick the fruit when it is dry, particularly if it is to be used for making jam. Do not touch the berries when picking; simply break off the stem about 2 cm [¾"] behind the fruit and put it carefully into a punnet or basket. Always remove damaged fruit and burn it to minimize the risk of infection. Summer fruiters will produce a first year crop.

After cropping, cut back the top growth of the plants of both ordinary and perpetual varieties with shears to about 7.5 cm [3"] above the crown and burn the cuttings to destroy any pests or disease spores. Remove straw and weeds and then water the bed if the soil is dry. Hoe the soil lightly and scatter general garden fertilizer as recommended for tomatoes around the plants, following the maker's instructions, or mulch with garden compost.

Summer fruiters should be grown on a 3-year rotation, with the bed divided into four strips. Remove 3-year-old plants after cropping, leave the site fallow for a year, and plant maiden runners in the fourth strip, which has had a year's fallowing, so that you always have one, two and

correctly planted planted too high planted too deep

1. *The crown of the plant must be just level with the surface of the soil. If planted too high, the roots may dry out; too deep, the crown may rot.*

2. *If planting after autumn, always cut off the first season's blossom.*

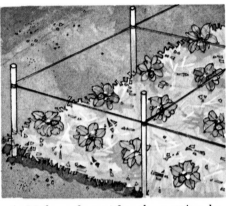

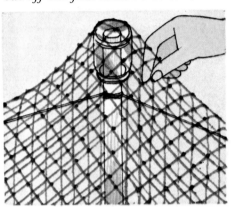

3. *Protect the ripening fruit with a layer of thrashed barley straw.*

4. *Make a frame for the netting by stretching wires between the posts.*

5. *Jars inverted over posts support the netting and stop it catching.*

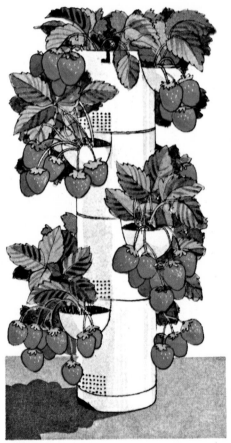

6. *Pick ripe berries when dry. Snap off stems; avoid bruising fruit.*

Forcing under cloches; make sure insects can fly in to pollinate.

Choose strong, healthy runners for propagation; pot them in individual pots, peg them down and keep moist.

A few weeks later sever the rooted runner from its parent plant, using a sharp knife to cut off the stolon.

If space is limited, an excellent alternative method is to grow this fruit in special 'tower pots'.

three year-old plants cropping in your garden.

Propagation

Strawberry runners are very easy to root but should only be used if they are definitely healthy and the parent plants are free from any sign of disease. Reserve some plants for propagation and cut the berries off before they start swelling, so that the plants' energy goes into the runners.

For root runners, sink small pots containing seed compost or a mixture of equal parts loam, peat and sharp sand at convenient points around the parent plants. Peg each runner down with a piece of bent wire, one per pot, so that the tip with leaves on it is held in close contact with the soil. Keep the pegged-down runners moist and they will root rapidly and in a few weeks can be cut from the parent plant, though not dug up. Transfer the rooted runners to their fruiting quarters a week after cutting.

EARLY CROPPING

An extra early crop can be grown under cloches or plastic tunnels or in a greenhouse. An unheated greenhouse has no advantage over cloches, although a heated one can advance cropping by several more weeks.

Forcing under cloches or plastic

Outdoors, crops can be forwarded by three or four weeks using glass cloches, or by two or three weeks with plastic cloches or tunnels. Many varieties crop earlier than usual in their first year, so do protect your new plants.

The plants are smaller in their first year, so they should be planted 23 cm [9″] apart, allowing 90 cm [3′] between rows — the wider spacing makes the placing of cloches and tunnels easier. After the maiden crop has been picked, pull out alternate plants and leave the rest uncovered.

There is no point in using cloches or tunnels too early; the beginning of late winter is quite soon enough. Before covering, weed the bed and scatter slug pellets around the plants. There is no need to 'straw' the bed but the plants must be protected from birds with netting when the cloches or tunnels are opened during the ripening period.

Using tunnels will lead to poor berry development unless insects are allowed to fly in to pollinate the blossom. Open the tunnels wide in the middle part of the day when the flowers are out. Most glass cloches have spaces through which insects can enter, but in very hot weather, open the cloches or space them 5 cm [2″] apart.

In the heated greenhouse

Use very early rooted runners (*see* Propagation) for greenhouse forcing. By the end of midsummer these should be planted singly in 15 cm [6″] pots filled with rich potting compost. Keep the pots outdoors until early in mid winter, making sure that the plants always have enough water and the pots are not cracked by frost. Once inside the greenhouse, keep the plants quite cool with no artificial heat until signs of growth can be seen, usually ten days or two weeks later. Now raise the temperature very gradually, reaching a maximum of 10°C [50°F] by the end of mid winter, and increase humidity by damping.

Once the flowers have set and the berries begun to swell,

allow the temperature to rise, ideally to 18°C [65°F], and maintain moister conditions until the fruit starts to colour, when the air should again be drier. Feed the plants occasionally with dilute liquid manure or fertilizer as the berries swell. Forked sticks or bent galvanized wire can be used to hold the fruit trusses up and keep the berries clean. Plants cannot be used again once forced.

CONTAINER GROWING

Summer-fruiting and perpetual varieties can be grown in barrels with drilled holes, patio pots and other strawberry containers. (*See* diagram). By growing in such a barrel or pot, a large crop is obtained in a small space. Smaller containers can be moved under cover for earlier cropping. Use a rich potting compost and work upwards, inserting the roots of the plants from the outside as each planting hole is reached. Make sure the strawberries are not planted too deeply or too shallowly and firm the compost layer by layer to minimize soil settlement after planting.

ALPINE STRAWBERRIES

Alpine strawberries are raised from seed. Sow in a greenhouse between mid winter and early spring at 10 to 16°C [50 to 60°F], or in a cold frame or beneath cloches in mid spring, or in the open in late spring. However, the later the sowing, the less certain is the first season's crop. In the greenhouse fill a seed tray or pan with fine seed compost, scatter the seed as thinly as possible and just cover with a sifting of compost. Germination may be rather erratic and is slow without heat. Prick off separately into another box, placing them 5 cm [2″] apart each way, using potting compost.

Alpine strawberries need a partially shaded site with soil rich in organic matter. Glass-raised seedlings should be set outdoors at the end of spring, while those sown in the open should be transferred to their final quarters in early summer or midsummer. Transplant alpine strawberries as early as possible in their development.

Set the alpines 30 cm [1′] apart in both directions and make sure that they are never checked by drought.

PESTS AND DISEASES

Strawberries can be infested by a variety of troubles, but grey mould *(Botrytis cinerea)* on the berries is the most likely. Ground or seed beetles may eat the pips and surface flesh of the fruit, doing this at night. They are usually black beetles, 1.5 cm [½″] long, and control is difficult. Keeping the bed and surrounding area free of rubbish helps; if you have serious trouble every year, a barrier of plastic sheeting round the bed can be put up in late spring, the lower edge penetrating into the soil for a few inches.

Red core is a serious soil-borne fungus disease invading the roots. Plants wilt during summer, and roots are dark brown with a red centre. There is no control. Plants should be destroyed and the land uncropped for at least 13 years; some varieties are partially resistant. Tarsonemid mite is a minute transparent mite which feeds on both surfaces of the young leaves. Plants look short of water and cease to grow, and the mites multiply fast in hot dry weather, so always keep the plants well supplied with

A south-facing, open but sheltered site
is the ideal place for strawberry beds.

(Right) Decorative containers provide a
feast for the eye as well as the table.

GROWING IN A BARREL

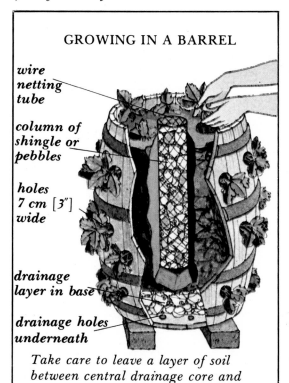

wire
netting
tube

column of
shingle or
pebbles

holes
7 cm [3"]
wide

drainage
layer in base

drainage holes
underneath

Take care to leave a layer of soil
between central drainage core and
base drainage or water will run out.

Plump, juicy berries ripe for picking. This luxurious summer fruit is only at its best fresh from the garden.

water. Dust with flowers of sulphur at weekly intervals. Strawberry blossom weevil bites through the stalks of flower trusses, and buds and flowers are left lying on the ground; derris or pyrethrum can be used.

Eelworm attack can be serious, giving puckered leaves and small plants with hollow centres; such plants should be destroyed, also their runners, and ground left free of strawberries for at least a year. Leaf spot shows as small, dark red-brown spots with a white centre; Royal Sovereign is the variety mainly infected, but the disease does little harm although it looks alarming. Removal of the worst-affected leaves is advisable. Lopsided fruit result from poor pollination and frost damage.

String Bean

SEE FRENCH BEAN.

Swede

Among the hardiest of all vegetables, swedes can withstand the rigours of the worst winters. This hybrid cousin of the turnip is ideal for stews.

Swede is an abbreviation of Swedish turnip, the name by which the plant was originally known. It was developed from the turnip for use in Sweden and other northern countries around 1780, possibly earlier. One of its chief qualities is extra hardiness — it can be left in the soil throughout winter and will be perfectly wholesome and edible after being frozen solid for weeks.

In some northern areas the swede has almost completely superseded the turnip — when a Scotsman talks about 'turnips' he will almost certainly be referring to swedes. In the United States it is called rutabaga.

Although the crop is grown primarily for its roots, any roots left in the ground till spring will produce a mass of pale green leaves which can be cooked as greens.

Cultivation

Although swedes will grow almost anywhere, a fertile soil is needed for a good crop, and in this respect they are rather more exacting than turnips. One which was manured for a previous crop is the best, but if this is not available give a light dressing of a compound fertilizer about 10 days before sowing. Swedes do well in a heavy soil, provided it is not acid, though acidity can be corrected by an application of lime.

Swedes can be sown at almost any time from early spring to autumn but early crops, except in countries with a cool summer, will almost certainly be attacked by leaf mildews, especially if they are being grown in well-drained, dry soils. In cool countries sowings can be made in late spring; in warmer (though still only moderately temperate) regions sowing should be delayed until about early summer. After that, a succession of sowings can be made, but those varieties which are sown too late (after midsummer) will have insufficient time to produce good-sized roots and will have to be used solely for greens.

Scatter the seed 1.5 cm [½″] deep in drills 45 cm [18″] apart. Germination temperature is 4-40°C [40-100°F]; time from sowing to germination varies according to weather conditions but is about 7-12 days. Swede seedlings, having short stems, sit closer on the ground than those of most other brassicas. They are not transplanted but are thinned at intervals, the final spacing being about 30 cm [12″] between plants.

Once the plants have become well established, little cultivation is necessary beyond hoeing to control weeds. Water well in dry weather.

Harvesting, storing and aftercare

Although swedes may be of sufficient size for harvesting in

Swede
Brassica napus napobrassica (fam. *Cruciferae*) also known as rutabaga and 'turnip'.
Hardy biennial.
Size: at its best for eating when 7.5-12.5 cm [3-5″] in diameter and 12.5-17.5 cm [5-7″] long, though it will grow much larger.
Climate: cool temperate.
Sowing to harvesting time: 20-24 weeks.
Yield: 0.5-1 kg [1-2 lb] per root, but can be much heavier.

1. *Scatter seed at depth of 1.25 cm [½″] in drills spaced 45 cm [18″] apart.*

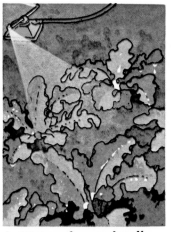

2. *Thin at intervals with a draw hoe to leave final spacing of 30 cm [12″].*

3. *Water often and well, especially in dry weather.*

4. *Pull swedes as needed through winter, or store.*

HOW TO PRODUCE BLANCHED SHOOTS

layer of packed soil

dry straw

drainage trench

5. *Storing in a clamp. To take a few swedes just remove a plug of straw. To take more, break open a soil layer.*

1. *Put roots in moist soil; keep dark and quite warm.*

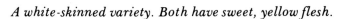

2. *Cut blanched shoots when 20 cm [8″] long.*

A purple-skinned variety showing the usual ridged neck.

A white-skinned variety. Both have sweet, yellow flesh.

early autumn, they are usually left undisturbed until all the summer vegetables have been harvested and frost has set in. They can then be pulled as required throughout the winter whenever the ground is not too hard to dig. Those left over till spring will produce a head of greens which may be welcome in a time of scarcity.

Gardeners with an adequate stock of swedes and sufficient storage space often take the precaution of storing a few in boxes or in an outdoor clamp, simply to ensure that a supply will be available when the rest of the crop is frozen hard into the soil. An outdoor heap covered with straw and encased in a layer of soil makes an adequate clamp. It is feasible to persuade swede roots to produce 'chicons', after the manner of chicory, for winter salad. Dig the roots up, cut off any top growth and place them in moist soil or peat in a box or barrel. Keep dark and moderately warm as for chicory when forced. Cut the blanched shoots when about 20 cm [8″] long. (*See* CHICORY).

Any residue left by the swede makes good compost. Clear as soon as crop is finished to avoid flea-beetle.

Pests and diseases

The flea-beetle (*Phyllotreta* species), a common scourge of brassicas, is almost always active when the seedlings are emerging and can cause trouble (*see* CABBAGE).

The swede is also vulnerable to other brassica pests and diseases, though some of these do not thrive in the high northern latitudes which the swede finds congenial. Soft rot and mildew may be troublesome, as well as dry rot (*Phoma lingam*) caused by using manure containing rotten roots.

Sweet corn

The plump kernels of the sweet corn cob, one of the most delicious of vegetables, must be eaten freshly harvested.

Sweet corn is a refined variety of Indian corn, or maize, and notable for its higher sugar content. Originally an American crop, corn was widely cultivated in Central America at the time of the Spanish Conquest and was introduced to Europe by Columbus. Today corn is grown as a crop, for both human and animal consumption, over vast areas of the tropics and has extended its range into the temperate zones. However, it does prefer a longer, hotter and sunnier summer than is usual in cooler temperate zones, and even with the newest varieties it is worthwhile extending the growing season as long as possible by the use of cloches and greenhouses.

Suitable site and soil

Sweet corn revels in sun, so an open, sunny site is best, but it is a tall plant with a shallow root system, so it also needs some shelter from high winds. It will grow in almost any kind of soil but prefers a light, sandy and reasonably fertile one. Prepare the ground in advance by digging in plenty of well-decayed farmyard manure, garden compost or any other organic matter, as well as bonemeal or soot. Correct an acid soil by the use of lime and, just before sowing or planting, work in a compound fertilizer at about 125 g per sq m [4 oz per sq yd]. Sweet corn is botanically a grass, and grasses like to be well fed, so give a further application of a quick-acting nitrogenous fertilizer about six weeks after sowing or planting at the rate of 30 g per sq m [1 oz per sq yd].

Sowing and planting out

The germination temperature for sweet corn is from 10-35°C [50-95°F], preferably above 16°C [60°F]. If kept watered and at a satisfactory temperature, seed should germinate within six to twelve days of sowing. Except for cool temperate zones, successional sowings may be made outdoors from mid spring at intervals of two or three weeks until well past midsummer, protecting the earlier sowings if cold threatens. Alternatively, early, mid and late season varieties may be sown at the same time and, by reason of their varying times of coming to maturity, will provide a succession of harvests. In cool temperate areas sowing outdoors is limited to late spring, so that there is little scope for a succession, although crops can be obtained earlier than normal by sowing in 7.5 cm [3″] peat pots under glass in mid spring.

Draw out a drill 5 cm [2″] deep and sow in the bottom at the rate of 5 or 6 seeds per 30 cm [1′]. The drills should be 75-90 cm [30-36″] apart. (This allows for the normal germination rate of about 75%.) Start thinning when the plants reach a height of about 20-25 cm [8-10″] so that

> **Sweet Corn**
> *Zea mays* (fam. *Gramineae*) also known as Corn, Indian Corn or Mealies.
> **Half-hardy annual.**
> **Size:** plant grows to about 1.2-2.4 m [4-8′] or more; cobs are 15-20 cm [6-8″] long.
> **Climate:** temperate to sub-tropical.
> **Sowing to harvesting time:** 9-14 weeks.
> **Yield:** 2-6 ears (or cobs) per plant; 2 the maximum in cool temperate areas.

1. *Immerse peat pots in water so that they expand, then sow 2 seeds in each.*

2. *As seedlings grow, remove the weaker ones and leave the strong ones to develop.*

3. *If dry when transplanting dig hole and flood before planting pot and plant.*

4. *As plants grow, put heavy mulch of straw around the plants to retain moisture.*

5. *To hand pollinate, shake tassel (male) onto the 'silks' (female flower).*

just ripe over ripe

6. *Just-ripe, green cob with green to brown silk, and overripe, faded cob.*

7. *To test for ripeness, use thumbnail and press seeds. 'Milk' spurts out if ripe.*

8. *To pick, grasp cob then split it from the stalk, pulling downwards.*

they are eventually spaced 25-35 cm [10-14″] apart. Take care when thinning to avoid disturbing the roots of the remaining plants.

An alternative, however, to growing in single rows is block planting. This involves sowing or planting in a rectangular block, allowing 25-35 cm [10-14″] between the plants in each direction. The advantage of block planting is that it gives the silks (the female flowers) a better chance of being pollinated — pollen from the male flower, on the top of the plant (the tassel), must fall onto the silky stigmas of the female flowers on the stems below. If wind blows strongly across a single row when the pollen is falling, most of the pollen will be wasted. On very still days, an occasional shake will ensure pollination.

In a cold climate cloches give sweet corn an earlier start. Place cloches over the soil about ten days before sowing, to warm it up. Alternatively many gardeners bring on their earliest crops in a heated greenhouse, in frames or even in

pots in the home. Peat pots filled with potting compost serve the purpose well, as transplanting can take place with the least possible interference to the root system. Sow two seeds per pot and eliminate the weaker plant.

Transplant outdoors when the likelihood of frost is past. If dry, dig a hole for each plant and flood with water before setting the plant. Avoid disturbing the roots. Plant 25-45 cm [10-18″] apart if grown in rows or blocks. Alternatively, two rows can be set fairly close together without access between them.

Care and development
Sweet corn is well able to smother most weeds when growing vigorously and approaching maturity, but in the early stages it often grows slowly, especially during dry weather, and is then very vulnerable to weed competition. Keep the plants well watered and hoe frequently, but take care not to disturb or sever the shallow, spreading roots.

A sweet corn bed in flower. Mature plants will smother most weeds. If they grow tall they may need staking.

Some gardeners carefully earth up their sweet corn plants, as with potatoes, to a height of a few centimetres (inches). This encourages the production of more roots and so a stronger plant. Others aim to retain moisture around the roots by means of a strawy mulch.

Liquid feeding is beneficial, at regular intervals from pollination time to harvest. Tall plants may need staking.

Harvesting and aftercare

A common mistake is to leave the cobs too long before harvesting. In general, cobs will be ready for harvesting about three weeks after the silks have first appeared on each plant. To determine when the cobs are ripe, watch the silken tassels on the cobs. While the grains are growing they are moist and pale green. When ripe they turn dark brown but still remain damp. If they become dry and shrivelled they have been left too long. The sheath of the cob should be dark green and should on no account be left to turn yellow or faded brown.

You can test one of the grains, or kernels, by piercing it with a thumbnail. If 'milk' spurts out, the cob is ready. If cobs are left too long on the stalk, the sugars they contain will start turning to starch. Because the conversion from sugar to starch takes place, in most varieties, as soon as the cob is parted from its parent plant, it is important to leave picking the cob until just before it is needed in the kitchen. However, certain varieties of sweet corn have been developed which improve rather than deteriorate for a few hours after picking. These extra-sweet varieties should not be grown near other types, as cross-pollination will affect their flavour. To pluck the cob, grasp it firmly and split it downwards from the stalk. It should break off easily. Cobs on the same plant will ripen at intervals of a few days.

Unlike field corn (or maize), which can be stored in a dry place for indefinite periods, sweet corn is harvested while succulent and is best used almost immediately (or prepared for the deep-freeze) although it will keep for up to two days if stored in a cool moist place. Do not remove the husks until you are ready to cook the cobs.

The dry stalks of sweet corn after harvesting form a kind of straw which can be used as litter for domestic animals, or

Sweet corn was first grown in Central America but today it is successfully cultivated in many temperate areas.

added to the compost heap; it makes excellent compost.

Pests and diseases

In tropical and sub-tropical countries sweet corn is troubled by a variety of pests and diseases, from rusts and smuts to weevils and ear-worms, but gardeners in temperate climates will mostly only have trouble with the seedlings, which may be attacked by rabbits and birds. Once the plant is established, the only pest which may then cause serious trouble is frit-fly, the larva of which eats out the growing point, stunting the plant. Seed treated against this pest will also discourage mice.

Mulch between rows, using manure or peat. This prevents weeds and preserves moisture.

In a dry summer, watering plants will make a lot of difference to leaf size.

Harvest when leaves reach a large enough size. Pull from the base carefully.

In winter put dry bracken over plants to protect them from frost damage.

Swiss Chard

Rarely grown commercially, Swiss chard is an easy vegetable to raise in the garden. It thrives in a partly shaded site — usually the most difficult part of the vegetable patch to fill.

Swiss chard was derived from a wild species that grows in some coastal areas of Europe. Closely related to beetroot and sugar beet, Swiss chard is grown for its foliage rather than its roots. The stalks and mid-ribs of the leaves are

---

Swiss Chard
Beta vulgaris cicla (fam. *Chenopodiaceae*)
Also called seakale beet, silver beet, seakale spinach.
Hardy biennial, useful for year-round cropping.
Size: 38 cm [15″] high, 30 cm [12″] across.
Climate: cool temperate to sub-tropical.
Sowing to harvesting time: 16 weeks.
Yield: about 10 plants per 3 m [10′] row, each giving 250-375 g [½-¾ lb] leaves.

Ruby chard is a variety with showy scarlet stems.

unusually wide, and these are tasty and tender to eat when cooked like asparagus or seakale. The green part of each leaf, high in vitamin content, is torn off and served separately. When boiled quickly the greens resemble spinach in texture but have a much milder flavour.

Suitable site and soil

Chard is ideal for the partly shaded area of the vegetable garden, which is the most difficult spot to fill. Any well-drained garden soil will be suitable. Unless it is well-broken-down clay, double dig the chosen patch in autumn or early winter, working in plenty of manure and, if available, a fish manure may be applied as a topdressing.

Sowing and thinning

A mid spring sowing will provide plants for summer and autumn eating, and some leaves for winter, and a late-summer sowing will give good winter and spring crops. Seed is station-sown 30 cm [12″] apart in 2.5 cm [1″] drills which are made 38 cm [15″] apart, and later the seedlings are thinned to one good one at each station. Germination occurs readily in open ground during normal spring weather, and seedlings appear in 12-21 days.

Cultivation

Weeding is best carried out by regular hoeing along the rows. Another method is to place black plastic between the rows of plants, keeping it on the soil with stones. If the ground has been well-prepared before planting, additional feeding will not be necessary. In a dry summer, however, watering with a can or hose will make a noticeable difference to the size of the leaves.

Harvesting and aftercare

Remove a few leaves from each plant at regular intervals when they are large enough, but pull them up carefully from the base. Do not strip it or pull it up.

A succession of pickings may be made throughout the late summer and autumn from the spring sowing. In the following spring, remove any dead or rotting outer leaves from the overwintered plants and hoe in a topdressing of nitrogenous fertilizer. Within a few weeks a new harvest of leaves can be gathered. In autumn it is advisable to put some straw or bracken over the plants so that the new leaves which are growing are protected in winter. In early summer, the plants will start to produce flower stems and should be dug out and placed on the compost heap.

Growing in containers

A few plants can be grown in a large tub or trough if there is between 30-60 cm [1-2′] depth of soil for the deep roots. Mix well-decayed manure into the potting compost, if obtainable: rabbit manure is ideal. Water regularly. Plants in tubs may need soaking twice a day during the height of summer. Containers can be put in a cold frame or greenhouse for winter protection.

Pests and diseases

Swiss chard is virtually trouble-free; slugs may attack and seedlings occasionally dampen-off.

Tarragon

Tarragon leaves are used to flavour wine vinegar and, either fresh or dried, they are excellent with chicken, in egg recipes and in Hollandaise sauce.

Tarragon (*Artemisia dracunculus*) is a member of the family *Compositae*. The name tarragon is derived from a French word meaning 'little dragon', because the herb was thought to cure poisonous bites. French tarragon, an aromatic, shrubby, hardy perennial, 1 m [3′] high and wide, is best for kitchen use. It is a native of southern Europe. Russian tarragon may grow twice as tall, but lacks the tang of the French type and is decidedly inferior as a culinary herb.

Cultivation

Tarragon must be grown where there is sun for most of the day and shelter from cold winds. Good drainage is essential as persistent damp causes root rot and the plant dies quickly. Add plenty of organic material before planting.

Do not try to grow tarragon from seed; in any case in cool climates the seed will not be fertile, and the flavour is always inferior to plants propagated vegetatively. The best means of propagation is division of the roots from a mature plant in late spring. Any small piece of root with a shoot on it will grow. Otherwise, cuttings may be taken in spring or late summer.

Plant bought roots or cuttings outdoors in late spring or early autumn 60 cm [2′] apart. In extremely dry weather water the plants lightly from time to time. In moderate or severe winters protect the plants with cloches; also protect them in winter if planted in autumn.

After four years, transplant tarragon to a new situation so that the soil is not impoverished and the flavour of the leaves does not diminish.

Harvesting

Fresh leaves may be taken any time during the growing season, from spring to autumn. If dried tarragon is required, shoots should be taken in late summer just before the plant produces its greenish white flowers. An

Tarragon will grow prolifically in a sunny, sheltered spot. Always transplant to a new site every four years.

alternative in cool temperate areas is to lift the plants and overwinter them in a cool greenhouse or a frame where they will provide fresh leaves throughout the year.

Thyme

Common thyme (left) and lemon thyme (right) are strongly aromatic herbs. Common thyme is an essential ingredient of 'mixed herbs' and bouquet garni.

Common or garden thyme *(Thymus vulgaris),* a member of the family *Labiatae*, is one of many species grown for its leaves. One of the standard herbs, it is well known as a flavouring for lamb, pork and fish. It is an ornamental plant often grown in the rock garden, between paving stones or in a border. Most species are low-growing, reasonably hardy perennials. Common thyme grows up to 20 cm [8″] high, with a spread of about 30 cm [1′], and it bears small lilac flowers from mid to late summer. Lemon thyme *(Thymus x citriodorus)* is a slightly higher, looser bush with deeper pink flowers in late summer and broader, lemon-scented leaves.

Cultivation

Thyme grows best in a sunny and sheltered position. All types grow well on gravel or chalk but a clay soil should be avoided. Work over a heavy soil to improve drainage and add fibrous garden compost. Do not give it an over-rich supply of organic material, however, because this promotes sappy growth that will not endure the winter.

Common thyme (but not lemon thyme) can be grown from seed, although cuttings from a nursery are more reliable. Sowing must be done carefully because the seed is extremely fine and needs the barest covering of fine soil.

The typical small lilac flowers of common thyme. Thyme is a pretty plant to grow in a rockery or in a border.

Sow in moist seed compost in trays in late spring and keep warm, about 16°C [60°F], until germination takes place. Pot on to deeper trays or singly into 5 cm [2″] pots until the plants are growing strongly. Plant these (or bought plants) at a spacing of 30 cm [1′].

Thyme seldom needs watering. Because it is small, watch it to ensure it is not choked by weeds. For more vigorous leaf growth in young plants, sprinkle nitrate of soda round them but only in damp weather. Remove any flowers.

Cuttings of young shoots, about 5 cm [2″] long, can be taken from established plants in early summer. Put three cuttings into a 7.5 cm [3″] pot and, when rooted, plant them out in early autumn. A quicker method of propagation is to lift and divide the roots of a mature plant during spring. These will produce plenty of leaf growth in the first season, while seedlings and cuttings will not do so until the following spring.

Under good conditions, thyme will usually grow in the open for many years. However, lemon thyme will need protection in the winter and so will common thyme in severe winters. Use a cloche or overwinter indoors.

Harvesting

Fresh sprigs of thyme can be harvested throughout the summer as long as the weather is dry, until the plant flowers. Dried thyme keeps its flavour well. Cut the leaves off in sprigs and put them in a dark, warm, dry and airy place. After a few days crush and store.

Tomato

Perhaps the most delicious and versatile of the vegetable fruits, tomatoes are well worth the care they require.

The tomato is one of the most intensively bred vegetables grown, and there is a wealth of varieties and types from which to choose. It flourishes in hot climates, but often needs artificial heat and light to induce growth in the cold, short days of early spring in cool climates. Yet even in quite inhospitable areas you can raise a successful tomato crop out of doors provided you choose the newer, hardier F_1 hybrids.

Tomatoes can either be raised from seed, or plants can be bought when they are between 6-8 weeks old. The latter method has the advantage of saving the cost of the heat needed to raise the seed and eliminates the risk of failure, but it means you are limited to the nursery's choice of varieties. The best course for a novice tomato grower would be to buy plants the first year and, if they do well, attempt to raise them himself the following year.

GROWING OUT OF DOORS

Growing tomatoes out of doors will produce excellent crops provided care is taken in the choice of site, as heat and light are essential.

Suitable site and soil

Ideally the bed should be made on a site which is in the shelter of a south-facing wall. It is unwise to grow tomatoes on land previously used for potatoes because of the risk of the microscopic potato eelworm *(Heterodera rostochiensis)*, which attacks the roots of tomatoes also.

Enrich the soil with rotted manure or garden compost in the autumn or winter before planting. The soil should be slightly acid (pH 6.5). If too acid, add lime at the rate of 125 g per sq m [4 oz per sq yd] two weeks before planting. Very alkaline soils are not suitable

Sowing and planting out

Sow from mid February onwards, depending on the light and heat in your district. Seed can be sown in a greenhouse, in a thermostatically controlled propagator, inside a slightly cooler greenhouse or in a heated frame. The temperature must remain steady at 18°C [65°F] until the seeds germinate, which takes about eight days, and can then be reduced at night to 13-15°C [55-60°F].

Either sow seeds singly in seed compost in a tray, covering with 0.5 cm [¼″] compost, and prick out the seedlings into 7.5 cm [3″] pots filled with a potting compost, or sow individually in peat pots filled with compost. In this case the plants do not have to be transplanted until they are moved to the garden. Whichever method is followed, the growing plants must never be allowed to dry out.

The plants should be at least 15 cm [6″] tall, compact, and

> **Tomato**
> *Lycopersicon esculentum* (fam. *Solanaceae*)
> **Perennial,** grown as an **annual.**
> **Size:** plants from 15 cm-1 m [6″-3′] tall, depending on variety.
> **Climate:** cool temperate to sub-tropical.
> **Planting to harvesting time:** from 8-15 weeks, depending on variety.
> **Yield:** about 3.6-5.4 kg [8-12 lb] per plant (greenhouse); 1.8 - 2.7 kg [4-6 lb] outdoors.

Outdoor bush varieties need no staking and very little pruning. Fruit should be kept off the soil with straw.

This bush variety bears straight-sided fruit. Bush tomatoes are ideally suited to cloche cultivation.

An F₁ hybrid greenhouse variety. This ripens early and is resistant to the diseases greenback and leaf mould.

The many tomato varieties bear fruit of different shape, size and colour. This one has round, yellow fruit.

GROWING OUT OF DOORS

1. *Sow seeds 1.5 cm [½"] apart in a propagator from late winter onward.*

2. *Prick off seedlings into 7.5 cm [3"] pots of potting compost.*

3. *Plant in moist warmed soil and tie to stakes with fillis string.*

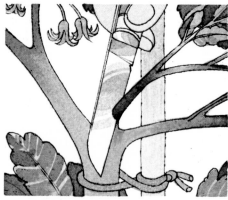

4. *Remove side-shoots of single-stem types using a clean knife.*

5. *Give liquid fertilizer every two weeks from start of fruit swelling.*

6. *Put dry straw under bush types to keep them from soil and slugs.*

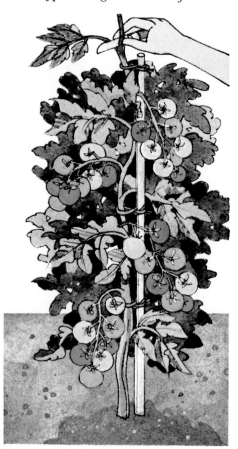

7. *When four trusses are ripe, cut main stem one leaf above top truss.*

8. *Harvest tomatoes as they ripen, leaving the calyx on the fruit.*

9. *Pick by severing the stalk at the knuckle just above the calyx.*

10. *Lay plants on straw and cover with cloches to ripen green fruit.*

dark green, not leggy and pale, preferably with the first flower truss well formed at the planting out stage. This can only take place once all reasonable danger of frost is past. The plants can go straight into the garden if they have the protection of cloches which have been in position for two or three weeks beforehand to give the soil a chance to warm up. If no cloches are available, harden off the plants in a frame two weeks before planting out.

Water the soil ball the day before planting, and make sure that the soil into which the plants are going is also moist. Take care to disturb the roots as little as possible if planted from pots. Plant in holes 45 cm [18″] apart in rows 75 cm [2½′] apart. Firm the soil around the plant by hand, and replace the cloches, if used, for two or three weeks. Do not water in immediately after planting, but water the soil ball only, as required, until plant begins to grow well.

Care and development
Make sure that the plants are adequately supported by tying them gently to canes or poles with fillis (a soft but strong twine). Remove all sideshoots as soon as they appear, to encourage the formation of fruit rather than foliage. Feed with liquid fertilizer every two weeks from the time the fruits begin to swell, using one with a high proportion of potassium which is vital for good quality fruit. Keep the plants regularly and adequately watered, otherwise they will suffer from dry set and blossom end rot (*see* **Pests and Diseases**). Remove any yellowing or rotting basal leaves and keep the weeds under control.

The above applies to plants grown as single stems, but some varieties, called 'bush' types, have a main stem which ends in a flower truss at about 38 cm [15″] tall, so that it stops growing upwards. All the sideshoots which then grow carry the rest of the crop but, as a plant can become a very leafy tangle, it is advisable to thin them out a little. Those kinds can be laid flat on the ground, and will need straw or wire netting to keep them off the soil and away from slugs.

Pollination
In dry weather, spray the flower trusses with water, early in the day, to encourage the flowers to set fruit. When the required number of trusses has been produced the main stem is cut (pinched out) at one leaf above the final truss, so that the plant's energies can concentrate on fruiting, not growing.

Harvesting the crop
Pick tomatoes as they ripen, removing them from the plant with the calyx still attached. Towards the end of the season, before there is any danger of frost, take any still green tomatoes indoors to ripen or, preferably, cover the plants with cloches to hasten natural ripening. Cut the fillis supports and lay the plants along the ground on straw to keep them off the damp soil and then cover with cloches.

GROWING IN A HEATED GREENHOUSE
Tomatoes are usually grown in greenhouse borders in soil that has been properly prepared: sterilized each winter, well watered, properly drained and periodically renewed.

Prepare the soil by digging in well-rotted horse manure, garden compost or rotted seaweed in the autumn or early winter at the rate of 5 kg per sq m [11 lb per sq yd]. Rectify any lime deficiency with a dressing applied not less than six weeks after manuring; the pH of the soil should be about 6.5. Flood with water about one to two months before planting, to ensure the subsoil will be sufficiently moist. Rake in a proprietary tomato base-fertilizer according to the manufacturer's instructions, shortly before planting. If it has been necessary to sterilize the soil with formaldehyde, flooding, manuring and any liming should follow, in that order.

Sowing and planting
Sow seed as described for outdoor tomatoes, the time of sowing being late autumn to early winter. The main crop is usually planted between late winter and early spring. Heat the greenhouse for about 14 days before planting to achieve a soil temperature of 15°C [60°F]; cold soil checks growth and encourages root decay. Plant as for outdoor tomatoes, and when the plants are at the same stage. Allow 30-45 cm [12-18″] between plants, depending on the variety, and 45 cm [18″] between rows. Do not plant too close to the edge of the border or the heating pipes.

Supporting
Greenhouse plants can reach approximately 2 m [6′] in height, and when in full cropping, are very heavy. It is most important that the house is structurally sound and firmly based if it is to be filled with tomatoes. One method of support is to run a horizontal wire along a row, 5 cm [2″] above the soil, and another directly above it, 15 cm [6″] from the glass of the roof. A length of soft 4-ply fillis string is then knotted to the lower wire and to the top wire, by each plant, and twisted around the plants as they grow. The string should be loose to start with — the plant will take up the slack as the stem is twisted round the string. An alternative method is to replace the lower wire with a stout 30 cm [12″] wire stake, placed by each plant and hooked at the top end. It should project by about 5 cm [2″], and the string is then attached to the hook and taken up to the roof as before.

Care and development
Tomatoes require a warm but well-ventilated atmosphere. The air temperature should average 15-16°C [60-62°F] during the day, but must be regulated to outside conditions; in dry but dull winter weather raise to 18°C [65°F], higher when sunny. Night temperatures should be 13-14°C [55-57°F] until the end of winter, rising to 16°C [62°F] in early spring and 18°C [65°F] from then on. Maintain a soil temperature of 13-15°C [55-60°F] and avoid draughts.

Remove the leaves below the bottom truss, in stages during the first three weeks, to provide a clear space below the crop and to allow the air to circulate freely above the soil.

Remove all sideshoots as soon as they appear. Smokers should use a sharp knife which is cleaned before touching each plant, as tomatoes are related to the tobacco plant and nicotine-stained fingers can transmit disease.

GROWING IN A GREENHOUSE

1. *Support plants by twining with fillis string tied to horizontal wires at top and bottom of greenhouse. Tie string to top wire as in inset for easy removal later.*

2. *Remove leaves below bottom truss in stages during first three weeks for free air circulation.*

3. *If dry and sunny, spray plants with water in mornings to encourage pollination of flowers.*

4. *Mulch plants with peat to conserve moisture, and keep well-watered. Shade from hot sun with blinds.*

5. *Remove growing tip at top wire at least three leaves beyond last truss, to ensure truss sets.*

Water lightly until the plants have set about 1½ trusses. Too much water in the early stages leads to soft, sappy growth. But take care not to let the roots get dry; lack of water is one of the greatest causes of failure. When the plants need water they must be thoroughly soaked; from mid- to late summer they might need soaking twice a day, and may take 4.5 L [1 gal] of water at a time. A peat mulch helps conserve moisture. Protect the plants from fierce summer sun with shading blinds.

Tomato flowers do not set well in a dry atmosphere so spray the plants with water in the mornings if it is sunny. This overhead damping should begin when the first flower opens and continue until the last flower has set. Although this will also help dislodge pollen, a further insurance is to either tap the trusses sharply, or use the tip of a small clean paint brush or a pellet of cotton wool to transfer the pollen from one flower to another.

Liquid feed the plants regularly according to manufacturer's instructions; it is usually advisable to start feeding when the fruits are the size of a marble, but if they are growing very well, feeding can be delayed for a little while. In general, tomatoes require high-potash feeds for the first half of the season, and high nitrogen towards the end of it. Greenhouse tomatoes can develop up to ten trusses, though it is usual to stop the growing tip when it reaches the top wire. When pinching out the tip, do so at least three leaves beyond the last truss, to ensure that it sets. If top growth is spindly and there is a heavy set of fruit on the first four trusses, it is wise to cut out the spindly growth to just above one leaf.

Harvesting and aftercare

Pick tomatoes as they ripen, breaking the stalk off at the knuckle. Yellow or green tomatoes will ripen if picked and put in single layers in trays in a warm place. The tomato haulm will make good compost-heap material; the roots should be removed completely and destroyed, in case they are infected with soil-inhabiting fungus diseases.

RING CULTIVATION

Rings are bottomless containers usually made of 'whale-hide', 23 or 25 cm [9 or 10"] in diameter and 23 cm [9"] deep. Place the rings 38 cm [15"] apart in rows 45 cm [18"] apart on a bed of aggregate (coarse sand, pebbles or gravel) at least 15 cm [6"] deep. Fill the rings to within 1.5 cm [½"] of the top with a good potting compost two weeks before planting, to give the compost time to warm up. Water the compost and the aggregate two days before planting, which takes place at the same time as border-grown tomatoes.

The roots will draw their nutrients from the compost, but take up most of the liquid they need from the aggregate. Once the plants are in the rings give each about 1 L [2 pt] of water but do not water them again unless they wilt on a hot day. The roots should reach the aggregate, which should be kept watered, in 10 days; after this, only the aggregate should be watered. In hot dry weather each

The single-stemmed variety Moneymaker is a heavy cropper that can be grown outdoors or in a greenhouse.

METHODS OF TOMATO GROWING

Grow plants in potting compost in bottomless rings on a bed of aggregate, such as gravel. Once established, plants are watered via aggregate and fed via the rings.

Set bush tomatoes near back of slightly shaded, sun-facing frame and train them forwards.

Grow single-stem tomatoes on stakes in a trench and protect them with raised cloches until midsummer.

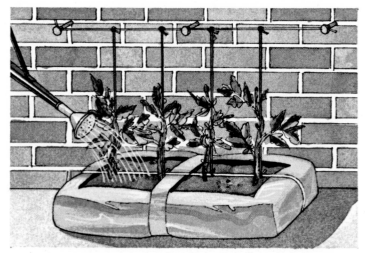

Single-stem plants can be grown in a peat bag against a sun-facing wall. Water as manufacturer instructs. Loop a fillis string around base of each plant stem and tie other end to a horizontal wire held on wall with nails.

plant will need about 2 L [3¾ pt] of water each day; less in cool, dull weather. Feeding is always given through the rings. Begin the regular weekly feed of a proprietary liquid feed high in potash when the fruit is forming on the first truss, at the rate of 1 L [2 pt] per plant. Make sure that the plants are adequately supported, with stakes put in about a week after planting, if growing outdoors, or with wire and fillis as for border plants. Topdress the plants with fresh potting compost or granulated peat halfway through the season, about 2.5 cm [1″] deep.

COLD GLASS AND CLOCHES

Germinate seed in late winter by one of the methods described in GROWING OUTDOORS, or buy in young plants. For a frame, choose a slightly shaded, south-facing site, or up against a south-facing wall. Prepare the soil during winter as for outdoor plants then, two weeks before planting, water generously, put the lights on and let the soil warm up. Just before planting in mid spring, give a topdressing of garden compost mixed with a quarter part of granulated peat and a sprinkling of bonemeal. Set the plants towards the back of the frame, with 45 cm [18″] between them if bush types and train forwards; otherwise plant 45 cm [18″] apart each way and support with a stake. Keep the bush types off the soil with a layer of straw or wire netting. Thereafter treat all types as for outdoor varieties.

Cloches can be used in two ways: they can be left on to protect bush types throughout the season, or they can be put over single-stem plants from planting time until midsummer, and then taken off or up-ended along the row for the rest of the season. Prepare the soil for both methods as for outdoor cultivation; then, for the second method, dig a V-shaped trench 15 cm [6″] deep, 30 cm [12″] wide at the top and 15 cm [6″] at the bottom, a week before planting, and mix the same topdressing into the bottom of the trench as was used for frame growing. In warm districts, planting can take place from mid spring, a little later in cooler areas. Plant bush varieties 90 cm [3′] apart, and single-stemmed kinds 45 cm [18″]. The cloches can be raised even more by putting them on bricks, and tall barn cloches will give greater height still. Remove them when the growing tip of the single-stemmed kinds is about to touch the top, and then treat as for outdoor tomatoes.

CONTAINER GROWING

Even without a garden a small quantity of tomatoes can be raised in containers such as pots, peat bags or troughs on patios and balconies. Tomatoes grown out of doors in containers require the same treatment as those grown in the open garden. They can be grown by ring culture outdoors. If grown in any container except a peat bag, they must have 17.5 cm [7″] minimum depth of compost. Supply a reliable growing compost and feed regularly with a proprietary liquid fertilizer. Take care that tomatoes grown in peat bags do not become waterlogged or dry out, by watering exactly as the manufacturers instruct.

PESTS AND DISEASES

Tomatoes, especially those grown in greenhouses, are

vulnerable to a host of pests and diseases, the most serious and common of which are: leafmould, *Verticillium* wilt, canker, sundry viruses and whitefly.

Leafmould (*Cladosporium fulvum*) is a fungus disease producing pale yellow spots on the upper surface of the leaves, with a brown fur on the undersurface in these areas. The leaves die completely and plants can be destroyed. A stagnant moist atmosphere is often responsible, especially if this occurs at night. Remove the most badly affected leaves and spray the plants with benomyl.

Verticillium wilt, or sleepy disease, is a soil borne fungus disease which invades the roots. The plant wilts at the top during the daytime, but recovers at night, then the bottom leaves do the same and start to turn yellow; finally the whole plant wilts permanently and dies. The stem is stained brown internally from the base upwards. Badly affected plants should be removed complete and destroyed; others may be helped by spraying overhead during the day, shading the greenhouse, and mulching close against the stem to induce new roots. The soil should be sterilized before planting tomatoes again.

Canker (*Didymella lycopersici*) affects the stems, first at the base and higher up later in the season, as brown sunken streaks, and the plant dies. Painting with maneb solution as soon as seen may stop it spreading.

Virus diseases are numerous, for instance fern leaf, in which the leaves are reduced to thread-like growths; spotted wilt, which produces brown leaves at the tip, a stunted plant and brown spots on the fruit; mosaic, which turns the leaves mottled yellow and green; and streak, resulting in plants spotted and streaked with brown. Destroy all infected plants completely.

Whitefly can be very troublesome, feeding on the undersurface of the young leaves as the plant grows, so that growth is stunted, leaves curled, grey-green and sticky, with black patches; in a bad infestation the plants die. Spray with resmethrin as soon as seen, or use the parasitic wasp *Encarsia formosa*, if available. The green-brown caterpillars of the tomato moth can do great damage to the leaves; two sorts of eelworm can infest the roots and potato blight the top growth (*see* POTATO). Grey mould may be a problem, also greenfly and red spider mite.

Fruits with green shoulders which do not turn red are afflicted with greenback, due to lack of potash, or too much or too strong sun. Blotchy ripening, in which fruit is yellow and red, can be due to lack of potash also, and too great a contrast between day and night temperatures. Blossom-end rot of fruit shows as sunken black patches at the blossom end, due to irregular supplies of water; cracking of nearly ripe fruit is for the same reason. Leaves bright yellow between veins, gradually yellowing all over and withering is due to magnesium deficiency, and often occurs where too much potash has been given, which the plant takes up in preference to magnesium. Spray the plants with a solution of 60 g [2 oz] Epsom Salts (magnesium sulphate) in 4.5 L [1 gal] of water, using a fine mist spray, as soon as the first yellowing is seen. The condition known as dry set results in flowers falling or fruits remaining the size of a pinhead; this is due to a dry atmosphere at pollination; spray with water in morning.

Turnip

The hardy turnip can be grown all year round. The swollen root stores well, while the leafy tops are a useful spring green, rich in iron and vitamin C.

Cultivated in Europe since the earliest times, the turnip root consists of about 90% water, but has the same vitamin C content as potatoes. The leaves have a significant iron content and are rich in vitamin C.

Turnips were formerly regarded as autumn and winter crops, but with good cultivation and the correct choice of varieties they can now be harvested all year round. In the gardening cycle they can be regarded as three distinct crops and different varieties are selected for each. Early turnips are those which, as quite small roots, are ready to harvest from mid spring to early summer. They may be grown in a hot bed in a frame, or started in greenhouses or outdoors under cloches. Maincrop turnips are sown in summer to produce roots 7.5-10 cm [3-4"] in diameter in the autumn. These can be used straight from the garden or stored for winter use. Finally, there are turnips grown, either in spring or autumn, for their leaves, which are cooked like cabbage. Roots left in the ground through the winter will produce leaves in early spring unless the weather is severe.

Suitable site and soil

Turnips require an open, sunny position. If grown in the shade of trees they will produce foliage rather than roots.

Turnip
Brassica rapa (fam. *Cruciferae*)
Hardy biennial.
Size: roots harvested when 7.5-10 cm [3-4"] across, but can grow much larger; leaves to 30 cm [12"].
Climate: temperate.
Sowing to harvesting time: maincrop 10-12 weeks; early crops 4-6 weeks.
Yield: average root weighs 250-450 g [½-1 lb], but can be much heavier.

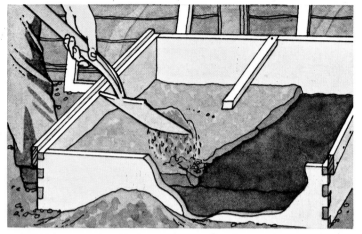

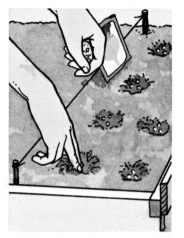

1. Prepare a hot-bed in a frame for growing early turnips, covering the 15 cm [6″] layer of manure with good soil.

2. Sow 3 seeds in each hole, spaced 12.5 cm [5″] apart.

3. Thin seedlings to one per hole. Give plenty of air.

For early spring sowing, choose an early, quick-growing variety. Sow thinly.

Maincrop turnips are sown in drills and thinned to 22-30 cm [9-12″] apart.

Hardy varieties can be left in the ground until needed, but pull less hardy.

Pull green 'turnip-tops' when they are 15 cm [6″].

This early turnip variety has purple-topped roots.

Many of the early varieties of turnip, which mature quickly have white roots.

Though they will grow in most types of soil, turnips do best in a rich loam. They like calcium and are grown extensively on chalk and limestone soils; they also need a soil well supplied with phosphates. Supply any enrichment that the soil may need in autumn or early winter, in the form of rotted organic matter, well before sowing time, and avoid the use of unrotted farmyard manure. If lime is needed, allow at least six weeks to elapse before an application which follows farm manure. If the maincrop follows early potatoes or any other crop for which the land was manured, there is no need to give further dressings.

Sowing and care
In theory the gardener can grow a succession of crops from early spring to late autumn. Two crops are more practical, an early one harvested in spring or early summer, and a maincrop harvested in autumn and stored through the winter. An intermediate crop would coincide with the main summer vegetables.

For early spring sowing choose an early, quick-growing variety and start under glass or cloches. For the maincrop, sow in mid to late summer, again selecting a suitable variety. A further sowing in early autumn will provide green turnip-tops in spring, with a cutting if required in late autumn, within a few weeks of sowing.

The early varieties generally have white roots. A succession is provided by more white varieties, by white turnips with red or purple tops, and by golden ones. Certain white varieties with green tops are among the hardiest and the best for overwintering to supply early spring greens.

Sow seeds thinly 1.5 cm [½"] deep in drills 30-40 cm [12-16"] apart, thinning plants to a spacing of 23-30 cm [9-12"] for the maincrop. Early crops and turnips for greens can be grown with a narrower spacing of 15 cm [6"] between plants and rows. The germination temperature is 4-40°C [40-104°F]. The sowing to germination period varies according to temperature, but in reasonably warm weather germination is rapid and can be less than a week, otherwise it may take up to 12 days. Turnips should not be transplanted.

Turnips are susceptible to drought and should be kept well watered, especially in the early stages. Good, well-flavoured, tender turnips will only be obtained if they are kept growing fast and continuously. Hoe frequently to aerate the soil and control weeds.

Growing in frames
A quick crop of early turnips can be grown in a garden frame, using compost from which some previous crop has been removed. Alternatively, you can put a 15 cm [6"] layer of warm, decaying farmyard manure in the frame and cover it with good soil. Insert seeds, two or three together, in holes about 12.5 cm [5"] apart in late winter. Thin to one per hole when the plants are large enough to handle. The bed can be covered by sacks or mats to help retain the heat and promote quick germination, but these should be removed after seedlings have appeared. Allow plenty of air after this and water moderately every day. It should be possible to harvest a crop within four to eight weeks.

Harvesting and aftercare
Turnips should grow quickly and be harvested while still young and tender. If they are allowed to remain in the soil too long, or if growth is checked (by drought, for example) the interior of the roots will become fibrous and tasteless. Turnips are pulled from the ground, and the leaves cut off. When harvesting for storing, leave about 2.5 cm [1"] of green attached to the root. The less hardy types of turnips should be out of the ground before the onset of hard frosts, but the hardier varieties can withstand a moderately mild winter and may be pulled as required. The spring crop of leaves may be picked or cut at any time after they are about 10-15 cm [4-6"] high.

For winter use, grow hardy varieties which can remain in the ground until needed. Alternatively, store in layers in boxes of dry sand or peat, or in heaps or clamps covered with a layer of soil and straw. The tops should first be cut off, but not too closely.

It is possible to leave a few small plants in the ground and harvest the leaves which they produce next spring. As soon as they form flowerheads, however, scrap them.

To avoid pests and diseases, clear away all surplus roots and the remains of vegetation after harvesting and take them to the compost heap.

Pests and diseases
Turnips are subject to all the pests and diseases of brassicas; the most troublesome is the turnip flea-beetle (*Phyllotreta* species). For their treatment *see* CABBAGE. Soft rot may attack roots in store.

Zucchini

Appreciated for their delicate flavour, zucchini are marrows which are picked while still very young and tender.

The popularity of zucchini as a vegetable delicacy has increased enormously in recent years. In addition to the traditional dark green variety there is a less well-known type which bears gold-coloured fruits. Both are equally delicious lightly steamed or fried, used in vegetable or meat dishes or raw in salads. Zucchini may also be stuffed, like marrows, with a savoury meat or cheese mixture.

Suitable site and soil
Since zucchini are baby bush marrows, the plants from which they come require the same growing conditions as those which provide adult marrows. For preparation of the site *see* MARROW. Remember that an open sunny position and a rich soil are essential.

Sowing and planting
Follow directions for MARROW. Take care to harden off the young plants gradually as a sudden drop in temperature can be fatal. A cold frame is valuable for this process, which usually takes place in late spring. Remove the top of the frame during the daytime only, then gradually expose the plants to the night air.

If no frame is available, expose the plants to outdoor temperatures for an hour or so during the day, increasing the length of time slowly. The plants should be ready for planting out in early summer, when the risk of frost is minimal. Space them 60 cm [2'] apart.

Care and development
Remember that plants providing zucchini should be grown like marrows without check — generous watering is vital if the embryo fruits are to swell; otherwise they are shed prematurely and the plants themselves take time to recover from the lack of water.

Keep the soil moist but not sodden and water regularly, particularly during dry weather. Take care not to splash the young stems with water because of the danger of collar rot (*see* CUCUMBER). Pollination by hand is unnecessary. Weed when necessary, taking care not to damage the young fruit. Give regular doses of liquid manure as soon as fruiting begins.

Harvesting the crop
Pick zucchini as soon as they are 5-10 cm [2-4"] long. Fruit can be left on the plants to grow into mature marrows, to a maximum length of 25 cm [10"], but this practice is not desirable as it discourages further fruit production.

Pests and diseases
Plants providing zucchini are vulnerable to cucumber mosaic virus (*see* CUCUMBER) and mildew (*see* MARROW). Red spider mites and slugs may also be a problem.

The yellow zucchini flower. Keep picking young fruits regularly and more female flowers and fruits develop.

The golden zucchini is a less familiar variety, but its butter-yellow fruits are just as tender and delicious.

Zucchini
Cucurbita pepo ovifera (fam. *Cucurbitaceae*), also known as courgette and baby marrow.
Half-hardy annual.
Size: Fruits at their best when 5-20 cm [2-8"] long; plant kept by pruning to 1.2 m [4'] square.
Sowing to harvesting time: 10-14 weeks.
Yield: About 20-30 fruit per plant.

BASIC GARDENING GUIDE

Planning your garden

Start by listing the crops you want to grow. For planning, it helps to divide them into four basic categories:

1. Quick-return, seasonal crops: greens, root crops and salads.

2. Quick-return, permanent crops: herbs, cane fruit and strawberries.

3. Long-term, permanent crops: apples, pears, plums, rhubarb.

4. Luxury crops: e.g. asparagus, globe artichokes and cardoons.

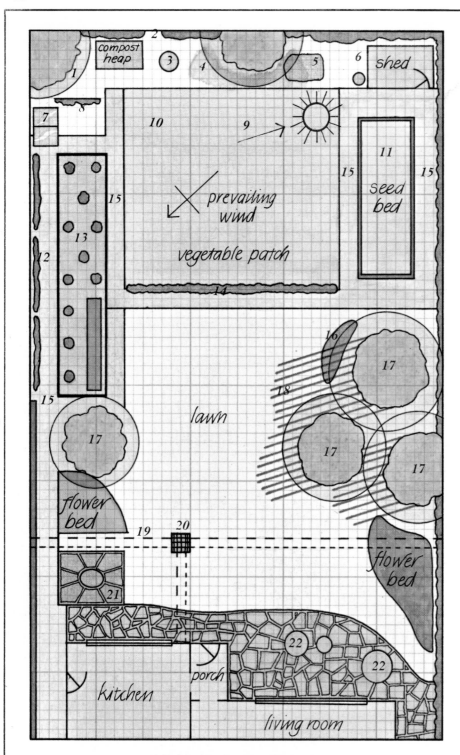

DRAWING UP A PLAN

KEY TO PLAN

1. Measure extent of main roots of trees and allow for this.
2. Gap in hedge at bottom of sloping garden to allow frost to escape and prevent frost pocket developing.
3. Incinerator sited far enough from crops for heat to do no damage.
4. Wet area of garden avoided.
5. Rhubarb will tolerate shade from trees and damp ground.
6. Garden shed and waterbutt accessible via path.
7. Cold frame sited against sun-facing wall for maximum warmth.
8. Loganberry grown on trellis to hide compost heap and incinerator from view.
9. Work out which areas receive the most sun.
10. Vegetable patch sited in sunny part of garden, protected from prevailing winds by hedges and trees, well drained.
11. Seed bed sited next to vegetable patch, protected from strong sunlight (kills seedlings), well drained.
12. Tender fruit (e.g. peaches) grown against sun-facing wall.
13. Soft fruit grown within protection of fruit cage.
14. Hedge grown to screen view of vegetable patch from house.
15. Paths laid down (and use made of existing ones) to link important areas of garden and to link garden to kitchen: paths should be wide enough to take wheelbarrow etc.
16. Alpine strawberries will tolerate partial shade from fruit tree.
17. Fruit trees planted in frost-free positions; allow for future spread of trees.
18. Measure shade cast by trees and allow for it when planning.
19. Locate house drainage system and avoid it when cultivating.
20. Locate house drainage inspection chamber and do not cover it (or cover it with a movable container).
21. Herb garden sited in dry, sunny part of garden near kitchen.
22. Fruit or vegetables growing in containers. Fit these with castors to make them movable.

Siting the plot

Once you have decided which crops you would like to grow, you must gather facts about your garden. Where you would like to have the plot is not necessarily the best place for suitable growing conditions. There are several factors to consider in determining the position of vegetables.

Good light is essential; most vegetables and fruit will not grow in shade.

Soil drainage is important; waterlogged soil will cause crops to rot and encourages many diseases.

Frost pockets tend to form at the base of sloping sites against solid fences, walls and hedges, and it is safer to avoid such pockets when planning the garden. Frost damage in spring is associated with fruit crops, but it can be just as destructive to any newly-emerged vegetables.

Drawing up a garden plan

1. Find out the overall dimensions, the exact shape of the garden and the position of the house.
2. Note where house drains are. If in doubt, try to obtain the plans of your house. The vegetable garden will have to be placed to avoid these drains.
3. Note the position of trees, and especially the area of shade they cast on the ground. Try to estimate the spread of their roots; extensive root systems of trees will compete with vegetables for water nutrients.
4. Mark in areas that receive most sun.
5. Note any wet areas where drainage may be needed.
6. Find out the direction of prevailing winds. This is important if screening is desired for the protection of crops on very exposed sites.
7. Mark the position of existing paving borders, shed and any other structures if you do not intend to move them. From all this information you can make an accurate drawing of the garden to assess which parts are most suitable for vegetable and fruit growing and how large a plot can be planned. Graph paper, marked out in squares, will make the job much easier. Use a simple scale and keep the plan big.

Having decided on the size, the next step is to find out how to make the best use of the space. Look up in the A-Z section the amount of space to allow between individual plants and between the rows of specified crops, their sowing time and their harvesting time. In addition, the expected yield of each crop given here helps you plan on a row-by-row basis in relation to your eating requirements.

Understanding crop rotation

The purpose of crop rotation is twofold: to gain the best possible return from the soil and to keep certain devastating pests and diseases in check. Growing the same crop on the same patch of soil year after year is inefficient, because the crop will gradually use up the nutrients it needs most, while the other nutrients will be very little depleted. Also the roots of different crops grow to different depths, so that growing only one crop will exhaust the nutrients at one level.

Crop rotation makes more economic use of garden compost and manure because some crops respond best to fresh application of rotted organic material, while others do well on land that has been prepared for previous crops.

Crop rotation can also solve the problem of disease. For example, club root, a fungus disease which attacks brassica crops, is highly infectious. Control is very difficult because the disease can linger in the soil for years, even when brassicas are no longer grown there. Severe attacks are brought on by continuous cropping of the same piece of ground, causing a slight infestation to increase rapidly. Crop rotation prevents the disease from building up.

Always move vegetables around every year, even if the garden is too small to group crops into separate, neat beds. A rotation system can extend over as many years as you want, but the simplest method is to divide a vegetable garden into three plots, of roughly the same size, excluding any perennial beds. (Perennials such as globe artichokes and asparagus have to stay in one place and so do not enter a rotation system.)

The cycle of one of the plots over three years follows this outline:

First year: Everything except roots and brassicas. Manure or garden compost is applied during the winter and the ground is dug over well. On this plot grow crops that need the richest soil conditions — peas, beans, celery, leeks, lettuces, onions, beet and spinach.

Second year: Roots. Now the plot will be used for raising root crops — beets, carrots, parsnips and potatoes, but not swedes and turnips because they are brassicas. All these do well on soil that has been manured the previous year. The breaking up of the lower layers of

the soil by deep-rooting crops helps improve its structure for subsequent crops of shallow-rooting vegetables.

Third year: Brassicas. In the last year of the cycle the plot is used for shallow-rooting brassicas — cabbages, cauliflowers, broccoli, Brussels sprouts, kale, swedes and turnips. All brassicas like a firm soil to encourage stable root systems. Since the soil has been cultivated in the first two years, it is only necessary to fork it over lightly for most brassicas. Cauliflowers, Brussels sprouts, swedes and turnips, however, like deeply-dug, well-manured ground. Cauliflowers also do best in freshly-manured soil.

Intercropping and catch cropping

Quickly-maturing crops, such as lettuce and radishes, may be 'intercropped' between rows of maincrops. They will be ready for harvesting when the maincrop is still growing. Such quick growing vegetables can also be 'catch-cropped' on a bed left vacant between maincrops.

A flexible system

You may choose to start with all three beds at once, starting each one at a different 'year'. Alternatively you may begin with one first year bed, turn it over to roots in the second year and start another first year bed, gradually building up a three-bed rotation system. If you have room for only one plot, simply follow the cycle through, starting with the First Year crops.

While some potatoes can be grown in a Second Year bed, to grow a year's supply for the average family requires as much as 9 sq m [30 sq ft]. Those with large enough gardens can work to a four-bed rotation system with potatoes grown alone as the second of four crops. The potatoes leave behind a clean, enriched and finely broken-up soil that is ideal for the root crop to follow.

Successional sowing

If you sow all the seed of a particular vegetable variety on the same day, you will be faced with a glut of the crop during the few weeks of harvesting time, and nothing at all during the rest of the year.

Instead, by making several smaller 'successional' sowings of the crop at intervals during the growing season, you will be able to harvest the crop over a longer period; also the plants have more chance of surviving pests, diseases, drought or other troubles if the sowing is spread out in this way.

Another method of achieving the same result is by sowing different varieties which need different lengths of time to mature. The first sowing is of an early variety, the next of a maincrop type and the final one of a late variety.

BASIC CROP ROTATION THREE YEAR CYCLE

	Bed 1	Bed 2	Bed 3
First year	Other Crops	Brassicas	Roots
Second year	Roots	Other Crops	Brassicas
Third year	Brassicas	Roots	Other Crops

Choosing your fruit

Both fruit and vegetables have their proper place in the kitchen garden. Fruit trees give a very high return in relation to the area of ground occupied, and fruit requires less continual attention and number of hours' work than vegetables. Although the initial outlay for fruit is greater than with vegetables, and there is usually a couple of years' delay before the first crop, soft fruit continues to crop for 10 to 15 years once established, and tree fruits will continue for 20 to 50 years.

Where to grow
When planning your garden think, if possible, in terms of grouping all your fruit together in one plot. This makes protection against birds easier; it facilitates spraying and reduces the risk of spray damage to adjacent crops. It also makes manuring easier.

Do not be deterred, however, if you have no orchard space. In an average garden there are many suitable spaces that are impractical for vegetables but useful for fruit. Fans, espaliers and cordons can be trained against the house outbuildings and boundary walls. Fruit can be made an ornamental feature. Cordon apples and pears, and in suitable climates chinese gooseberries and grapes, can be trained over pergolas. Both tree and cane fruit can be trained on wire fences separating one part of the garden from the other, and low one-tier espaliers make an attractive edging to the kitchen garden.

Fruit in general require full sun. Raspberries, blackcurrants, blackberries and loganberries are the most tolerant of partial shade. Shaded walls may be used for training gooseberries and red and white currants as cordons, and for blackberries, loganberries and Morello cherries. Remember that your trees — and fruit grown on fences — will themselves cast a shadow, so plan their positioning to avoid your vegetable garden losing much-needed sun.

Planning your requirements
Think very carefully about your planning; it may be some years before mistakes are revealed, and then you have lost both time and money. Check the yield of the mature tree, bush or cane before buying it, and plan to spread out your harvest over the maximum period without a glut. If you have a home freezer or plan to bottle fruit, use your space intelligently; your family will tire of a single crop.

Many species crop over a couple of months at least. Choose varieties that will spread your harvest, and spread out the season to the uttermost for favourite fruit. In a very small space, it may be better to rely on shop produce at the height of the season, and grow your own for the early and late seasons, when the bought price is higher.

Take care with tree fruit, however. With apples, pears and many of the best plums, you will have to select varieties that flower at the same time (and therefore crop near together) in order to get cross-pollination. Even self-fertile varieties of these trees crop better when cross-pollinated.

Types of tree
When buying, choose three-year-old bush trees and two-year-old soft fruit. Do not imagine that by buying an older tree you will shorten the waiting time before mature cropping. Young trees transplant better, and if you buy those on dwarfing rootstock they will quickly come to bearing. Maiden trees, that is unformed one-year-olds, are cheaper and you can train them to your chosen shape, but cropping is more delayed.

Dwarfing rootstocks are available for apples and pears. These induce early cropping and ensure that the tree will never become too large for its garden surroundings. A standard, half-standard or even a full-size bush on a vigorous rootstock is too large for the average garden; it would require a ladder for picking and pruning, and many of the branches would be out of the reach of ordinary garden sprays.

Rootstocks are carefully classified and are bred vegetatively, so that they are always true to type. They influence the growth and behaviour of the tree, while having little effect on the flavour, size or appearance of the fruit.

The top part of the tree (known as the scion) is worked onto the rootstock by budding or grafting. To bud a tree, the nursery will make a slit in the bark or the stem of the rootstock soon after midsummer and bind into it a growth bud from the chosen variety with a little shield of bark.

Rootstocks conform to government standards and offer protection against disease. Scions are also taken from virus-tested mother trees where available. Rootstocks can also be chosen to suit a particular climatic area, to make the variety chosen more suitable to local conditions.

CROPPING SEASONS FOR FRUIT

Late winter:	Forced rhubarb.
Mid spring:	Strawberries forced in heated greenhouse, early forwarded rhubarb.
Late spring:	Early strawberries under cloches or tunnels, the first thinnings of gooseberries for cooking, rhubarb.
Early summer:	Gooseberry thinnings for cooking, strawberries in the open, early sweet cherries, black, red and white currants, raspberries.
Mid summer:	Early apples and pears, sweet cherries and cherry plums (Myrobalan), early plums, early peaches, nectarines and apricots. Loganberries and other hybrid berries, black currants, red and white currants, gooseberries, raspberries, strawberries, blueberries.
Late summer:	Early apples and pears, mid season peaches and nectarines, plums and gages, apricots, later sweet cherries and cooking cherries, blackberries and later hybrid berries, black currants, figs, gooseberries, late summer raspberries, perpetual strawberries, blueberries, mulberries, grapes from greenhouse and outdoors.
Early autumn:	Apples, pears, plums, damsons and grapes, late peaches and nectarines, blackberries, figs, autumn raspberries, perpetual strawberries, last of the blueberries, greenhouse, cloche-grown grapes and outdoor grapes.
Mid autumn:	Apples and pears, bullaces, quinces, perpetual strawberries, outdoor and greenhouse grapes, the last outdoor figs.
Late autumn:	Bullaces, apples, perpetual strawberries under cloches, late grapes.
Winter:	Stored apples, pears, grapes with stalks in water.

Garden hygiene

Cleanliness in the garden leads to healthy, heavily cropping plants, just as much as hygiene in the home ensures freedom from human and animal disease. Key points to remember are:

1. Keep the garden clear of various kinds of debris — bricks, stones, wood, logs, glass, old machinery and rotting weeds and leaves that are not made into a proper compost heap. Otherwise they will harbour slugs, woodlice and particularly mice.

2. Tools and machinery should be kept scrupulously clean.

3. Be on the alert for the first pest or rotting leaf on a plant. Destroy virus-infected plants as soon as seen; also badly diseased vegetation. Do not put them on the compost heap.

4. Roots of vegetables should be dug up when the tops have been harvested, die-back shoots on fruit pruned off and bonfire material burnt frequently instead of leaving it for months at a time.

5. Constant vigilance and control of weeds -- deal with them before they set seed. Out-of-the-way and unused patches of ground should be kept tidy and free from weeds, too.

Sterilization of the soil will free it from soil-borne pests and diseases. Wash down the interiors of greenhouses, frames and cloches and all greenhouse equipment with sterilizing solution.

DEALING WITH WEEDS

There are three groups of weeds: annuals, biennials and perennials.

The annuals have shallow roots and abundant seed. Annual weeds can usually be fairly easily controlled by regular hoeing off and digging up before the flowers develop and set seed, as they die when their tops are removed.

Biennial weeds tend to develop a swollen root or stem below the ground which stores food for flower and seed development in the second year. Few of these are troublesome; they should be destroyed in the first year.

Perennial weeds are difficult to deal with, as they mostly have tenacious and spreading root-systems, and will spread rapidly by means of these if not treated. Sporadic digging, hoeing and hand removal are ineffective, although regular removal of the top growth by cutting or mowing will eventually eradicate them. This prevents food being stored in the roots of rhizomes, which therefore die of starvation. Mulching the top growth heavily is a long term method of control.

Using weedkillers

Modern weedkillers fall into three groups also. Firstly the **non-selective** or total kinds; they kill all plant growth, weeds or not, and in general are applied to the soil, to be absorbed through the plants' roots. The use of these is limited to uncultivated areas such as paths, or ground which needs to be cleared for future use, and they include sodium chlorate, dichlobenil and simazine. One or two, however, are suitable for use around crops, at much less concentrated rates. Secondly, there are the **selective** or hormone types, which are applied in solution to the top growth through which they are absorbed and then circulate round the plant's system in the sap. These mostly deal with broad-leaved plants. If painted or sponged carefully on to the weeds growing amongst crops, there should be no harm to the crop, as its top growth will not have been treated. Such weedkillers include those known as 2,4-D, 2,4,5-T, MCPA, mecoprop and so on. Finally there are the **residuals,** which are formulated to control and kill weed seeds in the soil as they germinate. These are applied in solution to the soil, and can usually be put on before or, with care, after sowing or planting. They can be effective for up to ten weeks. The residual herbicides include chloroxuron, chlorpropham and propachlor. With all these it is extremely important to follow the manufacturers' directions exactly.

STERILIZATION

Soil used for potting, propagation and greenhouse growing does not have the normal benefit of crop rotation. The soil becomes 'unhealthy' and pests and diseases associated with a particular plant can accumulate. These must be destroyed by sterilization if good growth is to continue. The alternative is to change the soil every three years — a costly and laborious job.

Soil can be sterilized by heat or by chemicals. Although heat sterilization is more thorough and heat-treated soil is ready for immediate use, chemicals are more convenient and less expensive for the home gardener.

Chemical sterilization

The main chemical sterilants are formaldehyde and cresylic acid, which are diluted according to the maker's instructions and watered into the soil where they change into gases. Another chemical sterilant is dazomet, which is applied in solid form. These are all selective in their action — formaldehyde is more effective against diseases than pests, while cresylic acid destroys pests more thoroughly than fungi. Remember that all chemical sterilants can irritate the skin, eyes, nose and mouth, so use them with care.

Method

1. Sterilants cannot spread properly through soil that is too wet. It should be just wet enough to retain its shape when pressed in the hand.

2. The temperature of the soil should be between 16-26°C [60-80°F].

3. If dealing with the soil of the greenhouse floor, dig it 15-20 cm [6-8"] deep before sterilizing it. Make sure the soil is free from clods and lumps.

4. Sterilization is perfectly safe in the open air, but in the confined space of the greenhouse it should not be done near growing plants. Add 5 L [1 gal] dilute solution of formaldehyde to 0.03 cu m [1 cu ft] soil, and mix thoroughly with a spade. The best results are obtained from sandy soils; soils high in clay and humus may need a higher dosage. Cover the heap with a plastic sheet or sacking for 48 hours.

5. Remove the cover and spread the soil out to dry. Turn the soil over several times during the next few weeks to clear the fumes. The soil must not be used for planting for at least six weeks.

6. As pests and diseases can be harboured in cracks, apply the chemical thoroughly around walls and any supporting posts. Remember to spray or wash the inside of the greenhouse before starting on the soil.

Heat sterilization

Soil treated with heat can be used immediately. There are a number of different methods. A **steam sterilizer** consists of a galvanized water tank enclosing a metal soil container which fits tightly over a water trough, heated electrically from below. Follow the maker's instructions. **Boiling** is an alternative. Trays of potting compost can be sterilized by thoroughly drenching with boiling water. To sterilize very small quantities of soil, bring 0.3 L [½ pt] of water to the boil in a 3.4 L [6 pt] saucepan, then fill to within 1.5 cm [½"] of the top with very dry soil, cover tightly and boil for 7 minutes. Remove from heat. Be sure to follow quantity and timing instructions exactly. Cool for another 7 minutes before removing the lid. **Electrode sterilizers,** made from metal, consist of a box containing electrical plates. Soil is packed around these, and a current is passed through it, warming it up. Follow the maker's instructions.

Tools

A gardener's tools will be in constant use, so buy the best tools you can possibly afford — they do a better job and last much longer. The basic tools are the spade, fork, hoe, trowel and rake. Apart from the tools described below, there are a few other items which are very useful. For hoses and watering cans, *see* WATERING. A pair of gardening gloves is essential for pruning and can be worn for almost any gardening job to protect the hands. A wheelbarrow is usually indispensable. Choose a galvanized barrow and not a painted steel one. There are many different makes available; balance is the most important factor to bear in mind, so try out the barrow with something in it before buying. If you have a small garden and no room for a barrow, a sturdy plastic bin will do instead.

A sieve or riddle, of 1.5 cm [½"] mesh will enable you to refine your own soil, compost or leaf mould, thus saving you money. A ladder or step-ladder is very useful for pruning or harvesting large fruit trees; this should be either hardwood or rustproof aluminium. When you finish using any tools, always clean them. Rinse off all dirt, dry and then wipe with a little oil. After cleaning, tools should be put away somewhere reasonably dry and clean. The tidiest method of storage is to hang them on sturdy nails or hooks in a shed or on a protected wall. Smaller implements can fit on a shelf. Never leave tools lying on the ground or floor — they can cause accidents.

1. Watering can
This is the most useful shape. Metal cans are more serviceable than plastic. *See* WATERING section.

2. The spade
The spade, the most basic of all garden tools, is used for heavy digging. A full-sized standard spade with a blade 30 cm [1'] long and 20 cm [8"] wide is ideal. Make sure the join between the shaft and blade is strong. Spades come in different weights, so choose one to suit you. The 'D'-shaped and 'Y'-shaped handles are least tiring to use.

3. Digging fork
The fork breaks the soil into small lumps. A digging fork usually has four tines (prongs). As with spades, there are different sizes, weights and types of handle. The tines of a good fork should twang like a tuning fork.

4. Potato fork
Used for lifting potatoes, this will spare the potatoes but let the soil through.

5. Manure fork
Farmyard manure will be difficult to shake off from an ordinary fork when it is to be spread. The answer is a manure fork which has three short, round tines from which the manure slips off.

6. The rake
The rake combs out small stones from the surface of the soil, producing the fine tilth needed for sowing seeds. Rake heads come in various sizes but a 23 cm [9"] one is a good size. There are different-shaped heads but those cut from one piece of metal are strongest. A wooden rake is also useful for clearing up garden refuse.

7. Dutch hoe
Hoes loosen the top layer of compacted soil and cut off young weed seedlings. Ideally, you should have a small and large hoe for different row sizes.
The Dutch hoe, which should be the smaller one, is held with the handle low enough to keep the blade nearly parallel with the soil surface, skimming just beneath it to cut or uproot weedlets. Work pushing the blade away from you.

8. Draw hoe
The handle of a draw hoe is held higher than the Dutch hoe, and is worked towards you with an up-and-down chopping movement. This should be the larger hoe. The draw hoe is also used for 'earthing-up' and making seed drills.

9. Five-pronged cultivator
This is a very useful tool that does the same job as the hoes, but covers a larger area more quickly.

10. Hand trowel
The hand trowel is for potting and planting out seedlings. Short-handled types are much less tiring than long-handled ones. Buy a trowel with a tough blade welded or riveted to the handle; pressed steel blades are cheaper but are a false economy.

11. Hand fork
This complements the hand trowel and can be used for sticky clay soils.

12. Dibber
The dibber makes clean neat holes for planting seedlings. Metal tipped or wooden types are available, or you can make your own from the top of an old wooden spade handle.

13. Garden line
The garden line is essential for making straight and parallel drills. You can make it yourself with two sharp sticks, about 30 cm [1'] long and a piece of thick, strong cord a little longer than the rows you are planting.

14. Measuring stick
Some gardeners dispense with this, and guess sowing distances. However seeds are becoming expensive and it is annoying to find you have some left over because you misjudged distances. You can buy a stick but it is much cheaper to make your own; use a 2 m [6'] length of lath and mark it with paint or cut notches every 15 cm [6"].

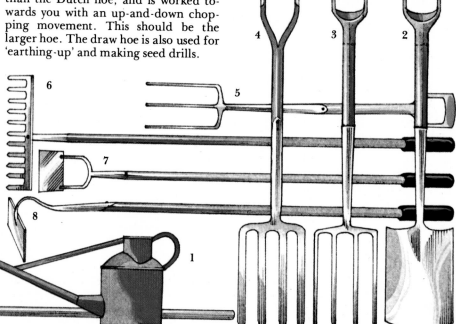

15. Secateurs
Secateurs are essential if you are growing fruit. Only buy the best, as blunt blades do irreparable damage.

16. Long-handled pruner
This is used for pruning high branches of fruit trees. It works on a lever system, with a handle at the bottom to move the small hook blade at the top.

17. Pruning saw
For thick branches which secateurs will not cut, use a pruning saw. This has a sharp blade which may be slightly curved.

18. Gardener's knife
The gardener's knife has many uses, from pruning small branches to crop harvesting. Buy a good quality knife and always keep it sharp.

19. Syringes and sprayers
Both of these have two functions: to apply liquid insecticides when needed, and also water when moisture is required. The best types have 2 or 3 nozzles, for fine and coarse sprays. The barrel should be of non-corrodible alloy. Sprayers with double-acting pumps give a continuous spray after initial pumping. Syringes are useful for applying small amounts of liquid. Both syringes and sprayers should be washed out with clean water after spraying a chemical.

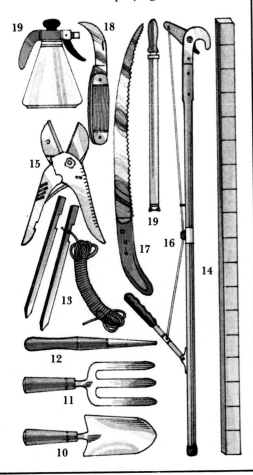

Improving the soil

The importance of humus
Humus is an organic substance obtained from decayed plant and animal matter. Manure, compost, seaweed etc. are all humus-supplying materials. Humus is essential to good soil texture and there is seldom enough already in garden soil. It must be added regularly in proportion to the intensity of cultivation.

Types of soil
The basic soils are clay, sand and loam, and these fundamentally differ only in the size of the grains that make up their structure.
Loam is a soil composed of clay, silt, sand and organic matter; it is ideal for the majority of crops — well-drained, warming up quickly and retaining nutrients over a long period. Improvements to other types of soil are made to bring them nearer to the composition of loam.
Clay soil is made up of small particles, which are closely packed. Because of its physical properties, water is held in it and it can become wet and waterlogged. Properly conditioned clay soil can be very fertile because it retains nutrients. To improve a clay soil, add rotting organic, fibrous material and some coarse sand to open up the structure, mixing both well into the top spit. You can help break up a clay soil further by adding lime in winter if it is at all acid (then leave about two months' gap before adding any farm manure), or gypsum if already alkaline, as this has a neutral reaction. Never attempt to work a clay soil when it is wet — it may set like cement and be very difficult to break down subsequently.
Sandy soil is made up of comparatively large particles. Water runs through it rapidly, carrying away plant foods, and it dries very quickly. Properly conditioned, it has the advantage of excellent drainage and easy penetration by plant roots, as well as warming up quickly in spring, making it very suitable for early crops. To improve a sandy soil, again add coarse organic material, to give it sponge-like bulk and hold it together.
You can tell, with practice, which kind of soil you have by feeling it when wet. A clay type will be definitely sticky and clinging; a sandy one will feel gritty, and a loam, if squeezed in the hand when moist but not saturated, should fall apart with a gentle tap.

Soil testing
Beyond basic improvement of soil types, the most common problems are highly acid and highly alkaline soils. In a too-acid soil many nutrients dissolve in large quantities, which are damaging to plant roots. In an excessively alkaline one, some plant foods are insoluble so that, although they are present, the plant roots cannot absorb them. The plant then suffers from a deficiency and shows symptoms of illness accordingly.
A simple soil test kit bought from a garden centre or garden shop will help assess the soil to determine the degree of acidity or alkalinity — the pH value. Inexpensive soil test kits are based on indicator solutions — coloured dyes that change in tint during the test. Precise instructions are given with each type of kit sold, but the principle is that samples of soil are taken from the area in question, shaken up with water and indicator solution and allowed to settle. The colour of the resultant solution is then compared to a test card of colour bands. The band which matches gives the reading of pH value.

Redressing the balance
If the soil is too acid, add lime at the rates suggested in the directions. The addition of lime to a very acid soil not only ensures that plants do not suffer from poisonously great quantities of nutrient, but it also helps a great deal in improving the soil structure of heavy clay soils. Further, some vegetable diseases thrive in acid soils, and lime is a necessity if vulnerable crops are to be grown. Lime also supplies calcium, a necessary nutrient.
There are various types of lime: chalk (calcium carbonate), good for light soils; hydrated lime (air-slaked lime); ground lime, like chalk but slower-acting; quicklime (calcium oxide), caustic and best used on vacant ground; gypsum (calcium sulphate), neutral in reaction, and magnesium limestone, containing magnesium.
If the soil is too alkaline, build up the soil depth if possible and add an acid-reacting fertilizer such as sulphate of ammonia and/or organic matter, which buffers the effect of the alkalinity.

Making a compost heap

Garden compost is a mixture of vegetable waste materials which are collected together in a special container or an enclosed heap and left to rot down. Properly made and well rotted, it can take the place of animal manures and do just as much good when added to the soil. It is always necessary to add some organic matter to the soil to supply plants with nutrients and to give the soil a good structure. Fertilizers will provide food but no humus; only rotted organic matter can supply this substance. It is vital if plants growing in soil are to develop satisfactorily, especially vegetables.

Making your own garden compost
Animal manures and other organic matter are often difficult to obtain and sometimes rather expensive. If you cannot obtain any or want to cut down on expenses, you can make your own garden compost very easily and at virtually no cost.
In order to make good compost, certain conditions will be necessary:
1. Air to supply oxygen
2. Moisture
3. Warmth, both within and outside the heap.
4. Nitrogen
All these enable the bacteria which work on the organic matter to live and multiply. A closely compressed heap without air, with too much or too little water, or with not enough warmth or nitrogen will not allow the heap to rot because the bacteria cannot live.

What goes on the heap
You can make the heap of any soft vegetative material: leaves, stems, grass mowings, flowers and so on. All these will supply nitrogen. Large stalks and roots, like those from cauliflowers, Brussels sprouts and similar plants will only rot quickly if they are split in half from top to bottom. If you do not think this worthwhile, leave them out of your heap. Equally, tough woody stems, leathery or evergreen leaves, bark and wood do not rot quickly enough and should not be used. Nor should the heap be regarded as a dump for stones, glass, plastic or any other rubbish. Disease and pest-ridden plants should be burned, as should really bad weeds, any

self-propagating rhizomes and all weed seeds, in case the heap does not heat up sufficiently to kill them. You can also put kitchen vegetable waste on the heap — potato peelings, fruit skins, cabbage leaves, and so on. Crushed egg shells will not rot down but are good to add for their calcium content. Coffee grounds and tea leaves are also excellent additions. Bones, fat, cheese rind or similar waste must not be put on the heap because they will attract rats and mice.
The size of the heap will depend on how much garden material you have. Grass cuttings are best to form the main part of it. The usual size is 90 x 90 x 90 cm [3 x 3 x 3′], which will provide about half a ton of compost. But it can be 1.2 or 1.5 m [4 or 5′] high and the same width and length, or as small as 45 x 45 x 60 cm [1½ x 1½ x 2′]. The more quickly the heap is made up the more quickly it will heat up and rot. Heaps made from spring to late summer should be ready for use in about 6-12 weeks; the late autumn ones will not finish breaking down until the following mid spring.

Constructing the heap
When you begin to build the heap you can either contain it with wire netting, corrugated iron or wood, or use one of the commercially sold compost containers. A square container of 5 cm [2″] wire netting supported at each corner with wooden posts is made easily and quickly. The lower 23 cm [9″] of each post should be treated with a wood preservative, and the netting attached by nails. The two front posts should be 1.5 m [5′] long, the other two 1.2 m [4′]. The heap is built directly on to the soil, but aeration is helped if you make a base about 2.5 cm [1″] deep from woody stems. Build the heap in layers 15-20 cm [6-8″] deep of vegetative material followed by 2.5 cm [1″] of soil with a sprinkling of lime on top of this to prevent the heap becoming too acid. Repeat these layers to the height you have decided on. Cover the heap with a sack each time you finish adding to it. When it is completed, cover it with a roof of corrugated iron to keep out the rain. This should be laid on top of the posts and project over the sides by about 10 cm [4″]. The higher front posts of the

heap will give the roof a backwards slant so that rain will run off. Site it so that rain does not drain into the heap.
When making the heap tread it a little to get rid of large air pockets and keep the surface even and level, not mounded up in the centre and sloping at the sides. If the weather is dry, spray each layer lightly with water. You can also use commercially sold activators to speed up the rotting down process. These are sold in the form of powders which are scattered over the heap as the makers direct on top of each new layer.
The sides of the heap should be turned to the middle occasionally so that the whole heap rots evenly and completely. This will also prevent an unpleasant odour from developing.
When the heap is ready it should consist of dark brown, crumbly material, rather like fibrous soil. If you can still see the shapes of the original plant material, it is not yet fit for use.

Using your garden compost
Garden compost is dug in at the rate of about 5 kg per sq m [10 lb per sq yd] if the soil is very short of humus as with a stony, sandy or town soil. Otherwise, on a reasonably good soil it can be used at 2.5 kg per sq m [5 lb per sq yd]. As with other kinds of organic matter this is done either in autumn when preparing for vegetables or about a month in advance of planting tree or soft fruit.

Mulches and top dressings
Garden compost can also be used as a mulch or topdressing. A mulch is a thin layer of material spread evenly over the soil surface around the plants, covering the area to which the roots extend. Mulches keep the soil moist and blot out weeds, and are put on in late spring to early summer. This function is distinct from any addition of nutrients. Any material which has not been absorbed by autumn is forked in.
Top dressings are very similar, but heavier. They are put on in autumn or early spring mainly for the purpose of supplying food and humus. (The term top dressing is also used in gardening to mean the addition of powdered fertilizer around growing plants.)

Long term value of a compost heap
To start with, you may find that your garden does not supply sufficient vegetative material for composting to make good the lack of humus in the soil. In this case, farmyard manure or other organic matter is worth buying at first. The quantity of vegetative material from your own cropping will gradually increase, year by year. As the application of compost continues it will build up, and the garden will eventually become self-supporting.

HOW TO MAKE A SIMPLE HEAP

(see illustration below)

A square container of 5 cm [2″] wire netting supported by wooden posts is quick and easy to make. The lower 23 cm [9″] of the posts should be treated with wood preservative and the netting nailed to the posts. The two front posts should be 1.5 m [5′] high and the two back posts 1.2 m [4′] high. The heap can be built directly on the soil, but a base of woody stems about 2.5 cm [1″] deep laid on top of the soil helps aeration. Build the heap in layers 15-20 cm [6-8″] deep of vegetative material, followed by 2.5 cm [1″] of soil and a sprinkling of lime on top of this. Spray the heap lightly with water if it is dry, and turn it occasionally. Cover the heap with sacking each time you finish adding to it. When it is completed, cover it with a roof of corrugated iron. The higher front posts make the roof slant so that rain runs off. Add extensions as shown below for continuous composting.

Wooden slats make a neat and effective bin. Leave ventilation gaps between slats.

A three-sided brick-walled bin is more permanent and is tidy and handy to use.

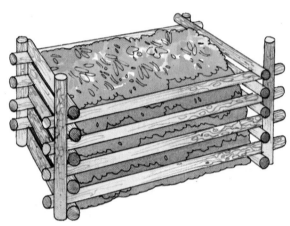

Poles make an easily constructed bin. Remove poles in turn to reach compost.

A strong circular wire container is well-ventilated and easy to lift away.

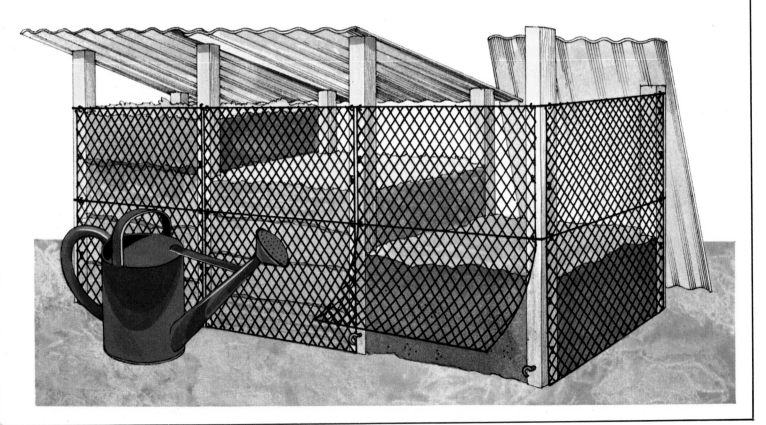

Fertilizers

The fertility of garden soils was traditionally maintained by the use of large quantities of farmyard manure. This kept the soil in good physical condition and supplied adequate amounts of mineral nutrients. Today, this is no longer always practical and other methods of feeding have been evolved, using a combination of natural and chemical substances.

A plant's mineral requirements
There are various mineral elements essential to plant growth which must be present in the soil. Three which are required in fairly high quantities are: nitrogen (N), phosphorus (P) and potassium (K). These key elements, NPK, form the basis of plant feeding and constitute most proprietary fertilizers. Supplies of magnesium (Mg) are also needed in some instances; calcium (Ca) and sulphur (S) do not, on the whole, need topping up as most soils contain plenty of these, although calcium is commonly added as lime.
Other mineral foods such as iron, manganese, copper, zinc, boron and molybdenum are classified as trace elements. These are just as important but are only needed in minute quantities by the plant. Most soils contain adequate reserves of these.

Functions of individual elements
Each of these elements has its own role to play in the plant. Nitrogen favours vigorous vegetative growth, whilst potassium gives sturdiness and en-

courages flowering and fruiting. Phosphorus is important in all parts of the plant but is of special value for healthy root growth. Magnesium is important for the production of chlorophyll. The roles of the remaining two elements, calcium and sulphur, are more general. The trace elements as a group are involved in many of the key growth processes. Deficiencies of any show up in a variety of ways such as regular yellow patterns, browning, stunting or malformed growth.

Factors affecting plant nutrition
The type of soil can have major affects on the availability of plant foods; all soils contain mirco-organisms which break down organic matter such as manure, or garden compost. Regular applications of this type of material will improve the soil structure, thus making it easier for plant roots to grow and absorb as much of the available food as they need.
Most plants are tolerant of fairly wide differences in soil acidity (pH) although they generally do best in soils near neutrality. For this reason the fertility of very acid soils is increased by the addition of lime.
Excessive applications of one plant food can lead to a deficiency of another in the plant. For instance, in the case of potassium, too much will be absorbed at the expense of magnesium, especially with tomatoes.
Weather conditions can affect the uptake of nutrients by plants. In cold frosty weather, there is little or no up-

take, so fertilizer applied then will not be of use until spring. Also, the more soluble plant foods may be washed out of the root zone by winter rain. Dressings are therefore best given during the growing season.

Types of fertilizers
Fertilizers are commonly divided into two main types, namely "organic" and "inorganic". They are distinguished by the fact that, generally speaking, the former are obtained from animal or vegetable materials whilst the latter are either natural minerals or manufactured products.
The most commonly used nitrogenous fertilizers are sulphate of ammonia (21%N), dried blood (12%N) (both quick-acting), and hoof and horn (12-14%N) (slow-acting). Phosphatic fertilizers consist of: bonemeal (16-32% P_2O_5), very slow-acting even when finely ground; superphosphate of lime (13-18% P_2O_5), quick-responding because of its ready solubility, and basic slag, slow-acting and an industrial by-product which has a variable content of phosphate and also supplies lime. The potash salt generally available to the gardener is sulphate of potash (48-50% K_2O), fairly quick-acting; wood-ash is also good (up to 10% K_2O).
Magnesium is available as Epsom salts (10% Mg) or as Dolomite limestone. The former, although quick-acting, has relatively short persistence, whilst the latter acts slowly but lasts longer.

Application
It is important that fertilizers should be used at the recommended rate and the dressing applied evenly all over the treated area. Too high a concentration can cause serious damage to roots and may kill off seeds and seedlings.
Fertilizers can be applied either as solids or liquid. The solid fertilizers provide fairly high quantities of plant food which are sufficient for several weeks or months. Liquid feeds supply rather small quantities of immediately available plant food and are valuable for producing quick bursts of growth, as a method of changing the NPK balance at critical stages in the growth of plants and for the correction of minor element deficiencies.
Normally liquid feeds are watered on to the soil but some can be applied as foliar feeds. Very frequent applications are needed for worthwhile effects. This method of application, however, can be of value in cases where root development has been restricted.
It is a legal requirement in the UK that the plant food content of a fertilizer be given on the pack, the quantity of each nutrient being expressed as a percentage of the total weight.

FERTILIZER MIXING CHART

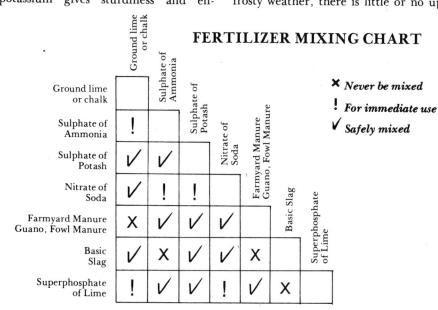

	Ground lime or chalk	Sulphate of Ammonia	Sulphate of Potash	Nitrate of Soda	Farmyard Manure Guano, Fowl Manure	Basic Slag	Superphosphate of Lime
Ground lime or chalk							
Sulphate of Ammonia	!						
Sulphate of Potash	✔	✔					
Nitrate of Soda	✔	!	!				
Farmyard Manure Guano, Fowl Manure	✗	✔	✔	✔			
Basic Slag	✔	✗	✔	✔	✗		
Superphosphate of Lime	!	✔	✔	!	✔	✗	

✗ *Never be mixed*

! *For immediate use*

✔ *Safely mixed*

Seeds and seed beds

Quality
Buy from reputable seedsmen whenever possible. Their seed will have a minimum germination percentage and most firms date-stamp their packets to prevent old seed being sold. As seeds are seriously affected by storage and age, some firms pack them in sealed humidity-proof packets. Seeds packed in these will remain fresh for several years but once the packets are opened, normal ageing begins.

Many seeds are described as F₁ Hybrids, and cost more than the others because the plants which produce them have to be hand-pollinated. However, they are much stronger, or have other worthwhile characteristics. As seeds saved from F₁ Hybrids will not yield plants true to type, buy new seeds yearly.

Saving your own seed
It is sometimes useful to save seed from your own plants but only from 'fixed' species, which will not hybridize with other species. Collect the seed when the plants are ready to shed it, clean it and keep it in a dry, cool place until needed.

Seed separation and germination
Seed should be sown as near the correct time as possible in the year in which it is bought, unless specially packed, otherwise leave the packets unopened in a reasonably steady, cool temperature. Never store in a damp place.

The most suitable germination temperatures for the common outdoor vegetables is from 7 to 16°C [45 to 60°]. If germination is likely to be difficult, soaking the seed overnight will help when the seed has a thick skin or shell, or the skin can be chipped with a razor blade. Seed can be protected with special powder dressings in case of attack from fungi or pests.

'Damping off' is a fungus disease which infects seedlings, so that they turn black at soil level and fall over. Crowded, damp conditions and unsterilized soil encourage it. Prevent or cure it by watering with Cheshunt compound, a copper fungicide.

SOWING UNDER GLASS
Many half-hardy crops are best sown in a greenhouse or frame where the temperature is about 18°C [65°F]. It is more economical to use a propagator for this, consisting of a heated base plate, a plastic tray and clear plastic dome, than to heat the whole greenhouse or frame. Seeds can be sown in trays or pots; the modern plastic trays retain heat and moisture better than the traditional wooden ones. Pots can be made of clay, plastic, peat or polythene sheet. All should have adequate drainage holes.

The soil mixture used for the seed should be seed compost, consisting either of a mixture of sterilized loam, peat and sand, with a little chalk and fertilizer added, or of mostly peat.

In seed trays
Fill the seed tray with moist compost to within 1 cm [½″] of the rim, firm it with the fingers and then level with a board. Water the compost by putting the tray in a shallow container of water and letting it soak upwards, then put aside to drain. Sow the seed thinly on the surface, sift a fine layer of compost over it, and firm gently. Label and date the seed, and cover with black plastic sheet until germination occurs. If you do not need the whole tray for one type of seed, you can divide it into sections with thin wooden slats and sow several types.

In pots
The bigger seeds, and seedlings likely to have sensitive roots, can be sown in pots. Put broken pieces of clay pot in the bottom of clay pots (unnecessary for other kinds), fill with seed compost to within 1 cm [½″] of the rim, and sow two seeds per pot. When they germinate, remove the weakest. Peat pots are buried whole.

Pricking out and hardening off
Seeds sown in trays will soon outgrow the space available. They must then be pricked out, i.e. transferred to another tray, with a spacing of 5 cm [2″] each way between each seedling. Use potting compost for this and prick out when two seed leaves have been produced, and the first true leaf is beginning to appear.

Lift each seedling gently, holding a leaf, not the stem, and replant, using a seed label as a dibber, so that the stem is buried up to the seed leaves.

As the weather gets warmer, the young plants can be gradually acclimatized to the outside. Put them in a cold frame, leaving the frame light a little open at first during the warm part of the day, but closed otherwise. Gradually increase the exposure before planting out.

SOWING OUTSIDE
An open but sheltered, sunny site is nearly always preferable as it suffers less from waterlogging and warms up earlier in the year than a shaded site.

Preparing the plot
The ground should have been dug for clearing, and limed, if necessary, preferably some months previously. Now break down lumps with a fork, remove large stones and any remaining weeds, and form a reasonably level surface by forking lightly and evenly. Leave the soil to settle for a few weeks, and then sprinkle with superphosphate or a compound fertilizer a few days before sowing, and rake it in.

Choose a day to sow the seed when the weather is mild and calm, and if possible with rain forecast. Seed germinates more quickly in warm soil, so do not be in too much of a hurry to sow the seed early in the season. The soil should be moist, but not wet or sticky. Tread it to firm it, then rake the plot gently to give the surface soil a fine texture, like breadcrumbs. Stand on boards laid alongside each row as you work, and cross-rake the plot. Generally rake to a depth of about 2.5 cm [1″] deeper than the drills need for the seeds.

Sowing procedure
Almost all vegetables are best sown in rows. To help you sow in a straight line, use a garden line (*see* TOOLS) close to the ground. Make a shallow furrow or drill by drawing the corner of the draw hoe along the line of the cord. Lining the drills with moist, granulated peat is often a great help to germination if the soil is sandy, or the weather hot and dry after germination.

Large or pelleted seeds can be sown individually at specific intervals, or stations. Put several together at each station to allow for possible germination failure. Later remove the weakest.

Sow fine seed thinly in a line down the drills; even so, some thinning will always be necessary. Too thick sowing will delay germination and lead to excessive thinning, which can damage the roots of the retained seedlings.

After sowing
Cover the row of seed by drawing the back of your garden rake along the drill. This tips the ridge of soil along each side of the furrow back into the centre and levels off the soil. Water the row immediately with a rosed can until the soil is quite moist. Light but continuous moisture must be maintained before and after germination. Be sure to label each row clearly.

Cloches and frames

CLOCHES

Cloches are used to protect plants from unfavourable weather. They may be moved around the garden to provide protection when and where necessary. Used intensively, cloches will give year round benefit, but if two or more crops are to be grown in the same plot in the year, remember to double the amount of organic matter incorporated.

There are a large number of designs available today, made either out of glass or plastic glass-substitutes. The simplest

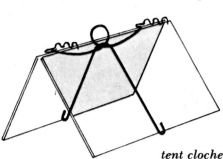

tent cloche

cloche design is the tent type which consists of two sheets of glass held in an inverted V shape. More sophisticated are the T, or flat-topped barn cloche with three sheets, and the pitch-roofed barn cloche with four.

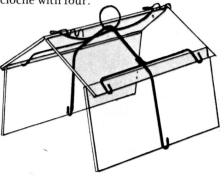

barn cloche

Usually, the glass is made in standard lengths of 60 cm [2'] and the cloches themselves are 23-60 cm [9"-2'] wide. Plastic cloches are made either from thin plastic sheets or from more rigid plastic or PVC. The thinner materials are held in place by half hoops of galvanized wire, dug into the ground for anchorage. The thicker types may be held between metal sections or framed like glass. The lengths of these cloches vary considerably from about 45 cm

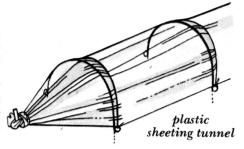

plastic sheeting tunnel

[18"] to 90 cm [3']. Widths also vary, but 45 cm [18"] is the most popular.

Choosing which cloche

Plastic cloches are cheap to buy, light to handle and easy to store. But they lose

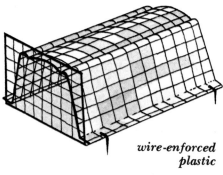

wire-enforced plastic

heat too quickly to help in frosty weather and all but the most expensive deteriorate quicker than glass. Glass cloches give more protection and are better in winter. They are more substantial and easier to use in more exposed gardens but are also more vulnerable to breakage. They can be bought in a greater variety of sizes and some incorporate ventilation panels, for growing a wider range of plants to maturity. Some commercial cloches can be bought with adaptors which raise their height. The cloche is held on wire stilts with the gaps at the sides filled in with two extra sheets of glass.

Use of cloches

Cloches fulfil many useful functions. During wet or cold weather, they can be used to cover soil to keep it warm and dry. This will enable you to sow or plant much earlier than in open beds. They will protect plants and seedlings from cold and wind, extending your growing season significantly and bringing plants through the winter. Ends of rows of cloches should normally be kept sealed

with sheets of glass or plastic to stop the row becoming a wind tunnel.

FRAMES

Frames are more permanent structures than cloches but like them they make use of trapped sun heat. They protect plants on four sides and have removable tops or lights. This enables you to sow earlier than in the open. They can also be used to shelter tender plants during the wetter and colder winter months, to force certain crops out of season and to 'harden off' greenhouse-raised plants.

Types of frame

Many different types of frame are available. Some have brick or concrete bases

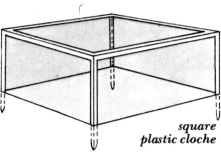

square plastic cloche

with glass sides; others have brick, concrete or wooden sides. The top of the frame, the light, may be hinged or sliding and the framework made either of wood or metal. All frames have a deep back and shallow front. The dimensions vary considerably, but there should always be adequate room between the tops of the plants and the light. The Dutch frame has a single light made of a large pane of glass, supported on a wooden frame. The light

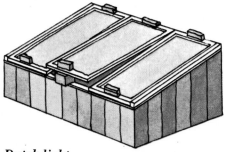

Dutch light

slides into grooves in the inside faces of the timber and is secured by a short wooden strip screwed into the base plate of the frame. No putty is used, making it simple to replace broken glass.

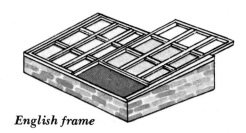

English frame

The English type is larger, with several smaller panes of glass supported by longtitudinal glazing bars. The latest frame designs use plastics or fibre-glass. The former are quite cheap to buy, the

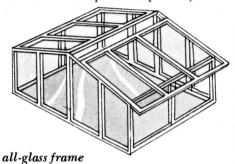

all-glass frame

latter expensive. Plastic sheets may be used instead of glass panes, and require only a light wooden framework. A few designs have clear side and end sections as well; these give good results except in cold weather.

Heated frames
Frames are usually unheated, but the development of safe electric warming cables has made it quite easy to convert cold frames by laying cables in the soil or around the walls. Adding heat increases the versatility of the frame considerably making it in effect a miniature greenhouse.

Watering
Watering can be a problem in frame gardening, as the soil can dry out quickly in warm weather. The best solution is mist irrigation which involves a rigid plastic water pipe fixed to the frame roof. The pipe has a series of brass nozzles which provide an even, fine mist of water.

Siting the frame
It is very important to put the frame in the best possible growing position. Ideally it should face the sun, but if this is not possible it must be sited where it is sheltered from cold prevailing winds and will receive maximum sunlight.

Soil preparation
The soil for the frame needs careful preparation. The area should be dug out to a depth of 30-40 cm [12"-16"] and the bottom of the hole covered with a 10 cm [4"] layer of small rubble and weathered cinders. If the subsoil is heavy, break it up with a fork before putting in the drainage material. The rest of the hole should be filled with a specially prepared compost. The formula used depends on whether the frame is for seedlings or for growing plants to maturity. In small frames it is a good idea to use seed trays or pots for seed raising, and to grow plants to maturity in the prepared frame soil.

Watering

Water in the soil
Water not only keeps plants upright (if they lack moisture they will wilt) but also carries with it nutrients from the soil, some of which are used in the leaves for photosynthesis. Thus plants deprived of water cannot grow, but it is equally important that they never become waterlogged. The roots must be able to breathe, which means that some air pockets must always be left in the soil. As water drains from the soil after rainfall it pulls air in behind it, supplying roots with the air they need. Drowning a plant with water will suffocate the roots. All soils have water tables (natural water levels). To ascertain a water table, dig down into the soil until the bottom of the hole fills with water. The top of the water is the same level as the water table. Generally, water tables rise in winter as there is more rain and less evaporation than in summer. Never plant fruit trees and bushes in ground with high water tables in the winter, as the roots will suffocate.

How much water
Water should be given in large quantities, and only when necessary. Roots follow water, so proper irrigation and heavy rains keep the roots down, searching for water at low soil levels. A daily trickle of water is inadvisable as this keeps the surface roots supplied, but leaves the plant prone to real drought in dry conditions. A lot of water every four or five days is the best method. The question of how much and when is more critical for container-grown crops than for those grown in open ground. Water must be given *before* the plants wilt.

When to water
Water should be given very early in the morning and always before the sun is strong. This is because water droplets on the leaves have a lens effect, so that the sun shining through them would scorch the foliage. Evening is another good time to apply water, so that the plants absorb as much as they can hold, ready for the next day's heat.

Watering cans
For the patio and container gardener a watering can is all that is needed. Test for size and weight when full of water before buying. Plastic watering cans are lighter and less expensive than metal types, but become covered in green algae on the inside. A good size for general garden use is a 6-9 L [1½-2 gal] capacity can. This is not too heavy and carries sufficient water to cover quite a lot of ground. Use a fine rose fixed to the spout of the can when watering seeds and young plants.

Sprinklers
Static sprinklers are attached to a hose and mains supply. They have a fast rate of delivery, and need to be moved every 15 minutes. Depending on the water pressure, they will water a circle 3.6-6 m [12-20'] in diameter.
Revolving sprinklers have a fairly even distribution and rate of delivery. They cover a diameter of 7.15 m [25-50'].

Drip irrigation and spray lines
Plastic pipes are fitted with nozzles at regular intervals and water drips slowly and continuously through the nozzles. There are some disadvantages: holes can become clogged, and the pipes are awkward to move. The main advantage is the slow rate of delivery of water, like fine rain. They are particularly suitable for plants which need a good deal of water and have many fine roots such as tomatoes, cucumbers or strawberries. Spray lines are used for large areas of gardens or growing crops. Metal or plastic pipes are pierced with holes at regular intervals.

Soaking the soil
Irrigation ditches are particularly suitable for level beds or small gardens where the gardener wants to avoid sprinkling certain vegetables. It also avoids compacting the whole surface of the garden, saving a lot of cultivation. Dig the ditches before planting, 30 cm [1'] wide, 15 cm [6"] deep, making them as level as possible. Trample bottom of ditches to harden them or line with heavy plastic sheetings. Divide long ditches into 1.8 m [6'] segments on sandy soils and 3.6 m [12'] segments on heavier soils. Use a dam (e.g. a piece of metal, a board or a shovel) to slow the flow of the water and enable it to thoroughly soak that section. (Plants should be only 7-10 cm [3-4"] from the shoulder of the ditch.) Watering basins are a good method for fruit trees. Dig out a shallow basin around the base of the tree — some of the roots may be exposed. Water the basin thoroughly, replace soil, then mulch to help retain the moisture.

The greenhouse

The greenhouse will be a permanent fixture and it is quite a sizeable capital asset, so it is worth taking care about the place where it will be erected.

Suitable sites
It should not be too far from the house, otherwise it tends to be neglected, especially in cold or wet weather. Don't put it where it is likely to be in shade for even part of the day; the glass or plastic alone will cut down the light, even when perfectly clean. So watch for trees, buildings, high walls, or even possible future building on a nearby site.

Put the greenhouse where it is sheltered from strong winds, so that heat is not lost unnecessarily, and if possible align it so that it runs north to south, to get the maximum light. A position handy for a tap or stand-pipe will save a great deal of walking to and fro with heavy cans of water; during hot weather you will really need a hose, as it will probably be necessary to water all the plants every day, sometimes twice, and to damp down the inside of the house. Don't put it at the bottom of a slope, however slight, which is backed by a wall or hedge; cold air will collect there, and make it particularly costly to keep the temperature high enough at night.

Easy access to mains electricity is often important, especially if you are planning to heat the greenhouse electrically or install mist propagation. (*see* under **Watering** on this page).

A greenhouse is often put to one side or another of a garden; if you do this, make sure there is plenty of room behind the greenhouse for any necessary work to be done.

Choice of greenhouse
When you are choosing a greenhouse, there are various pros and cons to be considered, not always obvious if you have never owned one before. For instance, look at the number of ventilators; are the adequate for the size of the house? There should be at least two in the roof and another in one of the sides. The more there are, the more control you will have over the temperature and humidity. Houses with solid walls often have ventilating grids spaced along the walls below the staging level. Houses are sold with hinged or sliding doors; remember that with some sliding doors it is very easy for the door to become jammed with soil at the bottom, and there may be draughts where it does not fit tightly. Make sure the doorway is wide enough for a wheelbarrow.

Various materials are used for the greenhouse structure. Wood needs regular upkeep, besides being treated with preservative, in the form of painting or oiling, but it is much more convenient than metal alloys when hooks, supporting wires and plastic sheeting need to be attached to it. The glazing bars however, being wider than metal ones, cut down the amount of light available to the plants.

Metal alloys, such as aluminium, make for a very well-lit greenhouse and need no upkeep, but the temperature variations can be greater — they can get very hot very quickly. Aluminium greenhouses are relatively expensive. Concrete is also used; it can make a very heavy-looking structure unless carefully designed, and tends to reduce the light. However, it is extremely long-lasting, needs absolutely no maintenance, and is much more stable.

Plastic walk-in tunnels are cheap and easy to put up, but do not have a very long life, generally two to four years before the plastic deteriorates and the light transmission becomes poor as a result of the sun shining on the plastic. If you want one of these, get the expected life span of the plastic from the manufacturer before you buy, and get a comparison of the light transmission through various kinds of plastic. Decide whether you want to grow plants on staging, in the soil of the greenhouse floor, or a bit of both. There are models which will suit all these. Those with glass down to the ground are best if you will be growing in the soil, but lose more heat, and will need plastic sheet insulation in winter. With brick or wooden half walls, tubular electric heaters can be used.

If you are going to be away in the daytime, a model with automatic ventilators is well worth considering; besides electrically operated kinds, there are those which rely on a chemical only.

Greenhouse management
It should be possible to manipulate the greenhouse environment so that the plants are always in first-class condition.

Watering
Watering is crucial; never let the plants run short whether in containers or the ground. Do not water late in the day so that there is a damp atmosphere by night, when the temperature is dropping, otherwise disease will thrive. Water container plants only when the soil surface has dried. There are a number of different automatic watering systems on the market. The capillary system involves a feed tank, operated by a ball valve, installed either inside or just outside the greenhouse, connected to the mains. Pipes from the tank feed water gradually into a bed of sand on the staging — commonly using a system of adjustable nozzles. Plants then take up water as and when they need it from the sand. Plastic pots are best. If you use clay pots, insert a fibreglass wick into the drainage hole of each pot. The sand is best contained in plastic trays and a depth of 2.5 cm [1″] is needed. A more sophisticated device is the mist propagator, which releases a spray of fine mist from overhead nozzles in response to an automatic device. This is intended to maintain a moist atmosphere.

Heating and ventilation
Increase the ventilation as soon as the temperature goes above 16°C [60°F], and leave one ventilator open a crack all through winter unless the temperature is very low. Try to maintain as even a temperature as possible by manipulating the ventilation. In dull weather keep the house almost closed; when sunny give it plenty of air. Maintain moisture in the atmosphere; if the greenhouse feels comfortable to be in, it will suit the plants as well as you, and keep a good many pests at bay.

In hot weather, spray the paths, staging, soil and walls with water two or three times a day to damp them down.

When heating in winter, try to keep the temperature at 7°C [45°F] or more; low night temperatures in spring especially hold plants back and you will quickly lose the earliness of your crops. A maximum and minimum thermometer is essential, for showing the night temperature, as well as the day.

Heating for greenhouses can be powered by electricity, gas, paraffin, or solid fuel, which heats hot water pipes. Whichever you choose, make sure that it will provide the degree of warmth needed for the crops you are growing. In very hot summer weather, shading will be needed, from the simple greenhouse shading paints to the sophisticated automatic roller blinds, otherwise many plants will be literally scorched. Keep the greenhouse clean at all times, throw out decaying vegetation, and wash down with a sterilizing agent every year.

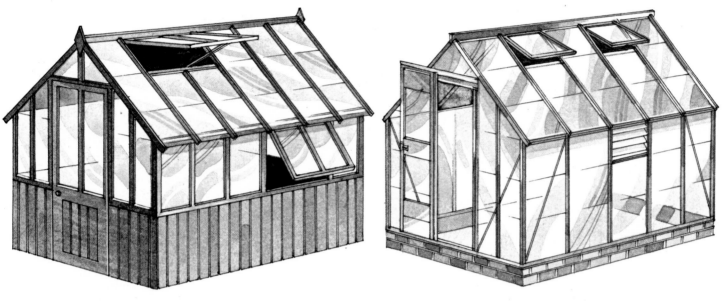

In a half-wall model, plants are grown on staging;
it is warm but less well lit than an all-glass house.

The all-glass house has panels set in a metal frame.
It admits the maximum amount of light, but loses heat.

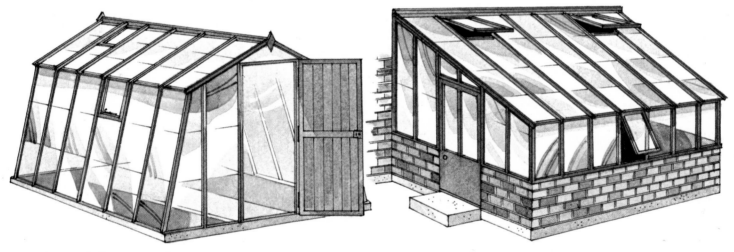

The Dutch-light type of house encloses the maximum
floor space in relation to glass, but also loses some heat.

Lean-to models are warmer than free-standing houses,
and may consist of half of any other model.

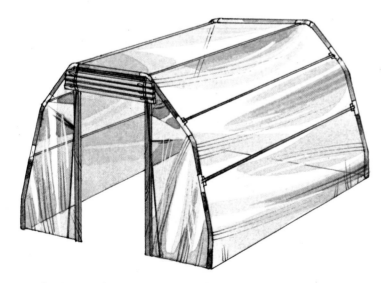

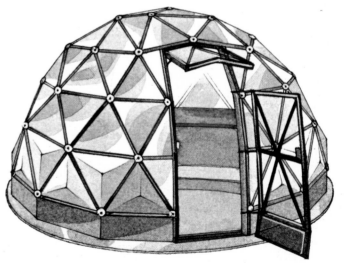

Plastic stretched over a frame offers some protection;
it is cheaper but less long-lasting than glass.

Multi-angular glass models are good for windy sites.
They offer the maximum ground space and use of light.

The first chart, SYMPTOMS AND CAUSES, helps you to pinpoint exactly which pest or disease is affecting your plant. Once you have identified the culprit, look up the suitable treatment. Treatment for those listed in *italics* is given in the A to Z cultivation entry for the plant concerned. Otherwise, treatment is given in the second chart COMMON TROUBLES. This describes the common pests and diseases that affect many plants and outlines suitable treatment.

Pests and diseases

SYMPTOMS AND CAUSES

BRASSICAS (except swede and turnip): large-headed broccoli, Brussels sprouts, cabbage, cauliflower, kale, kohlrabi, sprouting broccoli.

Leaves

Large holes in outer leaves, green caterpillars present.	cabbage white butterfly
Large holes in central leaves, some in outer leaves, green caterpillars present.	cabbage moth
Large holes in leaves near ground.	slugs
Large holes in outer leaves, no caterpillars.	birds
Many tiny round holes in seedling leaves and leaves of young plants.	*turnip flea beetle*
Small white flying insects on under surface; leaves greyish, sticky, may have black patches.	whitefly
Powdery white patches on leaves.	downy mildew
Round, light brown spots 1.5 cm [½"] wide mostly on outer leaves — leaves yellow and wither.	*ring spot*
Yellow areas between leaves, dark green bands alongside veins, particularly cauliflowers.	mosaic virus
Leaves long, thin and whip-like, all vein and no leaf blade, plant stunted and possibly blind, little or no curd — cauliflower and large-headed broccoli.	*whiptail*
Lots of small, slowly-moving, grey-blue insects on leaf under-surface.	mealy aphid
Leaves of young plants turn grey-green and collapse; roots swollen and misshapen; white maggots inside when cut open.	*cabbage root fly*
Leaves turn bluish and wilt; roots swollen, turn black and rot, smell unpleasant.	*club root*

Stems

Stems bitten off at or just below soil level, plants collapse — in young plants.	cutworms or leatherjackets
Seedlings: base of stem withers and browns. Seedling dies or produces poor, stunted plant.	*wirestem*

Flowers

Florets of cauliflower brownish on surface of curd, extending down into stem below.	*boron deficiency*

LEAFY VEGETABLES (not cabbage family): cardoon, chicory, Chinese cabbage, endive, lettuce, New Zealand spinach, seakale, spinach beet, Swiss chard.

Leaves

Holes in leaves of young plants and sometimes in older ones.	slugs
Leaves pale green or yellow, curled and twisted; tiny green or black insects on undersurface and on stems.	aphids — greenfly and blackfly
Tiny rust-coloured bumps — spinach beet.	*rust*
Large, pale green or pale yellow patches on leaves, white mould on leaf under these areas — especially lettuce.	downy mildew
Furry grey mould in spots and patches on leaves — especially lettuce.	grey mould (*Botrytis cinerea*)
Leaves mottled dark and light green, very crinkled, no heart, plants stunted — lettuce.	mosaic virus
Young leaves, later older ones, yellow, pucker roll inwards, lie limp on ground; plant dies.	spinach blight virus

Leaves yellow at tips, black leaf veins, black streaks in roots when cut across — seakale.	*black rot*
Leaves become slimy, turn brown and rot when being forced; also stems — seakale.	soft rot

Stems

Stems of young plants bitten through and plants topple over.	cutworms and leatherjackets
Leaves turn yellow, wither and plant dies; when lifted, purple felt-like growth all over outside of roots — seakale, chicory.	violet root rot
Leaves poor colour and wilt, plants small for no apparent reason, cease growing; dug up plants have small white woolly patches on roots with tiny greyish insects beneath.	root aphid

Roots

Plants stunted and slow-growing; if dug up may have small lumps on roots.	*eelworms*

LEGUMES: asparagus pea, broad bean, French bean, lima bean, pea, runner bean, soya bean.

Leaves

Edges eaten into half-moon-shaped holes.	*pea/bean weevil*
Large chocolate-coloured patches on leaves, stems and pods.	*chocolate spot*
Covered in small black insects.	blackfly
Leaves curled and pale or yellowed.	greenfly
Pinprick holes with brown edges in young leaves, leaves later tattered, growing points blind.	capsid
Small transparent spots with a wide pale yellow ring around them, which join up, and leaf may wither; spots also on pods and stems.	*halo blight*
Pale and dark green areas on leaves, which are curled; whole plant stunted.	mosaic virus
Powdery white patches on upper surface of leaves, and on pods — peas.	powdery mildew
Irregular holes in seedlings and young leaves.	slugs
Leaves wilting and becoming grey-green.	*Fusarium wilt*
Seed leaves misshapen, seedlings stunted, small round holes in seeds, may be gaps in row.	*pea and bean seed beetle*

Stems

Long, dark brown, sunken patches on stem, leaves wither, pods with reddish-brown spots.	*leaf spot (anthracnose)*

Pods

Holes in peas in pods, small white maggots present in peas.	*pea moth*
Silvery-white streaks on outside of pods, also leaves and stems — peas.	*pea thrips*
Pods torn with holes in them.	birds

STEM VEGETABLES: asparagus, celery, leek, rhubarb

Leaves

Needle-like leaves completely eaten, small slate-coloured grubs present.	*asparagus beetle*
Pale brown blisters and tunnels in leaves.	*celery fly*
Leaves turn white and tips die, plants stop growing — leek.	*white tip*
Leaves yellow and wilt.	*onion fly*
Leaves yellow and wither or fall, purple felt on outside of roots — asparagus, celery.	violet root rot
Small or large brown spots on leaves, may spread so that leaf withers; plant stunted.	*celery leaf spot*
Leaves mottled yellow and green, plant stunted.	mosaic virus

Leaves grey-green, stems thin with swollen bases, crown turns brown internally — rhubarb.	*crown rot*
Small, powdery, raised, red-brown spots.	*rust*

Stems

Stems of young plants with holes, or older plants with holes in centre.	slugs
Stems in centre brown, soft and slimy.	soft rot

ROOT AND TUBER VEGETABLES (except potato): Jerusalem artichoke, beet, carrot, celeriac, Hamburg parsley, onion, parsnip, radish, salsify, scorzonera, shallot, swede, turnip

Leaves

Pale brown blisters; leaves which shrivel.	*celery fly*
Leaves curled and stems twisted, small black or green insects on undersurface and on stems.	blackfly and greenfly
Leaves have red tinge then turn yellow, plant grows poorly; pale yellow maggots in roots.	*carrot fly*
Leaves yellow from tip, wilt and can easily be pulled off bulb; tiny white maggots in bulb.	*onion fly*
Brown spots on leaves, which wither — celeriac.	*celery leaf spot*
Mottled yellow and green, plants stunted.	mosaic virus
Greyish-white patches; turn yellow and wilt.	downy mildew
Leaves of young plants distorted and twisted, sometimes swollen; plants small.	*eelworms*
Leaves turn yellow and wilt later; white mould on base of bulb, roots small or non-existent.	*onion white rot*
Leaves yellowish between veins at first, turning brown later — beet.	*speckled yellows*
Yellow streaks on leaves or yellow all over, crinkled; plant small — onion, shallot.	*shallot virus*; *yellows* or *yellow dwarf virus*
Slight yellowing and stunting; roots with purple felt outside — beet, carrots.	violet root rot
Dark spots — seedlings and young plants.	*onion smut*
White patches — salsify and scorzonera.	*white blister*
Small round holes in leaves of seedlings and young plants; plants may be defoliated.	*turnip flea beetle*

Roots

Small round tunnels in roots from outside, shiny yellow worms in them or in soil round them.	wireworms
Bulbs become soft, slimy and smell bad in store — onions and shallots.	soft rot
Centre of root mottled with brown or grey, soft and slimy — swede and turnip.	soft rot
Brown sunken elongated canker-like areas on side of root — swede.	*dry rot (Phoma lingam)*
Round swellings on upper part of root, with white maggots inside — swedes and turnips.	*gall weevil*
Reddish-brown patches on shoulder — parsnip.	*canker*
Neck of bulb rots and grey mould appears on it — onion and shallot.	*neck rot*

FRUITING VEGETABLES (except tomatoes): globe artichoke, cucumber, eggplant, gherkin, marrow, okra, peppers, squash and sweetcorn. ALSO MELON.

Leaves

Yellow or grey-yellow speckling on leaves, webs underneath, leaves wither, plant wilts and ceases to grow.	red spider mite
Young leaves pale green and curling, small green insects on undersurface.	greenfly
Yellowing patches on leaves with grey furry mould on top; also flowers and young fruit.	grey mould *(Botrytis cinerea)*
Leaves curling and wilting, turning greyish, many tiny white insects beneath, sticky substance on leaves with black patches on it.	whitefly
Pale green or yellowing mottling of leaves, possibly also puckered; plant stunted.	mosaic virus
Powdery white patches on young leaves, later on older ones, growth stunted.	powdery mildew
Leaves wilt, stem becomes dark at base of plant, plant dies.	*collar rot*
Tiny pale green spots on leaves which spread and turn grey, then brown, leaf withers.	*cucumber leaf blotch*

Stems

Holes in stems of young plants.	slugs
Tips of stems eaten, plants blind and stunted — sweet corn.	*frit fly*

Fruit

Young ones wither from the tip and fall off — marrows and cucumbers.	*wither tip*

TOMATOES

Leaves

Small round, pale yellow spots, with brown fur on underside; spreads rapidly and plant dies.	*leafmould*
Yellow areas between veins of leaves, leaf becomes completely yellow and withers.	*magnesium deficiency*
Top leaves wilt in daytime but recover, then lower leaves, followed by yellowing of lower leaves; finally complete plant wilts permanently; inside stem streaked with brown from base up.	*Verticillium wilt*
Dark brown blotches on leaves, stems and fruit.	*potato blight*
Irregular holes in leaves, may be brownish-green caterpillars; leaves may be skeletonized.	*tomato moth*
Leaves greyish green, limp and curling, sticky with black patches, tiny white flies on undersurface; plants cease to grow.	whitefly
Leaves fern-like, very long and narrow; spotted and streaked with brown; mottled yellow and crinkled; bronze-brown spots.	viruses: fern leaf, streak, mosaic, spotted wilt

Stems

Long dark brown streaks and patches on stems, at leaf joints; stem rots.	*canker (Didymella)*

Fruit

Fruits set but remain size of pinhead, flowers and buds may drop without setting.	*dry set*
Transparent spots with 'halo' round them.	grey mould *(Botrytis cinerea)*
Hard green patches on fruit round calyx.	*greenback*
Yellow patches on red fruit.	*blotchy ripening*
Hard, round, sunken, dark brown or black patch on fruit at blossom end.	*blossom end rot*

Roots

Growth of plants stunted and slow; if dug up may have lumps on roots about the size of a pea, or brown 'cysts' as on potato roots.	*root knot eelworm, potato root eelworm*

POTATOES

Leaves

Dark brown-black patches on leaves; later on stems and tubers.	*potato blight*
Large irregular holes in leaves, may be skeletonized; reddish-brown caterpillars present, possibly also black and yellow striped beetles.	*Colorado beetle*
Discoloured and yellowing, curled; small green insects on undersurface and shoot tips.	greenfly
Leaves rolled inwards, mottled yellow or pale green, or crinkled; plants stunted.	viruses: leaf-roll mosaic, crinkle.
Leaves yellow on occasional plants, stem black at soil level.	*black leg*
Leaves pale green or yellow, small plants weak and stunted; brown 'cysts' on roots.	*potato root eelworm*

Tubers

Dark brown or black, rough patches on skin.	*scab*
Tubers with cauliflower-like growths on them; tubers rot and turn black.	*wart disease*
Large irregular holes in tubers.	snails and slugs
Small, round tunnel-like holes in tubers.	wireworm
Irregularly-shaped hollow in centre.	*hollow heart*
Irregular dark brown or black lines in flesh.	virus disease

MUSHROOMS

Tiny round holes in cap of mushroom.	*mushroom fly*
Large irregular holes in cap edge and centre.	slugs
Mushroom completely misshapen, with white web over cap, smells bad.	*bubbles*
Stalks with tiny holes, almost hollowed.	*mites or spring tails*

Casing appears covered in white powder.	plaster moulds

STONE FRUITS: apricot, cherry, greengage, nectarine, peach, plum.

Leaves

Leaves silvery-white on upper surface, on whole shoots or branches; wood stained internally with irregular purplish colour, brown or purple shelf-like growths appear on trunk.	*silver leaf*
Grey-green withering leaves, minute reddish dots on undersurface.	red spider mite
Irregular holes in leaves, spring and early summer; green or brown caterpillars present.	leaf-eating caterpillars
Small black or green insects appear on undersurface of leaves and at tips of shoots, leaves curled and discoloured pale yellow and green.	blackfly, greenfly
Small brown 'shot holes'; leaves yellow and die, bark cracked and gumming.	*bacterial canker*
Thickened, wrinkled lighter green patches, later reddish-pink, blister-like, with bloom; leaves drop off; growth checked and stunted.	*peach leaf curl*
Pale green speckling in patches on upper surface; small green hopping insects may be seen.	leaf hopper
Pin-prick holes with brown margins in young leaves and tips of shoots, leaves tattered later; tips of shoots blind, growth checked.	capsid
Much curled over and twisted at tips of shoots; mass of blue-grey insects on under-surface.	*mealy plum aphid*

Stems and trunk

Tips of shoots and leaves die, shoot dies back towards parent stem, and turns brown.	*die-back*
Small brown raised spots on bark of trunk and on stems of shoots; clear sticky substance on leaves on which black patches appear.	scale insects
Patches of brown gum ooze out of bark.	bacterial canker or *irregular water supplies*

Fruit

Hole in fruit, oozing brown liquid, seen in mid or late summer, fruit drops prematurely, red maggot in flesh near stone.	*red plum maggot (plum fruit moth)*
Fruitlets have tiny holes, with sticky substance at entrance, and drop in early summer; white maggots feed inside fruit on flesh.	*plum sawfly*
Patches of brown with white concentric rings of raised spots on them; fruit rots; may drop or mummify.	brown rot
Fruitlets hollowed out by small green caterpillars; flowers may also be attacked.	*cherry fruit moth*
Small dirty-white maggots in ripening flesh.	*cherry fruit fly*

VINES: grape.

Leaves

Powdery white patches on youngest leaves and tips of vines, growth stunted; spreads to fruit.	powdery mildew
Yellow speckling on leaves which wither and fall; minute pink-red insects on under-surface, also webs; growth ceases.	red spider mite
Leaves pale green and curl at shoot tips; small green insects on under-surface, and on stems.	greenfly
Grey mould in patches: leaves may fall; mould on young or mature fruit.	grey mould (*Botrytis cinerea*)

Regular half-circle holes in edges of leaves, top growth becomes poor for no apparent reason, roots infested with white maggots.	*vine weevil*

Fruit

Berries shrivel without ripening, after stalks have turned brown or black.	*shanking*
Light brown patches on fruit, which wrinkle and do not ripen.	*scalding*

Bark

Small dark brown oval or round raised spots on bark, and on skin of shoots; growth is slow; leaves may be grey-green with black patches.	scale insects
Small oval insects with grey-white mealy fluff on upper surface living on bark, moving slowly.	*mealy bug*

BUSH FRUIT: black, red and white currants, blueberry, gooseberry.

Leaves

Young leaves and tips of shoots tightly curled and twisted over, leaves yellow later, new growth severely stunted; small green insects on undersurface of leaves.	greenfly
Irregularly-shaped reddish blisters on upper surface; small cream insects on lower surface.	red currant blister aphid
Pin-prick holes with brown edges on young leaves and in tips of shoots, leaves later much torn; shoots stop growing, may be blind.	capsid
Leaves discoloured, fall prematurely; fruit small and poor quality.	red spider mite
Small angular dark brown spots on the leaves, which may wither and fall early; new growth slows, fruits shrivel.	*blackcurrant leaf spot*
Powdery white patches on under surface of leaves which curl upwards, and later turn brownish, also on fruit and stems where it becomes brown felt; growth stunted.	*American gooseberry mildew*
Powdery white patches on upper surface of leaves and shoot tips, also on fruit later.	*European gooseberry mildew*
Leaves very pointed and rather nettle shaped, fewer main veins than normal, cropping poor.	*reversion virus*
Leaves severely eaten until only main vein left, from centre of bush outwards; green and black caterpillars present.	*gooseberry sawfly*

Buds

Swollen and rounded large buds, easily visible in winter — blackcurrants.	*big bud mite*

Stems

Shoots have dead leaves at tip and along rest of stem from tip downwards; stem is dead, tiny red pustules may appear.	*die-back*

Fruit

Large irregular holes in fruit near ground.	slugs
Large pointed holes in fruit at top of bush.	birds

CANE FRUIT: blackberry, loganberry and other hybrid berries, raspberry.

Leaves

Tied together with webbing at tips of shoots, holes in leaves, brown caterpillars present; buds destroyed and blossom eaten.	bramble shoot webber

Cabbage club root

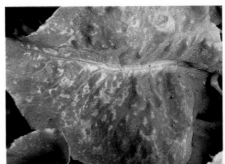

Mosaic virus

Pea moth caterpillars

Pin-prick holes with brown edges in leaves at shoot tips and in stems, later much torn; growth checked. — capsid

Young leaves curled, may be mottled yellow; small green insects on under-surface. — greenfly

Leaves markedly mottled yellow and curled, canes stunted, fruiting poor, sideshoots few. — mosaic virus of raspberry

Canes

Canes much stunted, develop many blind shoots; leaves may be mottled yellow and distorted. — blackberry dwarf virus

Long silvery-grey patches on canes extending from spurs, easily seen in winter; spurs do not produce leaves or sideshoots. — *spur blight*

Small round purple spots on canes late spring onwards, bark splits; tips of canes often killed. — *cane spot*

Fruit

Green fruits become brown and remain hard and unripe or may become distorted, white grub inside; ripe fruits misshapen, much less blossom. — *raspberry beetle*

STRAWBERRY

Leaves

Powdery-white patches on upper surface of leaves, purplish beneath, leaves curl upwards; white powder on berries. — powdery mildew

Small round dark reddish-brown spots on leaves. — *leaf spot*

Grey-green and look short of water; minute pale pink or transparent insects on lower surface, webbing may also be present; plants cease to grow and fruit does not swell. — *tarsonemid mite*

Crinkled and reduced in size, or with yellow edges; plants stunted and fruit poorly. — viruses: crinkle, yellow edge

Small, reddish leaves, outer ones brown during growth season; plants small, roots dark brown, with a red centre. — *red core*

Leaves puckered, plant stunted; secondary crowns produced, few flower buds. — *eelworm*

Young leaves curled and puckered; small green insects on under-surface, growth checked. — greenfly

Fruit

Pale brown patches on pale green fruit; grey furry mould on ripe fruit, often starting from stalk end; also mould on stalks and leaves. — grey mould (*Botrytis cinerea*)

Flesh eaten on surface, pips removed. — *seed or ground beetles*

Irregular dry holes in flesh. — slugs or birds

Fruit lopsided and misshapen. — *poor pollination or frost damage*

Flowers

Petals green and leaf-like. — green petal virus

Black 'eye' in centre; will not set fruit. — *frost damage*

Flower buds and stems lying on ground. — *strawberry blossom weevil*

Crown

Young plants eaten at soil level any time from autumn to spring, also roots. — leatherjackets, cutworms

PIP FRUITS: apples, citrus, fig, mulberry, pear, quince.

Leaves

Black spots and brown marks on upper side of leaf, leaves may fall early; hard black spots on fruit, which crack; 'blisters' on shoot stems. — scab

Powdery white patches on leaves and shoot tips in early spring; flowers creamy-yellow; infected dormant buds grey and pointed, easily seen in winter. — powdery mildew

Large irregular holes, in spring and summer. — leaf-eating caterpillars

Young leaves and shoot tips curled, growth much stunted, small green or grey insects on the underside. — greenfly, other aphids

Leaves speckled dull pale yellow or grey-green, wither and fall early, may be webbing; minute pale red insects on under-surface; new growth stunted, tree looks sick and short of water. — red spider mite

Pin-prick holes with brown edges in young leaves and shoot tips; fruitlets very misshapen. — capsid

Patches of light green on upper surface. — leaf hopper

White mottling on leaves in spring; flowers may fail to unfold. — *apple sucker*

Upper surface of leaf has green-yellow or reddish blisters turning black, and leaves fall early; fruit similarly affected. — *pear leaf blister mite*

Leaves dark brown at edges or sometimes in patches over whole leaf, tattered — pear. — *wind damage*

Fruit

Holes in side of fruitlets with sticky mess at entrance, ribbon-shaped corky scars on skin, fruitlet crops without maturing; white maggot with brown head inside fruit. — *apple sawfly*

Holes at calyx end, sometimes at side from mid-summer onwards; fruit highly coloured and drops early; pale pink caterpillar eats pips. — *codling moth*

Skin with sunken spots, small brown dots in flesh, flesh bitter — apples. — *bitter pit*

Holes in mature fruit. — birds

Brown patches on outside of fruit, extending to flesh which rots; later rings of white pustules on brown part; fruit may drop or dry up. — brown rot

Fruitlets suddenly get very big after setting and are misshapen; eventually blacken, rot and fall; inside are tiny white maggots. — *pear midge*

Mature fruit are dimpled and pitted on outside, flesh has small hard woody areas without taste or juice — pear. — stony pit virus

Grey furry mould on berries and fruit. — grey mould

Bark

Cracks and splits, breaks off, becomes sunken; shoot or branch encircled by canker dies, leaves gradually become yellow above it. — *canker*

Small dark brown oval or round raised spots on bark, and on skin of shoots; growth is slow; leaves may be yellow, yellowish-green or grey-green, with sticky substance and black patches on them. — scale insect

Masses of white fluff on bark, at forks, junctions and crevices; tiny grey insects underneath; swellings on stems and branches. — woolly aphid (American blight)

Small oval insects with grey-white mealy fluff on upper surface live on bark, move slowly. — *mealy bug*

Buds

Buds torn off in winter, no blossom in spring. — birds

Potato blight

Gooseberry sawfly larvae

Pear scab

Cherry black fly

Greenfly (type of aphid)

Brown rot on apples

Caterpillar of cabbage white

Wireworms on a carrot

COMMON TROUBLES

Remember that weather conditions, rather than a particular pest or disease, can often be the cause of trouble. Wind can cause leaves to go brown, wither or fall early; frost can produce black centres in blossom; wilting may be the result of drought; cold and drought can cause fruit to crack. A plant dying for no apparent reason may be the result of a too wet soil.

Use as few chemicals as possible but, where necessary, use the least harmful to natural predators, bees and humans, eg. derris, pyrethrum, resmethrin, quassia, soft soap. Alternatively use chemicals that break down quickly, eg. malathion, trichlorphon.

APHIDS: *Blackfly, greenfly, currant blister aphid, mealy aphid, woolly aphid (American blight) etc.*
Tiny insects 2-3 mm [$\frac{1}{8}$-$\frac{1}{16}$"] long, with wings when adult. Grow in stages, moulting a skin each time, which remains on plant as a white 'ghost'; green, black, grey, rosy or white in colour, depending on species; root aphid and woolly aphid are greyish with fluffy white coating.
Overwinter as tiny black oval eggs.
Damage occurs in spring and summer.
Feed by sucking the sap of young leaves, stems and flowers through needle-like mouth parts with which they pierce the plant tissue; root aphids attack roots and live in the soil. They secrete a sticky substance called honeydew, which falls to leaves below and on which sooty mould fungus grows.
Treatment: Finger and thumb; cut off completely heavily infested shoot tips and leaves; wash or wipe off honeydew and sooty mould; keep plants well watered, especially in dry weather; ladybird larvae are predators.
Spray with resmethrin, derris or malathion, or treat winter eggs with tar oil winter wash, but only if plants are dormant and woody. Treat woolly aphids with methylated spirits and a stiff brush, and water plants infected with root aphid with malathion or derris.

BIRDS: Peck out fruit buds from late autumn to early spring; peck holes in fruit, including tomatoes when ripening; feed on leaves of brassicas, peck up onion sets, tear off bean flowers, pull out seedlings, eat newly sown seed, feed on peas in pods.
Treatment: Protect with 1.5 cm [$\frac{1}{2}$"] netting; spray with harmless but bitter-tasting-to-birds repellants containing quassia or alum. Put paper bags or nets round individual fruits; criss-cross cotton above newly sown seeds or use proprietary bird scarers such as aluminium foil, scarecrows, mobiles.

BROWN ROT: Fungus disease which infects fruit, either in store or on the tree. Mummified fruits can serve as a source of infection for following year. Disease enters through wounds caused by birds, insects, weather, other fungus diseases.
Treatment: Destroy all infected fruit as soon as seen, and do not store diseased or injured fruit.

CAPSID: Comparatively large insects to 0.7 cm [$\frac{1}{4}$"] long, green, quick-moving, like gigantic greenfly, rarely seen as they move fast and drop to the ground when disturbed. Feed like greenfly, but as they are much larger, do much more severe mechanical damage. Damage occurs from late spring to end of mid summer.
Treatment: Spray thoroughly with malathion or derris as soon as first pinholes are seen, and spray surrounding ground; repeat as makers instruct.

CATERPILLARS, LEAF-EATING: Green, brown, yellow, black, spotted and/or striped, sometimes hairy, 1.5-4 cm [$\frac{1}{2}$-1$\frac{1}{2}$"] long; larvae of moths or butterflies.
Treatment: Hand pick; spray with derris or fenitrothion.

CATERPILLARS, ROOT-EATING, WIREWORMS: Leatherjackets are legless, grey-brown caterpillars 2.5 cm [1"] long when fully grown (adult is cranefly). Cutworms grey, with legs, 3 cm [1$\frac{1}{4}$"] long, usually in a curved position; larvae of the turnip moth, the heart and dart moth, and yellow underwing; all feed at night. Wireworms are yellow, thin, shiny, 1.5 cm [$\frac{1}{2}$"] long and slow moving, the larvae of brown beetles.
Treatment: Hoe regularly to expose to birds; hand pick, keep weeds down, since they provide cover for moths; dust soil with bromophos or diazinon before planting.

GREY MOULD: *(Botrytis cinerea)* Fungus disease which infects many plants, entering through injuries caused by pruning, insects feeding, weather conditions, bird and spray damage. Can destroy complete plants, e.g. lettuce, tomatoes, melons, or fruits such as those of aubergine, strawberry, or cape gooseberry.
Treatment: Disease spreads rapidly in cool, damp crowded conditions so improve aeration or ventilation and raise temperature. Cut out infected parts on healthy tissues then spray with the systemic fungicide benomyl, and

spray the flowers of fruiting plants mentioned to prevent later fruit infection.

LEAF HOPPERS: *See* APHID for treatment.

LEAF SUCKERS: *See* APHID for treatment.

MILDEW: There are two kinds of this fungus disease, powdery and downy. The former is more common and infects very many plants.
Treatment: Cut off affected growth as soon as seen, well back into healthy tissue. Then spray powdery mildew with dinocap, sulphur or benomyl, and downy mildew with thiram or zineb.

RODENTS AND SMALL MAMMALS: Eat bark from trees, feed on vegetables particularly brassicas, lettuce and any others with tender leaves, take ripening fruit especially strawberries, marrows and cucumbers; eat large seeds; eat fruit and vegetables in store.
Treatment: Use proprietary baits or traps baited with cheese, nuts or fat. Spray repellants as for birds.

RED SPIDER MITE: Minute oval creatures, pale red in colour, which need a hand lens to be seen. Found on the undersides of leaves, near the main vein. Fruit tree species overwinter as bright red eggs on bark of trees and hatch in late spring; greenhouse species overwinter as a hibernating adult, emerging to feed during suitably mild spells in winter. Mites feed by sucking sap like aphids and take a month to complete their life cycle.
Treatment: Maintain humid atmosphere round plants and keep well watered, especially during drought, as mites thrive in hot dry conditions; spray plants with water daily; treat with the predator *Phytoseiulus persimilis* or spray with derris or malathion.

SCALE INSECTS: Brown, sometimes grey, oval, round or shell-shaped, raised-spot-like pests about 2 mm [$\frac{1}{8}$"] long, stationary. Mainly on bark of stems and trunk, but also on undersides of leaves, especially if tough and leathery. Feed by sucking the sap from plants. Container-grown plants may be killed. Because they are immobile and frequently the same colour as the bark, these pests are often missed until there are a great many, when they are difficult to control.
Treatment: Scrape off as many as possible with the back of a knife on to paper laid beneath the plants, then spray thoroughly with malathion, and repeat once or twice more at 10-day intervals, depending on the degree of infestation. Sponge off any sooty mould.

SLUGS AND SNAILS: Snails are easily recognized by their shells, but slugs are often mistaken for pebbles at a casual glance. They feed at night and hide during the day.
Treatment: Put rings of gritty material round plants, at least 15 cm [6"] wide; trap in containers of stale beer or sweetened water sunk in soil near plants. Put down methiocarb pellets. Eliminate possible hiding places and improve drainage.

SOFT ROT: Bacterial disease which infects roots and centres of plants, and those in store. Worst in wet seasons.
Treatment: No chemical control, but infected parts should be cut out or plants destroyed. Avoid injury to plants so that bacteria cannot enter; slug damage in particular is dangerous.

VIOLET ROOT ROT: Fungus disease infecting plant roots.
Treatment: Lift and destroy infected plants, removing all the root. Do not grow any of these plants in the same soil for four years, and keep weeds away, particularly bindweed, dock and dandelion, which are susceptible.

VIRUS: There are many kinds of virus diseases, which become part of the nucleus of the plant cells, hence the difficulty of chemical control. Particles of virus are often easily spread by clothes, tools, hands and sap-sucking insects from infected plants to healthy ones; some are carried by soil-inhabiting pests. Very many plants are attacked. There is no control, so plants are best destroyed at once. Do not confuse with nutrient deficiency symptoms, in which discolouration occurs in regular markings and patterns.

WHITEFLY: Adults 1 mm [$\frac{1}{25}$"] long, snow-white, moth-like insects found under leaves; young and eggs flattened, circular, pale green almost transparent, on underside of leaf. Feed by sucking sap from leaves and stems, stationary until adult, then fly moves off to lay eggs on fresh leaves. Plant becomes very messy in bad infestation, especially tomatoes, and can be killed.
Treatment: New insecticide resmethrin gives good results, otherwise whitefly difficult to deal with, because of need for insecticide to penetrate to young through protective scale, and because all stages present all the time. There are several generations in a season.
The parasitic wasp *Encarsia formosa* is a biological control in some countries; destroy heavily infested plants, increase water supplies to remainder.

WIREWORMS: *See* CATERPILLARS, ROOT-EATING.

Grey mould (Botrytis cinerea)

Mildew on apples

Red spider mite damage

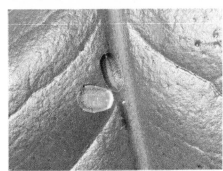
Scale insects (Coccus coryli)

Whitefly damage on tomatoes

Varieties

Each entry lists a number of recommended varieties, indicating their different characteristics and giving, where applicable, the essential information on sowing times, pollination, cropping etc. Where no entry appears for a particular crop, this is an indication that most merchants list only one variety. This applies to the majority of herbs and to a small number of fruit and vegetables.

APPLE

To set a crop, most apples need to be cross-pollinated. Most varieties have plenty of pollen and will pollinate one another, *provided their flowering seasons coincide or overlap.* Some have little pollen — they are known as triploid. They need a suitable pollinator to help them set their fruit, but they themselves will not pollinate the other tree. In this case there should be a third variety present (not triploid) to ensure a good crop on all three. A few varieties are self-fertile though they crop better with a suitable pollinator.

Dessert:
Beauty of Bath: small, heavily striped bright red apple, crops prolifically; ready late midsummer; not advisable for planting in frosty gardens; does not store, slightly tip-bearing; *flowers early.*
Egremont Russet: medium, yellow, heavily covered in brown russet; crisp and well-flavoured; suitable for small gardens — makes good cordons; ready mid autumn to early winter; heavy cropper and disease resistant; *flowers early.*
Tydeman's Early Worcester: medium, pale green heavily flushed with red, crops well; ready late summer; slightly tip-bearing; *early to mid season flowering.*
James Grieve: medium to large, yellow, striped and flushed red; good cropper; ready early autumn; tends to canker on heavy soil; *flowers mid season.*
Fortune: medium size, yellow with long red stripes; crisp, good flavour; ready early to mid autumn; crop moderate; *flowers mid season.*
Cox's Orange Pippin: medium size, yellow-orange with red flush and stripes; crisp, superb flavour; ready mid autumn, stores to late mid winter; crop moderate to heavy; spurs well but not advisable in wet areas, *flowers mid season; proven best pollinator James Grieve.*
Winston: medium, green, covered in stripes and flush of dull red; good flavour, slightly sharp; ready mid winter, stores till mid spring; crop moderate to light; good as a cordon; *flowers mid season. Self-fertile.*
Cooking:
Grenadier: medium to large, yellow-green, very good flavour; ready late summer to mid autumn; crop heavy and regular; good for small gardens; not prone to disease; *flowers mid season and is self-fertile.*
Bramley's Seedling: large, green but flushed red in the crimson-skinned sport; excellent flavour and cooks very well; ready late autumn and stores until mid spring; crop mostly heavy, but makes large tree and not suitable for small gardens; *flowers mid season; N.B. triploid.*
Crab apples:
Dartmouth: small, deep red fruit; mid autumn; good jelly; spreading head; *flowers mid season.*

John Downie: small conical yellow fruit flushed bright red; ready early autumn; also good for preserves; upright head; *flowers mid season.*

APRICOT
Breda: hardy, good cropper.
Bulida: fine South African variety.
New Large Early: one of the earliest ripening.
Moor Park: very hardy, juicy, sweet fruit.
Shipley (or Blenheim): early.

ARTICHOKE, GLOBE
Purple Globe, Green Globe: the two commonest varieties, distinguished by their colour.
Grand Beurre: new, very fleshy heads.
Gros Camus de Bretagne: sometimes obtainable.

ARTICHOKE, JERUSALEM
Fuseau: purple-skinned.
New White: white-skinned.

ARTICHOKE, CHINESE
White: white-skinned.
Old Red: red-skinned.

ASPARAGUS
Brock's Imperial: new F_1 hybrid; early, vigorous.
Connover's Colossal: good standard variety; large heads, slender tips.
Martha Washington: large size; prolific cropper over longer period than average.
Sutton's Perfection: high quality.

BEAN SPROUTS
Mung: crisp and slightly bland in flavour.
Triticale: tender and sweet.
Adzuki: crisp, nutty flavour. Brown seeds.

BEET
Early Bunch: early; resistant to bolting; round.
Globe: good maincrop; round; dark crimson.
Detroit (Little Ball): for successional sowings, especially for storing for autumn and winter.
Boltardy: early, resistant to bolting.
Cheltenham Green-top: long root; green leaves; maincrop; keeps well.
Golden: golden skin and flesh; a novelty.
Snow-white: white; crisp; does not bleed; typical beetroot flavour; a novelty.

BLACKBERRY
Bedford Giant: crops midsummer, good flavour, good size, vigorous, heavy cropper, less seedy.
Oregon Thornless: mid season, sweet flavour; medium-sized fruit; moderately vigorous, needs good soil conditions.
Himalayan Giant: late; good flavour; medium-sized fruit; vigorous; good variety to use for cooking and bottling.
John Innes: mid to late season; large fruit; juicy; good, sweet flavour; heavy cropper.

BLACKCURRANT
Amos Black: very late; fairly frost resistant.
Baldwin: late; compact bush; large berries; good for making juice; high Vitamin C content.
Boskoop Giant: early; large fruits; heavy cropper; high Vitamin C content; forms big bush.
Wellington XXX: early to mid-season; large berries; sweet; popular; forms large bush.
Westwick Choice: late; medium to large fruit;

heavy cropper; grows in a compact bush.

BLUEBERRY:
Berkeley: large, sweet berries; low, wide bush.
Bluecrop: most reliable variety for cool temperate areas; early; large berries; good flavour; slender, upright growth.
Coville: late; highly flavoured; for warm areas.
Herbert: best for flavour; large, dark blue berries; medium sweet; easily managed.

BROAD BEAN
Longpod:
Aquadulce: suitable for autumn sowing; early.
Bunyards: heavy cropper; popular.
Colossal: excellent cropper; high quality.
Dreadnought: long pods; heavy cropper.
Windsor:
Express: for early spring sowing; very quick maturing; good for deep freezing.
Green Windsor: for spring sowing; later maturing than Longpods; about 5 beans in every pod; excellent flavour.

BROCCOLI (WINTER CAULIFLOWER)
Divided into groups, according to winter hardiness and season of harvest. The earliest or **Peerless** strains suit only mild areas.
For cutting early winter to mid spring:
Angers: a series of varieties, labelled Nos. 1 to 5; mid winter to late spring; No. 1 earliest.
Snow White: early to mid spring; a **Peerless**.
For cutting mid spring to early summer:
Walcheren: several varieties prefixed by Walcheren; late spring to early summer. Very hardy.
Late Queen: extremely hardy; late spring; dwarf and compact. Suitable for cool temperate areas.
June Market: early midsummer; solid; large head. Suitable cool temperate areas.
Roscoff: a group for harvesting throughout winter in mild districts of cool temperate areas. For harvest from late autumn to mid spring, but only limited frost resistance. High quality; large, solid heads, well protected by leaves. Includes **St Agnes, St Bunyan** and **St Keverne**.

BRUSSELS SPROUTS
Achilles: good basic variety; holds its crop over long period; harvest mid autumn to late winter; medium size tight buttons; a F_1 hybrid.
Cambridge No. 5: large sprouts; prolific cropper; mid winter to early spring.
Peer Gynt: early variety — mid autumn but will hold its crop; moderately dwarf so suitable for small garden; dark green sprouts of small to medium size; uniform; prolific; F_1 hybrid.
Vremo: a prefix attached to a group of varieties specially developed for deep freezing.

CABBAGE
Divided into three main groups: those for sowing in early spring, those for sowing in late spring and early summer, and those for sowing in late summer and autumn.
For early spring sowing:
Golden Acre-Progress: mature late spring; round-headed; good colour and flavour.
For late spring and early summer sowing:
Greyhound: very early point-headed variety; ready mid summer; quick-growing; compact.
January King: a very late, round-headed variety; large; very frost resistant — will stand a severe winter; cut mid winter to mid spring.
Primo: good, popular, round-headed variety; late summer to early autumn; compact.
Winnigstadt: an old favourite; ready late summer to mid autumn; compact, with few outside leaves;

point-headed, grey-green colour.

Hispi: F_1 hybrid; point-headed, compact; ready early summer; very quick-growing; can be grown at almost any season; ideal for sowing under glass mid winter for early outdoor planting.

For late summer and autumn sowing:

Early Giant: sow in late summer for cutting in late spring; large pointed heads.

Harbinger: ready very early spring; small hearts; excellent flavour.

Wheelers Imperial: an old favourite; compact; early to maincrop in spring.

Red Cabbage: a round-headed variety, deep purple or red, grown for pickling; winter.

CARROT

Stump-rooted for early crops under glass:

Amsterdam Forcing: very early; succulent.

Chantenay Red-cored: large; suitable for successional sowing throughout season.

Note — there are several Chantenay varieties.

Early Nantes: small, succulent; suitable for successional growing.

Early Horn (Scarlet Horn): also good for successional sowing; almost coreless.

Intermediate-rooted for early outdoor and main crops:

James's Scarlet Intermediate: an old favourite; excellent flavour; stores well.

Juwarot: new; deep red-orange colour; claimed to have very high carotene (Vitamin A) content.

Long-rooted for maincrop and late:

St. Valery: an old favourite; heavy cropper; stores well.

CAULIFLOWER

For early summer harvesting, usually sown under glass:

All the Year Round: dwarf variety with large compact heads; early but may also be sown for a succession of crops.

Alpha: from which a number of others, including *Polar Ice* and *Climax,* have been evolved; large heads; snow-white; quick-maturing; useful for direct sowing (as opposed to transplanting).

Snowball: very early, dwarf; pure white; solid heads; excellent quality; good for freezing.

Autumn varieties:

Autumn Giant: from this original variety a group of varieties have been developed, including *Majestic* and *Superlative Protecting:* large, solid white heads; cut early autumn to winter.

Veitch's Self-Protecting: late autumn to early winter — snow-white heads well protected by leaves; an old favourite.

Australian varieties:

A group of autumn varieties recently introduced to UK and now very popular. Dwarf growth; pure white heads; high quality; uniformity. Harvest early autumn to early winter. Includes *Bondi, Barrier Reef, Canberra, Kangaroo* and *Manly.*

CELERY

Giant Pink, Giant Red, Giant White: usually sold according to colour.

Golden Self-blanching and *American Green:* two self-blanching varieties.

CHERRY

Pollination rules are very complicated. There are no fully proven self-fertile varieties of sweet cherry and only certain groups of sweet cherry are able to cross-pollinate each other. The acid *Morello* cherry, which is self-fertile, will pollinate all the varieties recommended here, except *Early Rivers.* If you wish to grow varieties other than those suggested here, be sure to consult the nur-

sery catalogue very carefully for suitable pollinators.

Early Rivers: sweet, red-black fruit; crops early summer; excellent flavour; vigorous; *pollinator: Waterloo or Merton Heart.*

Kent Bigarreau (Amber Heart): sweet; pale yellow with red mottlings; good flavour; crops late midsummer; trees spread and arch; moderately vigorous; *pollinator: Waterloo.*

Waterloo: compact tree; sweet juicy fruit; crops midsummer; *pollinator: Kent Bigarreau.*

Merton Heart: sweet black; rich flavour; crops midsummer; *pollinator: Early Rivers.*

Morello: popular acid variety, now divided into many other varieties; red to black fruit; crops mid to late summer; prolific; self-fertile.

CHICORY

Witloof: grown for forcing.

Red Verona: also for forcing, but with crimson or purple foliage.

Sugar Loaf: grown for fresh green salad in autumn and winter. Very hardy; not for forcing.

CHINESE CABBAGE

Pe-tsai: the original variety, most generally available. Others are *Sampan, Nagaoka, Michihli.*

CHINESE GOOSEBERRY

Common Chinese Gooseberry: most available.

Bruno: early; elongated fruits; good cropper.

Hayward: very large; not heavy cropper; late.

Monty: heavy-yielding mid-season.

CORN SALAD

Large-leaved English: good general variety.

Verte de Cambrai: particularly frost hardy.

CRESS

Curled, Broad-leaved and *Plain* are the varieties usually sown with Mustard for cutting for salad while still seedlings.

CUCUMBER

Greenhouse varieties:

Telegraph: an old favourite greenhouse variety; suitable for cold or heated houses.

Butcher's Disease-Resisting: popular for cold or heated houses; easy to grow; heavy cropper.

Femdan: F_1 hybrid; all female flowers; very heavy cropper; resistant to most diseases.

Ridge varieties:

Patio-Pik: early F_1 hybrid; bushy; prolific.

Long Green: standard; prolific; excellent quality.

Burpless Tasty Green: one of several *Burpless* types which are low on acid — hence the name; hardy; good cropper; excellent flavour.

Venlo Pickling: grown for producing gherkins for pickling; heavy cropper.

Apple-shaped: produces apple-shaped fruit; pale green; prolific; good flavour; novelty.

Japanese Cucumber: a recently introduced range of Japanese varieties; long fruit; prolific croppers; easy to grow; outdoor.

DAMSON

Shropshire Damson: most commonly grown; harvest mid autumn. Self-fertile.

Merryweather: late summer and early autumn; for dessert or bottling; large fruit; good flavour. Self-fertile.

EGG-PLANT (AUBERGINE)

Long Purple: the most popular variety.

Moneymaker: New F_1 hybrid; very early.

Black Beauty: Early; prolific; almost round.

ENDIVE

Moss Curled: early variety.

Green Curled: standard summer variety.

Winter Lettuce-leaved: standard winter variety.

FIG

Outdoor:

Brown Turkey: mid season; medium size; dark skin, light dots; deep red flesh.

Brunswick: mid season; large; pale green skin flushed with brown; flesh red at centre.

White Marseilles: early; large; skin pale greenish yellow; flesh white; for mild districts.

Indoor:

The above, with the addition of:

Negro Largo: mid season; large deep-black skin; deep crimson flesh at centre.

Bourjassotte Grise: late; fairly large; dark, reddish-blue skin with strong 'bloom'.

FRENCH BEAN

Dwarf:

Canadian Wonder: an old favourite; good maincrop; prolific; heavy cropper; vigorous.

Glamis: very hardy; ideal for cool temperate conditions; heavy cropper; stringless.

Masterpiece: early; suitable for forcing; prolific; long straight pods; prolonged cropping period; well-established and popular.

Waxpod: several varieties; round-sectioned golden pods; excellent flavour; stringless.

Haricot:

Comtesse de Chambord: harvest late; slow growth; heavy crop; rather small beans.

Climbing:

Earliest of All: Heavy cropper; medium-sized pods; prolonged harvesting season.

Kentucky Wonder: very hardy; disease resistant; heavy cropper; excellent flavour.

Purple-podded: several varieties; gourmet bean; excellent flavour; easy to grow; pods, although purple, are green when cooked.

Coco Bi-colour (Pea Bean): has very broad pods; turns green when cooked if gathered young; seeds may also be used as Haricot Beans.

GHERKIN: see CUCUMBER.

GOOSEBERRY

Careless: second early; excellent all-purpose; milky-green.

Lancashire Lad: mid-season; large red; sweet.

Leveller: mid to late season; high quality; fine flavour; yellow.

Lancer: late; yellow-green; excellent flavour.

GRAPE

Black Hamburg: most popular variety for cold or heated greenhouses; outside on sun-facing walls in mild areas only; blue-black, juicy.

Buckland Sweetwater: for cold greenhouses and west or sun-facing walls; light green fruit, large, juicy, very sweet.

Muscat of Alexandria: heated greenhouse; large, greenish-yellow fruit; a dessert grape of fine quality and flavour.

Madresfield Court: greenhouse variety; early; perhaps finest flavour of all black grapes.

Riesling Sylvaner: outdoor; fruit, light amber; good dessert quality, and for wine.

Siegerrebe: outdoor; fruit, golden or tawny brown; medium size; excellent quality and flavour; good for dessert or wine.

Pirovano 14: outdoor; dual-purpose; fruit, deep red, large; reliable cropper.

Precoce de Malingre: outdoor; early; good wine and fair dessert; green; consistent cropper.

GRAPEFRUIT

Marsh Seedless and *Foster:* two original varieties from which others are constantly being developed.
Shaddock: an early type with very large fruits, thick skin and many pips.

GREENGAGE

Like plums, all except self-fertile varieties need cross pollination. Choose two with the same flowering times.
Jefferson's Gage: yellow flecked with red; crops early autumn; *flowers early.*
Ouillin's Golden Gage: late summer crops; golden yellow; *self-fertile; flowers late.*
Cambridge Gage: round, yellowish-green; crops early autumn; *flowers late.*

KALE

Curled Scotch (marketed by different merchants under similar names): dark, curled leaves on stem of medium height; heavy cropper.
Dwarf Curled: dark curled leaves; heavy cropper; dwarf growth; suitable exposed situations.
Thousand-headed: a plain-leaved variety; once very popular; extremely hardy; heavy cropper.
Pentland Brig: a new cross between plain and curled varieties; very hardy and prolific.
Hungry Gap: dwarf variety for use in late winter and early spring; hardy; crinkled leaves.
Asparagus: curled leaves; produces asparagus-like shoots; hardy and prolific.

KOHLRABI

Purple and *White:* no difference except in colour.

LEEK

The Lyon: long, thick stems; hardy.
Musselburgh: another old favourite; long, thick stems; very hardy.
Giant Winter: for late use; very hardy; very large, with white stems and dark green leaves.
Colossal: good early variety with long stem.

LEMON

Lisbon: vigorous, almost seedless.

LETTUCE

Cabbage varieties:
For spring and summer sowing, for summer and autumn harvesting:
All the Year Round: solid; compact; white crisp heart; slow to run to seed.
Appia: quick-maturing; high quality; resistant to mildew, so good for midsummer sowing.
Buttercrunch: large; compact; slow to seed.
Webb's Wonderful: an old favourite; crisp heart with crinkly leaves; large; solid; slow to run to seed even in hot, dry conditions.
Great Lakes: crisp-hearted and solid; slow to bolt.
Windermere: smaller version of *Great Lakes,* but quicker maturing; popular variety.
For autumn sowing, to harvest in spring:
Arctic King: rather small; very hardy; compact.
Imperial Winter: large; very hardy.
Varieties for forcing under glass:
Kordaat: for heated greenhouse; matures winter.
May Queen: for cold or heated greenhouse; early spring harvest from autumn sowing.
Loose-leaf varieties:
For spring and summer sowing:
Salad Bowl: curved leaves, non-hearting.
Cos varieties:
Lobjoits Green Cos: very large, upright, solid hearts; tightly folded; very slow to bolt.
Winter Density: dwarf; compact; very hardy.
Little Gem: dwarf; crisp; compact; bright green.

LIMA BEAN

Fordhook: new variety; very early and very hardy.

LOGANBERRY

The ordinary type, and the thornless loganberry are the only kinds listed.

MARROW

Bush:
Green Bush: an F_1 hybrid; ideal for producing Courgettes; early; small and tender; prolific.
Golden Zucchini: early maturing, midsummer; golden yellow in colour.
White Bush: creamy-skinned fruit; early maturing; very productive.
Trailing:
Long Green Striped: produces heavy crops of large marrows; good for storing for winter use.
Vegetable Spaghetti: marrow-like fruits containing spaghetti-like pith.

MELON

Dutch Net: orange flesh, netted skin; good size; cloche, frame cultivation. Cantaloupe type.
Emerald Gem: green-fleshed; fine flavour.
Ha-Ogen: yellow flesh; green striped, yellow skin; small but heavy cropping; cloches, frames.
Hero of Lockinge: flesh white; small; good flavour; succeeds in cold frame or greenhouse.
Charantais: flesh scarlet, skin green; medium size; good flavour. Greenhouse or cloche.
Florida: favourite watermelon; large fruits with green skin and pink flesh.

MUSHROOM

There are three types of mushroom, classified according to colour — white, cream and brown. The white look most attractive, but the brown are probably easiest to grow.
Darlington's: white; popular variety.

NECTARINE

Early Rivers: flesh white; large fruits; ready mid to late summer; usually grown under glass; excellent flavour.
Humboldt: flesh yellow; late summer.
John Rivers: midsummer; white flesh.
Lord Napier: flesh white; mid to late summer; large fruits; usually grown under glass.
Pineapple: flesh yellow; early autumn.
Elruge: late summer; white flesh.

OKRA

Long Green; Green Velvet; Clemson Spineless; Perkins Spineless: little to choose between them.

ONION

Ailsa Craig: an old favourite; may be sown in either autumn or spring; large bulbs; mild flavour; long-keeping.
Bedfordshire Champion: very reliable; long-keeping; fine flavour; heavy cropper.
Giant Zittau: semi-flat bulbs; medium size; brown-skinned; very long-keeping.
White Lisbon: the variety usually grown for spring onions; quick-growing; white-skinned.
White Spanish (A1): very large bulbs; flat, will keep for a very long time.
Silver-skin: a small, silver-skinned onion, grown for pickling; quick-growing; ripens early.
Japanese Onions: a new introduction, for sowing in late summer to grow throughout the winter and produce bulb onions in the following early to mid-summer. There are several varieties, two of which are *Kaizuka* and *Express Yellow.*
Onion sets:
Rijnsburger Wijbo (Giant Fen Globe): early; heavy cropper; mild flavour; long-keeping.

ORANGE

Sweet:
Embigno: navel; pale pulp; large good fruit.
Valencia: good size and flavour; will jam.
Sour:
Seville types: used for marmalade; hardier than sweet oranges.

PARSLEY

Paramount: closely curled; compact; dark green; very hardy; slow to seed.
Green Velvet: quick-growing; heavy cropper.

PARSNIP

Avonresister: small, conical; very canker-resistant.
Tender and True: good general variety; smooth skin; marked resistance to canker.

PEA

Early varieties:
Feltham First: sow in late autumn or early spring (but not later, for successional sowing); round-seeded; very early; dwarf.
Early Onward: very popular; round-seeded; useful for successional sowing; very heavy cropper; good for freezing; 60 cm [2'].
Kelvedon Wonder: one of the earliest of the wrinkle-seeded varieties; good for successional sowings; heavy cropper; freezing; 45 cm [1½'].
Second early varieties:
Hurst Green Shaft: very heavy cropper; ideal for freezing; excellent flavour; 75 cm [2½'].
Onward: popular and very reliable; very heavy cropper; good for freezing; 60 cm [2'].
Purple Podded: small pods; peas are green; excellent flavour; 1.6 m [5'].
Maincrop varieties:
Lord Chancellor: heavy cropper; 1-1.2 m [3-4'].
Senator: medium-sized pods but very heavy cropper; outstanding flavour; 1 m [3'].
Recette: a new variety, claimed to be an exceptionally heavy cropper; 60 cm [2'].
Petit Pois:
Gullivert: small pods; delicate flavour.
Sugar Pea (Mange-tout):
Oregon Sugar Pod: good flavour; maximum yield.
Dwarf de Grace: very sweet; heavy crop.

PEACH

For outdoors in cool and warm temperate areas varieties fruiting by early autumn are suitable. In cold temperate areas, you should choose varieties that fruit no later than late summer.
Bellegarde: yellow-fleshed; early autumn.
Duke of York: white-fleshed; midsummer; suitable for outdoors or indoors.
Peregrine: white-fleshed; mid to late summer; favourite outdoor variety.
Rochester: yellow-fleshed; late summer; good outdoor variety.

PEAR

The notes on pollination in the APPLE varieties section (*see* above) apply to pears. In addition there are a number of diploid pears which will not pollinate each other. Always check carefully with the nursery when ordering. The varieties listed here will all cross-pollinate, but always *choose two with overlapping flowering periods.*
Conference: very reliable; resistant to frost and disease; pick in early autumn, keep for use later; fruit rather long in shape. Some degree of self-fertility but is best cross-pollinated; *flowers early.*
Marguerite Marillat: hardy and fertile; large golden fruits flushed with scarlet; juicy and sweet; *flowers early.*

Packham's Triumph: very heavy cropper; green ripens to yellow; juicy and sweet; pick in mid autumn for eating later; *flowers mid season.*

William's Bon Chretien (Bartlett): very high quality dessert pear; melting, juicy flesh; ripe in early autumn, for immediate eating, or for canning or bottling; *flowers mid season.*

Dr. Jules Guyot: very heavy cropper but small fruit; pick in early autumn and eat at once; *flowers late.*

Doyenne du Comice: another favourite; excellent flavour; not easy to grow, needs careful cultivation; susceptible to scab; pick early to mid autumn; fruit will store till early to mid winter; *flowers late.*

PEPPER (CAPSICUM)

Canape: early, strong growth; outdoors in mild districts: F_1 hybrid.

New Ace: F_1 hybrid; early; high-yielding; best grown under glass.

Mexican Chilli: a hot pepper which must be grown in a greenhouse.

PLUM

Varieties other than self-fertile need a suitable pollinator. Choose overlapping flowering periods.

Czar: dark blue, with attractive heavy bloom; good cropper; good cooker; quality not high; late summer. Self-fertile.

Marjorie's Seedling: dark purple; large; late, ready in early to mid autumn. Self-fertile.

Pershore: yellow cooking plum; ripe late summer to early autumn. Self-fertile.

Victoria: very popular; bright red; good for dessert, bottling and jam-making; heavy cropper; susceptible to silver-leaf; self-fertile.

POTATO

First early:

Home Guard: white-skinned; excellent quality; good cropper.

Arran Pilot: white-skinned; floury; high quality; good cropper.

Second early:

Kerr's Pink: pink-skinned; good for areas with high rainfall and/or heavy soil; good cropper.

Pentland Lustre: new variety; firm, yellow flesh; heavy cropper; eelworm resistant.

Red Craig's Royal: red-skinned; tubers of uniform shape and size; high quality.

Maincrop:

Arran Banner: white-skinned; large, round potato; heavy cropper; floury.

Desiree: red-skinned; heavy cropper in all kinds of soil; high quality.

Golden Wonder: kidney shape; white to yellow flesh; lemon skin; good flavour and cropper.

Majestic: the most widely grown variety; large tubers; very heavy cropper; kidney shape; rather waxy when cooked; suits most soils.

PUMPKIN

Hundredweight: the commonest variety; huge fruits; good for winter storage.

QUINCE

Vranja: large yellow fruit; crops when young; mid autumn cropping; good flavour.

RADISH

Cherry Belle: bright red; mild in flavour; globe-shaped; early; keeps well.

French Breakfast: half-red, half-white; olive shaped; quick-growing.

Scarlet Globe: most popular variety for outdoors; very quick-growing; red.

White Icicle: long, white roots; quick-growing.

Winter Radishes:

Black Spanish: black skin; white flesh; two varieties — one long, one round.

China Rose: oval shape; rose skin; white flesh.

RASPBERRY

Malling Jewel: prolific cropper; medium-sized dark red fruit; medium height; crops midsummer.

Malling Promise: tall-growing to 2 m [6']; heavy cropper; large fruits; flavour moderate.

Zeva: late, ripening in autumn; dwarf growth; vigorous; fruit of high quality; red and juicy; good for dessert, jam-making or freezing.

RED AND WHITE CURRANT

Laxton's No. 1: red; early; heavy cropper with medium to large berries.

Red Lake: harvests mid season; very heavy cropper; large berries.

White Dutch: a mid-season variety.

White Versailles: early; very prolific; large berries; rich flavour.

RHUBARB

The Sutton: good maincrop; reluctant to seed.

Timperley Early: good variety for forcing.

Victoria: best variety for raising from seed.

RUNNER BEAN

Enorma: very heavy cropper; pods slender and smooth; excellent for freezing.

Goliath: heavy cropper; large; high quality.

Kelvedon Marvel: very early.

Sunset: pink flowers; early; heavy cropping; medium length pods.

Hammond's Dwarf Scarlet: dwarf form, requiring no supports; very early; long cropping season; usually grown only by commercial growers.

Streamline: popular; long pods; high quality.

SPINACH

Greenmarket: large, dark green leaves; heavy cropper; slow to run to seed; sow in spring or autumn, to stand the winter; very hardy.

Cleanleaf: heavy cropper; leaves carried well above soil, thus avoiding contamination.

Monnopa: a new variety, low on oxalic acid content; very bolt resistant; winter hardy.

Long-standing Round: good general variety; quick growth; needs regular picking of leaves.

Long-standing Prickly: winter and early spring; quick growth; bolt resistant; hardy.

SPROUTING BROCCOLI

Green sprouting varieties (Calabrese):

Green Comet: very early; heavy cropper, with tight broad main head and few laterals; F_1 hybrid.

Late Corona: very similar to *Green Comet*, but much later in maturing; F_1 hybrid.

El Centro: matures autumn from spring sowing; has both central and side shoots.

Corvet: medium early; large rounded heads; good for freezing.

White sprouting varieties (small white spears):

Early White Sprouting: early-mid spring.

Late White Sprouting: late spring-early summer.

Purple sprouting varieties (small purple spears; hardier than other types):

Christmas Purple Sprouting: very early; matures mid-late winter.

Early Purple Sprouting: matures late winter-early spring.

Late Purple Sprouting: matures late spring-early summer.

Perennial sprouting varieties:

Nine Star Perennial: each plant produces 6-9 pale green heads in mid-late spring yearly.

SQUASHES

Hubbard squash: hard golden skin; medium size; ready autumn, will store in winter.

Scalloped summer squash: (Custard Marrow) thick, round and flat, with scalloped edges, white or yellow; summer.

STRAWBERRY

Early:

Gorella: large; good for cloches and tunnels.

Cambridge Vigour: good flavour; medium cropper; resistant to red core.

Second early & mid-season:

Royal Sovereign: old favourite; rich flavour and moderate cropper; excellent for forcing.

Grandee: immense berries, particularly in second season; excellent flavour; good for forcing.

Talisman: heavy cropper; mid-season; large berries; reliable.

Perpetual:

Gento: good all-rounder; good yields; largish berries; excellent flavour.

Alpine:

Baron Solemacher: very good flavour; fruit the size of a very large wild strawberry; crops mid summer to mid autumn; not runner.

SWEDE

Purple-top: excellent for both eating when young and for winter storage.

SWEET CORN

Earliking: one of earliest maturing. F_1 hybrid.

Kelvedon Glory: popular variety; second-early; cobs set well; excellent flavour. F_1 hybrid.

Sugar King: mid-season or late crop; high sugar content. F_1 hybrid.

SWISS CHARD

Also listed as **Seakale Beet** (Silver Beet)

Lily White: green-leaved, white-stemmed kind.

Ruby Chard (Rhubarb Chard): bright red stems.

TOMATO

Ailsa Craig: early; hardy; can be used for both indoor and outdoor cultivation; medium-sized fruit; good flavour.

Eurocross BB: early; heavy cropper; large fruits; moderately disease-resistant; greenhouse only; F_1 hybrid.

Harbinger: popular outdoor and indoor variety; early; moderate to heavy cropper; high quality.

Golden Queen: Golden yellow: indoor or outdoor; medium-sized fruit; sweeter flavour than red tomatoes.

The Amateur: bush variety for outdoor; early heavy cropper.

Outdoor Girl: probably the earliest for outdoor cultivation; heavy cropper; sweet flavour.

Tiny Tim: outdoors, dwarf to 38 cm [15"]; small, marble-sized fruit; bush type.

Mixed Ornamental: small fruits, red or yellow, currant, plum and pear shapes; dwarf, outdoors or under glass; usually eaten whole.

TURNIP

Early Snowball: early; medium-sized globe root; mild flavour; good quality.

Golden Ball: yellow globe variety; very hardy; best variety for winter storage.

Purple Milan: early; quick-growing; dwarf; flat roots; medium size; good under frames or cloches; quality excellent.

Green-top White: round; top of root green, lower half white; good for winter use and leaving through winter to produce green tops in spring.

ZUCCHINI *see* **Marrow.**

311

Glossary

Cross references in capitals refer to sections of the Basic Gardening Guide

Acid *(soil): see* IMPROVING THE SOIL.

Alkaline *(soil): see* IMPROVING THE SOIL.

Annual: a plant that completes its life cycle in one year and then dies.

Anther: in the flower, the part of the *stamen* that contains the *pollen* grains.

Axil: the angle formed between a leaf, flower or shoot stem and the parent stem from which any of these arise; usually refers to that formed between the leaf stem and parent stem.

Biennial: a plant that completes its life cycle in two years and then dies. Many vegetables are biennials but are treated as *annuals,* harvested in their first year, before they have had time to flower and seed.

Blanching: the process of excluding light from growing plants to make them white and less bitter.

Bleeding: the loss of sap from plant tissues that have been cut or damaged.

Blind: a seedling or mature plant that has lost its growing tip before it flowers, and so ceases to grow.

Bloom *(on fruit):* the downy or white waxy covering on grapes, peaches and other fruit.

Brassica: the botanical *genus* to which members of the cabbage tribe belong.

Budding: a method of propagating a fruit tree by uniting a bud, with a slip of bark attached, to a host plant.

Bulb: storage organ of a plant, composed of fleshy leaf bases wrapped around an embryo shoot, and sometimes also an embryo flower, from which new growth comes.

Bulbil: a miniature bulb, which forms either at the base of a mature bulb or on a stem by a flower-head (as in certain onions).

Calyx *(pl. calyces):* the outer series of modified leaves of a flower, made up of sepals, which are usually different in appearance from the petals.

Catch crop: quick maturing crop raised in a plot where a later crop is to be grown.

Chlorosis: the loss of colour (usually green) from a plant, often due to a mineral deficiency, resulting in the production of leaves that are yellow, white or mottled.

Clamp: a mound of straw and soil heaped over a store of harvested roots, such as carrots or potatoes, to preserve them.

Clone: a group of identical plants obtained by vegetative propagation from a parent.

Compost *(garden):* decayed vegetable matter, forming a valuable organic manure.

Compost *(potting):* a mixture, usually of loam, sand and peat, with the addition of plant foods, used for growing plants in pots and other containers.

Compositae: the botanical family whose flowers consist of a cluster of many 'florets' in a 'composite' head. The daisy is a typical member; examples are chicory and lettuce.

Cordon: a fruit tree or bush restricted by pruning to form a single main stem.

Cotyledons *(or seed leaves):* the first leaves to appear in a seedling; they usually look quite different from the mature leaves.

Crown: the heart or base of a perennial plant, which grows both roots and shoots.

Cruciferae: the botanical family of plants, the flowers of which have four petals arranged in the form of a cross. Examples are cabbage and radish.

Cross-pollination: the transference of pollen from one flower to another, either on the same plants or between different plants.

Cucurbits: plants of the botanical family *Cucurbitacae,* with tendrils for climbing; examples are marrow and cucumber.

Cutting: a small section of a stem, root or leaf cut off the parent plant and given the conditions it needs to produce roots, and become a new plant.

Deciduous: a tree, shrub or other plant whose leaves fall at the end of the season.

Dibber: *see* TOOLS.

Drawn: a term applied to plants which, because they are sown too thickly or in a badly-lit place, become long and sickly.

Drill: a straight furrow, usually shallow, in which seeds are sown.

Earthing-up: the process of drawing soil around a plant to exclude light, as with potatoes and celery. It is also done to protect a plant from frost, or to support it.

Espalier: a type of trained fruit tree in which a vertical trunk has pairs of horizontal, opposite branches arranged in tiers.

Eye: an undeveloped growth bud, used particularly of those on potatoes.

Family: a botanical term for a group of related *genera* of plants.

Fan: a tree or shrub restricted by training to produce a fan-shape.

Fallow: an area in which no plants are grown during a growing season. During this rest period the soil is usually cultivated, to aerate it and to destroy weeds.

Fertilization: the fusion of the pollen of the male plant with the ovule (or undeveloped seed) of the female, to form a seed.

F_1 Hybrid: the first generation of a new hybrid plant produced by cross-pollination.

Foliar Spray: a liquid containing plant nutrients which plants can absorb through their leaves, when sprayed over them.

Forcing: encouraging plants to grow more quickly than normal or at an unnatural time by use of heat.

Friable *(of soil):* crumbly, neither too moist, nor too dry; easily worked.

Frame: *see* CLOCHES AND FRAMES.

Fungicide: a chemical to kill fungi.

Gall: an abnormal growth on a plant, caused by insects, bacteria or fungi.

Germination: the first stage in the growth of a new plant from a seed.

Genus *(pl. genera):* botanical name for group of closely-related *species* of plants; related genera form a *family.*

Grafting: a method of propagation whereby the stem of one plant is united to a branch or root of another to form a new individual.

Green Manure: growing plants dug into the soil while still green to assist in providing plant food and improving the soil structure.

Hardy: refers to plants able to survive temperatures at or below freezing.

Half-hardy: refers to plants which will grow outdoors in summer but which will not survive temperatures below freezing.

Hardening off: the process of gradual acclimatization of plants that have been grown indoors to outdoor temperatures.

Half-standard: a tree, the stem of which grows vertically to a height of about 1.2 m [4'] before sending out lateral branches.

Haulm: the surplus green parts of a vegetable crop, such as the stems and foliage of potatoes or peas.

Heeling-in: the process of temporarily storing plants by placing their roots in a shallow hole and covering them with soil.

Herbaceous: a plant with tender green stems and foliage as distinct from woody growth. Commonly used of perennials which die down in autumn, forming new growth in spring.

Herbicide: a chemical to kill weeds.

Hot-bed: a prepared garden plot, often protected by a frame, in which the temperature is raised by the addition of organic matter which generates heat as it rots.

Humus: organic matter which has decayed to produce a brown or black substance. One of its most important properties is to improve the soil structure, whether the soil is basically clay or sand. The bacteria which it contains continue to break it down; it therefore has constantly to be replaced.

Hybrid: a plant grown from seed, produced by the pollen of a flower on one plant fertilizing the ovule of the flower on another, usually between two varieties or species.

Inter-cropping: the practice of growing a quick-growing crop, between rows of slower-growing plants; or of growing two crops in the same plot of ground.

Lateral: a branch or shoot growing from a larger stem.

Leaching: the loss of soluble minerals from the soil through water washing them away.

Leader: a major stem of a plant through which it extends a branching system; the central leader is one which continues growth of the trunk vertically.

Leafmould: a rich soil formed from decayed or decaying leaves of trees.

Leguminosae: botanically, the plant family to which peas and beans belong.

Light: *see* CLOCHES AND FRAMES.

Lime: a chemical compound supplying calcium to the soil.

Loam: *see* IMPROVING THE SOIL.

Maiden: a one-year-old fruit tree or bush ready for training; rooted strawberry runners are also called maidens.

Maincrop: the heaviest yielding crop of the season of a particular fruit or vegetable, as distinct from the early or late crops from specialized varieties.

Manure: originally farm manure, but now any bulky material that supplies humus and plant nutrients.

Mulch: any material used to cover the soil to aid cultivation. Organic mulches such as peat, straw and garden compost add food to the soil, help prevent the soil from drying out by reducing evaporation from its surface, keep the soil surface warm in winter and cool in summer and suppress weeds. Inorganic mulches such as plastic sheeting do not add food to the soil, but have all the other advantages of organic ones.

Neutral soil: see IMPROVING THE SOIL
Nitrogen: see IMPROVING THE SOIL.
Node: a stem joint from which leaves, buds and sideshoots emerge.
Nodules: tiny round swellings on the roots of leguminous plants, such as peas and beans. They contain bacteria which are able to convert nitrogen gas from the air into nitrogen compounds useable by plants.
Offset: a sideshoot that develops naturally into a young plant, as with many bulbs.
Ovary: botanically, an unripened seed-pod.
Ovule: an unfertilized seed in an ovary.
Parthenocarpic: able to bear fruit without pollination.
Peat: a substance formed in bogs and fens from partially decayed organic matter.
Perennial: a plant with an indefinite life-period, longer than two years. Usually applied to herbaceous plants.
Petal Fall: the stage at which fruit trees shed their flower petals.
pH Value: a numerical scale for measuring the acidity or alkalinity of the soil, ranging from 1 to 14. Acid soil has a pH of less than 7, alkaline soil a pH greater than 7, while soil with a pH of 7 is neutral.
Phosphorus: one of the essential plant foods, usually supplied by phosphates — these are compounds of phosphorus and other elements.
Pinching out: the removal of the growing point of a plant stem, to encourage it to branch out lower down or form new buds.
Pistil: the female organ of a flower, consisting of an ovary, stigma and style.
Pollen: the male cells of a flower.
Pollination: the transference of pollen from a male flower to the stigma of a female flower. Normally done by bees or other insects but may have to be done by hand.
Potassium: see IMPROVING THE SOIL.
Potting on: a term used for removing a plant and the soil around its roots to a larger pot, to allow more space for the roots.
Pricking out: the operation of transferring seedlings from the pots or trays in which they were raised from seed to other containers or to outdoor beds.
Propagation: the increase of plants, by sowing seed, root division, cuttings, grafting or other means.
Propagator: usually applied to a glass-covered container, artificially heated, for promoting the growth of seeds when outside conditions are unfavourable.
Pruning: the cutting back, usually of a tree or bush for various purposes. In winter this is often done to shape; in summer to encourage the development of fruit buds.
Pyramid: a fruit tree, usually a pear, but also cherries, plums and apples, trained to a pyramid shape.
Ring culture: a method of growing plants, particularly tomatoes, in which they are made to produce two root systems, one absorbing mainly nutrients and the other water. *See* TOMATO.
Rhizome: a part of a plant which looks like a root but is actually a creeping, underground stem, as in the weed *Agropyron repens* (couch grass).
Rogue: an alternative name for a mutant, or plant which does not conform to type.
Root-crop: vegetables grown for their roots.
Rootstock: A fruit tree used for its roots alone, onto which a fruit-bearing variety, the scion, is grafted.

Rootstock, dwarfing: a fruit tree rootstock that will produce a smaller tree than is natural to the variety grafted on to it.
Rotation of crops: see PLANNING YOUR GARDEN
Runner: a trailing stem of a plant which produces roots at the *nodes* where they touch the soil and eventually forms a new plant.
Salt: Sodium chloride used as a fertilizer for crops derived from maritime plants. Sold as agricultural salt. Has the property of making insoluble potash already in the soil available to plants. Also used as a weed-killer.
Scion: the uppermost *variety* of a fruit tree which determines what kind of fruit the tree will bear, grafted onto the stem of the *rootstock* of another variety or *species.*
Scorching: the effect of too much heat, too much sunlight or sometimes dry chemical fertilizer on the foliage of plants. White, brown or shrivelled patches appear.
Seed, pelleted: see SEEDS AND SEED-BEDS.
Seed-leaf: see *Cotyledon.*
Selective (of weedkillers): *see* GARDEN HYGIENE.
Self-fertile: of a plant variety whose flowers produce *pollen* that will pollinate the *ovules* of the same or other flowers borne by plants of that variety. It does not need another variety to act as a pollinator.
Self-sterile: a plant *variety* whose flowers are sterile to their own *pollen;* such a plant needs a different variety nearby to act as a pollinator and so enable it to produce fruit.
Sepal: botanically, the outer layer of modified leaves which comprise a flower, the inner one being made up of the petals. Sepals are usually green and protect petals.
Set: of potatoes, those tubers, or parts of them, used as seed and planted; of onions and related crops, small immature *bulbs* in a state of arrested development that are planted to shorten the growing period.
Setting: a term describing the appearance of a young seed or fruit after the *pollination* of a flower.
Soot: a black residue of fuel, resulting from imperfect combustion. It is a source of *nitrogen,* containing up to 6% and also acts as a deterrent to insects and slugs.
Species: botanically, a group of closely-related plants which collectively form a *genus.* Species will breed true from seed.
Spit: the depth to which soil is normally dug with a spade — about 23-30 cm [9-12"].
Spur: a short *lateral* twig or branchlet of a fruit-tree which bears a flower and subsequently a fruit. An established spur is one with several fruit buds.
Staging: shelving (permanent or portable) on which to place plants in a greenhouse.
Stamen: the complete male organ of a flower, consisting of an *anther,* which is borne on a slender stalk-like filament.
Standard: applied to fruit trees, a standard is a tree with an expanse of bare trunk, usually 1.5-1.8 m [5-6'], below the head of branches; it is produced by *grafting.*
Station: the position chosen for each plant in a row.
Stigma: the tip of the female organ of a flower, producing a sticky fluid when ready for *pollination.*
Stopping: the *pinching out* of the growing point of a stem to encourage branching or the production of more flower-buds.

Strig: of currants, one cluster of fruits with their stalks, including the central stalk of the cluster.
Subsoil: the soil beneath the *topsoil* layer, which is derived from it. Usually infertile and badly structured; unsuitable for growing plants.
Sucker: a shoot which emerges from a plant below ground-level, usually from the roots.
Succession: the sequence of crops in a garden — a matter which requires considerable planning to produce vegetables as they are needed and to avoid waste of space.
Sulphur: an element of which minute quantities are needed by some plants; these are normally obtainable through the sulphates supplied in fertilizers. Also used as a fungicide.
Systemic (of insecticide or fungicide): a chemical which, applied to one part of a plant, spreads to all other parts of it and, without doing the plant any harm, is lethal to any insect pests or fungus diseases.
Taproot: a root which penetrates directly downwards into the soil and is the main anchor of the plant, such as that of carrot, parsnip and other root crops.
Tender: a plant vulnerable to frost.
Tine: a prong, or spike of a fork or rake.
Tilth: the fine crumbly surface layer of cultivated, or tilled, soil.
Thatch: straw arranged to form a waterproof roof to a clamp or other construction.
Topdressing: the application of fertilizer to the surface of the soil; or the replacement of the surface layer of soil of a container with new potting compost.
Topsoil: the uppermost layer of soil in a garden. Varies from 5 cm [2"] to 60 cm [2'] or more deep.
Training: the art of shaping fruit-trees by pruning, stopping and other means.
Triploid: a plant whose pollen cells contain 1½ times the normal number of chromosomes (microscopic parts of a plant cell that give the plant its characteristic form). Such plants have less fertile *pollen* and need extra pollinators.
True leaves: the leaves of a mature plant, which succeed the *cotyledons,* or seed leaves, of the seedlings.
Truss: in some plants, eg tomato, a cluster of flowers or fruit.
Tuber: a storage organ, either a swollen underground stem, as in the potato, or a swollen root, as in the dahlia, by means of which the plant survives a period of drought.
Umbelliferae: a family in which the flowers form a kind of flattened dome, the flower stalks all linking with the main stem at the same point, eg. carrot and parsnip.
Union: the joint where a chosen variety (the *scion*) is grafted into the *rootstock.*
Variety: a subdivision of a *species.* A species has unique characteristics, which are always reproduced by its seedlings, but a variety will not breed true, and may or may not resemble its parents. Strictly speaking, the term now applies to those varieties which have arisen in the wild. Those which have appeared in cultivation, such as in gardens, nurseries or by deliberate breeding, are called cultivars; in gardening, however, the term is still used to include both kinds.
Virus: an ultramicroscopic organism which invades the nucleus of the plant cell, resulting in irreversible damage to plants.

Regional guide to seasons

A note on climate

In giving cultivation details, we have used such terms as 'early spring' and 'late winter'. By using the tables on this page you can find which months are equivalent to these terms in your region. Do remember that any unpredictable changes in weather can alter your plans; for example, an unusually long winter may mean delaying sowing times scheduled for 'early spring' months by a few weeks.

Your crops are affected not only by the regional climate, but also by the 'microclimate'. This is the individual climate of the garden, and depends on such factors as the slope of the site and the degree of shelter and shade from hedges or walls. You need to consider these factors — as well as the regional climate — in planning which crops to grow when.

UNITED KINGDOM

SEASON	South	North
Early spring	March	Late March/April
Mid spring	April	May
Late spring	May	June
Early summer	June	July
Mid summer	July	July
Late summer	August	August
Early autumn	September	September
Mid autumn	October	October
Late autumn	November	October
Early winter	December	November/December
Mid winter	January	January/February
Late winter	February	Early March

SOUTH AFRICA

SEASON	Western Cape & Cape Town	Transvaal Highveld	Durban & South Coast
Early spring	Late August/Early September	Late August/Early September	August
Mid spring	Mid-September	Mid-September	Early September
Late spring	Late September/October	Late September	Late September
Early summer	November/December	October/November	October/November
Mid summer	January/February	December/February	December/February
Late summer	March/April	April	April
Early autumn	Mid-April/Early May	Early May	May
Mid autumn	Late May	May/June	Early June
Late autumn	Early June	Early June	Late June
Early winter	Late June	Late June	June/Early July
Mid winter	July/August	July/August	Late July
Late winter	Early August	Early August	Early August

AUSTRALIA AND NEW ZEALAND

SEASON	Tasmania, mountains, Melbourne, Canberra, Armidale and South Island	Perth and Albany to Geraldton. N.S.W. Coast north to Kempsey, and North Island, New Zealand.	Coffs Harbour and north to Lismore, Brisbane, Bundaberg, Rockhampton & Mackay.	The Mallee, Wimmera, Riverina and the Darling Downs.
Early autumn	March	March	April	March
Mid autumn	April	April	May	April
Late autumn	Early May	May	Early June	May
Early winter	Late May	June	Late June	June
Mid winter	June/July	July	July	July
Late winter	August/Early September	August	August	August
Early spring	Late September	September	September	September
Mid spring	October	October	October	October
Late spring	November	November	October	November
Early summer	December	December	November	December
Mid summer	January	January	December/January	January
Late summer	February	February	February/March	February

Index

A

Actinidia Chinensis see
  Chinese gooseberry
adzuki bean 36-38
Agaricus bisporus see
  mushroom
Agaricus campestris see under
  mushroom
Allium ampeloprasum porrum
  see leek
Allium cepa see onion
Allium cepa aggregatum see
  shallot
Allium cepa perutile see ever-
  ready onion
Allium cepa proliferum see
  tree onion
Allium fistulosum see Welsh
  onion
Allium sativum see garlic
Allium schoenoprasum see
  chives
Aloysia triphylla see lemon
  verbena
American blight see woolly
  aphid
American cress 106
American gooseberry mildew
  46, 131, 304
Anethum graveolens see dill
angelica 10-11
Angelica archangelica see
  angelica
anthracnose (fungus disease)
  126
Anthriscus cerefolium see
  chervil
aphids 19, 25, 41, 44, 131,
  139, 203, 210, 304, 305,
  306
Apium graveolens see celery
Apium graveolens rapaceum
  see celeriac
apple 11-21
  cultivation 14, 15
  forms of trees **12, 13,** 16,
  18, 19
  harvesting and storing 19
  pests and diseases 19
  planting 14, **15,** 16, **18**
  pollination 13
  pruning 16, **17, 18**
  site and soil requirements
  12, 14
  spraying 19, 21
  varieties 12, 13, **20,** 308
apple cucumber 108
applemint 172
apple sawfly 19, 305
apple sucker 19, 305
apricot 21-23
  care 22-23
  harvesting and storing 23
  in pots **22**
  pests and diseases 23
  planting 21-22
  pollination 22, **23**
  pruning 23

site and soil requirements
  21
  varieties 308
Armoracia rusticana see
  horseradish
Artemisia dracunculus see
  tarragon
artichoke, Chinese **25,** 27
  varieties 308 (UK)
artichoke, globe **24-25**
  harvesting 25
  propagation **24,** 25
  site and soil requirements
  24
  sowing and planting 25
  varieties 308
artichoke, Jerusalem 25-27
  planting **26,** 27
  site and soil requirements
  26, 27
  varieties 308
asparagus **28-30**
  beds 28, **30**
  care of plants 31
  from seed 28, **30**
  harvesting **30,** 31
  pests and diseases 31
  soil requirements 28
  transplanting 28, **30,** 31
  varieties 308
Asparagus officinalis see
  asparagus
asparagus beetle 31, 302
asparagus pea **31-32**
aubergine see eggplant
Australian cress 105
autumn cabbages 61

B

baby marrow see zucchini
balm **33**
bamya see okra
bank cress 106
Barbarea praecox see land
  cress
barn cloche **298**
basic slag 296
basil **33-34**
bay **34-36**
bean seed beetle 198, 241, 302
beans in general 36
bean sprouts **36-38**
  varieties 308 (UK)
beetles 264, 305
beetroot **38-41**
  cultivation 38, **39**
  growing under cloche or
  frame 40
  growing in containers 40
  harvesting and storing 40
  site and soil requirements
  38
  varieties 38, **39, 40,** 308
Beta vulgaris see beetroot
Beta vulgaris cicla see spinach
  beet and Swiss chard
bigarreau see cherry
big bud gall mite 46, **47,** 304

bilberry 48, **50**
birds (as pests) 19, 46, 51, **59,**
  65, 85, **88,** 89, 101, 126,
  131, 139, 157, 176, 184,
  196, 203, 210, 217, 227,
  230, 233, 262, 273, 302,
  304, 305, 306
bitter pit 19, **305**
blackberry 41-44
  layering 43
  pests and diseases 44
  planting 41-42
  pruning 43
  site and soil requirements
  41
  training 41, 42, **43**
  varieties 308 (UK)
blackberry dwarf disease
  (virus) 44, 305
blackcurrant 44-47
  pests and diseases 46, 47
  planting 44, **45**
  propagation 46, **47**
  pruning **45,** 46
  site and soil requirements
  44
  spraying 46
  varieties 308
blackcurrant leaf spot (fungus
  disease) 46, 304
black dolphin aphid see
  blackfly
blackfly 41, 52, **53, 54**-55,
  179, 241, 245, 302, 303,
  304, **306**
black leg 223, 303
black root rot 198, 249, 302
blaeberry 48
blanching 312, see also
  cardoon, celery, chicory,
  Chinese cabbage, endive,
  Florence fennel, leek,
  lettuce, salsify and seakale
blight fungus 25, 220
blood orange 98
blueberry **48-51**
  cultivation 50
  planting 48
  pruning 50
  site and soil requirements
  48
  varieties 308 (UK)
bonemeal 296
borage **50, 51**
Borago officinalis see borage
borecole 142
botrytis (fungus disease) 51
Bowles' mint 172
boysenberry 157, **159**
brambles see blackberry
bramble shoot webber 304
Brassica chinensis see Chinese
  cabbage
Brassica napus napobrassica
  see swede
Brassica oleracea acephala see
  kale
Brassica oleracea botrytis see
  broccoli and cauliflower
*Brassica oleracea botrytis
  cymosa* see sprouting
  broccoli
*Brassica oleracea bullata
  major* see savoy
Brassica oleracea capitata see
  cabbage
Brassica oleracea caulorapa
  see kohlrabi
Brassica oleracea gemmifera
  see brussels sprouts

Brassica pekinensis see pe-tsai
Brassica rapa see turnip
broad bean 36, **51-55**
  cultivation 52, **53**
  growing under glass 54
  harvesting 52, 54
  pests and diseases 54-55
  soil requirements 52
  sowing 52, **53**
  spraying **53,** 54
  varieties 51, 52, 308
broccoli **55-57**
  harvesting and storing 57
  pests and diseases 57
  planting out 55, **56,** 57
  site and soil requirements
  55
  sowing 55, **56**
  varieties 308
  winter protection **56,** 57
brown rot (fungus disease) 19,
  204, 210, 304, 305, **306**
brown watercress 107
Brussels sprouts **57-61**
  'blown' sprouts 58
  container-growing 61
  cultivation 60
  early crops 58, 60
  harvesting **59,** 60
  pests and diseases see under
  cabbage
  site and soil requirements
  58
  sowing and planting out 58,
  59
  varieties 308
bubbles (fungus disease of
  mushrooms) 178, 303
bullace 112, 214
bush basil 33
butter bean see Lima bean

C

cabbage **61**-65
  feeding 62, 63, 65
  harvesting and storing **64,**
  65
  pests and diseases 65-66
  planting out **64,** 65
  soil requirements 61, 63, 65
  sowing **64,** 65
  spring greens 61, 65
  types 61, **63**
  varieties 308
cabbage club root **304**
cabbage moth 65, 302
cabbage root fly 55, 65, 144,
  302
cabbage white butterfly 65,
  302, **306**
calabrese 255, **256,** 257
calamondin 98
cane spot 230, 305
canker 19, 89, 103, 122, 172,
  176, 193, 204, 210, 283,
  303, 304, 305
cantaloupe see under melon
Cape broccoli 55
Cape gooseberry **66-68**
  cultivation and care 66, **67,**
  68
  harvesting and storing 68
  in greenhouse 68
Capsicum annuum see sweet
  pepper
Capsicum frutescens see chilli
  and red pepper

capsids 19, 44, 46, 131, 210, 219, 233, 241, 302, 304, 305, 306
caraway 68-69
cardoon 70-72
  blanching 70, **71, 72**
  cultivation 70
  sowing 70
carrot 72-75
  harvesting and storing 74, **75**
  growing in frames 74
  pests and diseases 74
  site and soil requirements 72
  sowing and thinning 72, 74, **75**
  varieties **75, 308** (Australian), 309 (UK)
carrot-fly 74, 81, 84, 191, 193, 303
Carum carvi see caraway
caterpillars 19, 44, 65, 68, 117, 183, 210, 304, 305, 306
cauliflower 76-79
  cultivation and care 77-79
  harvesting and storing **78**-79
  pests and diseases 78-79
  site and soil requirements 76
  sowing and transplanting **77, 78**
  varieties 76, 77, 309
celeriac 79-81
  cultivation **80, 81**
  harvesting and storing 81
  sowing and planting out **80**-81
celery 81-84
  blanching **83,** 84
  harvesting and storing **83**-84
  pests and diseases 84
  sowing and planting out 82, **83,** 84
  varieties 309
celery fly 81, 84, 193, 302, 303
celery leaf spot (fungus disease) 81, 84, 302, 303
Chenopodium bonus-henricus see Good King Henry
cherry 85-89
  choosing a tree 87
  harvesting 89
  pests and diseases **89**
  site and soil requirements 85
  training and pruning 88-89
  varieties 85, **86, 87,** 309
cherry fruit fly 89, 304
cherry fruit moth 304
cherry plum 214
chervil 90
chicons 90
chicory 90-92
  forcing **92**
  harvesting and storing 91-**92**
  site and soil requirements 91
  sowing and planting 91
  varieties 309
chilli pepper 210, 213
Chinese artichoke see artichoke, Chinese
Chinese bean sprouts 36
Chinese cabbage 93-94
  blanching **93**
  site and soil requirements 94

sowing and care 94
  varieties 309
Chinese gooseberry 94-96
  care 96
  growing under glass 96
  site and soil requirements 94, 96
  training and pruning **95, 96**
  varieties 309
chives 96-97
chocolate spot (fungus disease) 55, 302
Cichorium endivia see endive
Cichorium intybus see chicory
cider apples see apple
citrange 98
citron 98
Citrullus vulgaris see watermelon
Citrus aurantifolia see lime
Citrus aurantium see Seville orange
citrus fruit 97-103
  cultivation and care 98-101
  cuttings 103
  from seed **100,** 101
  harvesting 103
  in greenhouse 101
  planting out 101
  types 98, **99**
Citrus grandis see shaddock
Citrus limon see lemon
Citrus maxima = C. grandis
Citrus medica see citron
Citrus sinensis melitensis see blood orange
Citrus mitis see calamondin
Citrus nobilis deliciosa = C. reticulata
Citrus paradisi see grapefruit
Citrus reticulata see tangerine
Citrus sinensis see sweet orange
clay soil 293
clementine 98
cloches 298
clubroot (fungus disease) 55, 65, 78, 144, 146, 249, 302
codling moth 19, 305
coleworts see collards
collards 63
collar-rot 112, 172, 303, 304
Colorado beetle 224, 303
common cress 105, **106, 107**
composting 294-**295,** 312
  making a compost heap 294-**295**
  using compost 294
cooking apples 308, see also apple
coral spot (fungus disease) 234
cordon 312, see also apple, gooseberry and redcurrant
coriander 103-104
Coriandrum sativum see coriander
corn see sweet corn
corn salad 104
  varieties 309 (UK)
courgette see zucchini
cowberry 48
crabapple 105, 308, see also apple
Crambe maritima see seakale
cranberry 48
cress 105-107
  varieties 309 (UK)
crinkle (virus disease) 303, 305
crop rotation 289
crosnes see artichoke, Chinese

cross-pollination 312
crown rot 236, 303
cucumber 108-112
  care 110
  growing outdoors 110, **111**
  growing under glass 108, 110
  pests and diseases 110, 112
  sowing and planting out 108, **111**
  training 108, 110
  varieties 309
cucumber leaf blotch 303
Cucumis melo see melon
Cucumis sativus see cucumber
Cucurbita maxima see winter squash
Cucurbita mixta see Cushion pumpkin
Cucurbita moschata see squash
Cucurbita pepo see pumpkin and squash
Cucurbita pepo ovifera see marrow and zucchini
cultivator 292
curly cress **107**
currants 133
Cushaw pumpkin 224
cutworms 65, 68, 302, 305, 306
Cydonia vulgaris see quince
Cynara cardunculus see cardoon
Cynara scolymus see artichoke, globe

D

damson 112, 214, **215**
  varieties 309 (UK)
Daucus carota see carrot
dewberry 41, **43**
dessert apples 308, see also apple
dibber 292
die-back 23, 131, 269, 304
dill 112-113
Dolomite limestone 296
draw hoe 292
dried blood 296
dry rot 303
Dutch hoe 292
Dutch light **298**

E

early winter cress 106
earthing-up 312
earwigs 25
ear-worms 273
eau de cologne mint 172
eel worms 68, 74, 155, 190, 267, 302, 303, 305
eggplant 113-115
  care and harvesting 113, **114,** 115
  growing in containers 115
  growing under glass 115
  sowing 113, **114**
  varieties 309
Egyptian onion see tree onion
endive 115-117
  blanching **116,** 117
  site and soil requirements 116
  varieties 115, **116,** 309

Epsom salts 296
espalier 312, see also pear
ever-ready onion 188

F

fan 312, see also apricot, cherry, loganberry and peach
farmyard manure 296
fava bean see broad bean
fennel 118-119
fern leaf (virus disease) 283, 303
fertilizers 296
Ficus carica see fig
fig 119-122
  defruiting **120, 121**
  growing in a greenhouse 121
  growing in pots 121, 122
  planting and care 119, **120, 121**
  propagation 122
  site and soil requirements 119
  training **120,** 121
  varieties 309
finocchio see Florence fennel
flageolets 122, 124
flea beetle 65, 78, 94, 144, 146, 256, 269
Florence fennel 117-118
  blanching 117, 118
  sowing and planting 117, **118**
Florentine fennel see Florence fennel
Foeniculus vulgare see fennel
Foeniculus vulgare dulce see Florence fennel
forks 292
Fortunella japonica see kumquat
fowl manure 296
fox grape 131
Fragaria chiloensis see under strawberry
Fragaria virginiana see under strawberry
frames **298**-299
French bean 36, **122**-126
  care and harvesting **125,** 126
  pests and diseases 126
  site and soil requirements 124
  sowing and planting 124, **125**
  varieties 122, **123, 124,** 309
French horticultural beans 122
frit-fly 273, 303
fruit, general information 290
  cropping seasons 290
  siting and planning of garden 290
  types of trees 290
fruit flies 103
Fusarium wilt (fungus disease) 126, 302

G

garden cress 105
garlic 126-127
  varieties 309 (Australian)

gherkin 108, 111, **127**
  varieties 309 (Australian)
globe artichoke see artichoke, globe
glossary 312-313
Glycine max see soya bean
Goa bean see asparagus pea
golden cress 105
golden gram 36
Good King Henry 127-128
gooseberry 128-131
  cultivation 129
  pests and diseases 131
  planting 129
  propagation 129, **130**, 131
  pruning 129, **130**
  site and soil requirements **129**
  varieties 309 (UK)
gooseberry sawfly 130, 234, 304, 305
grape 131-139
  care 134
  double guyot method **136**-137
  in greenhouse 133, 134, **135**
  out of doors 136, 137, **138**
  permanent rod method 133, **135**
  pests and diseases 139
  pollination 134, 139
  propagation **138**, 139
  single guyot method **138**
  site and soil requirements 133
  thinning 136, **137**
  training and pruning 134, **135, 136**, 137, 139
  varieties 131, **132, 133, 137**, 309
grapefruit 97, 98, **102**
  varieties 310
greenback 283, 303
greenfly 41, 44, 46, 68, 74, 103, 110, 113, 115, 131, 139, 155, 166, 172, 174, 191, 198, 204, 214, 224, 231, 233, 251, 252, 283, 302, 303, 304, 305, **306**
greengage **139**, 214, **215**
  varieties 310
green gram 36
greenhouses 300-**301**
  heating and ventilation 300
  siting 300
  types of greenhouses 300-**301**
  watering 300
green watercress 107
grey mould (fungus disease) 68, 94, 115, 126, 139, 152, 166, 172, 198, 230, 264, 283, 302, 303, 304, 305, **306**-**307**
guano 296
Guinea squash see eggplant
gumbo see okra

H

halo blight 241, 302
Hamburg parsley 140-141
Haricot beans 36, 122, 124, **125**
  varieties 309 (UK)
Helianthus tuberosus see artichoke, Jerusalem
Hibiscus esculentus see okra

hoes 292
hollow heart 224, 303
honeydew melon see under melon
hoof and horn 296
horseradish 141-142
humus 293, 312

I

Indian corn see sweet corn
Irish potato see potato

J

Japanese plum 214
Jerusalem artichoke see artichoke, Jerusalem

K

kale 142-144
  harvesting and storing 142, 143
  site and soil requirements 146
  sowing and transplanting 142, **143**
  varieties 310
kiwi fruit see Chinese gooseberry
knives 292
kohlrabi 144-146
  site and soil requirements 146
  sowing and cultivation **144**, 146
  varieties 310
kumquat 98

L

Lactuca sativa see lettuce
ladies' fingers see okra
lamb's lettuce see corn salad
land cress 105-**106**, 107
large-headed broccoli 55
laurel see bay
Laurus nobilis see bay
leaf hopper 304, 305, 307
leafmould (fungus disease) 283, 303
leaf-roll mosaic (virus disease) 224, 303
leaf spot 267, 302, 305
leatherjackets 65, 155, 302, 305, 306
leek 146-149
  blanching 147, 149
  early crops 149
  harvesting **148**, 149
  pests and diseases 149
  site and soil requirements 146
  sowing and transplanting 146, **147**, 149
  varieties 310
lemon 97, 98, **99**, 101
  varieties 310
lemon thyme 275
lemon verbena 150

Lepidium sativum see common cress
lettuce 150-155
  autumn and winter crops 152, **153**
  blanching 152, **153**
  care 152
  growing in containers 155
  growing in greenhouse and frames 152, **153**
  harvesting **153**, 155
  pests and diseases 155
  site and soil requirements 152
  sowing and transplanting 152, **153**
  spring crops 152, **153**
  summer crops 152
  varieties 150, **151**, 152, **154**, 310
Levisticum officinale see lovage
Lima bean 155-157
  care **156**, 157
  growing in containers **156**, 157
  harvesting and storing **156**, 157
  site and soil requirements 155
  sowing and planting out 155, **156**
  varieties 310 (UK)
lime 98, **99**
lime (fertilizer) 296, 312
Lincolnshire spinach see Good King Henry
loam 293
loganberry 41, **157**-160
  care 160
  planting 158
  propagation **159**, 160
  site and soil requirements 158
  training 158, **159**, 160
  varieties 310 (UK)
long beet see beetroot
Lotus tetragonolobus see asparagus pea
lovage 160-161
Lycopersicon esculentum see tomato

M

Madagascar bean see Lima bean
Malus pumila see apple
Malus sylvestris see crabapple
mandarin orange 98
  varieties 310 (Australian)
mangetout 194, **195**, 197
manure 312
manure fork 292
marjoram 161-162
marrow 162-166
  care 166
  harvesting and storing **165**, 166
  pollination **165**, 166
  site and soil requirements 164-165
  sowing and planting out **164**-165
  training **164, 165**
  varieties 310
mealies see sweet corn
mealy aphid 65, 306

mealy bug 139, 305
Melissa officinalis see balm
melon 166-172
  care of fruit **167**, 170, 171-172
  growing in frames 170, **171**
  growing under cloches or plastic 170, **171**
  harvesting 172
  pollination **169**, 170
  site and soil requirements 168-169
  sowing and planting out **168**, 169, 171
  training and pruning **168**, 170, 171
  varieties **167**, 168, 170, 310
  watering **169**-170, 172
Mentha pulegium see pennyroyal
Mentha x piperita see eau de cologne mint
Mentha x spicata see spearmint
Mentha x suaveolens variegata see pineapple mint
Mentha x villosa see applemint and Bowles' mint
mercury see Good King Henry
mice (as pests) 196, 262, 273
mildew (fungus disease) 19, 117, 139, 155, 166, 183, 190, 198, 204, 210, 252, 269, 286, 302, 303, **307**
mint 172-174
mites 178, 303
morello see cherry
Morus alba see under mulberry
Morus nigra see mulberry
mosaic (virus disease) 224, 231, 283, 302, 303, **304**
moths 103
mulberry 175-176
  varieties 310 (Australian)
mulching 294, 312
mung bean 36-38
muscadine grape 131
mushroom 176-179
  care 178
  growing indoors 176, **177**
  growing out of doors 176, **178**
  harvesting **177**-178
  pests and diseases 178-179
  propagation 176, **177, 178**
  site and soil requirements 176, **177, 178**
  varieties 310
mushroom fly 178, 303
musk melon see under melon
mustard and cress 105, **106**
mustard greens 93
myrobalan see cherry plum

N

naartje 98
nasturtium 179
Nasturtium officinale see watercress
navel orange 98
navy bean 36
neck rot (fungus disease) 190, 303
nectarine 179-180, 198, **201**, 203
  varieties 310

New Zealand spinach 180-181
nitrate of soda 296

O

Ocimum basilicum see basil
Ocimum minimum see bush basil
okra 181-183
  harvesting **182,** 183
  sowing and cultivation **182,** 183
  varieties 310
onion 183-190
  care 184, **185**
  growing in containers 189, 190
  harvesting and storing **185, 187**
  pests and diseases 190
  site and soil requirements 181
  sowing and planting 184, **185**
  varieties 310
onion fly 184, 302, 303
onion white rot 303
orange **97,** 98, **99,** 101
  varieties 310
oregano 161
Origanum majorana see sweet marjoram
Origanum onites see pot marjoram
Origanum vulgare see oregano

P

pak-choi see Chinese cabbage
Panama orange 98
paprika 210-213
parsley 74, 190-191
  varieties 310
parsnip 191-193
  care and harvesting **192,** 193
  pests and diseases 193
  site and soil requirements **192,** 193
  sowing and planting **192,** 193
  varieties 310
Pastinaca sativa see parsnip
pea 193-198
  cultivation **196, 197**
  early crops 194, **196**
  harvesting **195, 197**
  late crops 194
  pests and diseases **196,** 198
  site and soil requirements 194
  sowing 194, **195**
  varieties 194, **195, 196, 197,** 310
pea moth 197, 198, 302, **304**
pea seed beetle 198, 302
pea thrips 198, 302
pea weevil 198, 302
peach 198-204
  care 200, 203
  growing under glass 202-203
  pests and diseases 203-204
  planting 200

pollination 200
site and soil requirements 198, 200
thinning of fruit 203
training and pruning 200, **201, 202, 203**
varieties 198, **201,** 310
peach leaf curl (fungus disease) 204, 304
pear 204-210
  buying and planting 204, 207
  care 207
  harvesting and storing 209-210
  pests and diseases 210
  site and soil requirements 204
  thinning fruit 209
  training and pruning **206,** 207, **208, 209**
  varieties 204, **205, 206,** 310-311
pear leaf blister mite 210, 305
pear midge 210, 305
pennyroyal 172
peppers 210-214
  care **213, 214**
  harvesting and storing **212,** 213-214
  sowing and planting out **212,** 213
  varieties 311
pepper cress 105
pests and diseases, general information 302-307
petit pois 194, 197
Petroselinum crispum see parsley
Petroselinum crispum tuberosum see Hamburg parsley
pe-tsai 93
Phaseolus angularis see bean sprouts
Phaseolus aureus see bean sprouts
Phaseolus coccineus see runner bean
Phaseolus limensis = *P. lunatus*
Phaseolus lunatus see Lima bean
Phaseolus vulgaris see French bean
Physalis peruviana edulis see Cape gooseberry
pickling onions 184, 189
pimiento see peppers
pineapple mint 172
Pisum sativum see pea
planning a garden 288-289
plaster moulds (fungus disease) 178, 304
plum 214-219
  care 217
  choosing a tree 214
  pests and diseases 217-218
  planting 217
  pruning and training **216,** 217
  site and soil 214
  thinning **216,** 217
  varieties 214, **215,** 311
plum fruit moth 219, 304
plum sawfly 219, 304
Poncirus trifoliata see under citrus fruit
poor man's asparagus see Good King Henry

potato 219-224
  cultivation 220, **221, 222,** 223
  growing in frames and containers **223**
  growing under plastic sheets **223**
  harvesting and storing 220, **221, 222,** 223
  pests and diseases 223-224
  planting 219-220, **221, 222**
  site and soil requirements 219
  spraying 220
  varieties 219, 220, **222,** 311
potato beetle 115
potato blight (fungus disease) 223, 303, **305**
potato fork 292
potato onion 189
potato root eelworm 224, 303
potato scab (fungus disease) 220
potato tuber moth 68
pot marjoram 162
powdery mildew 112, 302, 303, 304, 305, 307
pricking out 297, 313
pruner 292
pruning 313, see also apple, apricot, blackberry, blackcurrant, blueberry, cherry, Chinese gooseberry, citrus fruit, fig, grape, gooseberry, melon, mulberry, peach, pear, plum, pruning-tools, quince, raspberry and red currant
pruning saw 292
Prunus armeniaca see apricot
Prunus americana see under plum
Prunus avium see under cherry
Prunus cerasifera see cherry plum
Prunus cerasus see under cherry
Prunus damascena see damson
Prunus domestica see plum
Prunus insititia see bullace
Prunus italica see greengage
Prunus persica see peach
Prunus persica nectarina see nectarine
Prunus salicina see Japanese plum
Prunus spinosa see sloe
pummelo 98
pumpkin 224, 258
  varieties 311
pyramid 313, see also pear and plum
Pyrus communis see pear

Q

quince 224-226
  varieties 311

R

rabbit-eye blueberry 48
rabbits (as pests) 273

radish 226-228
  harvesting and storing 226, **227**
  site and soil requirements 226
  sowing and planting out 226, **227**
  varieties 226, **227,** 311
raisins 133
rakes 292
rape kale 142
Raphanus sativus see radish
raspberry 228-231
  care 228, **229,** 230
  pests and diseases 230-231
  planting 228
  propagation **229,** 230
  site and soil requirements 228
  training and pruning 228, **229, 230**
  varieties 228, **230,** 311
raspberry beetle 230, 305
raspberry dwarfs (virus disease) 231
red cabbage 61
red core 267, 305
red currant 231-234
  cultivation 233
  harvesting 233
  pests and diseases 233-234
  planting 233
  propagation 233
  pruning and training 231, **232,** 233
  site and soil requirements 233
  varieties 311
red currant blister aphid 233, 304
red kidney bean 36
red pepper (hot) 210, 213
red plum maggot see plum fruit moth
red spider mite 19, 23, 68, 110, 115, 122, 131, 139, 172, 183, 203, 204, 210, 213, 214, 283, 286, 303, 304, 305, **307**
reversion (virus disease) 46, **47,** 304
Rheum rhaponticum see rhubarb
Rhizoctonia (fungus disease) 126
rhubarb 234-236
  forcing 234, **235**
  harvesting **235,** 236
  planting 234, **235**
  site and soil requirements 234
  varieties 311
Ribes americanum see under blackcurrant
Ribes grossularia see gooseberry
Ribes nigrum see blackcurrant
Ribes petraeum see under red currant
Ribes rubrum see under red currant
Ribes sativum see under red currant
ridge cucumber 108, 127
  varieties 309 (UK)
ring culture 280, **282,** 313
ringspot (fungus disease) 65, 302
rodents (as pests) 51, 65, 307

root aphids 155, 302
root-rot 68
rosemary 236-237
Rosmarinus officinalis see
  rosemary
Rubus alleghaniensis see
  blackberry
Rubus argutus see
  blackberry
Rubus frondosus see
  blackberry
Rubus fruticosus see
  blackberry
Rubus idaeus see
  raspberry
Rubus loganobaccus see
  loganberry
Rubus strigosus see under
  raspberry
Rubus ursinus see under
  loganberry
Rumex scutatus see sorrel
runner bean 36, 237-241
  cultivation **240,** 241
  harvesting 241
  site and soil requirements
    239
  sowing and planting out
    239, **240,** 241
  supporting **240,** 241
  varieties **239,** 241, 311 (UK)
rust 149, 174, 255, 273, 302,
  303
rutabaga see swede

S

sage 242
salad onions 184, 187, 188
salsify 242-245
  blanching **244,** 245
  sowing 243, **244**
  varieties 311 (Australian)
Salvia officinalis see sage
sandy soil 293
Satureia hortensis see summer
  savory
Satureia montana see winter
  savory
savory 245-246
savoys (cabbage) 61
sawfly 19, 219
scab (fungus disease) 19, 210,
  219, 223, 303, **305**
scalding 139, 305
scale insects 19, 23, 36, 103,
  122, 139, 203, 304, 210,
  305,
    307
scorzonera see under salsify
  varieties 311 (Australian)
Scorzonera hispanica see
  scorzonera
Scotch kale 142
seakale 246-249
  blanching 247, **248**
  growing in containers 249
  site and soil requirements
    247, **248**
  sowing and planting out
    247, **248**
seakale beet see Swiss chard
seakale spinach see Swiss
  chard
seasons guide 314
secateurs 292
seed, general information 297
  germination 297, 312

saving seed 297
sowing 297
seed beds 297
Seville orange 98
shaddock 98
shallot 184, **186,** 187, **189**
  varieties 311 (Australian)
shallot virus 303
shanking 139, 305
silver beet see Swiss chard
silver leaf (fungus disease) 23,
  204, 217, 304
sleepy disease see wilt
sloe 214
slugs 25, 27, 31, 65, 72, 84,
  92, 94, 101, 107, 115, 117,
  126, 155, 157, 164, 166,
  178, 181, 183, 223, 228,
  241, 252, 262, 274, 286,
  302, 303, 304, 305, 307
smut 190, 273, 303
snails 31, 107, 303, 307
snap bean see French bean
soft rot (bacterial disease) 74,
  84, 190, 269, 285, 302, 303,
  307
soil testing 293
soil types 293
Solanum melongena see
  eggplant
Solanum tuberosum see potato
sorrel 249-250
sowing, general information
  297
  in pots 297
  in seed trays 297
  out of doors 297
  under glass 297
soya bean 36, 250-251
  cultivation 250
  harvesting and storing 250-
    251
  site and soil requirements
    250
  sowing 250, **251**
spades 292
spearmint 172, **173**
speckled yellows (deficiency
  disease) 41, 303
Spinacea oleracea see spinach
spinach 251-253
  care 252, **253**
  site and soil requirements
    252, **253**
  sowing and planting 252,
    253
  varieties 311
  winter crops 252
spinach beet 254-255
spinach blight (virus disease)
  252, 302
spotted wilt (virus disease)
  283, 303
spraing (virus disease) 224
sprayers 292
spray lines 299
spring cabbages 61
spring greens (cabbage) 61
spring onions 184, **188**
  varieties 311 (Australian)
spring tails 303
sprinklers 299
**sprouting broccoli 55, 255-
    257**
  harvesting and storing 256
  site and soil requirements
    255
  sowing and planting 255-
    256
  varieties 311

sprue (asparagus
  shoots) 31
spur blight (fungus disease)
  230, 305
squash 258-261
  varieties 311
squirrels (as pests) 262
Stachys affinis see artichoke,
  Chinese
staddle 87, **88**
sterilization of soil 291
stony pit (virus disease) 210,
  305
strawberry 261-267
  care and protection 262,
    263
  forcing early crops **263,** 264
  growing in containers **263,**
    264, **265**
  planting 262, **263**
  propagation **263,** 264
  site and soil requirements
    262, **265**
  varieties 311
strawberry blossom weevil 267,
  305
streak (virus disease) 283, 303
string bean see French bean
sugar peas see mangetout
suckers 210, 307, 313
sulphate of ammonia 296
sulphate of potash 296
sultanas 133
summer cabbages 61
summer savory 245
summer squash see marrow
superphosphate of lime 296
swede 267-269
  blanching shoots **268,** 269
  cultivation 267, **268**
  harvesting and storing **268,**
    269
  varieties 311
sweet corn 269-273
  care 270, **271**
  harvesting **270,** 271
  pollination **270**
  site and soil requirements
    269
  sowing and planting out
    269-**270**
  varieties 311
sweet fennel see Florence
  fennel
sweet marjoram 162
sweet orange 98
sweet pepper 210
Swiss chard 273-274
  growing in containers 274
  harvesting **273,** 274
  site and soil requirements
    274
  sowing and cultivation **273,**
    274
  varieties 311
syringes 292

T

tangelo 98
tangerine **97,** 98, **99**
tarragon 273, 274-275
tarsonemid mite 267, 305
tent cloche **298**
Tetragonia expansa see New
  Zealand spinach
Tetragonolobus purpureus see
  asparagus pea
thyme 275-276

Thymus x *citriodorus* see
  lemon thyme
Thymus vulgaris see thyme
tomato 276-283
  care and pollination **278,**
    279, **280**
  growing in a greenhouse
    279, **280**
  growing out of doors 276,
    277
  growing under frames and
    cloches 282
  harvesting and ripening
    278, 279, 280
  in containers 282
  pests and diseases 282-283
  ring cultivation 280, **282**
  site and soil requirements
    276
  sowing and planting out
    276, **278,** 279
  varieties **277, 281,** 311
tomato moth 283, 303
tools 292-293
Tragopogon porrifolius see
  salsify
tree onion 183, **188,** 189
Tropaeolum majus see
  nasturtium
trowel 292
turnip 283-283
  in frames **284,** 285
  site and soil requirements
    283
  sowing **283,** 284
  varieties 311
turnip flea beetle 285, 302,
  303
turnip-rooted cabbage see
  kohlrabi
turnip-rooted celery see
  celeriac
turnip-rooted parsley see
  Hamburg parsley

U

ugli 98

V

Vaccinium australe see
  blueberry
Vaccinium corymbosum see
  blueberry
Vaccinium lamarckii see
  blueberry
Vaccinium macrocarpum see
  cranberry
Vaccinium myrtillus see wild
  bilberry
Vaccinium vitis-idaea see
  cowberry
Valerianella locusta see
  corn salad
veitchberry 158
Versailles caisson **100**
Vicia faba see broad bean
vine weevil 139, 305
violet root rot (fungus disease)
  31, 74, 249, 302, 303, 307
virus spotting (of fig leaves)
  122
Vitis labrusca see under grape
Vitis rotundifolia see under
  grape

Vitis vinifera see grape
Vitis vulpina see under grape

W

wart disease (fungus disease) 223, 303
wasps 139, 203
watercress **107**
watering, general information 299
watering cans 292, 299
watermelon 166, **167**
  varieties 310 (Australian)

waxpod 122, **124**
weeds and weedkillers 291
weevils 273, 302, 303
Welsh onion 183, 188
whiptail 57, 79, 302
white beet see beetroot
white blister (fungus disease) 245, 303
white currant 231
whitefly 65, 68, 103, 110, 283, 302, 303, **307**
white rot 190
white tip (fungus disease) 149, 302
whortleberry 48
wild bilberry 48

wilt diseases 115, 172, 251, 283, 303
wineberry 158
winged pea see asparagus pea
winter cabbages 63
winter cauliflower see broccoli
winter moths 19
winter savory 245
winter squash 258
wirestem (fungus disease) 65, 302
wireworms 74, 223, 303, **306**
wither tip 112, 303
wood-ash 296
woolly aphid 19, 305, 306
Worcesterberry 129

Y

yellow beet see beetroot
yellow cress 106
yellow dwarf (virus disease) 190, 303
yellow edge (virus disease) 305
youngberry 157, **158**

Z

Zea mays see sweet corn
zucchini 285-286
  varieties 311

CREDITS

Photographs

T=top,   B=bottom,   L=left,   R=right, M=middle.

Bernard Alfieri: 17TL, 47TL, 60TL, 62, 209, 215TR.
Armstrong Nurseries, Inc.: 201TL.
Barnaby's Picture Library: 23BL.
BASF: 307M.
Pat Brindley: 93TR, 189TR.
W. Atlee Burpee Co.: 107TL, 237B.
Camera Press: 265T.
Roger Charity: 161BR.
Chevron Chemical Co./Ortho Division: 114B, 167T.
R. J. Corbin: 22L, 275T.
Eric Crichton: 12T, 24TR, 45TR, 50BR, 54TR, 63B, 67TR, 97, 111BL, 118TL, 128TL, 140, 141, 144, 151TL,BR, 154, 161TR, 175, 180, 192, 195TL, 227BL,BR, 239T, 243B, 246T,B, 251, 253, 254, 256B, 273, 277BL, 304M, 307B.

Dobies: 123, 124ML, 239B.
Mick Duff: 35.
Alan Duns: 75M. Front Cover.
Peter Dodd, HMSO Crown Copyright: 87B, 89TR, 306T.
Derek Fell: 29, 32BR, 43BR, 63T, 75TR, 76BR, 91BR, 107TR, 128BL, 133TL, 182, 210TR, 243T, 258T,B, 259, 260, 277TL,TR,BR, 286B.
Brian Furner: 71, 75TL, 80, 137, 169, 174, 222TR, 284R, 306MB, 307T.
Iris Hardwick Picture Library: 132.
Grant Heilman: 30BR, 86T, 99TL, TR,BR, 102, 111BR, 118B, 151BL, 156, 167BL, 173, 178, 195TR, 201BL, 211, 215BR, 230, 272, 275B.
George Hyde: 50TR, 56BR, 76BL, 82BL, 116BL, 191, 256T, 304R, 305M, 306MT,B, 307MB.
ICI: 305, 306M.
Jacana: 210BR.
Agnete Lampe: 73, 148, 222BR.
Patrick Matthews: 167BR.

May & Baker: 304L, 305R.
Merrydown: 133BL.
Ken Muir: 95.
Muriel Orans: 86BL, 145, 159.
Linda Palmer: 222TL.
Clay Perry: 40TL, 53B, 69, 91TR, 114TL, 124TL, 130TL, TR, 143BR, 163, 165, 186, 187, 188TL, 189TL, 235, 238, 271, 284L, 286T.
Spike Powell: 37BR.
G.R. Roberts: 32TR, 82TL.
Donald Smith: 86BR, 87T, 120BL, BR,158TR,BR, 201BR, 206TR, B, 232, 307MT.
Harry Smith Photographic Collection: 99BL, 109, 121T, 151TR, 188TR, 195B, 199, 205, 206TL, 215TL,BL, 218, 222MR, 229B, 237T, 266, 268L,R, 281.
J. Trehane & Sons Ltd.: 49.
Jerry Tubby: 43TR, 63M, 143BL.
Volmorin: 116TL, 124, 125.
Colin Watmough: 13R.
Liz Whiting: 265B.
Michael Wickham: 10.
ZEFA: 138.

Illustrators

Mike Baber
Terry Callcut, Ian Garrard/Linden Artists Ltd.
Barbara Firth
Ben Manchipp/Temple Art Agency
Gwen Simpson
Tony Streek/Spectron Artists Ltd.